100°E   120°E   140°E

40°N

C H I N A

Calcutta

P A C I F I C

BURMA

Hong Kong

BAY OF   Rangoon

BENGAL

20°N

Bangkok

Manila

Penang   MALAYA

O C E A N

Brunei

Equator   Singapore

Kuching

I N D O N E S I A

Djakarta

0°

Cocos
Islands

A   N

Darwin

N

20°S

A U S T R A L I A

Fremantle

0   500   1000   1500   2000
km

100°E   120°E   140°E   40°S

BRITISH DEFENCE POLICY
EAST OF SUEZ
1947–1968

The Royal Institute of International Affairs is an unofficial body which promotes the scientific study of international questions and does not express opinions of its own. The opinions expressed in this publication are the responsibility of the author.

The Institute gratefully acknowledges the comments and suggestions of the following who read the manuscript on behalf of the Research Committee: Michael Howard, Kenneth Hunt, and L. W. Martin.

British Defence Policy
East of Suez
1947-1968

PHILLIP DARBY

Published for
THE ROYAL INSTITUTE OF
INTERNATIONAL AFFAIRS
by
OXFORD UNIVERSITY PRESS
LONDON
1973

Oxford University Press, Ely House, London W.1

GLASGOW NEW YORK TORONTO MELBOURNE WELLINGTON
CAPE TOWN IBADAN NAIROBI DAR ES SALAAM LUSAKA ADDIS ABABA
DELHI BOMBAY CALCUTTA MADRAS KARACHI LAHORE DACCA
KUALA LUMPUR SINGAPORE HONG KONG TOKYO

ISBN 0 19 214992 X

© Royal Institute of International Affairs, 1973

Printed in Great Britain
by Hazell Watson & Viney Ltd
Aylesbury, Bucks

To
Sir Peter Gretton

Contents

MAPS

Preface

THIS book investigates the purposes and methods of the British deployment of power east of Suez in the two decades after the grant of independence to India. The consideration of purpose involves an examination of certain short-term factors which tied Britain to the area, of several shadowy conceptions of British interests, and of the nature of the military role during the devolution of empire. The shallowness of British assessments about the politics of the east of Suez role quickly becomes apparent and we are left with the question of what kind of nation policy-makers took Britain to be. Was she simply a European power with certain post-imperial interests and responsibilities or was she still a world power whose course had been set by the imperial experience? The consideration of methods involves a detailed discussion of the development of service programmes and an outline of the forces and equipment available. This is of intrinsic interest inasmuch as it charts the process of military adaptation to the changing problems of the area, which in turn forced the pace of political thinking. It is also essential for an appreciation of the substance of British policies, because for much of the period the government's approach was little more than strategic posturing in a vacuum. In its widest sense, the book is a study of the evolution of a structure of power which was originally built round the defence of India into a system of mobile forces designed to maintain stability round the rim of the Indian Ocean.

The approach is to examine what might loosely be described as the political and military aspects of the east of Suez commitment separately. In places this has meant twin chapters covering the same chronological period; at other times both aspects have been examined in the same chapter but in different sections. Although there is some overlap in the material, this procedure seems appropriate because the questions of ends and means are conceptually distinct. Ultimately, of course, the two cannot be separated and at various points in the text they are considered in conjunction, and frequently there are cross-references between the two.

A number of general periods have been identified in the evolution of British policies during the years 1947 to 1968. Inevitably this procedure has involved some arbitrariness, particularly since political and military developments did not always go hand in hand, and what was a milestone for one was not necessarily significant for the other. Thus 1962 saw the broadening of the British commitment east of Suez and for that reason it makes a dividing line from the diplomatic viewpoint, yet it has no particular significance in terms of changing strategic concepts.

Throughout the book, east of Suez or the Indian Ocean area—the phrases are used interchangeably—is taken to include the entire reaches of the Indian Ocean together with the lands bordering upon it. Hence the long coastline of east Africa, the Gulf of Aden, the coast of Arabia, the Persian Gulf, the Indian subcontinent, Burma, Malaya, the Indonesian archipelago, and Australia are within our area of interest. Africa other than the east coast, the main body of the Middle East, and China are excluded. At times, of course, the problems of adjacent areas impinge upon the region and it is therefore necessary to take a wider perspective. Egypt is a particular case in point, especially in the years before 1957 when Britain's position in the Indian Ocean was seen as hinging on control of the Suez Canal.

To generations of British policy-makers the Indian Ocean and the British territories bordering it formed a coherent strategic system. As the British consolidated their position in India the trading settlements and naval stations stretching from the Cape and Aden eastward to Singapore took on a broad strategic significance, and, albeit slowly, a system was fashioned in which India's defences began at oceanic gateways far removed from the subcontinent itself. In the fullness of this conception the parts were interdependent: Indian security depended on maintenance of the British position at these gateways; and to a less extent Britain's ability to hold them and to dominate the sea depended on control of the Indian subcontinent and its ports, communications facilities, and manpower resources.

In large part, Britain's defence responsibilities in the area after the Second World War can be traced back to this regional conception of Indian defence and to the independent momentum of the strategic footholds to which it gave rise. Interpreted in this way, the small war–counter insurgency strategy developed in the late fifties and early sixties can be seen as the indirect successor of the earlier oceanic strategy. However, this continuity should not obscure the fact that for much of the period the east of Suez concept was descriptive rather than analytic. Although from 1947 to 1968 the Indian Ocean was ringed by countries in which Britain had either interests or responsibilities the regional idea did not prevail throughout. After 1947—with India no longer a primary British responsibility and the main fear being Russia and global war—the Middle East, the Persian Gulf, and the Far East were seen as strategic units in their own right. To this extent, therefore, there is an element of artificiality in my use of east of Suez as the frame of reference. With the emergence of the Middle Eastern air and sea barrier in the late fifties, the area again acquired a measure of strategic coherence in the eyes of British planners. Slowly, and not fully until 1962, British political thinking broadened to encompass the whole area. In not much more than a decade the wheel had turned full circle.

The inadequacy of published sources made it necessary to draw on discussions and correspondence with persons involved in policy-making. For the most part, this was a matter of amplification of the public record and guidance as to the reliability of published reports. No specific attribution was possible in the text but in the main where material has been drawn from private discussion and correspondence this has been indicated.

I acknowledge with pleasure the very great help and kindness extended to me by politicians, senior officers, and officials. A number of policy-makers read the manuscript in full and made detailed comments. Others read certain chapters or discussed points with me. I am unable to mention by name all those who helped in one way or another but I can thank Sir William Armstrong, Air Vice-Marshal Neil Cameron, General Sir Michael Carver, Sir Michael Cary, Mr Frank Cooper, Air Chief Marshal Sir Alfred Earle, Marshal of the Royal Air Force Sir Charles Elworthy, Sir Allen Fairhall, Field Marshal

Lord Harding of Petherton, Sir Henry Hardman, General Sir Charles Harington, Viscount Head of Throope, Mr Denis Healey, Air Marshal Sir Maurice Heath, Admiral Sir Frank Hopkins, Air Chief Marshal Sir Edmund Hudleston, Field Marshal Sir Richard Hull, Major General W. M. Hutton, Admiral of the Fleet Sir Caspar John, Admiral Sir David Luce, Captain R. D. McDonald, RN, Vice-Admiral Sir Ian McGeoch, Mr Christopher Mayhew, Marshal of the Royal Air Force Sir Thomas Pike, General Sir Nigel Poett, Captain I. G. Raikes, RN, Mr Duncan Sandys, Lord Shinwell, Marshal of the Royal Air Force Sir John Slessor, Vice-Admiral Sir Richard Smeeton, Lord Strang, Field Marshal Sir Gerald Templer, Lord Thorneycroft, Colonel Hugh Toye, Lord Watkinson, and Lord Wigg.

I am especially indebted to Vice-Admiral Sir Peter Gretton, Sir Robert Scott, and Major General J. L. Moulton whose advice and encouragement I received from the outset. Each of them read successive drafts of manuscript and opened doors which would otherwise have remained closed.

My thanks go also to Professor Max Beloff and Professor Norman Gibbs of All Souls College, Oxford, and to Mr David Fieldhouse of Nuffield College and Mr Wilfrid Knapp of St Catherine's College, Oxford. Mr Michael Howard of All Souls, Professor Richard Neustadt of Harvard, and Mr George Anderson of Nuffield helped with certain material. Mr Josef Szwarc of the University of Melbourne worked closely with me on the revision of the manuscript and the book is much improved as a result. My research was made easier by the facilities of the Royal Institute of International Affairs, the Royal United Service Institution, and Nuffield College. The Royal Institute of International Affairs provided finance and Miss Rena Fenteman undertook the editing and made many suggestions of substance.

I should add that the views expressed are my own and that none of the persons or institutions mentioned above can be held responsible for any mistakes or omissions.

Melbourne   P. G. C. D.
March 1971

ABBREVIATIONS

AM	Air Ministry
Amer. polit. Sci. R.	*American Political Science Review*
BAOR	British Army of the Rhine
CENTO	Central Treaty Organization
CIGS	Chief of the Imperial General Staff
CO	Colonial Office
COI	Central Office of Information
DEA	Department of Economic Affairs
FO	Foreign Office
For. Aff.	*Foreign Affairs*
HC	House of Commons
HC Deb.	*Parliamentary Debates* (Hansard), 5th Series, House of Commons
HL Deb.	*Parliamentary Debates* (Hansard), 5th Series, House of Lords
Int. Aff.	*International Affairs* (London)
Int. Org.	*International Organization*
JRUSI	*Journal of the Royal United Service Institution*
LCA	Landing craft, assault
LCM	Landing craft, mechanical
LSL	Landing ship, logistic
LST	Landing ship, tank
MoD	Ministry of Defence
OEEC	Organisation for European Economic Co-operation
PM	Prime Minister
RIIA	Royal Institute of International Affairs
SEATO	South-East Asia Treaty Organization
VTOL	Vertical take-off and landing
WO	War Office

Introduction

When India has gone and the great Colonies have gone, do you sup-
pose that we can stop there? Your ports and coaling stations, your
fortresses and dockyards, your Crown Colonies and protectorates will
go too. For either they will be unnecessary as the toll-gates and bar-
bicans of an empire that has vanished, or they will be taken by an
enemy more powerful than yourselves.

From Lord Curzon's presidential address to the Birmingham
and Midland Institute, 1907 (reproduced in *The Nineteenth
Century and After*, Jan. 1908).

THE fall of Singapore on 15 February 1942 brought to a close
the period of British paramountcy east of Suez. For almost a
century and a half British possession of the gateways to the
region, the Royal Navy's control of the Indian Ocean and its
various passages, and the lack of any serious challenge from
Europe had enabled Britain to maintain a security system
which to a remarkable degree remained immune from the
shifts and tensions of other areas. In this system India was the
centre-piece: to some extent both the object and the source
of British power east of Suez. Although at times the protection
of the routes of communication, the defence of the Far Eastern
territories, or the maintenance of Britain's position in the
Middle East became the focus of attention it was generally
understood that the security of India was Britain's overriding
concern. In this sense the protection of India was part of an
ingrained pattern of thought. It was above politics: it went
beyond the issue of the moment. It was the touchstone to which
policy must return: the ultimate justification for a defensive
system which spanned half the world.

Both by independent action and by representation in Whitehall, the government of India played a crucial part in the

establishment of this system and in its maintenance. India had a Secretary of State in the British cabinet and thereby a measure of direct influence over United Kingdom policy. More important, India was an empire in its own right and made policy in accordance with its own interests. To the north-west and the north-east, from the Gulf of Oman along the boundaries of Persia, Afghanistan, and Nepal to Victoria Point on the Malay Peninsula, were territories which were included in the political, but not the administrative, sphere of competence of the Indian government. Lord Hardinge, writing of his journey to India in 1910, recalls that: 'On arrival at Aden I assumed, as is usual, the attributes of the Viceroy and hoisted the Viceroy's flag which was saluted by the shore batteries and by an Italian cruiser . . .'[1]

Although subordinate to Whitehall, the government of India pursued an imperial policy within its own sphere. On many occasions Indian policies were imperfectly co-ordinated with British policies and the initiative was often taken by the Indian government in strengthening its regional shield. Thus the protected states in the Persian Gulf and the colony of Aden were first brought into the system by the authorities in Calcutta and Bombay, not by Whitehall.[2] In addition, India assumed a considerable responsibility for the defence of the outlying bases and territories both to the east and the west. Indian military units were stationed at Hong Kong, Singapore, and Aden as part of the garrisons in those places. At various times Indian contingents were despatched to such distant points as Mombasa, the Sudan, Iraq, Persia, Malaya, China, and even New Zealand. In India itself a strategic reserve of nearly four divisions was maintained for the protection of imperial interests in the Indo-Asian area.

To point to the historical importance of the regional concept and the centrality of India is not of course to suggest that Indo-British policies can be understood simply in these terms. The detail of settlement and annexation, of maritime activity and diplomatic manoeuvring admits no neat order of this kind. In the early years direct economic motives and the drives to suppress piracy and the slave trade spearheaded policy in their

---

[1] *My Indian Years* (1948), p. 8.
[2] See Elizabeth Monroe, *Britain's Moment in the Middle East 1914–1956* (1963), p. 12.

own right.[3] Later, friction between the authorities at home and
in India and the separate requirements of Britain's lesser territories in the area brought cross-currents of interests and ideas.
Yet it remains true that the force of the imperial idea produced a
coherence which spanned the changing strategic circumstances
of the century before the First World War. Throughout this
period it was undoubted that India must be guarded from
afar. On land this meant buffers and protectorates, annexations
and alliances, but the method and the detail depended upon
circumstances and personality.[4] On the ocean a more consistent
pattern was discernible. British policy, it was said—and with
considerable truth—was throughout based on two main conceptions. First, that no other great power should be able to
establish bases or defended ports in the region.[5] In the Persian
Gulf this consideration provides a thread of continuity in the
history of Britain's diplomatic jostling and led eventually to
the whole of the southern coast of Arabia being brought under
British rule or protection.[6] Elsewhere the challenges to British
hegemony made little headway.[7]

The second conception, which followed logically from the
first, was that Britain should command the naval gateways
to the Indian Ocean. So long as these gateways were firmly
latched, it was argued, the Indian empire was secure and
Britain's naval supremacy unchallengeable. Thus Simonstown
at the Cape, and Singapore commanding the Malacca Straits,
became the sentinels of Britain's Indian Ocean preserve.
Later Aden and Fremantle closed the ring. The same pattern
of thinking led the British government to secure an interest
in the Suez Canal by purchasing the Egyptian stake in 1875.

In 1921 the British government took the decision to build a
large naval base at Singapore.[8] Changes in the Far Eastern
balance had made it necessary to guard against a Japanese

---

[3] A fascinating account of early British maritime and trading activities is given by
Prof. G. S. Graham in *Great Britain in the Indian Ocean 1810–1850* (1967). See also
his *Politics of Naval Supremacy* (1965), esp. ch. 2.
[4] K. M. Panikkar discusses some aspects of this policy in *Problems of Indian Defence*
(1960), pp. 23–5.
[5] RIIA, *Political and Strategic Interests of the United Kingdom* (1939), p. 247; also
Brig D. H. Cole, *Imperial Military Geography*, 10th ed. (1950), pp. 149–50.
[6] RIIA, *Political and Strategic Interests of the United Kingdom*, pp. 161–2
[7] See further K. M. Panikkar, *India and the Indian Ocean*, 2nd impr. (1962), ch. 6.
[8] Until the outbreak of the First World War Singapore remained a minor naval
base, in fact with fewer facilities than Simonstown.

naval threat and a number of general considerations led to
Singapore being selected as the site. Singapore lay astride
the routes of communication not only of the Indian Ocean but
also of the China seas and the southern Pacific, and was a point
from which all these communications could be controlled.[9]
However, the Indian Ocean loomed larger than the China
seas, and the decision owed more to Britain's position in the
Indian Ocean than to her role as a Pacific power.[10]

By these means Britain succeeded in organizing the defence
of India as a regional system. On the other side of the coin, it
was Britain's possession of India that made the system possible.
To borrow a cliché from strategic commentaries of the thirties,
India was the keystone of the arch of defence in the region.[11]
Geographically central to all the British territories in and
round the Indian Ocean, the focal point of communications
and administration, a place for acclimatizing troops, and a
great storage and supply centre, India was the base upon
which Britain built a second nucleus of power. The instrument
of that power was the army in India. Radicals might object
and Indian nationalists condemn, but from the middle of the
nineteenth century the Indian army was the real strategic
reserve of the British empire in the East. In the 1860s Lord
Salisbury had argued that India should not be used as an
'Eastern barrack in the oriental seas from which we may draw
any number of troops without paying for them'.[12] However,
this plea counted for little and from the Crimea to Mesopotamia
and in a succession of imperial policing expeditions, the Indian
army served in the defence of the empire.

In the inter-war years the role of the Indian army was clarified and more carefully defined but not fundamentally changed.
The Esher Committee, which sat in 1919, was categorical that
the army in India could not be considered otherwise than as
part of the total armed forces of the empire.[13] Predictably this
was hardly to the taste of Indian nationalists and in 1921 the
Legislative Assembly adopted a resolution repudiating the

[9] J. R. M. Butler, *Grand Strategy*, ii: *September 1939 – June 1941* (1957), p. 334.
[10] RIIA, *Collective Defence in South East Asia: the Manila Treaty and its Implications*
(1956), p. 33.
[11] A. G. Boycott, *The Elements of Imperial Defence*, 3rd ed. (1938), p. 263; Cole,
Imperial Military Geography, p. 169.
[12] Quoted in A. P. Thornton, *The Imperial Idea and its Enemies* (1959), p. 97.
[13] B. Prasad, ed., *Defence of India: Policy and Plans* (1963), p. 1.

assumptions of the Esher Committee, contending instead that the obligations devolving on India should be no different from those on the self-governing dominions.[14] In the face of growing hostility between the Soviet Union and the British empire, this resolution was unacceptable to Whitehall. However, if India's contribution to imperial defence were to continue to be of an altogether different nature from that of the self-governing dominions, it was apparent that India was entitled to some financial contribution from the United Kingdom government. This line of reasoning was accepted by the Garran Tribunal in 1933 and over the next few years India received a contribution of £1.5 million a year from the British Treasury. On the general question of India's role in imperial defence, however, the Tribunal was adamant:

The defence of India and the defence of the Empire cannot be dissociated. In a sense, everything done in the defence of India is also done in the defence of the Empire, and everything done in the defence of the Empire, whether in India or elsewhere, is also done in the defence of India.[15]

Despite the importance attached to the Indian army's role in imperial defence, in the period between the wars British strategic thought for the area had little of the tidiness ascribed by writers of strategic textbooks. As specific threats emerged, the services responded in their separate ways and the logic of events displaced the order of the regional concept. Two general observations may be made. In the first place, although India seems still to have been regarded as the hub of imperial defence most attention was paid to the spokes. Secondly, imperial defence itself increasingly took second place to national defence. To this extent, it is possible to discern certain similarities between the inter-war period and the early post-war years.

The heart of the matter was that there was no integrated strategic doctrine during these years. Each of the services had its own particular area of concern and therefore, especially in the twenties, each tended to view the overall picture quite differently. Another factor which worked to discourage the

[14] Ibid. p. 2.
[15] Tribunal on Certain Questions in Regard to Defence Expenditure in Dispute between the Government of India, the War Office and the Air Ministry, *Report*, Cmd 4473 (1933), para. 16(6).

development of any coherent strategic doctrine was the operation of the ten-year rule, which laid down that for ten years to come no great war need be expected.[16] The rule was first adopted in 1919 and although it was condemned by the Chiefs of Staff in each of their annual reports after 1928, it remained an article of official faith until March 1932.[17]

In the period between 1919 and 1936 the navy was primarily concerned with developments in the Far East. The elimination of the German fleet and the growth of both the American and Japanese navies during the war of 1914–18 resulted naturally in the focus of naval attention shifting from the Atlantic and the Mediterranean to the Pacific.[18] During the same years the army was preoccupied with India. Anglo-Russian relations had been strained since the end of the war and between 1925 and 1927 they became worse. Both the Secretary of State for India and the Chiefs of Staff believed that the Soviet Union was bent on a policy of encircling India. Accordingly plans were drawn up in 1928 and 1929 to defend India from a Soviet attack, the region believed to be threatened being the North-West Frontier.[19] The Manchurian crisis of 1931 focused attention on the weakness of Britain's defence in the Far East and provided the Chiefs of Staff with a lever with which to move the cabinet. Japan was now judged to be the more immediate danger though Germany was the greater one.[20] Thus the War Office and the government of India set about studying measures for strengthening the defences in the Far East. At this stage no immediate fear was entertained for the borders of India. So long as the eastern bastions were held, it was believed that India was secure.[21]

Developments in Abyssinia and the Rhineland in 1935 and 1936 forced some reordering of priorities. The navy now had no alternative but to rate the European danger first. The crises of 1935 and 1936 also had the effect of arousing fears regarding the western approaches to India. The possibility that

[16] N. H. Gibbs, 'British Strategic Doctrine 1918–1939', in M. Howard, ed., *The Theory and Practice of War* (1965), p. 201.

[17] W. K. Hancock and M. M. Gowing, *British War Economy* (1949), p. 45.

[18] Maj Gen S. Woodburn Kirby and others, *The War Against Japan*, i: *The Loss of Singapore* (1957), pp. 1 and 2.

[19] Prasad, pp. 15–28.

[20] Hancock and Gowing, pp. 63–4.

[21] Prasad, pp. 136–7.

British forces might be heavily committed in Europe led the government to expand India's overseas commitments, especially in the Middle East.[22]Hardly surprisingly the new developments led to an increased emphasis on the Royal Air Force. However, they effected little change in its pattern of strategic thinking. The RAF had always regarded its primary task as the defence of the United Kingdom, thus its plans were made on the supposition of war against Germany. The expansion programmes between 1934 and the spring of 1939 proceeded on that basis; later, the build-up overseas was sacrificed in the interests of home defence.[23]

Against this background of changing circumstances and assessments, it would be mistaken to interpret British thinking about the Indian Ocean area in the inter-war years primarily in terms of the regional concept. No doubt the security of India remained Britain's ultimate concern and behind the planning for the Middle East and the Far East lay still the recognition that the defence of India was best secured at its oceanic approaches. But the fact remains that for most of the period India was not seen as directly endangered except in the northwest;[24] and in the face of major threats elsewhere, and with limited resources for defence, strategic planning developed along piecemeal lines. To complicate the matter the three services pulled in different directions. The net result was that British strategy varied according to which potential enemy appeared the most threatening.

It took the war to weld the pieces into a coherent whole. On the one hand, India was exposed to the threat from the east and heavily dependent upon the sea routes in the western waters of the Indian Ocean. On the other, India played an invaluable part as a base and supply centre first for the Allied campaign in the Middle East and later for South-East Asia Command. During the war years, therefore, it again became apparent that the fate of India and that of the approaches to the Indian Ocean were intertwined: that Indian security rested on its oceanic flanks and that the defence of the Middle East

[22] Ibid. pp. 20–1 and 34.
[23] Gibbs, as cited in n. 16, p. 204.
[24] Concern with the North-West Frontier did not lend much weight to a regional conception of Indian defence. Indeed as Panikkar has implied, preoccupation with that area was usually associated with neglect of an oceanic strategy. *India and the Indian Ocean*, p. 7.

and the Far East were tied, if precariously, to the Indian sub-continent. With the end of the war the position quickly changed. The circumstances which forced British planners to adopt a broader perspective gave way to a situation in which particular areas raised distinctive problems and as a result strategic thinking broke into separate parts.

CHAPTER ONE

The Hold of Empire 1947–1953

In the early post-war years there was no clear conception of Britain's role east of Suez. It was plain that Britain had continuing interests and obligations in the area but their extent and likely duration remained largely unexplored. The Middle East and the Far East were seen as the pivots of British policy and attention was concentrated on the Suez area, the Persian Gulf, and the Malayan peninsula. Increasingly these wings of the old system became strategic entities in their own right but communications requirements, global considerations, and the habit of imperial thinking ensured that the whole area continued to be viewed as one of British predominance.

It is arguable that if the traditional understanding of Britain's regional involvement had had more meaning at the time, the debate about Britain's role might have taken place then, when it was really appropriate, instead of twenty years later. Equally to the point, had the Indian government had more success in the thirties in impressing upon Whitehall the relationship between India and the region, the removal of the hub in 1947 might have led to an immediate reconsideration of the role of the spokes. Thus account might have been taken of the diminished military importance of the Suez Canal, Aden, the Persian Gulf and Singapore, and Britain's strategic conceptions adjusted accordingly.

In the absence of a clear appreciation of what Britain was doing and why, no body of strategic doctrine was developed which defined the military tasks east of Suez. The main part of defence thinking was concerned with general war, and at the broad level of strategic analysis the Indian Ocean area was forced into this mould. British policies for the area, however, developed along more pragmatic lines. Lacking clear long-term foreign policy objectives and guided by the experience of an imperial past, policy as it emerged was largely a reaction to events: commanders trying to find a means of doing, with diminishing resources, what they were told they had to do – to win in Malaya, to put down the Mau Mau, to keep the oil flowing in the Persian Gulf.

At the time, the various moves on the Indian Ocean chess-board were viewed against a background of Europe, of the Communist threat, and of the fear of global war. The picture which emerges is of the three services taking up the remnants of the imperial system, making such adjustments as the post-war developments necessitated, and attempting to relate the whole to the global war theme. In short, the services were endeavouring, in the absence of any firm political guidance, to make sense of a system which had lost its *raison d'être*.

Yet more important from a historical perspective, each of the services, particularly the army, was adapting to the new conditions and building up a body of experience which was later to enable it to develop a strategy for limited conflicts. At this stage, however, the developments in Malaya and in Kenya made little impact on general thinking and the services failed to incorporate the lessons of these campaigns in their doctrine and training. As a result, the small-war potential of units such as the Royal Marines received little recognition and their role continued to be justified on the basis of a general-war function.

The Failure to Reappraise

The transfer of power to India and Pakistan on 15 August 1947 was the crucial event in Britain's post-war overseas policy. At a single stroke, the basis of Britain's position as an imperial power was gone. Without the Indian empire, Britain might still be a great power but it was no longer an imperial power in the full sense of that term. Nor were its responsibilities imperial as a matter of course. The need to secure the outer rim of India's defences, to maintain British dominance in the Middle East and the Far East, and to protect the route through the Suez Canal had lost their old compulsion. The diplomatic handiwork of a hundred and fifty years had served its purpose: the time had come to seal the retreat from empire.

The defence implications were scarcely less profound. Speaking in 1946, Lord Alanbrooke acknowledged that the loss of India would leave a great gap in the jigsaw puzzle of empire defence.[1] Whether empire defence was still an appropriate frame of reference was a point for argument but it was beyond dispute that the defence ledger east of Suez had changed dramatically. Although the withdrawal of British troops from India released some 55,000 men, that hardly compensated for the loss of the Indian army as a peace-time strategic reserve for the protection of imperial interests in the Middle East and Far East, and of a reservoir of manpower which could rapidly be drawn into service in time of war. Moreover, the loss of India's economic resources, communications facilities, opportunities for acclimatization and of its barracks, military installations, ports, and airfields went far towards undermining Britain's traditional strategy in the region. Certainly Britain was relieved of the onerous burden of maintaining internal security and she no longer had an automatic commitment to the defence of India but these gains, real as they were, could offset the strategic debits only if they were accompanied by a complete reconsideration of Britain's role and a reduction in the size of British forces deployed in the area.

To point to the crucial significance of 1947 for a redefinition of Britain's role is not to suggest that the entire defence network could have been dismantled overnight. The responsibilities of empire were not extinguished with the formal transfer of power. The fact was that transitional arrangements were required pending the development of indigenous defence capabilities. In addition, Britain had continuing commitments to the defence of her colonies and protectorates in the area. Although most of Britain's Indian Ocean territories had been acquired or developed because of her responsibilities in India, in the meantime they had become responsibilities in their own right. As Sir Robert Scott has observed, by 1947 Britain's defence tasks had diversified far beyond their primary purpose of the defence of India.[2]

In the background lay a moral obligation to assist in the defence of Australia and New Zealand. The Commonwealth link was reinforced by ties of kinship and culture and it was

---

[1] *Times*, 7 Nov. 1946.
[2] *Major Theatre of Conflict: British Policy in East Asia* (1968), p. 2.

accepted without question that an attack on Australia and New Zealand would be treated as an attack on the United Kingdom. There was also a more shadowy obligation to independent India and Pakistan. Although the formal defence commitment had come to an end, there was a general belief that Britain continued to bear some residual responsibility for the security of these states. Field Marshal Sir Claude Auchinleck, the last British Commander-in-Chief in India, gave expression to what others felt when he declared that 'Britain is still morally bound to aid India and Pakistan against an aggressor.'[3] Considering the sense of responsibility and the sentimental attachment which so many Britons felt, it was unthinkable that Britain would adopt any other attitude. One million British graves across the subcontinent, and varied mementoes of the days of the Raj on the walls and mantelshelves of countless British homes bore witness to the generations that had served in India and it could not all be in vain. The chapter could not so easily be closed.

There were some who envisaged a formal defence arrangement with India. The distinguished Indian diplomat and historian, K. M. Panikkar, pointed out that until the establishment of an indigenous defence system, India would need to work on the basis of intimate co-operation with Britain. He therefore advocated an Indo-British defence pact in which Britain shared with India responsibility for defence of the area.[4] The *Manchester Guardian* saw advantages in a formal defence alliance and wondered whether it might not become the basis of a wider Indian Ocean security system.[5] In the event no formal arrangement was negotiated, the reason no doubt resting, on the Indian side, with the fear that a defence agreement would compromise their newly won independence and be incompatible with their policy of non-alignment, and, on the British side, with the determination to avoid entanglement in any Indo-Pakistani conflict.

In the case of Burma and Ceylon, the grant of independence was accompanied by the negotiation of transitional defence agreements which involved the United Kingdom in continuing, though more limited, responsibilities. The precedent was thus

[3] 'The Defence of the British Commonwealth', I, *Daily Mail*, 20 July 1948.
[4] 'The Defence of India and Indo-British Obligations', *Int. Aff.* 22/1 (Jan. 1946), pp. 85–90.
[5] 29 Nov. 1947.

established for offering 'run-down agreements' to former British territories on or after the attainment of independence which were designed to safeguard them during the difficult transitional period when adequate indigenous forces were not available. On the British side, they also served to emphasize the amicable nature of the parting. The conclusion of such agreements was always a matter of discretion, but during the fifties it became the usual procedure. The defence agreement with Burma was signed in London on 17 October 1947, as an annex to the treaty transferring power to Burma. Under the agreement Britain agreed to send to Burma a joint service mission, which would provide instructional and other staff for service with the Burmese forces. Although there was no automatic commitment to the defence of Burma, it appeared that British support was envisaged in at least some circumstances.[6]

The agreement with Ceylon, signed on 15 November 1947, committed Britain more deeply to the security of that country, though in return Britain obtained important strategic facilities. The two governments agreed to give each other 'such military assistance for the security of their territories, for defence against external aggression and for the protection of essential communications, as it may be in their mutual interest to provide'. Further, Britain undertook to furnish assistance for the training and development of the Ceylonese armed forces while Ceylon agreed that British ground, naval, and air forces could continue to be based on the island and that the necessary ports, air strips, military establishments, and communications facilities would be available to British forces.[7] At a press conference, Sir Oliver Goonetilleke, the Home Minister, said there was no time limit to the agreement, which would continue so long as it was in the interests of both parties.[8]

In Arabia and the Persian Gulf, Britain remained responsible for the defence of Kuwait, Bahrain, Qatar, the Trucial Coast, Muscat and Oman and the South Arabian states by virtue of a series of treaties and other agreements made during the nineteenth century, which grew out of attempts to abolish

[6] FO, *Treaty between the Government of the United Kingdom and the Provisional Government of Burma regarding the Recognition of Burmese Independence and Related Matters*, Cmd 7360 (1948). The agreement was terminated by Burma in 1953.
[7] CO, *Ceylon: Proposals for conferring on Ceylon fully responsible status within the British Commonwealth of Nations*, Cmd 7257 (1947).
[8] *Times*, 15 Nov. 1947.

piracy and the slave trade and to safeguard the approach to India. In the Far East there was a continuing responsibility for the state of Brunei which was brought under British protection by a treaty in 1888 and reaffirmed by a new agreement in 1906.

Finally, Britain had a constitutional responsibility for the defence of her remaining colonial territories in the area. At the beginning of 1948 Tanganyika, Uganda, Kenya, Zanzibar, Mauritius, Aden, the Seychelles, the Maldives, Malaya, Singapore, North Borneo, Sarawak, and Hong Kong were within this category. These colonial defence responsibilities were especially significant because many of them seemed likely to continue for decades. Although self-government had long been the ultimate objective of British colonial policy, and it had been confirmed by the grant of independence to India and Pakistan in 1947 and to Ceylon and Burma in 1948, it was thought likely to be a matter of generations before the remaining British territories obtained independence. In a sense this was the lesson to be drawn from India. Ceylon was the exception which proved the rule. Sir Charles Jeffries, Deputy Under-Secretary of State for the Colonies from 1947 to 1956, has pointed out that in 1948 it was agreed that Ceylon was a special case because of its size, its economic strength, its advanced social organization, and its poltical experience. At that time no other colony seemed to be in sight of fulfilling these conditions.[9] As late as 1950, Colonial Office doctrine was explicit that political progress must be matched by corresponding social and economic development.[10] As a result, independence for the African colonies seemed decades away.[11]

Given these strands of continuing commitment, the implications of Britain's moral obligations and of her involvement in Malaya and in Africa were of a different order of magnitude from the implications of her withdrawal from India. The need for reappraisal was in no way lessened by the existence of these essentially ancillary responsibilities. On the contrary, it was these responsibilities which made reappraisal so necessary, for without the moral commitments and the Malayan and African ties, Britain's role east of Suez could never have survived the loss of India.

[9] Sir Charles Jeffries, *Transfer of Power* (1960), p. 12.
[10] W. M. Macmillan, *The Road to Self-Rule* (1959), p. 220.
[11] See Margery Perham, *African Outline* (1966), pp. 36–8.

What was required was a redefinition of Britain's objectives in the area: an adjustment of the imperial role to accord with the conditions of the post-imperial order. With hindsight, it is all too easy to speculate about the possibilities of such a re-appraisal. Yet it is central to our theme to show that there were openings for British initiative. Most plausibly, the old assumption of Britain's predominance in the area and the broad sweep of her responsibilities might have given way to a more limited conception of Britain's defence interests based upon the protection of particular territories and strategic areas.[12] Thus Britain's Middle Eastern commitment might have been scaled down and some formula devised to enable Britain gradually to withdraw from the Persian Gulf. At the very least, a long-term plan of general disengagement might have been drawn up, which could have served as a frame of reference when decolonization proposals and weapons procurements were being considered.

However, no reappraisal ever took place. At the time Britain's role was not seen in its historical perspective and it was not subject to inquiry in this light. In these circumstances a system which had stood the tests of a century and more could survive the removal of its linch-pin. While some modifications and some readjustment could hardly be avoided, the main workings of the system continued on into the fifties.

In retrospect the need for reappraisal seems so obvious that at first sight it is difficult to understand how Indian independence could pass leaving little more than a ripple on the placid surface of British political and strategic thinking. The reasons are complex: a combination of institutional factors, external circumstances, and patterns of thought which only slowly lost their hold on decision-making in Whitehall. To some extent the explanation spans two decades and is the continuing theme of this book.

In particular departments and on specific issues, studies and inquiries were undertaken which had some bearing on Britain's role, but their scope was limited and their overall effect was negligible. In addition, there were individuals who felt acutely the need for reappraisal but their efforts were

[12] In a leader 'The Indian Ocean' on 9 Aug. 1947, the *Manchester Guardian* foresaw such a pattern, though with the warning that it 'could hardly fail to increase international tension.'

nullified by a combination of short-term pressures and economic stringency. The resistance to change was so deeply rooted
that only a major reconsideration involving alike the services
and the overseas policy departments, and with firm cabinet
backing, could have launched Britain on a suitable post-
imperial course. On the broader issue the Chiefs of Staff took no
initiative, confining their attention to the problem of rebuilding
an imperial strategy from what remained of the pre-war pieces.
The practice of preparing an annual review of imperial defence,
which before the war occupied about a month, lapsed during
these years. It was not until 1951 that a major review was
prepared and even this was of limited scope. The 1952 global
strategy paper was more comprehensive and broke new ground,
but by then the main lines of Britain's Indian Ocean course
had been charted and a change of direction was hardly possible.[13]
In the service departments also there was very little rethinking.
Speaking in the debate on the Army Estimates in 1948, Emanuel
Shinwell, Secretary of State for War, acknowledged that the
British withdrawal from India, together with the changes in
the organization of the army which were now seen to be essential, had brought about a situation 'which demands a complete
review of our organisation and military plans.'[14] He went on to
announce certain reductions in infantry and armoured units,
and then moved to safer ground and nothing more was to be
heard about a review. According to one report, whatever was
done, there was very little questioning of basic presuppositions.
Judging from organization and deployment patterns, if any
review was made it can hardly have gone much further than
the files of the War Office. The other service departments were
less deeply involved in the imperial venture and no initiative was
forthcoming from those quarters.

Nor was there any inquiry in the Foreign Office or the Colonial Office. The question of Britain's role was an academic issue
and both departments had more pressing problems which
required immediate attention. As one senior official explained:
'Men like Sir Robert Scott would say turn your mind to what
is happening in Asia, but it didn't seem necessary to do anything about it.' Thus the old ideas lingered on and the collective outlook remained imperial.

[13] For further treatment of the 1952 paper see pp. 46–8 below.
[14] 448 HC Deb., 9 Mar. 1948, col. 1015.

In part the continuance of the old pattern of thought stemmed from the fact that neither department was equipped to examine long-term trends and the wider implications of day-to-day policy. In the Foreign Office, in particular, there was an in-built prejudice against forward planning and before 1949 there was no desk specifically responsible for carrying it out. In 1949 Ernest Bevin set up a Permanent Under-Secretary's Committee which was briefed to identify the longer-term trends in international affairs and to prepare studies on their implications for the formulation of British policy.[15] Although several studies were produced, the Committee was gravely hampered by the pressure of day-to-day problems and the lack of a permanent staff. About 1950–1, under the aegis of this Committee, a number of subcommittees were set up to con-sider areas such as the Far East and the Middle East and to recommend appropriate British policies. After having sat for several months a few hundred pages of typescript were pro-duced, a vote of thanks was received, and nothing more was heard.

At the political level there was no clear conception of defence contraction as an integral part of the process of decolonization. At various times there were ideas for withdrawal from certain areas and there was continuous pressure for a reduction in defence spending which led to periodic reviews, but these attempts at adjustment fell far short of a general reconsideration of Britain's role. Against a background of conflicting interests, ideas and personalities, the government adhered to a wider view of Britain's defence interests. In the absence of reappraisal, it was inevitable that the imperial instincts and the pressure of immediate events should stifle initiative and that policy should develop along established lines.

The tone of the government's approach to Britain's world responsibilities was set by Ernest Bevin, the Foreign Secretary. Speaking in the House of Commons in May 1947, he declared:

So far as foreign policy is concerned, we have not altered our commitments in the slightest . . . His Majesty's Government do not accept the view . . . that we have ceased to be a great Power, or the contention that we have ceased to play that role. We regard

---

[15] Lord Strang, *The Diplomatic Career* (1962), pp. 110–11.

ourselves as one of the Powers most vital to the peace of the world, and we still have our historic part to play.[16]

Inevitably the pressure to reduce defence spending and the opposition within the Labour party to National Service weighed heavily upon ministers, but in general the government accepted the need to maintain Britain's imperial position, though it was not always prepared to pay the strategic price. When the gap between the Treasury and the Foreign Office widened, 'service ministers simply got Cabinet orders to do this or that on existing resources.'[17]

For a time Attlee pressed upon the Chiefs of Staff and the Defence Committee the idea of withdrawing from the Middle East and concentrating in Africa.[18] However, the political and military obstacles were formidable, the opposition of the Chiefs of Staff eventually held sway, and the matter was allowed to rest.[19] Until the outbreak of the Korean war in June 1950 there was heavy pressure from the Treasury to reduce defence expenditure and the annual Defence White Papers laid emphasis upon a strong and sound economy as the first essential of Britain's strength. Both Hugh Dalton and Sir Stafford Cripps as successive chancellors made repeated attempts to reduce Britain's defence responsbilitites and hence lighten the economic burden of her military role but their efforts met with little success.[20] In 1947 or 1948, for example, Cripps set up the Harwood Committee under the auspices of the Imperial Defence College to examine the strategic implications of a defence budget of £800 million.[21] An interesting report was produced but as was so often the case it was shelved in the face of more immediate considerations. Again, under pressure from Cripps, Hong Kong was almost abandoned in April 1949.[22] However, within a matter of weeks British forces were increased because of the HMS *Amethyst* incident and in June it was decided to maintain the British presence, largely because of the ramifications of this incident.

[16] 437 HC Deb., 16 May 1947, col. 1965.
[17] Emanuel Shinwell, *Conflict Without Malice* (1955), p. 197.
[18] Hugh Dalton, *High Tide and After: Memoirs* [iii] *1945–1960* (1962), pp. 101 and 105.
[19] FM Viscount Montgomery, *Memoirs* (1958), pp. 435–6; see also pp. 36–8 below.
[20] See e.g. Dalton, ch. 23.
[21] Sir Edmund Harwood, Chairman of the Committee, was then Civilian Director of the Imperial Defence College.
[22] R. N. Rosecrance, *Defense of the Realm* (1968), p. 106.

In general, Parliament and press gave remarkably little thought to the possibility of limited withdrawals and, with some notable exceptions, criticism of the government's defence policies focused on the adequacy of the effort rather than the breadth of commitments. Of course there were some, mainly on the Labour benches, who questioned the extent of Britain's commitments, but until 1953 they were very much voices in the wilderness.[23]

The institutional responsibility for reappraisal rested with the Defence Committee, though it might reasonably have been expected that some prodding would come from the Chiefs of Staff. The Committee was set up in 1946 to replace the Committee of Imperial Defence and it was the central body where domestic, foreign, and military policies were examined concurrently and with an eye to both present and future needs. It was responsible for reviewing current strategy and it was charged with the co-ordination of the various departments in preparation for war. Its regular members were the Prime Minister, the Minister of Defence, the Lord President of the Council, the Foreign Secretary, the Chancellor of the Exchequer, the service Ministers, the Minister of Labour, and the Minister of Supply. The Chiefs of Staff attended all meetings and could be called upon to advise the Committee on defence aspects. Other ministers, officers, and officials were from time to time invited to attend meetings when specialized subjects were under discussion.[24]

On the evidence available, the Defence Committee's failure to reappraise reflected the inadequacy of the system rather than the weakness of the Labour administration.[25] In Whitehall, opinion was firm that the Committee was an ineffectual body for resolving issues involving long-term goals and crossing departmental boundaries. Indeed, according to one report, until its replacement by the Defence and Overseas Policy Committee, the Defence Committee in practice dealt almost exclusively with arguments about equipment and the allocation of resources. The broader issues were handled out of

[23] See e.g. the speeches of R. H. S. Crossman, 448 HC Deb., 1 Mar. 1948, col. 88, and Reginald Paget, 472 HC Deb., 16 Mar. 1950, col. 1609.
[24] PM, *Central Organisation for Defence*, Cmd 6923 (1946), paras 20-5. See also PM, *Central Organisation for Defence*, Cmnd 476 (1958), para. 4.
[25] In the absence of published sources, this section depends heavily on discussions with ministers, senior officers, and officials.

committee by the Prime Minister, the Foreign Secretary, and one or two other senior ministers and it was only rarely that military planners were involved. The root of the problem lay in the extreme reluctance of a ministerial committee to take decisions about role. To some extent, therefore, it can be argued that the lack of firm political direction on defence issues—a perpetual complaint of military leaders—was a by-product of the committee system and of cabinet government.[26] Perhaps the last word was expressed by one senior official when he explained that too many vested interests were involved for the Defence Committee to tackle the question of role. In his opinion, reappraisal was 'too fundamental to be practical politics'.

Among the background factors to be taken into account, the circumstances of India's independence seem fundamental. That India obtained independence by agreement greatly reduced the sense of change. Moreover, attention was fixed on India, not on Britain. As one official observed, 'from 1945 to 1947 we were preparing the Indians for the change but not ourselves.' Throughout, the transfer of power to India was the dominant concern and its sequel—the retraction of British power from the Indian Ocean—escaped attention.[27] Later the decision of India and Pakistan to remain in the Commonwealth and the transference of the assumptions of empire to the Commonwealth made it possible for British leaders to see the new situation as a continuation of the old.

A more general factor which worked against reappraisal was that after 1947 British interest in developments east of Suez was extremely limited. India had long been the focal point of British interest in the area and Indian independence inevitably downgraded the priority of the Indian Ocean in British eyes. Despite the continuing belief that Britain had a major role to play in Africa, Asia and the Far East, Indian Ocean problems were not widely discussed in Parliament or the press. The European Recovery Programme, NATO, and the Berlin crisis held the headlines. Certainly the Malayan

---

[26] This theme is elaborated on pp. 138–9 below.

[27] In India more attention was given to the other side of the coin. See e.g. Panikkar, *Int. Aff.* (London), 22/1 (Jan. 1946); Lt Gen G. N. Molesworth, 'Some Problems of Future Security in the Indian Ocean Area', *Asiatic Review*, 42/149 (Jan. 1946), pp. 26–34; and Sir V. T. Krishnamachari, 'Regional Arrangements – the Indian Ocean Area', *India Quarterly*, 2/3 (July – Sept. 1946), pp. 287–9.

and Mau Mau emergencies made some impact, but neither could be said to illustrate any sustained interest in the area east of Suez.

During 1948 Australia grew increasingly restless about Britain's neglect of Asian affairs and J. B. Chifley, the Australian Prime Minister, was reported to have voiced strong criticisms when in London.[28] Nor was Canberra alone in feeling that Britain was losing touch with developments east of Suez. Speaking in Delhi on 11 November 1948, on his return from the Prime Ministers' Conference, Jawaharlal Nehru reported that in London he had found only a very limited awareness of Asian issues: 'The people there were so concentrated on their immediate problems such as the Western Union that they did not see other problems which were not only important to themselves but mightily affected them.'[29]

Even more revealing was Admiral Sir Denis Boyd's disclosure that: 'After two and three-quarter years as C.-in-C. (Far East) I came home with a wide experience of the whole area and a great enthusiasm for the problems but, apart from the First Sea Lord, absolutely no-one took the slightest interest in my return.'[30]

Boyd asked to see the Foreign Office and the Colonial Office, but neither department showed any interest. Upon inquiry, Boyd learned from a previous C in C that not even the First Sea Lord had seen him on his return.[31]

Still, if British interest was on the decline, there were few who thought that Britain could stand aside from the problems of the area. Having just fought two long and exhausting campaigns, one to hold on to the Middle East and the other to eject Japan from her conquests, it was hardly the time to retreat unnecessarily. Arguments about withdrawal fell on deaf ears because the government and indeed the nation were still thinking in terms of Britain as a world power. To reduce commitments or to limit the traditional conception of Britain's role in Africa, Asia, and the Far East smacked of abdicating from world leadership and was too much at variance with Britain's history and tradition. To men brought up to a map of

[28] Patrick Maitland 'Commonwealth Criticism of Britain: "Neglect" of Affairs in S.-E. Asia', *Scotsman*, 13 Dec. 1948.
[29] Ibid.
[30] 'The Services in the Far East', *JRUSI*, 95/577 (Feb. 1950), pp. 41–2.
[31] Ibid. p. 42.

the world centred on the Indian Ocean and with so many of the surrounding lands coloured in red, it required an about-turn in outlook and thinking to accept such a far-reaching change in Britain's position and interests, and this could not be accomplished overnight. Sir Oliver Franks, the British ambassador in Washington from 1948 to 1952, has expressed the feeling of the time in a passage which is worth quoting at length because it so clearly portrays the habit of thought of the men who held the reins of policy-making over these years:

> . . . we assume that our future will be of one piece with our past and that we shall continue as a Great Power. What is noteworthy is the way that we take this for granted. It is not a belief arrived at after reflection by a conscious decision. It is part of the habit and furniture of our minds: a principle so much one with our outlook and character that it determines the way we act without emerging itself into clear consciousness.[32]

The course of events east of Suez worked to complement traditional patterns of thought in Britain. No sooner had the transfer of power to India been accomplished than pragmatism began to call the tune of British policy. The ink was scarcely dry on the Indian Independence Act when Communist violence in Malaya forced Britain to embark on a counter-insurgency campaign which was to tie her hands for twelve years. With a war to be fought and won there was very little stimulus for fresh thinking about political aims in the area. What was the use of asking questions about the purpose of deploying power east of Suez when the immediate problem was Malaya, was on the ground, and rested at the company and even the platoon level?

The outbreak of the Korean war in June 1950 had a more profound impact and put an end to all ideas that overseas forces might gradually be reduced. Although the primary fear was for Europe, the war heightened British perception of the Communist threat in the Far East and the Middle East.[33] Now that world Communism was thought to be on the march, a consolidation of Britain's position was essential. The huge rearmament programme and the revision of contingency planning spilled over from Europe to the overseas theatres, and the door

[32] 'Britain and the Tide of World Affairs', *Listener*, 52/1314 (11 Nov. 1954), p. 788.
[33] See Shinwell's speech, 478 HC Deb., 26 July 1950, col. 469.

was closed to pressures about the level of defence spending and National Service, which might otherwise slowly have eroded Britain's Indian Ocean role.

Against this background, it is hardly surprising that the negotiation of the ANZUS Treaty in 1951 provoked no re-thinking about Britain's role. With the United States now formally tied to the defence of Australia and New Zealand, the British commitment became a second string to the Antipo-dean bow of military dependence. The opportunity was therefore available for Britain to reconsider her defence obligations but both the government and the opposition chose to regard them as before. Herbert Morrison, the Foreign Secretary, declared: 'The United Kingdom Government regard the arrangement as complementary to the understand-ings of mutual support and co-operation between our country, Australia and New Zealand.'[34]

The general attitude was one of irritation that the United Kingdom had been excluded from the pact, and that later the ANZUS Council had refused to allow British observers to attend Council meetings.[35] While welcoming the pact, Morrison had no hesitation in declaring that Britain was a Pacific power and admitted that 'it would not have been un-welcome to us if we had been included in the proposed pact.'[36] The opposition wanted to know why the pact had not been widened to include Britain. After all, said R. A. Butler, we should certainly involve ourselves as far as possible with United States policy in the Far East.[37] Nor did Churchill conceal his dislike of the pact, and when the Conservatives came to power he made no secret of his hope that wider arrangements would be negotiated in which Britain could play a major part.[38]

In the absence of a major reconsideration, Britain's role and its purposes east of Suez remained largely undefined. The extent and nature of Britain's involvement was determined more by developments in the area and by the global power configuration than by a close examination of British interests and responsibilities. The crises and preoccupations of the time

[34] 486 HC Deb., 19 Apr. 1951, col. 2007.
[35] See generally D. E. McHenry and R. N. Rosecrance, 'The Exclusion of the United Kingdom from the ANZUS Pact', *Int. Org.* 12/3 (summer 1958), pp. 320–9.
[36] 486 HC Deb., 19 Apr. 1951, col. 2007.
[37] 491 HC Deb., 25 July 1951, coll. 490–1.
[38] *Times*, 18 June 1953.

led naturally to a concentration on three areas of particular
concern: the Middle East, the Persian Gulf, and the Far
East; and in the main British policy broke into these separate
parts. However, assumptions about the lines of communication
and empire defence provided certain linking threads and the
whole area continued to be regarded as a British preserve in
the context of the global struggle between East and West.

In the last years of the forties it was assumed, rather than
consciously spelt out, that developments around the Indian
Ocean were still of great significance to the United Kingdom
and it was accepted on all sides that Britain must be in a position to influence their outcome. That Britain had weighty
strategic and economic interests in the area was something
that everyone knew, and if they received little attention in
the House of Commons it was not because they were regarded
as unimportant but simply because most members took them
for granted. At first the imperial motive—a mixture of ideas
about power and responsibility, trade and communication—
provided an instinctive and sufficient underprop for the maintenance of British dominance in the area. Later as the force of
imperial thinking declined, fear of Russia, and to some extent
of China in league with Russia, became the mainspring of a
wider British involvement. Labour ministers, no less than
Conservative leaders, fell naturally into the habit of interpreting
Britain's interests more in the light of her position as a world
power than in specifically national terms. Attlee's writings
reveal how deeply he was influenced by this pattern of thought,
and it seems equally true of Bevin and Shinwell.[39]

The clearest statement of Britain's stake in the Indian Ocean
area was made by Major General Sir Ian Jacob in 1950. As
he put it, in a report endorsed by a study group of the Royal
Institute of International Affairs chaired by R. A. Butler:

The United Kingdom desires a tranquil Indian Ocean. Our
interests in Africa, the development of the new countries, the economic riches of Malaya, and the route to Australia and New Zealand
would all be seriously affected by the incursion of an enemy into
the Indian Ocean arena. We would like to see the creation of a
strong regional arrangement, capable of preserving the inviolability

[39] See C. R. Attlee, *As it Happened*(1954), espec. pp. 200 and 202. Also Francis
Williams, *A Prime Minister Remembers* (1961), ch. 11.

of the Indian Ocean, and the United Kingdom would be most ready to play its part in this.[40]

According to this line of thinking, Britain still possessed vital interests around the rim of the Indian Ocean. In the Far East it was assumed, though without any real investigation, that Britain's economic interests were safeguarded by a continued military presence and this argument reinforced Britain's general concern for the security of the area and the protection of the lines of communication to Australia and New Zealand.[41] The data relating to Britain's investment in the Far East are very unsatisfactory but it seems that for Malaya alone the pre-war figure was about £100 million and by 1950 it would have been rather higher.[42] This was almost entirely private capital, most of which was invested in rubber and tin. In addition, Australasia and the Far East accounted for about one-fifth of Britain's total overseas trade.

During these years the Persian Gulf remained a secure British enclave and therefore the need for a military presence was accepted almost without question, neither requiring nor receiving any full political justification. In the background of policy-making, however, the protection of the oil supplies was emerging as a prime consideration to be set alongside Britain's responsibility for the security of the Gulf States. One fear was that the supplies of oil might be physically cut off, thus gravely damaging the British economy. Some indication of Britain's dependence on supplies of Persian Gulf and Middle Eastern oil is given by the import figures for the financial year 1949–50. In that year Britain's imports of crude petroleum from Kuwait and Bahrain were valued at £22.1 million, and from Saudi Arabia, Iraq, and Iran at £25.4 million, while imports from the rest of the world amounted to only £8.4 million.[43] Another fear was that the British interest in the major operating companies—Kuwait Oil, Anglo-Iranian Oil, and Iraq Petroleum— and the dollar savings and high profits yielded might be lost

[40] 'The United Kingdom's Strategic Interests', in RIIA, *United Kingdom Policy: Foreign, Strategic, Economic* (1950), p. 54.
[41] See MoD, *Statement on Defence 1950*, Cmd 7895 (1950), para. 5.
[42] A. R. Conan, *Capital Imports Into Sterling Countries* (1960), p. 33. Also G. C. Allen and Audrey Donnithorne, *Western Enterprise in Indonesia and Malaya* (1957), p. 290, app. 3.
[43] Economic Cooperation Administration, Special Mission to the United Kingdom *The Sterling Area: an American Analysis* (1951), table 267.

if Arab nationalism were allowed to run an unchecked course.[44]

On both counts it was generally accepted that a continued military presence safeguarded Britain's interests. In this connection John Strachey's recollection of the advice he was offered as Secretary of State for War when the Abadan crisis broke out in 1951 is pertinent. According to Strachey, both the advocates of using armed force and the opponents of such a course advised that if the crisis were not resolved Persia would be unable to extract and refine the oil and that not only the Anglo-Iranian Company would be ruined but the British economy itself would be crippled for lack of oil.[45] The same assumptions appeared to have coloured Britain's approach to both the Persian Gulf and the Middle East, though the Abadan experience suggested that they were at least questionable.

The Middle East was held to be an area of vital concern to the United Kingdom, so much so that in January 1947, when Attlee challenged the Chiefs of Staff on the issue, all three were prepared to resign rather than give way over the area.[46] In the eyes of the Chiefs of Staff, the Middle East would provide the base from which British forces would be able to attack the Russian flank. Moreover, its significance as a focal point of imperial communications had been vindicated by the war and it was still seen to be of great value as a half-way house between the United Kingdom and the Far East. Oil was another important consideration in that control of the Suez Canal and of Aden was thought to secure the outlet from the Gulf and the route west. Finally, the Middle East was regarded as a convenient base from which Africa could be protected from a Russian invasion, and a counter-attack launched if necessary.[47] By the late forties these considerations were taken to be conclusive. Whatever political doubts existed in the earlier years of the Labour government, the service chiefs had steered the United Kingdom back to its traditional understanding of the need to hold the Middle East.

In Africa, although it was accepted that Britain's political

---

[44] For details of Britain's interest in the major oil companies see ibid. p. 513.
[45] *The End of Empire* (1959), p. 161.
[46] Montgomery, *Memoirs*, p. 436.
[47] See Gen Sir Leslie Hollis, *One Marine's Tale* (1956), pp. 155–7; Col The Hon. E. H. Wyndham, 'The Near and Middle East in Relation to Western Defence', *Brassey's Annual 1952*, p. 40; and Maj Gen L. O. Lyne, 'The Middle East', *Brassey's Annual 1953*, pp. 107–13.

and especially her economic interests had become more important than in the pre-war years, there was no attempt to examine them in detail and it seems unlikely that they figured large in British thinking. To some extent the scheme for a British base in Kenya in the late forties brought Africa into the mainstream of imperial defence, but British interest was not long sustained after the abandonment of the project, and in any case it was largely a consequence of developments in the Middle East.[48]

It went without saying that Britain would be the principal actor in imperial or post-imperial ventures in the Indian Ocean but it was expected that the Commonwealth and the colonies would make up the supporting cast. The interests to be protected were not Britain's alone and the effort required could hardly be unilateral. In the case of the successor states the hope was for a measure of co-ordinated action based on common interest while the colonies would play their traditional part by contributing to the central programme. To this extent Britain's approach remained imperial, and co-ordination with Commonwealth and colonial governments was a matter of fundamental importance.

Before the war the Secretaries of State for India and for the Colonies were regular members of the Committee of Imperial Defence and co-operation with Australia, New Zealand, and South Africa was secured by a network of informal liaison and periodic conferences.[49] In the early post-war years the assumption came naturally that this system of informal co-operation and the understanding of mutual obligation would continue under the mantle of the Commonwealth. However, although in varying degrees liaison between the member countries remained close, the hopes for extensive collaboration at the Commonwealth level were dashed by the policies of non-alignment of the Asian states and the increasing independence of the old dominions.

At the end of the Second World War the theory of Commonwealth defence still rested on the decision of the Imperial Conference of 1926. According to this decision, general defence, meaning the defence of the empire's lines of communication, was the responsibility of the United Kingdom and was to be

---

[48] See further pp. 36–8 below.
[49] See further Franklyn A. Johnson, *Defence by Committee: the British Committee of Imperial Defence 1885–1959* (1960), pp. 212–19.

carried out by the Royal Navy, assisted by such forces as the dominions could provide. Local defence was the responsibility of each dominion and the function of their respective land forces, while the United Kingdom assumed responsibility for the local defence of the colonies.[50] By the beginning of 1946 this scheme was manifestly obsolete but no alternative arrangement had taken its place.

During 1946 and 1947 the idea of allocating zones of responsibility within the Commonwealth appears to have been accepted in principle, though no clear-cut definition was forthcoming. At the Commonwealth Conference of 1946, J. B. Chifley proposed that Australia should take on larger responsibilities in the Pacific on behalf of the whole British Commonwealth. According to Chifley, this scheme for the Pacific had equal relevance to other areas.[51] Speaking at the Royal United Service Institution in 1947, Viscount Alanbrooke proposed that each dominion assume direct responsibility for land, sea, and air areas connected directly with the security and defence of that dominion. In addition, each dominion would formulate proposals as to the degree and nature of assistance required from other members of the Commonwealth in an emergency.[52]

The White Paper *Central Organisation for Defence* in 1946 was more guarded, but it accepted the idea of regional association and it proposed that regional questions be studied in the appropriate regional centre. Overall co-operation was to be obtained by a system of Commonwealth liaison officers.[53] The principle of regional association was used as an argument against the participation of the Dominions in the deliberations of the Defence Committee – a line of thinking that a number of observers found difficult to understand.[54] In view of the differing approaches of the various members of the Commonwealth, the White Paper saw no value in developing any alternative centralized machinery.[55] The looseness of these arrangements found little favour with Australia and New Zealand and there

[50] W. C. B. Tunstall, *The Commonwealth and Regional Defence* (1959), pp. 5 and 6.
[51] *Times*, 7 Nov. 1946.
[52] 'Empire Defence', *JRUSI*, 92/566 (May 1947), pp. 182–6. See also Alanbrooke's earlier speech, *Times*, 7 Nov. 1946, and Sir Arthur Bryant, *Triumph in the West 1943–1946* (1959), pp. 532–3.
[53] PM, *Central Organisation for Defence*, Cmd 6923, paras 38 and 39.
[54] e.g. Lord Hankey, 143 HL Deb., 16 Oct. 1946, col. 311, and Lord Altrincham, ibid. col. 143.
[55] PM, Cmd 6923, paras 36 and 37.

were many in the United Kingdom also who thought the scheme lacking in substance. Lord Chatfield expressed the general feeling when he declared that 'the connection with Imperial defence in this paper is weaker than it was, and it never was very strong.'[56]

As foreshadowed in the 1946 White Paper, consultative machinery was set up by Britain and certain of the dominions during 1947. United Kingdom service liaison staffs were established in Australia and South Africa in 1947, and in New Zealand in 1948. The Commonwealth Prime Ministers' Conference in 1948 expressed general approval of the existing arrangements, though certain improvements were recommended.

A development of greater moment occurred in 1949 when the governments of the United Kingdom, Australia, and New Zealand agreed to co-ordinate defence planning under the ANZAM arrangement. Although the precise nature of the arrangement has never been publicly clarified, it seems that ANZAM involves no formal governmental obligation and is primarily an arrangement for facilitating staff co-operation and joint planning.[57] In a television interview in Australia in 1963, General Sir Richard Hull, then Chief of the Imperial General Staff, explained that ANZAM covered no precise area, but its region of interest is known to include Australia, New Zealand, Malaya, and Borneo together with the adjacent sea areas.[58] According to one report, planning was at first limited to the defence of sea and air communications in the region, but was subsequently extended to cover the defence of Malaya.[59] Under the agreement a New Zealand flight of Dakotas was stationed at Singapore in September 1949 and in June 1950 RAAF aircraft arrived in Malaya. About the same time ships of the RAN began to operate on a more frequent schedule in the neighbouring waters. Reportedly, the differing approaches of the three governments at times led to delicate political problems and there were cases of friction.

[56] 134 HL Deb., 16 Oct. 1946, col. 284.
[57] A Committee, known as the ANZAM Defence Committee, has met in Canberra on an 'as required' basis. Although a small secretariat was set up, the Committee has been primarily a forum for representatives of the Chiefs of Staff of the three countries to discuss the Commonwealth Strategic Reserve in Malaya and other matters of general concern.
[58] Sir Alan Watt, *Australian Defence Policy 1951–1963* (1964), pp. 53–5.
[59] RIIA, *Collective Defence in South East Asia*, p. 20.

A second venture in closer Commonwealth co-operation, this time in the Middle East, was of a more limited nature. Following a conference held in London in June 1951, the governments of Australia, New Zealand, and South Africa agreed to participate in an Allied Command Organisation in the Middle East with Britain, the United States, France, and Turkey. As originally conceived, the idea was to 'internationalize' the Suez base within the framework of a regional defence organization but Egypt and the other Arab states rejected this proposal.[60] Despite the opposition of the Arab states, the Western countries pushed ahead with planning and Commonwealth air units were posted to serve with United Kingdom forces. On 6 March 1952 the Australian government announced its decision to send an RAAF fighter wing to the Middle East.[61] This was shortly followed by an announcement from Wellington that New Zealand would send a fighter squadron.

Defence arrangements in the colonies and their relation to the general scheme of Commonwealth defence attracted little public attention but they remained of considerable importance during the post-war period. The basic principle governing colonial defence was that the ultimate responsibility rested with the United Kingdom government but the overseas territories made such contributions as they could according to their means and resources. In both Africa and South-east Asia the various colonial forces were administered by the War Office, though the Colonial Office and the Colonial governments were consulted on questions of finance.[62]

The White Paper *Central Organisation for Defence* in 1946 proposed to revive the Overseas Defence Committee as a sub-committee of the Defence Committee in London. This body was to be charged with surveying the whole field of defence preparations in the colonies and their relation to the general picture of imperial defence.[63] When the Overseas Defence Committee was re-established in 1947, however, its terms of reference differed from the original intention. Under the revised arrangement, the task of co-ordinating the colonies with the general scheme of imperial defence belonged to the Chiefs of Staff

---

[60] See further John C. Campbell, *Defense of the Middle East* (1960), pp. 40–8.

[61] *Times*, 6 Mar. 1952.

[62] Sir Charles Jeffries, *The Colonial Office* (1956), p. 177.

[63] PM, Cmd 6923, para. 40.

who were advised by the joint planning staffs. The Chiefs of Staff reported to the Defence Committee, which then decided whether the proposals of the Chiefs of Staff affecting the colonies should be implemented.[64]

In South-east Asia, the position was slightly different because of the office of Commissioner-General. At the end of the Second World War the need to co-ordinate political, military, and economic policy in the area led to the appointment of a Governor General for the British territories in Malaya and Borneo and of a Special Commissioner for South-east Asia. On the retirement of Lord Killearn as Special Commissioner on 1 May 1948, the two posts were amalgamated and Malcolm MacDonald, the then Governor General, became Commissioner-General, South-East Asia.[65] The Commissioner-General was responsible for co-ordinating policy and administration between the various British colonial governments and represented the civil and political interests of the territories on the British Defence Co-ordination Committee, of which he was chairman. In addition, he was responsible for advising the United Kingdom government on the general problems of foreign policy in the area.[66] On a number of occasions recommendations were forwarded to Whitehall for similar appointments for the Persian Gulf and East African areas, but nothing came of these suggestions.

Adjusting the Defence System

At the end of the Second World War much of the apparatus of imperial defence remained in working order and that part which did not was quickly re-erected in fundamentally its pre-war form. British strategy east of Suez therefore hinged on the systems of bases, territorial commands, and trooping by sea. The main workings of this system continued into the fifties without serious challenge though the loss of India forced certain modifications to the traditional pattern.

In general the same strategic value was attached to the chain

---

[64] HC, *Second Report from Select Committee on Estimates ... Session 1948–49: Defence Estimates* (1950), p. ix, para. 18.
[65] See *Times*, 10 Mar. 1948, and RIIA, *Collective Defence in South East Asia*, p. 17.
[66] Statement by Secretary of State for the Colonies, 496 HC Deb., 27 Feb. 1952, coll. 155–6.

of bases[67] as before the war.[68] It could hardly be doubted that
bases had become more vulnerable because of the increased
range and power of modern weapons, but lest it be thought that
their usefulness had declined, a host of arguments was forthcoming in contradiction. The defence of the Commonwealth
was still regarded primarily as a problem of controlling the
lines of communication, and it was the belief of the time that
this soon came down to the matter of bases. In the past the
security of the lines of communication had rested with the
fleet, and bases had been essential because they provided safe
anchorage, repair facilities, and supply depots. For the present
this was still true and the navy's dependence on bases was no
less than of old; indeed it could be argued that it was greater
because of the increasing proportion of small ships in the fleet,
which being less self-reliant had greater need of base support.[69]
Even in these early post-war years, however, there were some
who looked to the day when aircraft would take over the role
of the fleet. But bases would still be needed—for without them,
as Viscount Trenchard explained, air power would lose its
mobility and hence its usefulness to Commonwealth defence.[70]
The instrument of power might change then, but it was the
principle that the lines of communication must be defended
which mattered and this was seen to rest firmly on the maintenance of the great chain of bases.

The army too adhered to the old outlook. Bases were required
to garrison troops for policing-duties in the area. The fact that
troops were required to maintain bases attracted much less
attention. Nor was the environment in which a base operated
a factor to be taken too seriously in these years. Thus all the
old garrisons were re-established much as before and the army
accepted its role as a garrison army in the East without much
questioning. B. H. Liddell Hart wrote that money and man-

[67] Throughout I have used the word 'base' in a broad sense to describe any location
where men are stationed and equipment stored, and from which an operation might
wholly or partly be conducted.
[68] DeWitt C. Armstrong, 'The Changing Strategy of British Bases' (unpublished
Ph.D. dissertation, Princeton Univ., 1959), p. 168.
[69] R Adm C. C. Hughes Hallett, 'Naval Logistics in a Future War', *JRUSI*,
95/578 (May 1950), p. 225. An alternative possibility was, of course, the development of a 'fleet train' or afloat support. However, limited resources forced the
Admiralty to delay development of ships and techniques which would make the
fleet independent of shore support.
[70] 166 HL Deb., 4 Apr. 1950, col. 805.

power were being wasted by scattering soldiers in non-operational packets throughout the world but the issue never really came alive at this time.[71]

Along with other elements of the old scheme of imperial defence, the system of territorial commands continued without substantial change. Such a system was natural enough when Britain was responsible for defending and policing a great empire, movement was slow, and communications were poor. Troops stationed abroad required commanders who were familiar with local conditions and who were empowered to make middle-range decisions. Similarly, the broad spread of naval forces necessitated some decentralization of naval command.[72] Whether the system might be modified or scaled down with the diminution of Britain's responsibilities in the area appears to have escaped question or even comment. The pages of the strategic journals reveal no discussion of the subject at all.

The extent to which the existence of separate service commands, each with different areas of responsibility and often with headquarters located in different places, seriously hindered the co-ordination of the various units is a question which is difficult to answer on the information available. What is clear is that the system as it existed in the late forties placed very considerable obstacles in the way of close co-operation. Mountbatten has recorded the difficulties to be faced when Commanders-in-Chief have their headquarters at different points and it is pertinent that, at the dissolution of his command in South-East Asia, he recommended that the boundaries of the commands of all three Cs in C be drawn to coincide, and that a Supreme Commander with a small unified staff should be established at Singapore.[73] Neither of these recommendations was in fact carried out, with the result that the command situation in the Far East lacked any order or coherence. At the end of the war the naval headquarters were re-established at Hong-Kong, while both the army and the air force had their headquarters at Singapore. One retiring naval Commander-in-Chief, Far East, hinted at some of the difficulties

[71] B. H. Liddell Hart, *Defence of the West*, (1950), p. 210.
[72] Maj Gen J. L. Moulton, 'Bases or Fighting Forces?', *Brassey's Annual 1964*, p. 145.
[73] V Adm Earl Mountbatten of Burma, *Report to Combined Chiefs of Staff by Supreme Commander South-East Asia 1943–1945* (1951), para. 30.

in a lecture delivered to the Royal United Service Institution:

Each C.-in-C. had a different area and title and responsibility. Some were Far East like myself with a station stretching from Christmas Island to the North Pole and from Fiji to Nanking. The Army C.-in-C. had Ceylon and South East Asia with Hong Kong. The Air C.-in-C. had South East Asia and Hong Kong.[74]

In 1948 some improvement was effected by moving the naval headquarters from Hong Kong to Singapore,[75] after a complaint from Montgomery.[76] In 1950 the possibility of establishing a unified command was considered and rejected, the view of the Naval C in C prevailing—that under the existing system Whitehall obtained the advice of 'three wise men'.

In the Middle East the situation was a little better. Both the army and the air force had their headquarters in the Canal Zone though again each had different areas of responsibility. The RAF had five subcommands, including one at Aden and another at Nairobi in East Africa. In 1948 the army command was reorganized and two subordinate commands were established, one of which was East Africa.[77] In June 1953 East Africa was formed into a separate command.[78]

As in pre-war days, the movement of troops to and from stations east of Suez was predominantly by sea. Immediately after the war, fairly large numbers of troops had been carried by Transport Command on routine trooping flights, but with the rundown of the command at the end of the forties the great bulk of trooping reverted to the sea.[79] In 1950–51, for example, 423,000 persons were moved by sea and 18,500 by air.[80] In 1952 at the initiative of the Air Staff and initially opposed by the other two services, a major policy decision was taken by the Chiefs of Staff and endorsed by the government to increase and encourage air trooping, even if this meant the withdrawal from service of some of the older troopships before

[74] Boyd, *JRUSI*, 95/577 (Feb. 1950), p. 43.   [75] *Times*, 10 June 1948.
[76] Montgomery, *Memoirs*, p. 458.   [77] *Times*, 23 Apr. 1948.
[78] WO, *Memorandum of Secretary of State for War Relating to Army Estimates 1954–55*, Cmd 9072 (1954), para. 54.
[79] See Lt Col T. S. Craig, 'Trooping Today', *Army Quarterly*, 76/2 (July 1958), p. 215. Also HC, *Sixth Report from Select Committee on Estimates . . . Session 1950–51: Ministry of Transport; Shipping and War Terminal Services* (1951, p. vii, paras 5 and 6).
[80] HC, *First Report from Estimates Committee . . . Session 1961–62: Trooping* (1962), p. iv, para. 4.

the end of their useful life.[81] At first only a limited expansion of air movement was possible because of the shortage of suitable long-range aircraft,[82] but the decision at least represented the first major departure from traditional procedure.

Although the framework of the imperial system withstood the transfer of power to India, certain adjustments could hardly be avoided. The withdrawal from India involved the loss of base facilities and large numbers of troops, and both were still required if Britain was to maintain her traditional strategy in the area. Speaking of the Middle East, though in terms at least partly applicable to the east of Suez area as a whole, A. P. Thornton sets the scene:

The Indian Army, underprop of British might in the Middle East, had gone. Some other must be found, and fashioned. Genuine bases must be established. The soldiers were to wander, sometimes in imagination, sometimes in reality, from the Canal Zone to Kenya, from Cyprus back to Haifa, searching, somewhere along this inner circle, for security for the British Empire, for the protection of its communications and the safeguarding of its supplies of oil . . .[83]

In the early years the need for bases was the smaller of the two problems. The loss of India was a grievous but by no means disastrous blow. Alternative arrangements could be devised and the base situation made reasonably satisfactory, if not all that the military desired. Without undue difficulty, Britain managed to piece together a strategic network which served its purpose well enough until the mid-fifties when the whole edifice began to crumble in the face of a militant nationalism. Shortly after independence, transit and over-flying rights were negotiated with India and with Burma. The Defence Agreement with Ceylon ensured continued use of the naval and air facilities on the island. In September 1945 Singapore was re-occupied, reconstruction was put in hand, and by early 1948 the base had been almost completely restored.[84] Hong Kong

---

[81] Craig, as cited in n. 79.
[82] WO, *Memorandum of Secretary of State for War Relating to Army Estimates 1953–54*, Cmd 8770 (1953), paras 94 and 95.
[83] *The Imperial Idea and its Enemies*, p. 334.
[84] In 1949 Adm Boyd argued (p. 43) that Australia, not Singapore, was the logical place for a Far Eastern base. He went on: 'Singapore is the last place on Earth to use as a main base in a modern war, but in the absence of Empire planning, it is the only one.

too had been re-established though its strategic importance was very much on the wane.

In the west Britain continued to hold the Simonstown base in South Africa under the terms of the Smuts-Churchill Agreement of 1921. Simonstown was a small base with one dry-dock, and was strategically situated to command the sea routes round the Cape and the southern waters of the Indian Ocean. In the north Aden was of considerable importance as a link in the chain of imperial communications. As yet little development had taken place, but its airstrips were useful to the RAF and its defended port, though lacking in facilities, was the only harbour of value on the southern coast of Arabia. In the Middle East the key to Britain's strategic position remained the great sprawling base in the sands of the Canal Zone, a confused mass of workshops, railways, and strongpoints valued at between £500 and £700 million. For a time its future was uncertain. On a number of occasions between September 1945 and January 1947 Attlee questioned the efficacy of a Mediterranean strategy and expressed the view that Britain should withdraw from the Middle East and make a line of defence across Africa from Lagos to Kenya.[85] Others were concerned that the loss of Britain's military installations and strategic facilities in India would strain the base at Suez and there were growing doubts about its value in view of the large number of troops tied down in its own defence. With Palestine and Kenya in mind as possible alternatives to Suez, in May 1946 the government offered to withdraw from Egypt subject to an agreement that the base could be reactivated by Britain in the event of war.

Despite instability in Palestine the army began the task of transferring stores and equipment there, but the move was cut short by the decision to abandon the Mandate in September 1947. The government's attention was then fixed on Kenya. The favoured site was McKinnon Road, an insignificant railway halt some seventy miles inland from Mombasa. However, the General Staff had always been doubtful about Kenya's suitability as a major base. Viscount Alanbrooke visited the area as CIGS in December 1945 and concluded that it was too distant from the Middle East and that the road, rail, and port facilities were too inadequate for it to serve as a replacement for Suez. At first the possibility of Kenya made a deep impression on Ernest Bevin but later his enthusiasm cooled. According to Liddell Hart the case for a move from the Middle East to Africa was presented in private memoranda and discussion, but opinion was very divided and the net effect was towards the deferment of any final decision.[86]

Nevertheless preliminary planning went ahead and a more limited scheme was authorized. In September 1947, 300 Royal Engineers arrived in Kenya from Egypt to build a depot for military stores to be moved from India and Egypt. At the same time work began on rail and road projects to improve communications between Nairobi and Mombasa.[87] Early in 1948 some 1,800 Italian workers, the first of a number of labour reinforcements, were brought in by air to help with construction.[88] The official position was that the McKinnon Road depot was intended simply as a reception base for evacuated stores. However, it was widely believed that the project was a first step in the establishment of a base in Kenya at which a strategic reserve could be stationed, not merely for the support of the Middle East but for any part of the Indian Ocean area as well.[89] Although construction was not completed, the depot was opened in November 1948. During 1949 work slowed down and army and civilian construction units were seriously under strength. In November 1950 a statement issued by East Africa Command put an end to speculation. The McKinnon Road establishment, on which £2 million out of a total visualized expenditure of £8 million had been spent, was to be closed down. The statement explained that additional storage centres were no longer required and it emphasized that the depot was too isolated to serve as a major base, for which purpose it had never been intended.[90] Intended or not, the possibility that McKinnon Road might have developed beyond a storage centre was a real one which had been ruled out only by the

[86] *Defence of the West*, p. 248. See also E. Monroe: *Britain's Moment in the Middle East 1914–1956*, p. 157, and 'Mr Bevin's "Arab Policy" ', in A. Hourani, ed., *Middle Eastern Affairs*, 2 (St Antony's Papers no. 11, 1961), pp. 9–48 esp. p. 16; Lord Strang, *Home and Abroad* (1956), p. 291; and Bryant, *Triumph in the West 1939–1946*, pp. 522 and 531.
[87] *Times*, 13 and 16 Sept. 1947.
[88] *Times*, 27 Mar. 1948.
[89] See e.g. *Daily Telegraph*, 25 June 1948, and *New York Herald Tribune*, 26 July 1948.
[90] *Times*, 15 Nov. 1950.

changed situation in the Middle East. The offer to withdraw from Egypt had proved abortive and as the European climate had deteriorated and fear of Soviet designs increased, the service chiefs resolved to retain forces in the Canal Zone come what may. Ideas that McKinnon Road might be maintained as a minor storage depot were abandoned in the face of financial pressures, the manpower demands of Hong Kong and Malaya, and practical difficulties such as water supplies, which became apparent during construction. One year later, the leader of a Northern Rhodesian government mission which visited the depot to inspect materials reported that stores were lying in the open, rusted and unusable, and that road rollers and electric motors were covered by thick vegetation.[91]

If the full impact of the loss of India as a military base could be staved off by moving the main British defence line southwards to run through the Middle East, Africa, Ceylon, and Malaya, the loss of the Indian Army could not so easily be overcome. In the early post-war years manpower was a scarce commodity for a nation confronted with formidable problems of reconstruction and industrial modernization, and men policing the beats of empire were men lost to the cause of economic recovery. Yet manpower was still the chief requirement if Britain was to maintain her Indian Ocean role on anything like the old pattern. In the absence of reappraisal, then, the problem confronting defence planners was to maintain service levels in the area in the face of heavy domestic labour demands and financial stringency.

One solution was of course conscription. Late in 1946, after strong representations by the army and a number of stormy cabinet meetings, the government agreed to the introduction of National Service in peace-time. The National Service Bill introduced in Parliament in March 1947 proposed a period of eighteen months' service, but opposition within the Labour party led the government to reduce the period to twelve months. This was reluctantly accepted by the War Office on condition that the period be increased if overseas commitments had not been liquidated by January 1949.[92] In the latter part of

---

[91] *Johannesburg Star*, 12 Nov. 1951.
[92] For the military side see Montgomery, *Memoirs*, pp. 476–80. A full discussion of the political debate and the division in the cabinet is to be found in C. R. Rose, 'The Relation of Socialist Principles to British Labour Foreign Policy 1945–51' (unpublished D.Phil. thesis, Univ. of Oxford, 1959), pp. 300–5.

1948 the issue was reopened and after the threatened resignation of the military members of the Army Council led by the CIGS,[93] and later by the acting CIGS, the government agreed to the eighteen months period. It was increased to two years in September 1950, as part of the general strengthening of the forces at that time.[94]

National Service was initially justified by the desire to maintain large reserve forces rather than by the requirements of overseas commitments. However, the decline in the Regular content of the forces and the increased manpower demands overseas led to a change in thinking. The Minister of Defence admitted to the House in 1949 that the restoration of the eighteen-months period for National Servicemen was made necessary because Britain's overseas commitments remained undiminished.[95] The following year the Secretary of State for War declared that overseas commitments, particularly those in the Far East, had made it necessary to use National Servicemen in overseas theatres rather than simply as a reserve, as had been originally intended.[96] By 1951 National Servicemen made up half the army's total manpower, and in a sense they had taken the place of the Indian troops.

The system was not without serious disadvantages and a number of critics, foremost among them Liddell Hart, argued that National Service was greatly reducing the effective strength of the army and making it unsuited to operations other than imperial policing.[97] Moreover, National Service necessitated a large training establishment, reduced Regular recruiting, and, in the opinion of some, weakened Regular morale. From the viewpoint of meeting commitments east of Suez, there were additional reasons why the system left much to be desired. The army, for example, was faced with the heavy administrative burden of constantly rotating personnel to and from the various stations, and the period of active service of the National

---

[93] Montgomery, *Memoirs*, p. 479.
[94] See Attlee's speech, 478 HC Deb., 12 Sept. 1950, col. 957.
[95] 462 HC Deb., 3 Mar. 1949, col. 548.
[96] 472 HC Deb., 20 Mar. 1950, coll. 1561–2. See also statement by Shinwell, 478 HC Deb., 26 July 1950, coll. 472–4.
[97] See e.g. Liddell Hart's *Defence of the West*, pp. 199–200 and letter to *Sunday Times*, 26 Mar. 1950; also Lt Gen Sir Gifford Martel, *East Versus West* (1952), pp. 56–61. Some critical observations are to be found in Brig C. N. Barclay, 'Historical Background, General Policy and Tasks of the Army', *Brassey's Annual 1950*, pp. 139–40.

Servicemen was relatively short. According to one estimate, a total of nine months had to be deducted from the useful tour of a National Serviceman in the Far East, and seven or eight months in the Middle East.[98] The position with respect to skilled men was even worse because of the longer period of basic training. It is difficult to generalize about the army's attitude to National Service but most soldiers appear to have been convinced that there was no alternative. However, as one senior officer explained: 'Professionally speaking, we hated National Service.'

A second solution was seen in the colonial empire. What was needed, it was argued in many quarters, was a fuller development of colonial forces, and perhaps a great colonial army in Africa which could replace the Indian army. R. A. Butler took up the call in 1946,[99] and his plea for tapping the manpower resources of the colonies was echoed on both sides of the House and outside over the next six years. The war had shown that African forces could be rapidly expanded once an effort was made, and their record in both the Middle East and South-east Asia surely put an end to the notion that Africans made second-class soldiers, even if, it was grudgingly admitted, they might not be the equal of the Indians. Here then was the answer to Britain's manpower difficulties. It was therefore a matter of dismay that the 1947–48 Army Estimates revealed that colonial forces were to be reduced during 1947 by about a quarter of a million men to the lowly figure of 87,000.[100] R. H. S. Crossman described the reduction as 'a major tragedy' and in this he had the support of most of the House.[101] Why, one speaker wanted to know, should such reductions be authorized at a time of severe labour shortages at home? After all, the colonial empire had only one man in every six or seven hundred of working age in the forces, whereas the figure for the United Kingdom was one in eighteen.[102]

From this viewpoint, a more encouraging development was the negotiation of an agreement with Nepal and India which

[98] 'Manpower and Defence', *Round Table*, 39/156 (Sept. 1949), p. 325.
[99] 420 HC Deb., 4 Mar. 1946, col. 55.
[100] *Army Estimates 1947–48* (1947), p. 9, Vote A. In the event the full reduction did not take place.
[101] 434 HC Deb., 13 Mar. 1947, col. 1622.
[102] Brig H. R. Mackeson, 435 HC Deb., 20 Mar. 1947, col. 673.

provided for the continued employment of Gurkha soldiers in the British army. Under the terms of the agreement, signed on 9 November 1947, the government of Nepal agreed that the United Kingdom could recruit Gurkha officers and soldiers up to the number required to maintain eight battalions, and the government of India agreed to the use by the British army of recruiting depots in India and promised to provide transit facilities between Nepal and an Indian port.[103]

This was welcomed as a step in the right direction but there was little else to please those who advocated a fuller development of colonial forces. Despite assurances by successive ministers that the government was as concerned as members to draw upon the manpower of the colonies, the numbers in the colonial forces steadily declined until 1951.[104] In 1949 the government announced that it was necessary to build up local forces to the extent necessary to deal with disturbed local conditions and that it was, in conjunction with the colonial governments, examining the size and composition of the forces required.[105] Following a review by the Chiefs of Staff Committee, consultations with the various colonial governments took place and in the case of the East and West African colonies a conference was held in London. The basic problem was one of finance as neither the colonial governments nor the United Kingdom were anxious to commit themselves to any proposals which might involve them in increased expenditure.[106]

No announcement was made regarding the outcome of the discussions and in the absence of any concrete programme of expansion, agitation mounted in Parliament and in military circles. A number of critics clung to the idea of raising a colonial army in Africa to be modelled on the pattern of the old Indian army. Others thought such a scheme too ambitious and would have been content with more limited measures to strengthen local forces. Trenchard suggested the opening of a big training school similar to Halton at which Africans could

---

[103] 445 HC Deb., 1 Dec. 1947, coll. 34–5, and *Times*, 2 Dec. 1947.
[104] The Army Estimates give the following figures: 1948: 151,000; 1949: 92,500; 1950: 69,100; 1951: 65,000.
[105] MoD, *Statement on Defence 1949*, Cmd 7631 (1949), para. 13.
[106] See MoD, *Statement on Defence 1950*, Cmd 7895, para. 17.

be trained in mechanical work.[107] All were agreed, however, that something should be done and that the government was moving too slowly.

By 1950 it was clear that the bolder scheme for a colonial army had been abandoned in official circles. Finance was the determining factor. The cost of colonial forces had increased as much as five-fold and it was agreed that it was no longer reasonable that each colony should pay the whole cost.[108] Opinion in the War Office was firm that the money available was better spent on British battalions than on African ones, the argument hinging on efficiency and flexibility of use.[109] No final decision had been taken regarding the more modest proposals for strengthening colonial forces, but for the time being at least the Colonial Office and the War Office decided against any action.[110]

If the government's interest had waned, back-bench pressure showed no signs of abating. In March 1951 an amendment to a private member's motion inviting the government to investigate the possibility of raising bigger forces in the colonies was passed with a majority of 182.[111] During the course of the debate Strachey, Secretary of State for War, stated that the government was proceeding with a development of the colonial forces.[112] Later events showed that this was true and colonial troops rose from 66,000 in 1951 to 78,000 in 1952, falling slightly to 75,000 in 1953. Yet the careful development of colonial forces in Africa and other parts of the Commonwealth which Strachey set in motion was a very different thing from the raising of a large expeditionary force from Africa, which was what so many politicians and strategists had advocated.[113] Welcome as this development was, it still disappointed those whose eyes had been fixed on an African version of the Indian army.

[107] 166 HL Deb., 4 Apr. 1950, col. 803. RAF apprentices are trained at Halton in Buckinghamshire.
[108] HC, *Second Report from Select Committee on Estimates . . . Session 1948–49: Defence Estimates*, pp. viii—ix, para. 17.
[109] Lord Ogmore later stated that the War Office had for years fought a rearguard action against the fuller use of colonial forces, 176 HL Deb., 8 Apr. 1952, col. 42.
[110] *Observer*, 28 May 1960.
[111] See 485 HC Deb., 16 Mar. 1951, coll. 1970–2066.
[112] Ibid. col. 2049.
[113] One interesting development occurred in 1952 when battalions of the King's African Rifles and the Fiji Regiment were posted to Malaya. *Times*, 22 Jan. 1952.

Strategic Doctrine and Service Practice

Before 1954 there was no body of strategic thinking specifically concerned with the defence problems of the Indian Ocean area. Initially this neglect was merely an aspect of the general pragmatism of British policy following the war. At this time defence planning was closely tied to day-to-day requirements. The Soviet Union was not seen as a definite foe, a major war seemed several years away at least, and, except for the nuclear weapons programme, there was not felt to be any urgent requirement for decisions on longer-term issues. At home demobilization was the main issue, while overseas Britain was preoccupied with operational responsibilities arising from the war. This lull in strategic thinking extended across the whole spectrum of defence policy. On Viscount Montgomery's account, in 1946 there was no clear conception in Whitehall about how Britain would fight a major war.[114] Discussions between the Chiefs of Staff produced little more than a re-affirmation of the traditional requirement to hold on to the Middle East and to maintain control of the sea lanes.[115] Thus Attlee admitted that the 1946 White Paper was 'something of a stop-gap';[116] the 1947 White Paper explained that 1947 was 'yet another transitional year';[117] while in 1948 the new weapon factor was seen 'as an emphatic reminder of the needs to preserve a flexible policy and a warning that there must be no rigidity in decisions about the future role of the three Services'.[118]

Two specific factors contributed to the postponement of a major strategic re-assessment. In the winter of 1946 the government adopted the ten-year rule, which directed the Chiefs of Staff to assume that there would be no major war for a decade. On the evidence available, it seems that this decision was taken on economic rather than strategic grounds, the idea being to force the services to postpone re-equipment and to make maximum use of their war-time stocks.[119] The second

[114] *Memoirs*, p. 435.
[115] Ibid., pp. 435–6.
[116] 420 HC Deb., 4 Mar. 1946, col. 40.
[117] MoD, *Statement Relating to Defence*, Cmd 7042 (1947), para. 6.
[118] MoD, *Statement Relating to Defence 1948*, Cmd 7327 (1948), para. 55.
[119] See further Cdr William J. Crowe, 'The Policy Roots of the Modern Royal Navy 1946–63' (unpublished Ph.D. dissertation, Princeton Univ., 1965), pp. 65–6; and Rosecrance, pp. 55–6.

factor, in practice probably more important than the first, was the uncertainty about the impact of atomic weapons on military strategy. Articles in the strategic journals and parliamentary discussions at the time reveal widely divergent views about the implications of nuclear weapons and apparently this was a major consideration underlying the reluctance to plan far ahead.

The neglect of broader strategic thinking was especially marked east of Suez because of the weight of Britain's commitments in the area. At the end of the Second World War Britain remained responsible for the maintenance of order in India; she assumed much of the responsibility for the clearing-up operations in the Far East; she provided forces for the occupation of the Netherlands East Indies and a token contingent for Japan. The result was that planners were heavily concerned with the problems of the area but mainly in terms of their immediate implications. Before Indian independence, planning was dominated by considerations of internal security in India while after August 1947 planning was primarily about operational commitments. It was this situation which no doubt lay behind Admiral Boyd's observation that there was a very definite feeling among thinking men in the Far East that there was a lack of Far Eastern policy.[120]

During 1948 defence thinking ran deeper, though east of Suez considerations played no part in the process. At the end of 1947 the Labour government abandoned its earlier attempts to co-operate with the Russians. The Czechoslovakian *coup* in February 1948 and the Berlin blockade in June removed any lingering doubts that a hard line was mistaken. Thenceforward planning proceeded on the basis that Russia would be the enemy and that the arena of conflict would probably be Western Europe.[121] The development of NATO now became the dominant consideration in British military thinking.[122]

With the emphasis increasingly on Europe, one factor which worked against the emergence of specific thinking for the Indian Ocean area was the widely held belief that 'modern war meant total war'.[123] By the late forties, strategic theory

---

[120] *JRUSI*, 95/577 (Feb. 1950), p. 41.
[121] Rosecrance, p. 77.
[122] Earlier the services had not been allowed to contemplate conflict with Russia.
[123] Lord Tedder, 'A Defence Warning to Britain', *Sunday Express*, 19 Oct. 1947.

both in Britain and the United States hinged on the assumption that the nations involved would devote their whole national effort to the object of winning the war and that campaigns would be waged on a global scale. At this level of discussion, the Indian Ocean area could never loom very large. In so far as the area was considered at all, it was seen as but a part of the overall strategic picture. Although it was assumed that policing tasks would continue on the traditional pattern, most strategists expected any serious fighting to draw in the major powers, who would then battle it out to the end. For this reason, old concepts such as the maintenance of sea communications continued to dominate Britain's approach to the security problems of the area.

Paradoxically, the outbreak of the Korean war reinforced the preoccupation with Europe and with general war. In Britain, as well as in the United States, the war was seen as an indication that Communist policy had hardened towards the West. Although this particular contest was being fought in Asia, it was widely thought that Europe would be the real battleground. As Churchill put it in a broadcast on 26 August 1950: 'My eyes are not fixed upon Korea ... the supreme peril is in Europe. We must try to close the hideous gap on the European front.'[124]

Essentially the government took the same view. Although it was alive to the dangers of the Far East and the Middle East and it attached great importance to a successful outcome of the Korean conflict, there could be no doubting that these were altogether secondary areas and that the main lesson derived was for the defence of Europe.[125]

The fear of general war led the government to embark on a major rearmament programme which, although subsequently curtailed, provided the forces with the weapons and equipment which were to be their stock-in-trade for several years.

[124] *Observer*, 27 Aug. 1950.
[125] See the text of Attlee's broadcast on 30 July 1950, *Times*, 31 July 1950; and Shinwell's speeches, 478 HC Deb., 26 July 1950, col. 469, and 484 HC Deb., 14 Feb. 1951, col. 409. On the basis of interviews with Labour ministers, Richard Rose has argued that one factor behind the rearmament programme was the attempt to show the United States that Britain was making great sacrifices for defence, and thus to ensure American assistance in the defence of Europe. In his 'The Relation of Socialist Principles to British Labour Foreign Policy 1945–51' he quotes one senior minister as saying: 'None of us was taking the American alliance for granted' (pp. 333–4).

The revised expansion programme of September 1950 was primarily directed towards strengthening the three services for a global conflict after the style of the Second World War. The general policy involved a switch from ambitious long-term projects to developments which quickly could be made operational. In the case of the army and the air force, the accent was on weapons and equipment for Europe. For the navy the emphasis rested on the threat of the submarine and the mine. From the viewpoint of Indian Ocean strategy, the net effect of the rearmament programme was to direct attention away from the area and to channel resources into projects and weapons which had little relevance to the needs of the area.

Equally significant for British policy east of Suez was the failure of Korea to generate any rethinking about the nature of wars to be expected or the way they would be fought. Although Korea was itself almost a classic case of limited war, most strategists assumed it to be a departure from the norm. In the United States particularly there was a strong inclination to attribute the difficulties of Korea to the political restraints which prevented full use of the West's military capabilities, and this produced a determination not to become involved in such a situation again.[126] This line of thinking was evident in Britain also and it led to a reaffirmation of the strategy of global war with its heavy emphasis on air power. The Secretary of State for Air made the point clearly in his statement to the House on 18 March 1952:

Do not let us draw false lessons from what is happening in Korea. The United Nations' Air Forces there have shown great stopping power. Indeed, without them our ground Forces must have been overwhelmed by weight of numbers. But air power has not been deployed in the way that it would inevitably be deployed in a major war; that is, against the whole war-making power of the opponent.[127]

Shortly after the return of the Conservative government in October 1951, it became clear that defence expenditure would have to be considerably reduced. One possible way of reconciling conflicting economic and military requirements was seen in an increased reliance on nuclear weapons. At the prompting of Churchill early in 1952 the Chiefs of Staff—Sir

[126] H. A. Kissinger, *Nuclear Weapons and Foreign Policy* (1957), p. 54.
[127] 497 HC Deb., 18 Mar. 1952, coll. 2108–9.

William Slim, Sir John Slessor, and Sir Rhoderick McGrigor—with Sir Ian Jacob, then Churchill's military assistant, withdrew to one of the staff colleges for about two weeks to review the major aspects of defence policy. The preliminary planning was done by the Chiefs themselves and their conclusions were set out in a paper which became the basis of British defence policy for the remainder of the fifties.[128]

The first part of the paper dealt with nuclear deterrence and was the key to the rest. To counter Soviet aggression, primary reliance should be placed on the nuclear deterrent. Although America's deterrent was formidable, the paper argued that Britain's strategic forces could make an important contribution. Section two was concerned with NATO, and its main conclusion was that manpower targets could be considerably reduced because of the advent of tactical nuclear weapons. As a concession to the navy, the notion of 'broken-backed' warfare was grafted on to the main concept. The thinking here was that as the initial exchange might not be decisive, it was necessary to make provision for continuing operations, particularly at sea. Apparently neither Slim nor Slessor took the concept seriously, but it was the price to be paid for McGrigor's acceptance of the paper.

The third section considered Britain's overseas responsibilities in resisting Communist expansion and recommended certain reductions in forces. The defence of the Middle East was still required in war, but given a settlement with Egypt, the Middle East base could be reduced to one division and 160 aircraft. In the Far East, the situation in Indo-China and the importance of the area to the defence of Australia and New Zealand were factors to be taken into consideration. For these reasons and others, the paper concluded that the Far East was of greater importance than the Middle East and that no reduction was possible in this theatre. Bearing in mind the requirements of both areas, the paper recommended a strengthening of Transport Command, including a proportion of tail-loading aircraft.[129]

[128] For the published record see Rosecrance, pp. 159–75; Crowe, pp. 111–13; Charles J. Murphy, 'A New Stategy for NATO', *Fortune*, Jan. 1953, pp. 80–5, 166, 168, 170, and 'Defence and Stategy', *Fortune*, Dec. 1953, pp. 77–8, 82, 84.
[129] Apparently the Chiefs of Staff particularly had in mind the need to reinforce the Middle East in an emergency and to withdraw troops from the Far East should a major war break out elsewhere.

Churchill expressed himself well pleased with the document, the primary point was accepted almost immediately, and the priority of the bomber force was established. For the rest, the full rigour of the paper was never translated into policy. Despite the acceptance of the logic of section two, the army maintained its NATO ground commitments, and it was much later that manpower shortages forced reconsideration. The proposals for overseas defence fared little better. Britain eventually withdrew from Suez but Cyprus was developed as a partial substitute. It was years before Transport Command made substantial headway. In that the global strategy paper superimposed a nuclear strategy upon a conventional strategy, its implications for British policy in the Indian Ocean area were profound. Although the full dimensions of the problem did not become apparent until after 1953, the adjustment of overseas strategy recommended in the 1952 paper was ancillary to the nuclear doctrine and the heavy demands placed on defence resources by the latter was one reason for the slow development of the former.

The 1953 Defence White Paper was in the tradition of its predecessors and revealed no new thinking about strategy east of Suez. Global war was still the theme, though it was now assumed to be less immediate – hence the concept of a 'prolonged pull'. What was interesting, however, was that the parliamentary debate on the White Paper broke new ground inasmuch as several speakers questioned cold war strategy. Although few of the issues were taken up by the press, the debate indicated that at least in some quarters serious doubts were held as to the efficacy of Britain's traditional policy for the area.

The disclosure that no strategic reserve was then available,[130] and the admission of the Security of State for War that an army of the equivalent of eleven and one-third divisions, which he stated as the present strength, was just too small having regard to Britain's overseas commitments,[131] led to some rethinking on both sides of the House. Air mobility was seen as one solution and several members pointed to the weakness of Transport Command. George Wigg, always a keen advocate for the army, moved an amendment urging the government

---

[130] 512 HC Deb., 5 Mar. 1953, col. 575.
[131] Ibid. coll. 845–6.

to relate the provision of an adequate force of transport air-craft to the strategic and tactical needs of the fighting services in peace and war.[132] In reply, the Parliamentary Secretary rather lamely cautioned against exaggerating the number of aircraft required.[133] The other and related possibility was a change in the army's deployment pattern. John Strachey, who knew the problems after his time at the War Office, led the way with an argument which was to become very much more famil-iar over the next five years:

We must concentrate. We must stop stationing all our available forces—land forces, at any rate—all over the world. . . .

What this means is a radical revision of the tradition of our world defence policy. It means ceasing to try to behave as if we were still the leading world empire. From the date . . . of India's assumption of independence a re-orientation of our whole attitude was abso-lutely necessary. We have begun to undertake it, but we have not carried it through in the military field, where to a very considerable extent we are still living in the past.[134]

To sum up the argument thus far: the main lines of strategic thought directed attention away from east of Suez and obscured the distinctive nature of Britain's military functions in the area. By way of corollary, no body of strategic doctrine was developed which defined the tasks and methods of internal security. Certainly the conduct of small wars and the handling of in-surgencies of various kinds had long been recognized as issues in their own right requiring methods which diverged widely from those of regular warfare.[135] Equally, the post-war operations in Malaya, Kenya, and other British territories were undertaken in accordance with this tradition and almost as a matter of course. What was lacking, however, was a con-ceptual formulation of the problems which could be incorpora-ted in the general strategic doctrine. There was nothing new about this, for, as Anthony Verrier has observed, the most valuable imperial tasks had always lacked intellectual analysis or justification.[136] Nor was it by any means a feature unique to British defence thinking. In the United States also, the

[132] Ibid. 12 Mar. 1953, col. 1575.
[133] Ibid. col. 1608.
[134] Ibid. 5 Mar. 1953, col. 637–8.
[135] See e.g. Col C. E. Callwell, *Small Wars*, 3rd ed. (1906), esp. p. 23, and Maj Gen Sir Charles W. Gwynn, *Imperial Policing*, 2nd ed. (1939), esp. pp. 4–5.
[136] *An Army for the Sixties* (1966), p. 158.

problems of guerrilla warfare received very little consideration during these early post-war years.[137]

This doctrinal neglect of the peacekeeping role must be considered against a background of the three services as separate empires, each with its own focus of attention and to a large extent determining its own role. The main direction of strategic policy was of course determined centrally, within a framework consisting of the Defence Committee, the Minister of Defence, the Ministry of Defence, and a number of sub-committees of which the Chiefs of Staff Committee was the most important. However, the Minister of Defence was essentially a co-ordinator, the Ministry of Defence was little more than a small secretariat assisting the various committees, while the Chiefs of Staff Committee seldom appears to have succeeded in deciding major defence issues except as a compromise between service interests.[138] Within the broad parameters thus established, the services remained responsible for their own procurement policies and strategic doctrine. It is therefore necessary to consider the approach of the three services separately.

The disjunction of theory and practice was most pronounced in the army. Although the army was deeply involved in maintaining internal stability in British territories in the area, this aspect of its role was overshadowed by global-war considerations and the theories of deliberately staged war. Working from the chain of military bases and drawing on National Servicemen and to some extent colonial manpower, the army developed its traditional policing concepts which were rooted in the garrison and the infantryman. In Malaya new techniques of counter-insurgency were evolved at the Far East Land Forces training centre. Under the leadership of men such as Lieutenant General Sir Harold Briggs and General Sir Gerald Templar, the Indian experience was adapted to the new conditions and certain general principles established which were later to be developed into a coherent theory of anti-guerrilla

[137] See William M. Kaufmann, *The McNamara Strategy* (1964), p. 17.
[138] Some aspects of the workings of this system are discussed more fully on pp. 72–3 below. For differing accounts of its efficacy see Montgomery, *Memoirs*, pp. 487–97, and MRAF Sir John Slessor, *The Central Blue* (1956), pp. 450–63. An interesting general discussion is to be found in Laurence W. Martin, 'The Market for Strategic Ideas in Britain', *Amer. polit. Sci. R.*, 56/1 (Mar. 1962), pp. 23–5.

operations.[139] However, partly because soldiers looked upon the policing role as familiar ground and therefore took it in their stride, there was little attempt to elevate thinking and tactics to the level of strategic doctrine.

Lacking any full conceptual formulation, the counter-insurgency role made little impact on thinking in the United Kingdom. At least in these early years, the developments in organization and tactical methods in Malaya were largely confined to Malaya. In the United Kingdom troops about to be sent to the Far East and the Middle East were still being trained in obsolete 'cordon and search' methods. Exercises on Salisbury Plain remained modelled on the campaigns of the Second World War.[140] In the words of one senior commander, units would come out to Malaya 'not knowing what it was all about'.

In Kenya also it took some time for the Malayan experience to make much impression. Early attempts to obtain effective unity of command met with very little success,[141] and ambush arrangements were primitive. During a visit to Kenya in February 1953 General Sir John Harding, recently appointed CIGS, strongly criticized the lack of co-ordination, the general tactics, and the absence of knowledge or interest in what had been achieved in Malaya.[142] Thereafter the situation improved. The following month a new organization was set up along the lines of Templer's scheme in Malaya which brought the army, the police, and the government together for co-ordinated planning and closer co-operation. The text book for the new force was reported to be Templer's *Conduct of Anti-Terrorist Operations in Malaya*.[143] The official statement outlining the scheme said the Governor had decided to use the methods

---

[139] In one important respect the Indian experience was reversed. By and large in India the army never considered it had any responsibility outside its cantonments, except in a purely military capacity. In Malaya, however, it became evident that the active support of the population was essential and the army's role was broadened to accomplish this aim—hence Gen Templer's insistence on 'winning the hearts and minds of the Malayan people'.

[140] Alun Gwynne Jones, 'Training and Doctrine in the British Army since 1945' in Michael Howard, ed., *The Theory and Practice of War*, pp. 318–19.

[141] See *Manchester Guardian*, 26 Feb. 1953.

[142] For Gen Harding's public comments see *Times*, 26 Feb. 1953.

[143] *Manchester Guardian*, 2 Apr. 1953. First published in 1952, this manual set out in detail the military role, organization and tactics, and was the official handbook for troops in Malaya.

proved successful in Malaya 'after many alternative ideas had been tried'.[144]

The RAF was not deeply involved in operations east of Suez and its strategic doctrine was scarcely affected at all. This was the era of the supremacy of air power, but it was a supremacy which rested on the bomber and only came into its own in conditions of general war. Hence RAF strategy was primarily concerned with general war and its forces were organized along appropriate lines. So long as British bases were held, however, the same forces would be able to handle limited conflicts, and the same general principles, suitably adapted, would apply.[145]

The RAF maintained small forces in both the Middle East and the Far East, though the aircraft were mostly obsolescent and their role does not appear to have attracted any close scrutiny. One line of thought about the Middle East, following pre-war tradition, saw the RAF as heir to the army's role of peacekeeper. Thus the system of air control developed in the twenties and thirties continued without substantial change, though it was now largely restricted to the Arabian Peninsula. Such a notion was never applied to the Far East.[146] In Malaya and to a lesser extent in Kenya, the air force's role was primarily one of support for the army. In both campaigns, however, airmen adjusted to this ancillary role slowly and with some reluctance. It took even longer for the idea of air support to gain general acceptance in Whitehall. In Malaya, as in Kenya, occasional bombing operations were carried out along the lines of Tedder's 'air carpet' theory, though without any real effect.

The great airborne operations of the later stages of the Second World War led some strategists to advocate air mobility as the basis of the army's future policing role. Although the Air Staff supported the principle, transport for the army was low on the list of air force priorities. As a result, Transport Command was allowed to run down during the late forties, and in 1950 it bore the brunt of economies necessary to strengthen Fighter and Bomber Commands.[147] The Korean war failed to shake RAF thinking, the Secretary of State for Air having no diffi-

---

[144] *Times*, 11 Apr. 1953. See more generally *Times* leader, 1 June 1953.
[145] See Viscount Trenchard's observations, 161 HL Deb., 2 Mar. 1949, col. 89.
[146] The different conceptions of the air role in the Middle East and the Far East are discussed at pp. 89–93 below.
[147] Ch. 2 below contains a full discussion of the early ideas about air mobility and of Transport Command's strength in these years.

culty confining that experience to its facts. He then went on to announce 'regretfully' that no expansion of Transport Command beyond its existing size was possible while the build-up of other operational commands was in progress.[148] One airman aptly explained the RAF's viewpoint in these years and later by an analogy to cricket. The RAF was in the position of a batsman confronted by a fast bowler and at the same time worried by a swarm of wasps. The wasps were conflicts east of Suez, the ball was nuclear war, and the bowler was Russia. Although the wasps were troublesome, 'we had to keep our eye on the ball'.

The navy's major role was less securely based than that of the air force, but even so the Admiralty, like the Air Ministry, made little attempt to incorporate a small war—local stability strand in its general strategic thinking. In these years naval thinking centred on the ship rather than the shore. At first the Admiralty clung to the traditional conception of the navy's role which gave pride of place to the defence of the imperial supply routes and lines of communication. The fleet's objective was thus to deny the sea to enemy ships and to ensure the 'safe and timely arrival of convoys'.[149] The task of the aircraft carrier was to protect the naval force from submarine, surface, or air attack. Little attention was paid to its scope for land offensive. Later the emergence of the Russian threat and the development of NATO led the Admiralty to place particular emphasis on anti-submarine and anti-mine measures. The Korean experience did little to advance the Admiralty's thinking. Although the navy played a major role in the operations and the aircraft carrier in particular emerged with an enhanced reputation, only a few officers argued for the development of a small role and they were 'voices crying in the wilderness'. In the words of one senior officer, Korea sowed the limited-war seed but it took some years to germinate.

In keeping with the general-war theme, naval discussion of the Indian Ocean area mainly focused on the serious shortage of larger warships. It was a matter of grave concern, for example, that during 1948 and 1949 not a single carrier was stationed in the Indian Ocean.[150] In general, however, the

---

[148] 497 HC Deb., 18 Mar. 1952, col. 2119.
[149] Crowe, p. 82.
[150] 'Hazarded by Default', *Navy*, 53/2 (Feb. 1948), p. 42.

area did not weigh heavily because the navy had no positive foe. In the east there was of course the insurgency in Malaya, but as one officer explained, this was a ball to the army; in the west there was the fear of a Russian march to warm water ports, but as another officer said, it was difficult to build a strategy on that. The Indian Ocean itself scarcely figured at all. As one officer put it, it was 'an empty hollow'; in the view of another, it was 'just a place to go across'. An indication of how the Admiralty looked upon the priorities of various areas was provided by the report of the Harwood Committee, which recommended that in economic extremis the fleet should withdraw from the Pacific and Africa and concentrate in Home Waters and the Mediterranean. In the event the report was never acted upon and later the Korean war led to a strengthening of naval forces east of Suez.

The post-war shortage of resources and the dominance of the role at sea led the Admiralty to neglect amphibious warfare. Ever since the Gallipoli failure, the Admiralty had shown little interest in this form of warfare. The war-time landings in Normandy and Sicily were discounted as a guide to the future, the belief of the time being that the advent of nuclear weapons had ruled out operations of this nature.[151] For these reasons and others, the Board of Admiralty's attitude to amphibious vessels was similar to that of the Air Staff towards airlift.[152] After lengthy discussions, it was decided to retain Combined Operations Headquarters and to maintain a skeleton amphibious squadron in commission to keep amphibious techniques alive.[153] For a time the Royal Marines were in danger of abolition, but eventually the Naval Staff agreed to place the Corps on a permanent footing, to be maintained at a strength of about 11,000.[154] At this time the Marines' role was threefold—to provide detachments for ships, to provide crews for landing craft, and to serve in the commando role. They had no specific responsibility for amphibious warfare and as yet their potential for policing operations was largely unrealized. Despite ambi-

---

[151] Bernard Fergusson, *The Watery Maze: The Story of Combined Operations* (1961), p. 384.
[152] Crowe, p. 79.
[153] Ibid. See also the statement of the First Lord of the Admiralty, 154 HL Deb., 8 Mar. 1948, col. 519.
[154] See further Hollis, pp. 161–3, and Capt J. R. Grindle, 'Combined Operations— Black Art or Common Practice?', *Brassey's Annual 1951*, pp. 167–8.

tious plans at the end of the war, training developed along Second World War lines and few new ideas circulated.[155]

The failure of the defence establishment to adjust its thinking to the requirements of limited conflicts east of Suez was symptomatic of the larger national failure to come to terms with the question of role. Until firm guidelines about the purposes of deploying power had been established, the military appreciation was bound to be piecemeal and lacking in structure. The root problem lay in the weakness of political thinking about the ends of policy and about Britain's position in the post-war world. So long as imperial considerations retained their hold on the official mind, there was a sufficient sense of purpose and direction to obscure the need for fundamental questioning. And against this background the essential pragmatism of Britain's approach ensured that policy was cast in the traditional mould. With the focus of attention thus fixed on the immediate and the specific, the opportunity for reappraisal passed by, and, in turn, the main military tasks went largely without recognition. In the circumstances of the time this was understandable enough, but the consequences were profound: the die was cast for Britain's involvement to continue at a substantial level without any searching examination of the basis of policy.

[155] See Maj W. R. Sendall, 'Royal Marines in the Future: Need for an Amphibious Striking Force', *Navy*, 56/1 (Jan. 1951), pp. 4–5.

CHAPTER TWO

The Old Power Structure and the New Strategic Policies 1954–1956

UNTIL the Suez débâcle challenged the assumptions of the past decade, nothing happened to jolt British political thinking about the purposes and extent of the east of Suez role. By the early fifties the course had been set and policy-makers found no reason in these interim years to question the direction of British policy. As imperial considerations receded into the background of thinking, the Communist threat outside Europe increasingly shaped British perceptions, and contemporary developments were therefore taken to confirm the traditional involvement. There was of course a difference in scale now that the Soviet Union and China figured larger but this was seen to require an adjustment through the development of alliances rather than a fundamental revision of Britain's role.

What distinguishes the years 1954–6 from the earlier period was the emergence of new strategic policies relating to the type of forces required east of Suez and the appropriate method of movement. The first new line of policy was the scheme for an airlifted strategic reserve and this was followed by the tentative development of a limited-war role for the navy. In the years after the Suez operation these two approaches to the problem of overseas security were to recast British strategy for the region. As yet, however, they were more important in theory than in practice as few transport aircraft were available, amphibious ships and equipment were of Second World War origin, and army manpower was still adequate for the maintenance of the traditional pattern of regional deployment. At this stage, therefore, the new policies were not much more than pointers to the future and they served to conceal the confused state of

British strategic thinking and the continuance of the main strands of Britain's pre-war policy for the area.

The one event that might have been expected to produce an immediate and far-reaching change in the deployment pattern and the structure of power east of Suez—the 1954 decision to evacuate the Suez Canal Zone—passed by, leaving the old system still functioning much as before and largely unchallenged. The House of Commons debate on the initialled agreement scarcely scratched the surface of British strategic policy. Churchill explained that the base no longer had any real strategic significance, while the best that the Opposition could do was to attack the agreement as a 'give-away'. And so Britain moved into the mid-fifties, the loss of India and Suez notwithstanding, with the bulk of the paraphernalia of imperial defence still intact. Strategic mobility had been grafted on to the old system but without any full examination and invested with little substance.

British Purposes and Regional Alliances

In the years before the Suez crisis the politics of Britain's role in the Indian Ocean remained largely unexplored. Commitment was the starting-point and not the subject of analysis. It is perhaps a truism to explain that the right questions were not then being asked. In retrospect the questions seem so logical and obvious: What was the purpose of the British commitment? What was the relationship between military power, diplomatic influence, and economic interest? Yet questions are a product of the time and the environment, and in Britain in the mid-fifties a military presence in the East was part of the accepted order of things. That Britain's role had changed was of course plain to all, and it was viewed differently by traditionalists and radicals. There was disagreement about both ends and means—Eden for example saw Britain's role in the Middle East in different terms from that in the Far East, and in both areas his conception of Britain's function was poles apart from Strachey's. But that a role—and a major role—remained was unchallenged, and as it was unchallenged the government had no need nor any interest in spelling out the sort of justification that might satisfy the academic observer. Thus when the Seato and Baghdad pacts came before Parliament the discussion was not about whether Britain had a role in the Far East and the Middle East, but whether these pacts were suitable instruments for British influence, and whether they offered the best hope for maintaining some sort of stability in these areas.

It is true that in Parliament there were some calls for a reduction in Britain's commitments and that each year in the defence debate one or two speakers could be relied upon to raise the issue of over-commitment, and to argue for withdrawal from Hong Kong or from some particularly anachronistic commitment left over from the days of empire. But this was strictly an intellectual exercise restricted to the Commons and to a few Labour rationalists, and it had little impact on general thinking. The press paid scant attention to the matter of commitments, and overall this issue never assumed any real political importance in the years 1954–6. The only sustained discussion took place during the debate on the 1954 White Paper when Emanuel Shinwell and R. H. S. Crossman came out strongly in favour of cutting back overseas commitments.[1] Thereafter the evacuation of Suez and the withdrawal from Korea seemed to satisfy most observers. The 1955 debate found scarcely a reference to the subject, and it attracted little attention in the debate the following year.

All this is not to say that the east of Suez role was never discussed during these years. Some discussion took place and attempts were made to explain the role in terms of British interests, but the arguments used were mostly superficial and they seldom went beyond the level of generalities.[2] The point is simply that these explanations cannot fairly be set alongside the basic questions outlined earlier because the issue of commitment was not a live one. There is also a very real feeling of a gap between the political level and the military level. Though the various political rationalizations can be made to fit the defence facts, the conviction remains that the two tended to be independent worlds. The defence system existed in its own right and had a dynamic of its own. It was not the military's place

---

[1] 524 HC Deb., 2 Mar. 1954, coll. 1043 and 1091.
[2] See e.g. the comments of Head, 538 HC Deb., 8 Mar. 1955, col. 361; Macmillan, 542 HC Deb., 15 June 1955, coll. 597–8; and Amery, 549 HC Deb., 28 Feb. 1955, col. 361.

to justify and explain and they were not much concerned with the attempts of others.

The Indian Ocean area as a whole seldom constituted the frame of reference for political discussion. Most commonly discussion and explanation of Britain's role centred on the Middle East and the Far East, though the point was always made that it was essential to maintain the lines of communication between them. Politically, as well as strategically, the Middle East and the Far East were seen as quite distinct areas and it was therefore natural that there developed separate explanations for Britain's military presence in the two areas. To some extent this was true of Africa also. There were differences between these various approaches, but generally speaking Britain's military presence was seen as having a threefold function.

In the first place, there was the assumption, never clearly spelt out, that if Britain was to be present in these areas in terms of diplomacy then she had also to be there in terms of military power. It is relevant that Eden saw Britain's accession to the Baghdad Pact primarily as a matter of strengthening her diplomatic position in the Middle East. In the House of Commons he explained: 'Our purpose in acceding to the Pact was a very simple one. I think that by doing so we have strengthened our influence and our voice throughout the Middle East.'[3]

That even by the mid-fifties military power was of diminishing diplomatic utility, seems to have made little impression on policy-makers and there is much to support the argument that, especially in the Middle East, Whitehall placed too great a premium on the military factor. It took the Suez crisis to generate some rethinking here.

Secondly, there were economic considerations. Both in the form of investment and trade, Britain still had important economic interests in the area and it was widely accepted that a military presence helped to safeguard these interests. In the Persian Gulf and in the Middle East generally, oil was always in the background of policy and there was a shadowy but persuasive idea that the military ought to be sitting around the places where the oil flowed up. In part this line of thinking

[3] 539 HC Deb., 4 Apr. 1955, col. 897.

lay behind Britain's interest in the Baghdad Pact. Anthony Nutting, Minister of State for Foreign Affairs, frankly told the Commons: 'Lately, the development of the oil resources of this area has added yet another compelling factor to the need for adequate and effective Middle East defence.'[4]

In the Far East, Britain's economic interests lacked the pull of oil and they were to a considerable extent shared with other Western powers. Still, as a study group of the Royal Institute of International Affairs pointed out, in 1954 the countries of South-east Asia exported 91 per cent of the Manila hemp, 89 per cent of the natural rubber, 76 per cent of the copra and coconut oil, 68 per cent of the tin, and 68 per cent of the rice that entered into international trade. Substitutes were expensive and who could tell, if South-east Asia were to come under Communist domination by subversion, what trade policy would follow?[5]

Finally, and of course this was the most important, there was the security interest. In British as in American eyes, Communist ambitions in Asia meant that the defence of the area was not only a matter of local importance, but one that affected the central balance. Over and above a concern for the future of the individual countries, there was the consideration that the loss of so large and populous an area to the Communist bloc would be a disaster of the first magnitude and one which must be averted at all costs. The problem presented itself differently in the Middle East and the Far East. In both areas the threat was Communist, but in the Middle East it was seen in the conventional terms of a military move southwards by the Soviet Union towards the Red Sea and the Persian Gulf, while in the Far East the most probable method by which the Communists might seek to obtain control of the area was thought to be internal subversion, exploiting internal dissension and the presence of racial minorities in most of the countries in the area.

Two facts were immediately apparent. In the first place, the prospects for an indigenous defence system or systems were remote. There was no likelihood that the major indigenous powers would be willing or able to change their traditional policies and commit themselves to the defence of the weaker

---

[4] 539 HC Deb., 4 Apr. 1955, col. 834.
[5] *Collective Defence in South East Asia*, pp. 30–1.

states in the area. And even if they did, their low level of national power could hardly present a credible deterrent to Communist expansionism. Secondly, it was clear that the problem of preventing aggression at a regional level was a matter for the West in general and not just Britain. Local stability aside, the days when Britain could play a unilateral role were over. And so Britain moved into the alliance market, though without the verve of the United States. What was needed was a co-operative effort between those local powers which could be made to see reason and the Western powers. The preference was for formal alliances, but where these were unobtainable, understandings which facilitated a sharing of the defence burdens were a useful second best. Viewed in this light, 1954 and 1955 were productive years for British diplomacy. The alliance structure of the West was extended across Asia in the form of SEATO and CENTO, and both South Africa and Australia were induced to play a more positive part in the defence of their own areas of special interest.

The British role in the foundation of SEATO was an important one, although the primary initiative came from the United States. The deterioration in the French position in Indo-China in early 1954 led the United States government to approach the British and French governments with a proposal that the powers involved should issue a warning to China, and that they should simultaneously set about organizing the collective defence of South-east Asia. Preliminary discussions took place during the Berlin Conference at the end of January, and these were followed by talks in London in mid-April between Dulles and Eden.[6] At the end of the talks, a statement was issued declaring that the two governments were ready to take part, with the other countries principally involved, in an examination of the possibility of establishing collective defence in South-east Asia. In the British view, however, no action should be taken which might prejudice the negotiations on Indo-China, about to take place at Geneva. On the question of membership, Britain favoured a wider grouping than did the United States and it was anxious that India and other Asian Commonwealth countries should be included.

Despite the tentative nature of British policy, military staff discussions took place in Washington in early June between

6 Sir Anthony Eden, *The Memoirs*, iii: *Full Circle* (1960), pp. 87–9, 95–8.

representatives of the United States, the United Kingdom, France, Australia, and New Zealand. A second step towards commitment was taken later that month when Churchill and Eden visited Washington for discussions on Indo-China. A communiqué issued by the President and the Prime Minister on the 28 June affirmed that they would 'press forward with plans for collective defence' in South-east Asia, irrespective of the outcome of Geneva.[7] Following the talks, an Anglo-American study group was set up in Washington to explore the question of South-east Asian defence and to investigate the possibility of the countries participating in the Geneva negotiations, together with other countries with interests in the area, underwriting any settlement reached.[8]

By the end of the Geneva Conference, however, it was clear that the Communist powers were unwilling to participate in any reciprocal guarantee of the settlement negotiated. The wider scheme was therefore abandoned, and British policy was directed towards establishing a defensive treaty which would underwrite the Geneva Agreement but which would command the support, if not the membership, of the principal Asian countries. After having secured the somewhat reluctant agreement of the United States, Britain approached the five Colombo powers with a request for their views. India had no hesitation in dissociating itself completely from the proposed pact, and Indonesia and Burma followed suit. Ceylon was more sympathetic, but eventually decided against attending the conference, though it was 'prepared to maintain an open mind on the subject'.[9] Pakistan, its interest heightened by the fact that India would not be going, agreed to attend. From there events moved swiftly. Representatives of the United States, the United Kingdom, France, Pakistan, Thailand, the Philippines, Australia, and New Zealand met in Manila on 6 September 1954, and the treaty was signed two days later.

In its final form the pact differed substantially from Eden's earlier conception of a wide system of military arrangements guaranteeing the Geneva settlement. To this extent, Britain's participation may be regarded as a *quid pro quo* for American endorsement of the cease-fire agreement. Put somewhat

[7] *New York Times*, 29 June 1954.
[8] Eden, *Full Circle*, pp. 132 and 143.
[9] *Hindu*, 14 Aug. 1954.

crudely, Britain agreed to underwrite the armistice partly as the price for getting the Americans to Geneva. The Russians then refused to co-operate, the Asian countries followed them, and thus the pact closely resembled the original American proposal. This, however, was not the whole story. At the risk of over-simplification, it is useful to consider the wider motives behind Britain's involvement in the SEATO enterprise.

Given the government's continuing view of Britain as a world power and as a diplomatic principal in Asia – and Eden's leading role at Geneva bears witness to this – membership of SEATO came naturally if hardly enthusiastically. The events in Indo-China had highlighted the fact that the South-east Asian situation was not only of regional importance, but could have momentous repercussions on the world stage. It was therefore accepted on both sides of the House and by the press that Britain must be in a position to make her voice heard, and if necessary to act as a brake on American policy. In this sense, Britain's participation was seen not so much as a military commitment but as an inevitable part of Britain's world role.

There was, of course, a military aspect also. The security of the area was an extremely important matter for the West, and as Kenneth Younger pointed out in the Commons, Britain could not 'possibly escape from her share of responsibility for it'.[10] During the early months of 1954 the fear was very real that the fighting in Indo-China might spread to other parts of South-east Asia. Within twelve months, it was believed, the Communists could control the whole of Indo-China, and thus Thailand would be in danger and Malaya threatened. Eden has recorded that at the beginning of 1954 his chief concern was for Malaya: 'I wanted to ensure an effective barrier as far to the north of that country as possible.'[11] The security of Thailand was also of concern to Britain, and in April Eden raised the possibility of an Anglo-American guarantee in the event of a total collapse in Indo-China and he was prepared to recommend this to Churchill.[12] The cease-fire eased the situation temporarily, but the belief was strong that unless the Geneva Agreement was underwritten by some military agree-

[10] 532 HC Deb., 8 Nov. 1954, col. 938.
[11] *Full Circle*, p. 87.
[12] Ibid. p. 101.

ment the 17th parallel might prove to be a very short-lived boundary indeed.

Finally, SEATO fulfilled two associated and long-standing aims of British diplomacy in South-east Asia. It committed the United States to the territorial security of the area and it removed the anomaly of Britain's exclusion from the ANZUS Pact. Ever since the spring of 1951 Britain had been anxious to be associated with ANZUS planning but the United States had blocked the various proposals advanced. The United States' stand, and the unwillingness of the Australian and New Zealand governments to carry insistence on British membership to the point at which the Americans might reassess the value of the alliance, had caused much heart-burning and misunderstanding in the United Kingdom. It was therefore a matter of satisfaction that in SEATO the substance of Britain's desire could be met.[13] More important was the fact that for the first time the United States was specifically committed to the defence of South-east Asia. Apart from what this meant in terms of reassurance, the door was now open for co-ordinated planning on a wider basis than formerly.

Both in Parliament and in the press Britain's membership of SEATO was greeted with mild approval. Although some doubts were expressed about whether the treaty would succeed in its aim, there was general agreement that it was the most that could be expected in the circumstances. SEATO came with so little publicity, however, that there was no great debate and the tendency was to regard it as unimportant.[14] What was most surprising was the lack of interest in the question of commitment, for the treaty had substantially increased Britain's obligations in the area. Under Article IV Britain and the other signatories undertook quite plainly, in the event of armed attack in the treaty area against any of the parties or designated states, to 'act to meet the common danger'.[15] At the time it was accepted that this could only mean that they would fight, and that the reservation about 'in accordance with . . . constitutional processes' could not absolve them from that obligation.[16]

[13] Ibid. p. 93, and *Times* leader 'The Importance of Manila', 8 Sept. 1954.
[14] Both *The Times*, 8 Sept. 1954, and the *Sunday Times*, 12 Sept. 1954, made this point.
[15] FO, *South-East Asia Collective Defence Treaty*, Cmnd 265 (1957), Art. IV (1).
[16] RIIA, *Collective Defence in South East Asia*, p. 144.

In the event of subversion the commitment was more tentative, the parties agreeing only to 'consult immediately in order to agree on the measures which should be taken for the common defence'.[17]

The negotiation of the Baghdad Pact in 1955 aroused more interest than had SEATO, though in the long term it was less important for British policy. Britain had long been anxious to establish an effective defence system in the Middle East. The failure of the Anglo-American scheme for an Allied Middle Eastern Command in 1951 had temporarily checked Britain's designs and for a time the initiative passed into American hands. After a fact-finding expedition to the Middle East in the spring of 1953, Secretary of State Dulles returned to the United States convinced that the climate of Arab opinion was such that a broadly based Middle Eastern defence network was not then possible. In his view, Western efforts would have to be concentrated on the 'nothern tier' states which were the most aware of the Soviet menace and were also best situated to provide protection for the area as a whole.[18] American initiatives were therefore directed to bringing Turkey and Pakistan together, and they were partly responsible for these two countries signing a treaty of friendship and security in April 1954. The treaty was specifically open to accession by other states and was in fact intended as a first step towards a broader alliance. The position of Iraq was now crucial. The United States had taken a decision on military aid to Iraq the previous year and a military assistance agreement was effected by an exchange of notes on 21 April 1954. However, while it was understood between the two governments that Iraq would play its part in regional defence, no formal commitment had been made. Not wishing to weaken the bonds of the Arab League, the pro-Western Iraqi Prime Minister, Nuri Pasha, made a vain attempt to enlist Arab support for a regional defence agreement. Finding the Egyptian door firmly closed to the West, Nuri settled for the bold course and on 24 February 1955 signed an agreement with Turkey which pledged the two countries to co-operation 'for their security and defence'.

It was at this stage that Britain took a hand in the proceedings. Until the signing of the Turko-Iraqi Pact Britain had

---

[17] Cmnd 265, Art. IV (2).
[18] Campbell, *Defense of the Middle East*, p. 49.

watched developments from the sidelines. The government had not shown any great enthusiasm for the northern tier concept and it had had reservations about the Turkish-Pakistan agreement, as the maintenance of good relations with India was still an important strand of Britain's policy. The Baghdad Pact, however, seemed to open the way for a regional defence organization in which Pakistan, Iran, and Jordan might participate and Britain play a predominant part. It seemed possible, Eden records in his *Memoirs*, 'that the pact could grow into a NATO for the Middle East'.[19] Another consideration was that the Anglo-Iraqi Treaty of 1930, under which Britain enjoyed the use of the air bases at Habbaniyah and Shaiba, was due to expire in 1957 and the Air Ministry was insistent that it needed a reliable staging post between Cyprus and Aden or Bahrain, as well as a station for desert flying practice.[20] To a government which accepted a power-oriented theory of international politics, particularly in the Middle East, these arguments were conclusive and on 4 April 1955 Britain acceded to the pact. At the same time, an agreement was reached with Iraq which affirmed the RAF's right to use the two air bases.[21] Pakistan acceded to the pact in September 1955 and Iran joined in October. Neither the United States nor France made the expected commitment, however, and Britain, as the only Western member, naturally assumed the role of leadership.[22]

In Britain the pact was accepted as an achievement of considerable importance and the House of Commons approved it without a division. The opposition was concerned about the effect the pact would have on Israel, but most Labour speakers agreed with the government that this was the sort of mechanism that Middle Eastern defence required. Patrick Gordon Walker put the issue in terms which made sense to both parties:

The Middle East is the Achilles' heel of Commonwealth defence . . . a vacuum has arisen since the war in the Middle East. It is a power vacuum, and, like nature, dictators abhor a vacuum. It is important that we should not leave this power vacuum in this part of the world.

[19] *Full Circle*, p. 220.
[20] Monroe, *Britain's Moment in the Middle East 1914–1956*, pp. 183–4.
[21] FO, *Special Agreement between the Government of the United Kingdom of Great Britain and Northern Ireland and the Government of Iraq*, Cmd 9544 (1955).
[22] For Macmillan's observations see his *Memoirs*, iii: *Tides of Fortune 1945–55* (1969), pp. 652-6.

The only way in which it can be filled up is by this sort of pact, by increasing local strength within the area.[23]

In Africa Britain's efforts to establish some form of regional alliance met with less success. Shortly after the meeting of Commonwealth Defence Ministers in London in June 1951, the Commonwealth Relations Office announced that the British and South African governments intended to convene a 'defence facilities conference' of African powers to 'discuss ways and means of facilitating communications and the movement of military forces and supplies, should need arise, in the Eastern and Central parts of the African continent'.[24] The conference met in Nairobi in August with representatives from Britain, South Africa, Italy, Portugal, and Southern Rhodesia together with United States observers. The scheme for a regional defence organization broke down, however, because of the refusal of the Union government to consider any scheme which involved employing part of the African population in the armed forces in such a way that they actually bore arms. None the less, the conference did bear some fruit in that it eventually led to the Anglo-South African Exchanges of Letters on Defence Matters, under which the South African government assumed a larger responsibility for the maritime defence of the area.[25] The Union government undertook to expand the South African Navy and to be responsible in peacetime for the 'South African area', a large stretch of sea similar to, though somewhat smaller than, the Royal Navy's South Atlantic Command. The Royal Navy continued to be responsible for the whole South Atlantic area.[26] Under Article 10 of the Agreement a joint maritime war planning committee was set up which would be responsible for co-ordinating the use of all military facilities in British and South African territories in the strategic zone.

In the Far East once the SEATO Pact had been signed Britain's attention was directed to Australia and New Zealand and to the very small defence burden that these states were carrying. During November and December 1954 reports appeared in several British newspapers that Britain was asking

[23] 539 HC Deb., 4 Apr. 1955, coll. 854–5.
[24] *Times*, 16 July 1951.
[25] Tunstall, pp. 47–8.
[26] For details see MoD, *Exchanges of Letters on Defence Matters between the Governments of the United Kingdom and the Union of South Africa June 1955*, Cmd 9520 (1955), pp. 4–10.

the Australian government in particular to provide ground forces for a strategic reserve for the defence of South-east Asia. Britain had long urged Australia to send troops to Malaya, it was said, but recently pressure had increased because of the instability in Indo-China.[27] It would seem significant that during November and December the three British Far Eastern Cs in C visited Australia and had discussions with senior cabinet ministers. Further discussion was reported to have taken place at the Prime Ministers' Conference in January and on 1 April 1955 the Prime Minister, Robert Menzies, announced that Australia would send to Malaya an infantry battalion with supporting arms, together with various air and naval forces.[28] Menzies went on to say that these forces would be part of a larger joint reserve which would include British and New Zealand forces. More information was forthcoming from the New Zealand Minister of Defence, T. L. Macdonald. Speaking in Wellington on 15 April, he explained that the reserve would be controlled by the United Kingdom Command structure in Malaya and would be within the ANZAM framework.[29]

Defence Resources and Service Priorities

It was one thing to accept a continuing role east of Suez on the basis of general political considerations but it was another to provide the defence resources necessary to make it effective. When it came to the practical matter of allocating forces and equipment there were grave difficulties because of the dominance of the nuclear deterrent in British defence thinking. Although there was some recognition of the distinctive nature of the military tasks east of Suez the main part of strategic thinking, now more sophisticated than ever, spiralled off in another direction and was lost in the clouds of the thermo-nuclear bomb. The maintenance of internal security and the protection of British territories from external attack were the areas where defence thinking was at its weakest. Nuclear deterrence not only held the centre of the strategic stage but its shadows extended to the wings. As a result, the overseas defence role remained inadequately formulated and the manpower and material needs

---

[27] See in particular *Observer*, 28 Nov. 1954, and *Scotsman*, 2 Dec. 1954.
[28] *New York Times*, 2 Apr. 1955.
[29] *New Zealand Government News Bulletin* (Wellington), 18 Apr. 1955.

of British forces east of Suez made less impression on defence planners in Whitehall than they deserved.

The 1953 White Paper recognized that defence must now be maintained at two levels. The first was concerned with a direct Communist attack and had two aspects: the build-up of the deterrent and the strengthening of the forces for global war should the deterrent fail. The second related to Britain's overseas commitments and to her cold war responsibilities in resisting Communist expansion through indirect actions and infiltration.[30] The order of priorities was indicated by the statement that the re-equipment of the armed forces, the expansion of the RAF, and the build-up of men and materials fell into the first category, while the forces stationed in overseas theatres fell into the second.[31] In short, overseas defence was to be maintained with existing forces while the strengthening of Britain's global war capability was to proceed steadily, though less dramatically now that the imminence of major war had receded. By 1954 the government had firmly settled on the view that continuation of the cold war was more likely than the outbreak of a major war at any particular time. However, despite a recognition of the separateness of the two roles, the 1954 White Paper went on, in line with Washington's theory of massive retaliation, to give priority to the nuclear bomber, to maintain the hot war capability of the Royal Navy, and to reduce expenditure on the army. The explanation was suggested by the curious statement that 'As the deterrent continues to grow, it should have an increasing effect upon the cold war by making less likely such adventures on the part of the Communist world as their aggression in Korea.'[32]

Yet, as Sir John Slessor pointed out at the time, there was no reason why the growth of atomic power should do anything of the kind—indeed quite the reverse could be expected.[33]

The next two years revealed no departure from the order of

---

[30] At the time the official label 'cold war duties' was used generally to describe the activities of British forces overseas. In fact, however, many of these activities had no connection with the East-West confrontation. The Kenyan campaign is a case in point.

[31] MoD, *Statement of Defence 1953*, Cmd 8768 (1953), para. 3.

[32] MoD, *Statement on Defence 1954*, Cmd 9075 (1954), para. 12.

[33] 'Air Power and the Future of War', *JRUSI*, 99/595, Aug. 1954, p. 347. Also *Strategy for the West* (1954), p. 154. For a similar view see the *Observer* leader 'Thinking Ahead', 21 Feb. 1954.

things established in 1953 and 1954. The 1955 White Paper placed an increased emphasis on the deterrent and the parliamentary debate was conducted almost entirely in terms of nuclear war with the Soviet Union. Given strict limits to the resources available for defence, the priority assigned to the deterrent dictated the form of the defence programme and where most of the money would be spent. Although the White Paper made the point that there was a continuing need for conventional forces and weapons for use in overseas defence, nothing was forthcoming save a few generalities along the now familiar theme. Nor did the 1956 White Paper offer much more hope. Certainly it enunciated a limited-war role for the navy but this did not involve the government in any additional expenditure and in no way interfered with the existing naval construction programmes. The same ships and much the same weapons would serve both purposes. No less than in earlier years finance was the limiting factor and the White Paper made it clear that defence spending must be stabilized. Paragraph 10 pointed out that the cost of new weapons was increasing and would continue to increase and that the only way expenditure could be contained within reasonable bounds was to reduce the numbers in the forces.[34] Thus manpower was to be cut in favour of new weapons, or to put it another way, conventional capability was to be reduced in the interests of the nuclear deterrent.

On the matériel side, all three services were forced to economize on weapons and equipment required primarily for the overseas defence role. The re-equipment of Transport Command was gravely hampered by lack of resources, with the result that the provision of air transport lagged far behind the government's announced priority for the strategic reserve.[35] Helicopters fared little better and only small numbers reached the air force and the navy over these years.[36] At the beginning of 1954 only two squadrons of under 20 aircraft were in service in Malaya and both had been seriously overflown. Moreover, the one squadron employed in Army Support was naval, and

[34] See further Eden, *Full Circle*, pp. 370–1.
[35] See pp. 78–82 below.
[36] In the case of the RAF it should be pointed out that this was not solely a matter of non-nuclear economies as there was a marked indifference (some would say dislike) on the part of the Air Staff to the development of this type of aircraft.

had been diverted from anti-submarine work.[37] Yet there was no mention of helicopters in the *Memorandum* on the 1954–55 Air Estimates and none had been ordered by the army, although the United States army had at that time more than 1,000 S55 helicopters. In March it was reported that General Sir Gerald Templer had sent a despatch to the War Office for an additional 40 helicopters,[38] and by the end of the year a third squadron had arrived. Slowly more helicopters became available, although the position was never wholly satisfactory. The production of new equipment for the army was mainly concentrated on the requirements of armoured units, and infantry forces drew most of their equipment from Second World War stocks. For communications, the army still depended on signal equipment which had been in use at the end of the war and was now rapidly wearing out.[39] In the navy one result of the global-war priority was that the anti-submarine and mine-sweeping programme used up resources which might otherwise have been employed modernizing amphibious forces.

A more general consideration which worked to discourage the development of specialized weapons and equipment for overseas defence was the understanding that as far as possible all three services should be equipped and trained to handle a range of different tasks and duties. This line of thought was particularly important in the case of the army. At various times proposals were advanced for certain sections of the army to be specially trained for cold war fighting. Similarly there were proposals for lightweight weapons and wireless sets and for specialized equipment, particularly for Malaya. As a matter of policy, however, the British army remained a general purpose army, and the War Office insisted that equipment must be suitable both for Europe and overseas. The same kind of thinking appears to have influenced RAF policy towards the helicopter. In the early fifties the helicopter seemed to the Air Staff to be a return to the Lysander concept, and opinion

---

[37] The other squadron (194, RAF) was employed in the ambulance role. See further Maj J. Ll. Waddy, 'Helicopters for the Army', *Army Quarterly* 69/2 (Jan. 1955), pp. 196–7, and Neville Brown, 'The Military Helicopter', *Brassey's Annual 1962*, p. 81.

[38] *Straits Times*, 20 Mar. 1954.

[39] WO, *Memorandum of Secretary of State for War Relating to Army Estimates 1954–55*, Cmd 9072, para. 128.

was firmly against the purchase of aircraft for use in un-
sophisticated theatres which would be unable to survive in a
European conflict.[40] The navy also adhered to a policy of
general purpose forces and its ships and equipment were
designed with a variety of tasks and conditions in mind. To
use the naval phrase, what was required was 'world-wide
capability'. Necessarily this involved some compromise, but
in the navy it appears to have had less significance for overseas
defence than in the other services.

The neglect of the overseas role was accentuated by the lack
of overall planning during these years. Two Conservative ministers expressed the view that before 1957 there was never a
global strategy in any full sense. Nor was the defence vote
allocated in accordance with agreed strategic priorities. The
picture which emerges is of each service determining its own
role and equipment programme without much outside interference; of a sum of money being voted for a strategy and of
that sum being split between the services in an arbitrary
manner.[41] The explanation of the lack of firm control must rest
largely in the position of the Minister of Defence. His statutory
authority was strictly circumscribed and his effectiveness was
limited by the size of his staff.[42] In Macmillan's view the
Minister's powers were entirely inadequate.[43] Others have
argued that the problem was compounded by an indifferent
Minister of Defence, another who was reluctant to assert the
authority of the office, and the remainder whose tenure of
office was too short to enable them to grapple with the difficulties
of conflicting service roles and equipment programmes.
However these factors may be weighted, there can be little
doubt that the predominance of service interests seriously
hampered the development of a balanced policy. With two
services backing the hot war and the other by no means wholly

[40] The Lysander was a high-wing monoplane ordered in 1935 at the urging of the
General Staff for army co-operation. However, it proved unable to defend itself
in war.

[41] On one account, when the cabinet cut defence spending there was little inquiry
into the service programmes and the result was a percentage cut all round. In
1958 Emanuel Shinwell gave a very similar description of the 1951 budgetary
process. 592 HC Deb., 28 July 1958, col. 1000.

[42] See Michael Howard, *The Central Organisation of Defence* (1970), pp. 7–9.

[43] When he was Minister of Defence in 1954, Macmillan was reported to have said
'I have no authority except my grey hairs.' His views are fully set out in *Tides
of Fortune 1945–1955*, pp. 560–2.

committed to the cold war role, it was inevitable that overseas defence thinking should develop along piecemeal lines.

Late in 1954 the lack of any clear overseas defence policy led Macmillan, then Minister of Defence, to direct an inquiry into the relevant strands of defence and colonial policy, particularly the requirement for good intelligence. Macmillan's concern was especially with the cold war situation and he observed in his diary: 'No one is wholly responsible—it's partly Defence, partly Colonial Office, partly Foreign Office. There's no central anti-communist organisation with any drive in it'.[44]

After obtaining authority from the cabinet, Macmillan appointed General Sir Gerald Templer to prepare a report on colonial security and intelligence, assisted by a Foreign Office official, Sir George Young.

The Templer report was called *Security in the Colonies*, and in its printed form was dated 11 May 1955. It was a study of the problem in the broadest terms, against a background of an assumed long period of cold war. It contained a range of recommendations the object of which was to improve the situation in the cold war, and also to ensure that, in the event of hot war, the colonial territories would be in a position to play whatever role was given to them. The report dealt in detail with the way in which colonial intelligence should be processed in Whitehall, the organization of the colonial police forces and of the armed forces, and it attempted to highlight the most likely areas of conflict. In addition, it made a strong recommendation for a mobile strategic reserve including civil administrators and police officials, and a number of more general recommendations on such subjects as the duty of the British overseas, education and subversion in the schools, and language training. The report appears to have had very little impact. Macmillan moved from defence to foreign affairs the month before the report was presented, and it seems unlikely that it made a deep impression on other politicians or on senior civil servants.

The shortage of resources for the overseas defence role primarily affected the army and various attempts were made by that service to increase the allocation. At one time Field Marshal Harding, the CIGS, together with Antony Head, the Secretary of State for War, argued that overseas defence ex-

[44] *Tides of Fortune 1945–1955*, p. 572.

penses should be separated from the main defence vote, and
be debited against the Colonial Office. Although no progress
was made on this front, a later scheme of Head's very nearly
succeeded. During the short period when he was Minister of
Defence in the last months of 1956, Head promoted the idea of
separating expenditure on certain ancillary programmes from
the main service vote. Thus expenditure on helicopters and
expenditure on landing craft would have been detached from
the RAF and navy votes respectively. However, Head resigned
before the scheme was approved, and his successor showed no
interest.

Against this background of restricted defence resources and
limited recognition, at the centre, of the distinctive nature of
the overseas defence role, the main lines of service strategy
followed the pattern established in the early fifties. For the
RAF, these were the high-water years of nuclear preoccupation,
and the air support role and the provision of air transport for
the army were regarded as distractions from the main task
in hand. Despite the evidence of Malaya that the use of air
power in the security role was subject to serious limitations,
very little thought seems to have been given in air force circles
to how air power could be more efficiently used east of Suez.

In the navy also overseas defence made little impact. The
security of sea communications continued to be the navy's
chief concern, and naval strategists pointed to the growth of
Soviet sea power to show that the danger here was as real as
ever. In any future war the mine and the submarine were seen
as the gravest threats, and the construction programmes concentrated on building up a fleet of minesweepers and anti-
submarine ships. Both in the services and in Parliament,
however, there were many who had misgivings about this
conception of the navy's role, and there were some who even
doubted whether the navy had a viable role at all.[45] Had not
the advent of nuclear weapons ruled out the possibility of a
long drawn-out war, during which it would be necessary to
defend sea communications? Was not the navy clinging to
strategy of the last war, a strategy which could have little
relevance to the next? In defence, naval strategists took up
the notion of 'broken-backed warfare', and it was on this basis

[45] Doubt about the navy's role came out most strikingly in the debate on the 1955
Navy Estimates. 537 HC Deb., 3 Mar. 1955.

that the navy managed in 1954 and 1955 to maintain its share of the defence budget.[46] Although the 1954 and 1955 White Papers paid lip service to the navy's task in limited war, this role could hardly be said to have weighed heavily on the Admiralty. At best, limited war was but a third-string justification for a strong navy —one reason for its low priority no doubt being that the dominance of nuclear war theories made it natural that naval strategists should look to the nuclear arena to find a new justification for the service which they never doubted was as vital as ever. By 1955 the Board of Admiralty had begun serious rethinking, but it was not until 1957 that the Board turned to overseas defence as the answer to the navy's search for a role in the nuclear age.

The army was more deeply involved in overseas defence than either of the other services, but it was mainly out in the theatres concerned that thinking and training were adjusted to its needs. In the War Office global war was still the priority. Army doctrine gave pride of place to the role of reserve armies, the need to reinforce BAOR in a crisis, and the adaptation of armoured groups to the conditions of nuclear war, at the expense of the bread and butter problems of maintaining internal and local stability in British territories overseas. As late as 1956, despite a wider recognition of the special requirements of overseas defence and the upgrading of that role contained in the 1956 White Paper,[47] the British army was still primarily organized and trained for major war in a European setting.[48] To give an illustration, new brigade commanders would arrive in Malaya from the United Kingdom and immediately set about planning large-scale operations, manoeuvring battalions in an almost unbroken jungle, much as they would have done during the Second World War or in exercises in Germany.[49]

The difficulty facing the army was that for many years, and especially since the end of the Second World War, the sort of forces required for major war and for local wars overseas had been steadily diverging. For the overseas role the infantryman with his personal arms and light supporting weapons

[46] See MoD, *Statement on Defence 1954*, Cmd 9075, para. 13 and *Statement on Defence 1955*, Cmd 9391, para. 29.
[47] MoD, *Statement on Defence 1956*, Cmd 9691, para. 15.
[48] Brig K. R. Brazier-Creagh, The Local Defence of Overseas Territories', *Brassey's Annual 1956*, p. 219.
[49] Brig Richard L. Clutterbuck, *The Long, Long War* (1966) p. 51.

was still the chief requirement. In Malaya, for example, a gunner unit had been reorganized as infantry, there being no requirement for it in its normal role.[50] Yet for major war the need was not men but armour and increased fire power. The economics of defence made some sort of choice inevitable, but from the east of Suez standpoint the policy of reducing army manpower in the interests of air power and new weapons was an unfortunate one. On average, about 1,000 patrol hours were being spent in Malaya for every contact with the enemy, and 1,600 for every man killed or captured,[51] and the army was always stretched during these years. After the publication of the 1954 White Paper and the statement that the government intended to reduce the total size of the army,[52] Lieutenant General Sir Brian Horrocks considered that if overseas commitments remained at their existing level, it was difficult to see how a smaller army could fulfil its obligations.[53] By 1956 there had been no diminution in Britain's overseas commitments, and yet the army had declined by some 45,000 men, and more drastic reductions were being implemented.[54]

The New Strategic Policies

Although the main body of defence thinking was concerned with global war, certain lines of policy were developed which offered fresh answers to some of the more pressing problems of overseas defence. In retrospect, the emergence of these policies was the most significant feature of the period inasmuch as in the years after 1957 they hardened into the central prongs of Britain's defence scheme east of Suez. The most important of the new developments was the plan for a central strategic reserve which could be airlifted to overseas theatres when trouble broke out. The idea was by no means new. Liddell Hart had mentioned it in 1946, and had advocated the replacement of ordinary infantry divisions by airborne divisions which could draw their heavier equipment from regional

[50] Brazier-Creagh, *Brassey's Annual 1956*, p. 223.
[51] WO, *Memorandum of Secretary of State for War Relating to Army Estimates 1955–56*, Cmd 9395 (1955), para. 13.
[52] MoD, *Statement on Defence 1954,*, Cmd 9075, para. 16.
[53] 'Calculated Risk in Cutting Army', *Sunday Times*, 21 Feb. 1954.
[54] The Army manpower figures were: 1954: 443,000; 1955: 422,000; 1956: 398,000 (estimate).

depots.[55] The concept had been quite widely discussed in the various strategic journals, and it had won the support of a number of army and air force strategists in the belief that it would permit considerable reductions in army manpower, minimize army deployments abroad, and reduce Britain's dependence on overseas bases. Since the end of the Second World War successive service ministers had cherished the hope that such a reserve could be established in the United Kingdom.[56] However, their hopes had been frustrated by the manpower demands imposed by the maintenance of the old system of bases and garrisons, and the continued heavy burden of Britain's overseas commitments. The result was that in 1954 Britain still had no strategic reserve and the army was 'strained and over-strained', its forces 'sprawled all over the world'.[57]

On 27 January 1954, after some press reports that London would like to follow Washington's example of reducing the number of troops stationed abroad by establishing a strategic reserve,[58] the Minister of Defence, Lord Alexander, announced that he intended to build up a central reserve 'ready to go off to deal with any emergency at any time'.[59] According to a *New York Times* report, believed to be based on an interview with one of the Chiefs of Staff or an official very close to them, this proposal was part of a long-range defence plan which aimed at a strategic reserve of at least two infantry divisions plus a paratroop brigade, a substantial proportion of which could be moved by jet transports to trouble spots in the Middle East or Far East within twenty-four hours.[60]

The White Paper, which appeared in February, was more reserved and spoke simply of the government's aim 'to reconstitute the strategic reserve at home, the lack of which is at present a serious, though unavoidable, defect in our defence readiness'.[61] The withdrawal of troops from the Suez Canal Zone and the reduction of the Commonwealth Division in Korea provided the government with an opportunity to give

---

[55] *The Revolution in Warfare* (1946), p. 89.
[56] See DeWitt C. Armstrong, *The Changing Strategy of British Bases*, p. 223, and *Scotsman*, 29 July 1954.
[57] Statement by Nigel Birch, Parliamentary Secretary to the Ministry of Defence, 524 HC Deb., 2 Mar. 1954, col. 1029.
[58] See especially *New York Herald Tribune*, 14 Jan. 1954.
[59] *Daily Telegraph*, 28 Jan. 1954.
[60] 9 Feb. 1954.
[61] MoD, *Statement on Defence 1954*, Cmd 9075, para. 16.

some substance to its policy. According to the War Office statement in July, two-thirds of the Suez garrison of 85,000 was to be brought back to the United Kingdom to reconstitute the strategic reserve.[62] Two months later, Field Marshal Harding's announcement of the reduction of the Commonwealth Division in Korea led *The Times* to conclude that: 'There will now for the first time since the war—except for a very brief period in 1951—be a substantial number of regular troops stationed at home'.[63]

It was not government policy to release the size of the strategic reserve; consequently no figures are available which chart this course. The 1955 White Paper said simply that reduced commitments 'now made it possible' to rebuild the strategic reserve.[64] Some progress was reported the following year,[65] and by 1957 an army brigade had been designated for the purpose.[66] In general, however, the pattern seems to have been that as soon as a start was made assembling troops for the strategic reserve, the units involved would be posted overseas to meet the demands of operational commitments.[67]

The provision of air transport for the reserve posed an equally difficult problem. Transport Command had been allowed to run down at the end of the war and when, early in 1950, economies were effected in the services, the main cut in aircraft production fell upon this Command. Over the next three years very few transport aircraft came into service, for the aircraft expansion programme was concentrated on the operational commands.[68] Although the 1952 global strategy paper stressed the requirement for transport aircraft and the Air Staff supported the principle, the Air Staff was reluctant to sanction the development of British aircraft as it feared that this would interfere with the V-bomber programme.[69] Instead it

---

[62] *Daily Telegraph*, 29 July 1954.

[63] 21 Aug. 1954.

[64] MoD, *Statement on Defence 1955*, Cmd 9391, para. 17.

[65] MoD, *Statement on Defence 1956*, Cmd 9691, para. 33.

[66] WO, *Memorandum of the Secretary of State for War Relating to the Army Estimates 1957–58*, Cmnd 150 (1957), p. 10.

[67] One senior officer thought this happened five times in these years.

[68] For a full account of the state of Transport Command over these years see John W. R. Taylor, 'Give the Army Wings', *RAF Quarterly* 4/1 (Jan. 1952), pp. 13–18 and Air Vice-Marshal W. M. Yool, 'The Changing Pattern of the RAF', *Brassey's Annual 1953*, p. 329.

[69] e.g. the Chief of the Air Staff strongly resisted the development of the Beverley.

was hoped that transport aircraft could be obtained from the United States under the military aid programme. Discussions in fact took place with United States officials, but without positive result. Thus in 1954 the RAF's airlift capability was extremely limited.

Transport Command had only about 40 obsolescent Hastings, of which probably not more than 25 were serviceable at any one time, and about 56 old and slow Valettas, of which perhaps 30 were serviceable at any one time.[70] Both the Hastings and the Valetta had been designed basically as civil airliners and neither had the speed, capacity, or loading and unloading features that were really required of modern transport aircraft.[71] When carrying its maximum of 34 troops, the Valetta had a range of only 360 miles, and in this role had never been intended as anything more than a stop-gap aircraft. The Hastings was a more useful aircraft as it could carry 50 troops for about 1,690 miles, but still it could carry nothing larger than a two-and-a-quarter-ton truck and a half-ton trailer. An order for 20 Beverleys was an encouraging development as this aircraft was a great advance on existing freighters and could carry 94 men with their equipment or up to 45,000 lb. of freight over short distances.[72] However, only 8 were due to be delivered in 1955, and even when the remainder came into service, air transport would still be far too limited for the strategic reserve to be anything more than a useful extra to Britain's traditional garrison strategy. The only other provision for air transport was certain new arrangements for the use of civil aircraft, but this scheme had many disadvantages and in any event the number of aircraft involved was fairly small. Although the 1954 White Paper made no mention of the strategic reserve being airlifted, it was clear from the government's plans that this was in fact the intention and the debate in the House proceeded on this assumption. That Transport Command was quite inadequate for the task attracted very little attention, and to read through the debate and also that on the Air Estimates leaves the impression that there were few parliamen-

[70] Lord Balfour's figures (186 HL Deb., 17 Mar. 1954, col. 465), which are broadly confirmed from other sources.
[71] For information about aircraft numbers, delivery dates, and performance see Owen Thetford, *Aircraft of the Royal Air Force Since 1918*, 4th ed. (1968).
[72] See further Capt A. J. V. Kendall, 'Air Mobility for the Soldier', *Air Power*, 7/3 (spring 1960), p. 182.

tarians who were aware of the plight of the Command, or if they were aware, were much concerned about it.

The first official announcement that the strategic reserve would be air-mobile came in February 1955.[73] Transport Command was then, however, very little stronger than it had been twelve months earlier. On a generous reckoning the strategic airlift was equivalent to a lift of about 1 brigade,[74] or to put it another way, equivalent to 78 Hastings loads.[75] Comets and Vickers-100 long-range jets were on order but the numbers were small and there were serious limitations to the kinds of military equipment they could carry, as both were military versions of commercial aircraft.[76] The delivery of the Beverley had been delayed by developmental difficulties, and capacity increased only marginally over the year. There was more improvement in 1956. The Beverley was now coming off the production line in reasonable numbers,[77] and a squadron of Comets was formed. The Comet was by no means an ideal transport aircraft as it was unsuitable for heavy freight, and its range hardly placed it in the true strategic category. Even so, an aircraft which could carry 44 men at 480 m.p.h. for more than 2,000 miles was a valuable addition to Transport Command's limited fleet. The general position was still far from satisfactory, however, and early in the year Transport Command was forced to use Coastal Command Shackletons to ferry troops to Cyprus. The Shackleton was a maritime reconnaissance aircraft which could be made to provide noisy and uncomfortable accommodation for up to 30 troops, but, as one critic observed, there was little point in flying troops to a

[73] MoD, *Statement on Defence 1955*, Cmd 9391, paras 17 and 41.
[74] Statement by Secretary of State for War, 538 HC Deb., 8 Mar. 1955, col. 202.
[75] MRAF Sir Dermot Boyle, 'The Next Ten Years', *Air Power*, 7/2 (winter, 1959–60), p. 95.
[76] The modification of commercial aircraft to serve as military transports involved many disadvantages and usually resulted in poor loading and unloading arrangements, limitations on the sort of equipment that could be carried, and difficulties in packing and securing loads. Army and air force opinion, therefore, strongly favoured the development of specialized military transports. However, conversion of civil aircraft was always much cheaper and financial planners could be relied upon to present a forceful case against specialized aircraft. Later there was constant argument between financial and strategic planners over this issue. See further HC, *Second Report from Estimates Committee ... Session 1963–64; Transport Aircraft* (1964), pp. xii–xiii, paras 28–34.
[77] Twenty-six were delivered in the period 1955–56 and 1956–57. See ibid. p. 119, table.

combat area if they were physically and mentally exhausted on arrival.[78] An order for 13 Britannias promised some improvement in the future, but the first of these aircraft was not expected to come into service until 1959 and, in any case, the number was too small to change the situation substantially.[79] By now the government's neglect of Transport Command was attracting more attention. *The Times* censured the government in February,[80] and the opposition expressed its concern by moving an amendment to the Air Estimates urging the re-equipment of the Command.[81]

In all, the airlifted strategic reserve was more important as a concept than as a policy over these years. The idea itself certainly broke new ground, but it was never fully worked out and there was little appreciation of some of the difficulties involved. One very senior army officer described the policy as 'prenatal', and he went on to explain that the army still had sufficient forces in the critical areas overseas to handle most situations that might arise. In the army's view, therefore, strategic airlift was not a 'first flight' concern, but mainly a matter of enabling rapid reinforcement. More importance was attached to tactical airlift, and most pressure was directed to this end. Another consideration was that the build-up of the central reserve proved a slower business than had been envisaged in 1954.

The shortage of transport aircraft was of course fundamental. So long as little headway was made with the re-equipment of Transport Command, the policy could never have much substance. Although senior air force officers argued that the Air Staff recognized the importance of the Command, the fact remains that transport aircraft remained a low priority. Nuclear deterrence was what defence was about, and the provision of air transport for the army drew off resources which were more urgently required for the build-up of Bomber Command. A general indication of the Air Staff priorities is

---

[78] J. W. R. Taylor, 'How Good are the RAF's New Aircraft?', *Air Power*, 3/4 (July 1956), pp. 257–8.
[79] An order had also been placed in 1955 for 3 Britannias for operation by the independent air operators. These were to be used for air trooping. 538 HC Deb., 8 Mar. 1955, col. 202.
[80] 'Selective Deterrence', 18 February 1956.
[81] 549 HC Deb., 5 Mar. 1956.

given by the table below, which compares expenditure on transport aircraft with total aircraft expenditure.

	1953–54 £m	1954–55 £m	1955–56 £m	1956–57 £m
Total aircraft expenditure	140	156	186	165
Value of transport aircraft delivered	4.25	7.5	6.25	14.75
Approx. value of transport spares delivered	2.0	2.25	2.5	3.5

Note: Light aircraft such as the Pembroke and Pioneer and helicopters are included as transport aircraft.

Sources: Line 1: annual *Air Estimates*; lines 2 and 3: HC, *Second Report from Estimates Committee . . . Session 1963–64: Transport Aircraft,* p. 119.

Although the V-bomber programme was the major factor behind the Air Staff's neglect of transport aircraft, other considerations appear to have worked in the same direction. The army still had mainly Second World War equipment, which was heavy and bulky, and there was a natural reluctance to provide air transport for men without proper equipment. The problem was accentuated by the fact that the transport aircraft then available were not fully satisfactory for military purposes. Generally, co-ordination between the army and the air force was poor and joint training was haphazard in the extreme. Only three airborne exercises were conducted in 1956.[82]

While the RAF remained cool about the overseas role, the navy began to see possibilities hitherto unexplored. About a year after the air scheme had made its appereance, the Board of Admiralty hesitantly took the first steps to develop a naval answer to the problems of overseas security. A number of circumstances contributed to the shift in naval attention. By the mid-fifties the broken-backed concept had become generally discredited. The defence vote had fallen in real terms and there was strong service competition for funds. Finally, the appointment of Mountbatten as First Sea Lord early in 1955 paved the way for the Admiralty to broaden its conceptual

[82] AM, *Memorandum by Secretary of State for Air to Accompany Air Estimates 1960–61,* Cmnd 950 (1960) para. 26.

horizons. The first indication of the navy's increased interest in overseas defence appeared in the 1955 White Paper where reference was made to its ability to support land operations as in Korea.[83] The following year a plan was announced to make available in limited war a force of aircraft carriers supplemented by cruisers and escorts.[84] However, it was not until after Suez that the scheme was adjusted to the needs of amphibious assault, and became a central feature of Britain's deployment of power east of Suez.

The only other policy which had much bearing on the east of Suez role was the development of air trooping. During 1954 and 1955 air trooping steadily increased its share of the total load and was extended to all stations in the Indian Ocean. Except for the movement of army units, air trooping became the normal means of travel for personnel of all three services between the United Kingdom and Aden, East Africa, and the Persian Gulf.[85] In October 1954 a new contract was placed for the operation of an air trooping service to Singapore, and by February 1955 the service was carrying about 1,000 passengers a month in each direction.[86] This resulted in a manpower saving of about one-seventh; thus out of 10,000 men moved on the Far East route in a year the army gained 1,400 or 1,500 in effective manpower in the field. There was in addition a financial saving as air passages to both the Far East and the Middle East cost less per head than sea passages. During 1955 the navy also made use of air trooping to increase the length of service of ships in Far Eastern waters. For some time ships of the American navy had been recommissioned by air, and the pressure on British ships now led the Admiralty to follow suit in some instances.[87]

The Base Strategy

No less than in the earlier period, British power east of Suez rested firmly on the chain of military bases. Command, communications, and arrangements for inter-service co-ordination

---

[83] See MoD, *Statement on Defence 1955*, Cmd 9391, para. 40.
[84] MoD, *Statement on Defence 1956*, Cmd 9691, para. 22.   [85] Craig, pp. 215–16.
[86] WO, *Memorandum of Secretary of State for War Relating to Army Estimates 1955–56*, Cmd 9395, para. 86.
[87] John Chappell, 'Trooping by Air', *Navy*, 61/9 (Sept. 1956), p. 273.

were tied to the base system. Each of the services drew its logistic resources from the base network, and none would have retained much semblance of overseas strength divorced from it. For the air force and the navy the exercise of power east of Suez was above all a matter of mobility: and mobility in these days of 'short-legged' aircraft and ships required airstrips, harbours, and refuelling and supply centres, at the very least in the east and the west and at some point near the middle of the Indian Ocean. For the army, bases were essential, not only because of its logistic dependence on the other two services, but also because of its need to station combat formations close to likely trouble spots. Notwithstanding the establishment of the strategic reserve the British army remained primarily a garrison army and it was dependent for its striking power on the string of garrisons from the Mediterranean to Hong Kong, on its theatre forces in Malaya, Kenya, and the Middle East, and on the supplies and equipment stored at these places. While this was pre-eminently true of the Far East, it was only to a degree less true in the west. During the slow withdrawal from the Suez Canal Zone, the base there remained the main source of army power in the Persian Gulf and Africa as well as in the Middle East. When the withdrawal was finally completed military power became concentrated in the Mediterranean, and the army's ability to carry out major operations around the western rim of the Indian Ocean declined correspondingly. The Chiefs of Staff were only too aware of this, and the move from the Middle East caused much heart-burning and led to renewed interest in a base in Africa.

In terms of strategic theory, the chain of military bases was now primarily a chain of airfields held in the first place for the deployment of bomber forces, and in the second for the deployment of airborne troops. Though it was hoped that the establishment of a strong central reserve would reduce the need to have large army garrisons dotted along the imperial life-line, there is no evidence to suggest that strategists believed the scheme would permit a gradual run-down of the base structure. It was admitted that the strategic reserve required a permanent chain of depots where heavy equipment, arms, and ammunition could be stored. Moreover, it was soon apparent that if the airstrips were to be secure, army garrisons were needed for their protection. Thus the effect of air doctrine was to tie down army forces to the defence of British bases. To some extent this was welcomed by the army as justifying its force levels, but doubts were expressed, particularly at senior commander level.

As British strategy at this time knew no alternative to the base structure, the outlook was not encouraging. The loss of the Middle East base was a serious blow and the expedient adopted of moving the main force to the substitute bases of Cyprus and Libya by no means solved the awkward problems created. Both in Parliament and in the press there was some discussion of the merits of a base in East Africa, and, in the debate on the Army Estimates in 1955, a few members on both sides of the House advocated setting up a base there to avoid the 'over-flying' difficulties in the Middle East.[88] In the army also there was some pressure for a base in Kenya. In the Indian Ocean the chain was still intact, but several of Britain's strategic footholds were rather less secure than they had been a few years earlier. In Ceylon and in Singapore there were difficulties with the governments over the position of the bases, and in South Africa control of the Simonstown base passed to the South African Navy. For the moment, however, there seemed no other course but to hold on wherever possible, to place the strategic above the diplomatic interest and to negotiate as favourable terms as could be managed, and to hope that the wave of nationalist feeling would abate before too much damage was done.

In Ceylon agitation against the agreement permitting Britain to use the Trincomalee and Katunayake bases had been mounting for some time, and the Ceylon government found it necessary to move warily. When in July 1954 a newspaper report quoted the new C in C, East Indies Fleet, Vice-Admiral Norris, as saying that 'Trincomalee will naturally be a naval base from which ships of the East Indies Fleet will operate in the event of a third world war', the Ceylonese Ministry of Defence and External Affairs was quick to issue a communiqué stating that there was no question of Trincomalee being used in the event of war without the permission of the Ceylon government.[89] East Indies Command later denied that Admiral Norris had made the statement, and in September the First Lord of the

---

[88] e.g. Hugh Fraser, 538 HC Deb., 8 Mar. 1955, col. 243, and C. J. M. Alport, ibid. col. 307.

[89] *Hindu*, 1 Aug. 1954.

Admiralty, J. P. L. Thomas, when visiting Ceylon was careful to stress that the base would be used only after consultation and with the full consent of the government of Ceylon.[90] Assurance of consultation and consent, however, fell far short of satisfying the more fiery nationalists and there were repeated calls for a British withdrawal. The government, being more sympathetic to the British interest, was placed in an awkward position and Sir John Kotelawala, the Prime Minister, attempted to justify the continued British presence by envisaging the possibility of a Communist invasion from South India.[91]

The victory of the left-wing opposition in the April 1956 elections brought little hope of any long-term future for the British bases. Solomon Bandaranaike, the new Prime Minister, immediately announced that the question of the bases was a subject which would have to be looked into at an early date.[92] A few weeks later he declared that the bases 'must go' and he said that he had written to the British government about them.[93] A temporary reprieve was won at the Commonwealth Prime Ministers' Conference in July when a rather indefinite agreement was reached which permitted the continuation of certain communications, movements and storage facilities enjoyed by Britain under the 1947 Agreement, in return for British assistance with the development and training of the Ceylon armed forces.[94]

A more satisfactory arrangement was made with the South African government over the Simonstown base. In July 1955, as part of a broader agreement on defence co-operation between the two governments, Britain agreed to transfer control of the Royal Navy base at Simonstown to the South African Navy.[95] In return, South Africa undertook to maintain the base efficiently and further to expand its facilities according to a detailed plan. After transfer, the Royal Navy would continue to enjoy the facilities of the base in peace-time and was guaranteed their use in time of war, even 'in a war in which the United

[90] Ibid. 30 Sept. 1954.
[91] Ibid. 8 Sept. 1954.
[92] Times, 7 Apr. 1956.
[93] Ibid. 5 May 1956.
[94] Ibid. 7 July 1956.
[95] MoD, Exchanges of Letters on Defence Matters between the Governments of the United Kingdom and the Union of South Africa, June 1955, Cmd 9520.

Kingdom, but not the Union, is involved'.[96] On 2 April 1957, after 143 years of occupation and control by the Royal Navy, the Simonstown base was transferred to the South African Navy.

The problem in Singapore was to find a formula which would reconcile Britain's strategic interest with the local demand for self-government. The broad lines of British colonial policy had never been in doubt. The end was self-government and the approach was through the recognized stages of parliamentary development. But ever since the first major territories gained their independence in the early post-war years, the concept had been developing that this general policy could not be applied to a number of small territories whose importance as strategic bases placed them in a different category.[97] In Singapore in 1956 the doctrine of the primacy of the strategic over all other considerations was put to the test and the government came down in its favour.

The background to the 1956 negotiations can be quickly told. In July 1955 the Singapore Legislative Assembly adopted a resolution calling for immediate self-government for the Colony. Discussion took place the following month between the Colonial Secretary Alan Lennox-Boyd, the Chief Minister of Singapore David Marshall, and the Governor Sir Robert Black, and it was agreed to hold a constitutional conference in London about April 1956. The conference opened at Lancaster House on 23 April but after three weeks of negotiations it broke down, mainly over the issue of responsibility for internal security after Singapore had attained self-government. According to Marshall, to cede control over internal security was to make a mockery of independence.[98] The British view was that external defence and internal security were inevitably intertwined in Singapore, and that at the very least it was necessary for the United Kingdom to retain some power to make Orders in Council on matters of internal security which affected the United Kingdom's responsibilities for external affairs and defence. The Australian and New Zealand govern-

---

[96] Ibid. p. 11, para. 4.
[97] 'We do not accept the principle of self-determination as one of universal application', Macmillan reported in the summary of the London Tripartite Conference on Cyprus, 7 Sept. 1955. Quoted in J. L. Moulton, *Defence in a Changing World* (1964), p. 100.
[98] *Keesing's Contemporary Archives*, 1955–6, vol. 10, 14909.

ments were equally convinced that it was necessary for the United Kingdom to retain some control over internal security, and both Prime Ministers issued statements endorsing the United Kingdom's stand. Marshall returned to Singapore a disappointed man and resigned as Chief Minister on 7 June. In a farewell speech to the Legislative Assembly he bitterly attacked the Colonial Office, dismissed the Australian government for hurrying to the support of the United Kingdom without ascertaining the views of the Singapore government, and accused the British government of making Singapore 'a live offering to their god of brass, SEATO'.[99]

The political uncertainties about the Singapore base led some officers and officials to favour the establishment of a British base in Australia. According to one report, the possibilities of an Australian base were discussed 'endlessly' in the mid-fifties, but the government never considered the matter seriously. The scheme would have involved developing an Australian base while at the same time maintaining Singapore, and the government would not countenance the financial burden of such a 'double stance'. Nor was it likely that the Australian government would have committed itself financially.

The negotiations over the future of Singapore and the continuing difficulties regarding the Cyprus base provoked during mid-1956 the first serious discussion of the whole question of bases. The government's position was now clear. The bases must be held, if necessary independently of the willingness of the local majority to co-operate. *The Times* accepted the government's view that the bases must be held, but it was anxious that some means be devised by which they would continue to fulfil their strategic function with the co-operation of the inhabitants.[100] The *Observer* adopted a similar position. It was now essential that the bases be secured by consent, and in some cases the only solution would be for them to be held in partnership with other allied or Commonwealth countries.[101] The *Manchester Guardian*, in a more reflective leader on 22 May, took up the question of purpose and concluded with an argument which was often to be repeated in later years:

[99] *Times*, 7 June 1956.
[100] 20 June 1956.
[101] 20 May 1956.

Ironically, the relinquishment of British bases round the Indian Ocean is a more serious matter for the Asian countries than for Britain. Once the British forces have gone they are unlikely to come back ... Certainly we shall not keep a large reserve ready in Cyprus or in England just because some day it might be wanted again in the Far East. The cost would be excessive.

Divergent Policies in the Middle East and the Far East

In earlier days the Middle East and the Far East had been side-pieces of a regional system, deriving their meaning and purpose from the defence of India. Once the centre-piece was lost this regional conception was quickly eroded and the two areas became in British eyes independent units, each with its own diplomatic pattern and strategic practice. By the middle fifties the distinctive nature of political thinking about the two areas was readily apparent but what is perhaps more interesting is that it was paralleled in the military sphere.

It is easy to exaggerate the difference in military thinking about the two areas but broadly speaking in the Middle East the accent was on air power and on air mobility, while in the Far East defence was seen largely in terms of the garrison and the infantryman. Certainly the use of air power in maintaining local stability was more deeply rooted in strategic thinking in the Middle East, and its use was much more widespread there than in the Far East. The dominance of air power in imperial policing in the Middle East went back to 1921 when the RAF, arguing on the basis of its success in Somaliland in 1920, had taken over from the army the responsibility for garrisoning Iraq.[102] Seven years later the RAF succeeded in wresting the defence of Aden from the army and the navy.[103] Broadly these changes involved the substitution of a system in which small tribal wars and other disturbances were quelled by air action for one in which they were put down by columns on the ground, operating from neighbouring garrisons. Promoted strongly by Trenchard, the air control method, as the former came to be called, became accepted as an economi-

[102] The RAF claimed that in 21 days air power had solved the Somaliland problem which had baffled the army for 21 years. See further *Gen Lord Ismay, Memoirs,* (1960), pp. 35 and 59; Andrew Boyle, *Trenchard* (1962), pp. 365–95; and Slessor, *The Central Blue,* pp. 51–70.

[103] For details see Boyle, and Slessor, as cited in n. 102, p. 570 and pp. 57–8, resp.

cal and efficient way of maintaining local stability in under-
developed territories throughout the Middle East. Building
on its experience there, and also to a less extent in the North-
West Frontier of India, the RAF developed a body of theory
which defined the techniques and scope of air policing.[104] In
many ways the air control system represented one of the most
notable doctrinal achievements of the RAF in the twenties
and thirties. However, the apparent failure of the method in
Palestine in 1937 and 1938 was a major setback, and as the
coming war approached, RAF interest declined and the bombing role increasingly dominated air force thinking.

After the Second World War the air control method was
not widely discussed in the RAF, but it continued to be employed in the Arabian Peninsula and the Persian Gulf. Most
commonly air power was used to quell local disturbances by
pin-point attacks on focal points such as forts, supply bases, or
buildings occupied by dissident groups or local dignitaries.
These targets were very easy to identify in the Middle East, and
for a time such attacks continued to be an economical way of
maintaining local stability. However, their effect was usually
transitory rather than permanent, and once the RAF was
forced to take action on a regular basis, the efficacy of the
method was called into question. Another consideration was
that the system involved very little contact with the local
population, and for this reason it was not possible for the military to identify themselves with local forces or to be linked in
efforts to improve the lot of the people.

In mid-1955 something of a feud developed about the air
control method on both military and humanitarian grounds.
In May RAF aircraft bombed five small villages in Southern
Arabia after rebel tribesmen had refused to pay fines imposed
for attacking a government convoy.[105] The issue provoked
sharp parliamentary exchanges and there was considerable
controversy in the press. Lord Lloyd, Parliamentary Under-
Secretary of State for the Colonies, did not mince words when

---

[104] See e.g. Wg Cdr J. A. Chamier, 'The Use of the Air Force for Replacing
Military Garrisons', *JRUSI*, 66/462 (May 1921), pp. 205–16; Capt J. B. Glubb,
'Air and Ground Forces in Punitive Expeditions', *JRUSI*, 71/484 (Nov. 1926),
pp. 777–84; Air Cdre C. F. A. Portal, 'Air Force Co-operation in Policing the
Empire', *JRUSI*, 82/526 (May 1937), pp. 343–58. Slessor, as cited in n. 102, sets
out the mechanics of the method in some detail.
[105] *Manchester Guardian*, 23 May 1955.

he declared: 'the destruction from the air of the property of lawless tribes, is, in our opinion, the most effective and probably the most humane way of punishing them when they refuse to pay a collective fine.'[106]

In June more serious clashes with dissident tribesmen and incursions from across the Yemeni border raised doubts about the adequacy of security arrangements in the colony and the protectorate. The responsibility for security still rested with the RAF, and reliance was placed on air sorties supported on the ground by the Aden Protectorate Levies, for which the RAF Regiment provided the officers. There were no regular troops in the territory and the only other force was the RAF Regiment of about 1,000.[107] The situation deteriorated during the latter part of the month and on 1 July the 1st Btn, the Seaforth Highlanders, and one squadron of the Life Guards were flown in from the Suez Canal Zone.[108] Later that month Major General C. L. Firbank visited Aden to make a special report for the Chiefs of Staff.[109] For some time the air force and the army battled over the issue but in February 1956 it was announced that an army battalion would be maintained at Aden.[110] In 1957 the army assumed responsibility for security in the territory and thenceforward army units were permanently stationed in Aden and army officers staffed the Aden Protectorate Levies. However, the air control method continued to be used much as before, and it was not until 1958–9 that it was modified to suit the new conditions.[111]

A second line of policy which found ready acceptance in the Middle East was that of airlifting troops to trouble spots from neighbouring bases or from the United Kingdom. A mobile force which could be moved into an area with speed was particularly suited to the conditions of the Middle East and the Persian Gulf, and once the aircraft became available the threat of Britain's intervening from outside became a

---

[106] 193 HL Deb., 15 June 1955, col. 111. For questions in the House of Commons and replies of Alan Lennox-Boyd, Secretary of State for the Colonies, see 543 HC Deb., 13 July 1955, coll. 1931–6 and 544 HC Deb., 20 July 1955, coll. 372–4.

[107] *Manchester Guardian*, 22 June 1955; *Daily Telegraph*, 2 July 1955.

[108] *Times*, 2 July 1955.

[109] *Sunday Times*, 17 July 1955.

[110] See *Times*, 28 Mar. 1956. Apparently the army argued that for some years the RAF Regiment had been used in an army role but this was disputed by the Air Staff.

[111] See pp. 131–33 below.

distinctive feature of her Middle Eastern strategy. It dove-tailed nicely with earlier thinking; it involved no continuing presence; it implied an occasional threat; and it seemed cheaper, at least in terms of political cost.

While in the Middle East strategic doctrine was heavily influenced by deterrence theory, the Far East may be regarded as building on the Indian tradition of 'watch and ward'. There was a different sense of time and purpose. The military presence was not so overtly military. Tactical doctrine was not about air power or armoured formations but was concerned with jungle patrols, mapping programmes, and co-ordination with the civil authorities. The emphasis was on men on the ground familiar with local conditions, thus there was close co-operation between British forces and the local population: to give one illustration, about 30 Sarawak trackers were normally allotted to each infantry batallion.[112] The result was a relatively immobile structure of power based on Singapore and extending through Malaya and Borneo, carefully shaped to maintain local stability and to protect the territorial borders, but not well suited to striking out beyond these areas.

Nor did the concept of air mobility fully take root in the Far East in these years. Apart from the practical difficulties of transporting units to the Far East by air, the military never saw themselves as threatened or unpopular. Singapore was the base and there was not the same requirement for inter-threatre mobility as in the Middle East. As one British general was reported to have remarked during confrontation (though the point might equally have been made in the earlier period), 'What good is strategic mobility to me? What I want is a platoon which can find its way in the dark and has one or two chaps who can speak the lingo'.

These differences in tactical doctrine partly reflected the different topographical conditions in the two areas. In the Middle East and the Persian Gulf the barren nature of the terrain favoured attack from the air and made concealment difficult, whereas in the Far East the thick jungle and mountain-ous hinterland greatly reduced the effectiveness of air action. Another factor was the degree of professionalism of the enemy. The Communist terrorist in Malaya was a full-time soldier, and

[112] *The Conduct of Anti-Terrorist Operations in Malaya* (1952), ch. 21. See also Richard Miers, *Shoot to Kill* (1959), p. 104.

a very different proposition from the tribesman of the Arabian Peninsula.[113] However, once Arab dissidents were organized from outside and had learned the art of dispersal, the air control method proved much less effective. A third factor was the differences in the degree of Britain's political and economic involvement in the two areas. In both the Far East and the Middle East Britain's initial contact had been almost solely strategic; but in the Far East British colonialism had taken root and the involvement had deepened, whereas in the Middle East, and particularly in Southern Arabia and the Persian Gulf, Britain's interest had remained largely strategic. In the mid-fifties, for example, Aden was still little more than a bunkering place. The result was that in the Far East Britain's military position was built upon a secure political and administrative structure and there was a sense of identification with the people and their problems. For all this there was no parallel in the Middle East.

To take stock of these years, one is forced to select and to order the various threads in the light of the subsequent development of British policy. At the time, the lines of policy and the cross-currents of thought admitted no coherent approach to defence east of Suez. The emergence of distinctive thinking about the Middle East and the Far East meant that the wider frame of reference was not seen as of contemporary relevance. The dominance of the deterrent and the fear of general war impeded recognition of the distinctive nature of limited threats to the peace and the development of appropriate forces. The existence of separate service strategies added to the general disorder—an air force with its eyes on Russia and nuclear retaliation and only peripherally concerned with defence east of Suez; a navy dispossessed of its old role and in search of a new; an army in practice concerned with one thing and in theory concerned with another. It was only in the last years of the fifties that a broader pattern took shape: that the east of Suez area regained a measure of conceptual unity; that the limited-war role was accepted as more pressing than the global role; and that the development of strategically mobile forces became a central concern of the defence establishment as a whole.

[113] Wg Cdr F. Norris, 'The Roles of the Far East Air Force' *Brassey's Annual 1955*, p. 309.

CHAPTER THREE

The Impact of Suez and the
Sandys White Paper

IF both the experience of the Suez crisis and the Sandys White Paper of 1957 appear to stand out as landmarks in the evolution of British defence policy, their significance for the east of Suez role is neither as direct nor as obvious as first appeareances might suggest. In point of fact none of the developments of the post-Suez year represented a sharp break with the past or substantially changed the main lines of British defence policy in the Indian Ocean area. Certainly the military weaknesses shown up during the Suez operation led to some measure of re-equipment and to an increased emphasis on mobility, but the main guidelines were already at hand and, in any event, these developments must be balanced against the downgrading of conventional forces which was implicit in the government's reaffirmation, with even more enthusiasm than in the past, of the primacy of the nuclear deterrent.

In retrospect, the Suez experience can be seen as significant less for its immediate impact upon British policy than for its longer-term influence on strategic thinking. On the mobility issue, for example, the operation produced relatively little in the way of concrete results in 1957 but it did become a reference point for much of the agitation for an increase in airlift capability, for larger strategic reserves, and for the development of amphibious forces in the subsequent four or five years. Equally important again from the longer-term viewpoint, were the changes the Suez crisis produced in the environment in which British defence policy had to work itself out. The emergence of the air barrier, and hence the division of the area of Britain's overseas responsibilities into two parts, and the increasing problems and precariousness of foreign bases were closely related to the Suez adventure and to the fact that Arabia, Asia, and Africa now found a British presence less acceptable than in the past. If the Suez crisis marks a watershed, then, it does so primarily in terms of those later developments which can be traced back to the events of October and November 1956, but which subsequently acquired a momentum of their own.

For our purposes the 1957 White Paper is important, not because it effected any immediate and basic change in British strategy but because it brought together and set out in fuller form the various strands of strategic thought since 1954. In this sense the White Paper can be seen as the logical outcome of the attempt to give some intellectual coherence to the strategic ideas of the previous three years—representing, as it did, the high-water mark of the theory of nuclear deterrence and the most optimistic assessment of the policies of strategic mobility. The next four years were largely concerned with working out the implications of the 1957 statement, re-weighting priorities, modifying some of the concepts, and developing others.

The Suez Operation

The shortcomings of the military operation at Suez stemmed largely from earlier failures to give some substance to the emphasis placed on mobile forces in official theory. To be effective, military action following Egypt's nationalization of the canal on 26 July 1956 needed to be swift, and to be swift it was necessary to have mobile forces already in being. However, despite all the urging in previous years, the mobile forces available at the outbreak of the crisis were altogether inadequate for the sort of intervention required. The strategic reserve, although on paper of divisional strength, in fact amounted to only one brigade, as many of the units earmarked for it were deployed in completely unrelated roles and others were already serving overseas. Moreover, before the available units could be used in action they needed to be brought up to strength, draw their mobilization stores and, if possible, undergo additional training, as very little air training had then taken place. Of the remaining mobile forces, a large proportion of the units not involved in training were committed to internal security duties in Cyprus and elsewhere. The 3rd Commando Brigade had two of its Commandos in Cyprus,[1] and two battalions of the 16th Parachute Brigade Group were also tied down in anti-terrorist operations there. All these troops eventually played an important part in the operation, but in early August their state of readiness was poor. According to one account:

> the parachutists had done no parachute training for months, the Commandos had not practised amphibious warfare or co-operation with tanks for over twelve months. There were no transport aircraft and none of the base organisations or specialists required for an amphibious operation were readily available.[2]

It was therefore necessary to spend a matter of months consolidating military strength. The period of preparation went back to 27 July, when the Chiefs of Staff were 'instructed to get ready a plan and a time-table for an operation designed to occupy and secure the canal, should other methods fail.'[3] It was immediately clear that the shortage of aircraft ruled out an airborne operation and that the main assault would have to be seaborne and launched from Malta. The Chiefs of Staffs' plan involved a build-up of forces at home and in the Mediterranean over a period of six weeks. Mid-September was the earliest date by which action could be taken. As Eden notes with resignation in his memoirs, this was the same period of preparation as was required for the invasion of Sicily from North Africa in the Second World War.[4] From the start it was accepted that a period of ten days would be needed between the receipt of orders and the start of the operation.[5]

Early in August steps were taken to strengthen Britain's position in the eastern Mediterranean and a number of army, navy, and air force units were moved into the area. Twenty thousand reservists were called up following a royal proclamation on 2 August. The shipping position was examined and found to be critical. This led to a period of frenzied activity

---

[1] The third functioned as a training unit in the UK.
[2] A. J. Barker, *Suez: the Seven Day War* (1964), p. 26; see also pp. 43–4.
[3] Eden, *Full Circle*, p. 427.
[4] Ibid. p. 430.
[5] In the event the Commander-in-Chief got little more than ten hours' notice. Despatch by Gen Sir Charles F. Keightley, 'Operations in Egypt—November to December 1956', suppl. no. 41172, 12 Sept. 1957, to *London Gazette* of 10 Sept. 1957, p. 5328.

during which warships were taken out of reserve, troopships diverted, and a number of merchant ships requisitioned from private firms. The shortage of tank landing ships was particularly serious and it was overcome only by adopting the unsatisfactory expedient of requisitioning any that could be found, including some which were being used to ferry vehicles to and from Northern Ireland.[6]

Before 1956 Britain's air transport weakness had not gone unnoticed but the government had managed to forestall many would-be critics by focusing attention on the position as it soon would be rather than as it was. The Suez operation, however, brought an end to the government's world of make-believe when the air transport fleet was shown to be but a shadow of the theory. Early in August the scheduled services of Transport Command were cancelled and considerable publicity was given to a 'great airlift' of reinforcements to the Mediterranean, undertaken jointly by Transport Command and chartered aircraft belonging to the independent air lines. In fact, however, the total number of troops carried accounted for only about a quarter of a division, and of these by far the largest number was carried by the independent air companies. When the airborne attack was made, at Port Said solely, although Britain had one brigade in the strategic reserve, the shortage of aircraft was such that only one British battalion (some 500 men) was dropped from the air, the other two being sent in by sea.[7] In his memoirs, Eden refers to a shortage of parachutists,[8] but in actual fact there was then available, between the British and the French, something in the order of six times the number of parachutists actually dropped.[9] The shortage was in transport aircraft, not in parachutists.

The amphibious force followed the Second World War pattern except that a large number of its parts were missing and the ships and equipment were considerably older. Although 32 tank landing ships had been retained on the navy's list, only 2 were in operational state and there were difficulties

[6] Generally see Eden, *Full Circle*, pp. 429 and 534, and Neville Brown, *Strategic Mobility* (1963), pp. 60–1.
[7] B. H. Liddell Hart, *Deterrent or Defence: a Fresh Look at the West's Military Position* (1960), p. 29.
[8] *Full Circle*, p. 534.
[9] FM Lord Harding, 221 HL Deb., 10 Mar. 1960, col. 1029.

and delays in taking the others out of reserve.[10] The one new feature was an improvised helicopter force which landed 400 Royal Marines at Port Said in 90 minutes.[11] However, the mixed helicopters carried only 100 men in each lift at about 60 knots, and neither the Whirlwinds nor the Sycamores were really suited to the operation. Landing such a small force involved considerable risk as the first 100 Commandos were very vulnerable while waiting for the follow-up lifts to arrive. At Suez there was no mishap, but it was clear that capacity would need to be substantially increased in any subsequent operation. With 22 Sikorsky S58s, for example, 300 men could be lifted at a time, and the second and subsequent lifts would arrive far more quickly than with the Whirlwinds.[12] Summing up later Major General J. L. Moulton, Chief of Amphibious Warfare from 1957 to 1961, observed that 'The operation bore the hallmarks of World War Two: the long assembly period; the slow approach of non-ocean-worthy ships; the long preliminary softening up; and the preoccupation with beach defences and forces in the near vicinity of beaches.'[13]

Viewed in wider perspective, the operation revealed the failure of the defence establishment to adjust to the changed conditions of the mid-fifties. The weeks of planning, preparation and re-equipment; the vast armada which eventually steamed from Malta; the five days of air operations which laboriously paved the way for the arrival of the assault force; all were legacies of the days of global-war thinking when it had been assumed that the international climate would be different and that political considerations would determine only the decision to act, not the methods. Such an approach had no place in a world of heightened sensibilities and ostensibly at peace. The debits were quickly tallied and the operation labelled a failure. Not all the blame can be attached to the military of course. Political indecision was a major factor contributing to the delay, and ships carrying vehicles and stores were loaded, unloaded, and reloaded because of cabinet equivocation. Although it was true that the services had shown little appreciation of the pre-

[10] Liddell Hart, *Deterrent or Defence*, pp. 29 and 30, and Barker, p. 49.

[11] Despatch (cited in n. 5) by the C in C, Gen Sir Charles F. Keightley, p. 5334.

[12] Capt T. M. P. Stevens, 'Troop-Carrying Helicopters', *Army Quarterly*, 75/2 (Jan. 1958), p. 203.

[13] 'Amphibious Warfare in the late 1960s: Seaborne/Airborne Operations', *JRUSI*, 107/625 (Feb. 1962), p. 19.

mium attaching to speed, surprise and mobility, the villain of the piece was the government and a succession of defence ministers whose words and strategic concepts had had so little relation to actions and appropriations.

More important than as an indictment of past policies, however, the Suez operation stood as a lesson for the future. The campaign had demonstrated both the irrelevance of nuclear power to limited conflicts and the inadequacy of Britain's conventional forces. Each of the weaknesses discussed above argued for more emphasis on mobile forces. The external restrictions on the movement of British forces pointed in the same direction. Libya was unusable as a base for offensive operations, and the 10th Armoured Division and the air units stationed there had to be struck from the order of battle. Britain's airfields in Jordan were closed to her. No sooner had the Anglo-French forces landed at Suez than Solomon Bandaranaike extracted an assurance from the British government that the bases in Ceylon would not be used for any purpose connected, however remotely, with the operation. In short, Britain found that many of her foreign bases were much less usable in times of crisis than under routine conditions.

On the positive side, the operation had confirmed the advantages of sea- and air-mobile forces. Planning at sea had been uncomplicated by political difficulties and restrictions. The helicopter experiment from HMS *Ocean* and *Theseus* had been a success. The effectiveness of seaborne aircraft had exceeded all expectations. The case for a strong air-mobile force had been strengthened by a consideration of what might have been accomplished if Britain had possessed a sizeable central reserve and an adequate air transport fleet at the outbreak of the crisis. As the military preparations dragged on *The Economist*, for example, declared that the lesson of the crisis was that Britain needed two fully equipped divisions poised permanently for a quick take-off.[14] The emergence of the air barrier did, it is true, create complications but the point here was surely that sufficient forces must henceforward be stationed east of the barrier, not that air mobility had lost its usefulness.

[14] 1 Sept. 1956. Liddell Hart wrote later that the surest way to save the canal from being blocked was to capture the keypoints along it, together with the airfields, by a surprise drop from the sky. In his assessment this would have required at least one airborne division, preferably two. *Deterrent or Defence*, p. 28.

In the interval between the cease-fire and the publication of the 1957 White Paper many of these points were taken up by the press, but no single line emerged on the reshaping of the defence machine or on the balance to be struck between conventional and nuclear forces. Time was needed to digest the material thrown up by the Suez operation and to rearrange the thoughts of a decade. Still, there was no disagreement with Alastair Buchan's conclusion that Suez had 'revealed the most serious weaknesses in the readiness and mobility of Britain's conventional forces',[15] and there was a measure of agreement that no time should be lost in making good these deficiencies. When the 1957 White Paper eventually appeared, however, the accent was on nuclear deterrence; mobile forces were decidely a second priority. To understand how this came about it is necessary to broaden the frame of reference and to take into account a number of other factors, two of which had hovered in the background of policy-making for some years but which came to the fore during these crucial months.

The Wider Background to the 1957 White Paper

Over and above the specific military lessons derived from the Suez experience, the campaign produced a mood of disillusionment and frustration which was widespread throughout the country. That the operation had failed because the services had been starved of the resources necessary to develop strong mobile forces was overlooked, or was regarded as less important than the fact that it had failed. It was of the essence of this line of thought that no amount of explanation or rationalization could alter the fact that the military establishment had proved incapable of fulfilling the demands of foreign policy. What is more, the feeling was that it had been conventional forces that had failed Britain, that had undermined her paramountcy in the Middle East, and placed her position as a world power in jeopardy. In this wave of disillusionment it was natural to turn to something unaffected by the stigma of Suez: a set of weapons which could restore national prestige and ensure some independence of action—a first essential, it was felt in many quarters, in view of America's perfidious role during the crisis. Alastair Buchan has argued that this

[15] 'Britain's Defence Problem', Observer Foreign News Service, 23 Jan. 1957.

feeling played a significant part in the further increase of
emphasis on the nuclear deterrent and there can be little
doubt that this was so.[16] That the reaction was patently irra-
tional and that it so clearly was based on a misreading of
Britain's position at Suez and indeed her position in the world,
makes it no less understandable or important. The relationship between the Suez experience and the 1957 White Paper was
not simply a matter of rational analysis and judgement, and
to limit the explanation to these terms can only obscure the
real motivations and distort the true picture. As in the making
of many great decisions, emotion played its part. Rationalization after the event can all too easily overlook this very human
element.

This mood of disillusionment was important in another way
in that it led to a public clamour for defence retrenchment.
George Brown, the Labour spokesman on defence, accurately
gauged the climate of the time when he referred to

the extraordinary kind of neutralist emotion which is growing, not
least in the party opposite. There is in every speech that is made,
in every newspaper that one reads, even the more responsible ones,
an emotion that Suez has shown that all this money has been wasted,
that it has not produced effective results, a feeling of, 'Let us cut it;
let us do away with it. Nothing is of any use, anyway.'[17]

In fact the economic burden of defence expenditure had weighed
heavily upon the government for some considerable time, and
before the Suez crisis erupted steps had been taken to ease the
strain on the economy.

Early in July 1955 the Minister of Defence, Selwyn Lloyd,
reported that unless existing programmes were revised, the
cost of defence would rise from £1,517 million in 1955 to
£1,929 million in 1959. Eden, then in office four months and
gravely concerned about the state of the economy, determined
to call a halt to this spiralling expenditure. A series of studies
for a revision of programmes was put in hand, as a result of
which cuts were made and the defence estimate for 1956–57
was stabilized at £1,535 million.[18] In Eden's view this was a

[16] 'Britain and the Nuclear Deterrent', *Political Quarterly*, 31/1 (Jan.–Mar. 1960),
p. 39.
[17] 564 HC Deb., 13 Feb. 1957, coll. 1288–9.
[18] Eden, *Full Circle*, pp. 370–1.

useful start but a more far-reaching investigation was required. Motivated mainly by economic considerations, though also by dissatisfaction with the existing machinery for decision-making, in the early summer of 1956 he set up a small Cabinet subcommittee to examine long-term needs. The committee's starting-point was the proposition that since the war the United Kingdom had attempted 'too much in too many spheres of defence', and that the time had come for effort to be transferred from defence preparations to the improvement of her economic position. In particular, the Prime Minister pointed out that means must be found of increasing the credit side of Britain's balance of payments by £400 million.[19] The committee met throughout July, and in October Eden announced that the strength of the services would be reduced from 800,000 to 700,000. Although no public announcement was made, the review led Eden to plan for reduction to about 445,000 by April 1960, or a year later at the outside limit.[20]

Before these reductions could be implemented the Suez crisis intervened. Its immediate effect was to thrust aside all thoughts of defence reductions, but even before the Anglo-French forces had withdrawn from Egypt it had injected a new note of urgency into the case for large-scale economies. A new economic crisis was in the making.[21] The military failure at Suez had focused public attention on the level of defence spending.[22] And the view was now widely held that Britain had not been getting full value for money. For the next few months defence was examined 'with a deeply sceptical eye'.[23] The *Financial Times* contended that unless the military budget came down, Britain could not return to prosperity.[24] *The Economist* drew attention to the fact that a larger slice had been taken out of Britain's national income than out of any other

[19] Ibid. p. 371.
[20] Ibid. p. 374. These reductions were to be made possible by increased reliance on nuclear deterrence. See especially Eden's letter to Eisenhower, ibid. pp. 372–3.
[21] The Suez crisis was a significant factor here. The Anglo-French invasion of Egypt led to a run on the pound in the world's financial markets. Britain's overseas reserves fell by $57m. in Sept., $84m. in Oct., and $279m. in Nov., the latter representing about 15 per cent of her total gold and dollar reserves. The operation itself raised defence expenditure in 1956–57 to about £1,700m.
[22] The Labour party made much political capital out of the fact that over £7,500m. had been spent on defence since 1951, and it missed no opportunity to push this point home.
[23] *The Economist*, 5 Jan. 1957.
[24] 1 Dec. 1956.

NATO country's except the United States. Moreover, much of this expenditure had been incurred abroad and had aggravated Britain's balance of payments difficulties. At home the burden had fallen particularly heavily on the engineering and electronics industries, and on research resources, with correspondingly adverse effects on exports and industrial re-equipment.[25] *The Times*, the *Guardian*, and the *Observer* joined the battle and even after February, when the emphasis changed, there could be no doubt that the consensus was for some cut-back. A number of ministerial statements during this period made it clear that the government was thinking along the same lines. In his first television address after becoming Prime Minister, Macmillan emphasized the need for defence economies.[26] The following week Duncan Sandys declared that Britain was spending more on defence than she could reasonably afford.[27]

Very closely linked with the economic argument was an issue which had been looming on the political and military horizon for some time—the abolition of National Service. For some years the arguments in favour of ending National Service had been persuasive. The strongest argument was financial. The maintenance of a large standing army was a costly burden, and unless substantial cuts were made or, alternatively, Britain's nuclear effort scaled down, there appeared little hope of reducing defence expenditure. From the viewpoint of the services, the system was uneconomical because of the large number of men tied up in training, the short useful life of the National Serviceman, the difficulty of successfully training the two-year man in many of the specialized skills, and the wastage due to personnel movements. Moreover, it was believed to be a considerable disincentive to Regular recruiting, particularly for the army.[28]

In the navy and the air force opinion was strongly in favour of a return to all-Regular forces. The navy had never looked on National Service as anything more than a 'necessary evil' and by 1957, with Regular recruiting almost meeting the navy's

---

[25] 5 Jan. 1957.

[26] *Times*, 18 Jan. 1957.

[27] *Times*, 27 Jan. 1957.

[28] For a full discussion see William P. Snyder, *The Politics of British Defense Policy 1945–1962* (1965), pp. 237–42, and Army League, *The British Army in the Nuclear Age* by a study group of which Richard Goold-Adams was rapporteur (1959), pp. 52–3.

manpower requirements, the Board, as a matter of policy, was prepared to go short rather than to continue the system. The RAF was more heavily dependent upon National Servicemen, but recruiting had improved, and the Air Staff was anxious to reduce its swollen training establishment.

The army's position was more ambivalent. On the one hand, there was the attraction of a large army and the conviction, at least in some quarters, that an all-Regular army would be too small to handle the commitments which would come its way. On the other, there were strong arguments and an even stronger sentiment which favoured a return to all-Regular forces. One very senior officer went so far as to declare that National Service was 'having a crippling effect on the army'. In his view, forcefully expressed at the time, the army 'had become nothing more than a sausage machine, with a small Regular cadre turning out the sausages'. Another relevant consideration was that the army faced a financial problem of its own. The desire to make use of the very large stocks of ammunition and equipment built up during the war and during the Korean emergency, together with a broad acceptance of the proposition that there would be no world war within ten years of 1948, had led to a calculated postponement of any large-scale re-equipping of the army. By 1957, however, these stocks had either been used or were becoming out of date, and their replacement was a matter of some urgency. To embark on a major re-equipment programme, and at the same time to go on paying, clothing, feeding and housing a conscript army was clearly beyond the resources of the army's budget.[29] Perhaps more important than these rational objections to National Service was the deep-seated emotional commitment to an all-Regular army. The tradition of the British army had been built around all-Regular forces and ten years of peace-time conscription had apparently done little to erode it. Thus in 1957 conscription remained an alien system, and, in the words of one senior commander, most officers 'were prepared to pay a considerable price to get rid of it.'

Politically, conscription was unpopular, and most politicians expected electoral advantages to accrue to the party responsible for bringing it to an end. During 1954 the need for conscription

[29] See A. Gwynne Jones, in M. Howard, ed., *The Theory and Practice of War*, p. 320, and *The British Army in the Nuclear Age*, p. 46.

was questioned by many Labour parliamentarians and by some Conservatives, and in the 1955 election campaign the Labour party proposed a reduction in the period of service. The government also was unhappy about the policy, but it refused to give any commitment either to reduce the period of service or to bring the system to an end.[30] A few months later a more serious challenge to National Service came from within the cabinet. In the late summer of 1955 Selwyn Lloyd proposed a reduction in the period of service, in the first instance to eighteen months, to be followed later by a reduction to twelve months. Reportedly, Lloyd argued the case strongly and he had the ear of the Prime Minister. After various preliminary studies a full debate took place during which the Secretary of State for War and the CIGS successfully argued the case for the retention of two years' National Service, on the grounds of efficient use of manpower. After the Suez operation, opposition to conscription mounted rapidly and by early 1957 only a sprinkling of voices could be heard defending the system. George Brown spoke not only for the Labour party but for a large section of the informed public when he declared in February:

It is National Service that makes the Army so costly, so inflexible and so immobile. We, on this side, believe that until a decision is taken on policy grounds to get rid of National Service, many of the other decisions that will raise the efficiency and purpose of our Services will never be taken.[31]

Each of these factors contributed to make the climate by no means favourable to an emphasis on conventional forces when the new government took office in mid-January. Policy-making now passed largely into the hands of two men who both had some definite ideas of their own on military policy. Harold Macmillan, the new Prime Minister, had previously served as Minister of Defence and later as Chancellor of the Exchequer and was known to favour defence economies.[32]

[30] Eden, *Full Circle*, p. 373.
[31] 564 HC Deb., 13 Feb. 1957, col. 1299.
[32] In 1956 he had dramatized the defence burden by claiming that Britain, as compared with her European allies, was carrying 'a second rifle'. If Britain cut defence spending to a comparable percentage of the GNP there would be a saving of £700m. He went on to speculate about the significance for the economy of such a saving, though admitting it was a pipe-dream. Emrys Hughes, *Macmillan: Portrait of a Politician* (London, Allen & Unwin, 1962), pp. 112–14.

He was a strong supporter of the nuclear deterrent, and his experience in the First World War almost instinctively inclined him against a large standing army.[33] Shortly before taking office as Prime Minister he had sharply disagreed with Antony Head, who was then Defence Minister, over the adequacy of an army of 165,000 men, and neither a cabinet meeting nor a conference between the two ministers had resolved the difference.[34] For his Defence Minister, Macmillan chose Duncan Sandys, a forceful personality and a man unlikely to be intimidated by senior officers or unduly perturbed by conflicting advice.[35] Sandys had a passionate interest in rockets,[36] he believed strongly in the future of nuclear weapons, and he was thought to favour economies on a scale which his predecessor considered either impossible or unjustified.[37]

It remained to invest Sandys with the wider authority to intervene in service matters which was essential if he were to be able to carry through the major reshaping of the armed forces that the Prime Minister considered necessary. Fifteen months earlier the first steps had been taken to strengthen the position of the Minister of Defence. Aware that in the past some holders of that office had found themselves acting as co-ordinators rather than as directors of policy, Eden expanded the role of the Minister to include a responsibility for ensuring that the composition and balance of the forces within the three services conformed to the overall strategic policy. For the first time the Minister was empowered to consider the content of service programmes as well as their cost. At the same time Eden appointed a permanent chairman of the Chiefs of Staff Committee.[38] Macmillan's views on these changes are unknown, but he had long been critical of the machinery for central control of defence, and apparently considered the new grant

[33] Verrier, *An Army for the Sixties*, p. 123.

[34] L. W. Martin, 'The Market for Strategic Ideas in Britain: the "Sandys Era" ', *Amer. polit. Sci. R.*, 56/1 (Mar. 1962), pp. 28–9.

[35] Sandys became the tenth holder of the Defence portfolio in eleven years, and the fifth in under two and a half years.

[36] In 1940 and 1941 he had commanded an experimental rocket regiment; from 1943 to 1945 he had been chairman of a war cabinet committee for defence against German 'V' weapons; in the early fifties, when Minister of Supply, he had been an enthusiastic supporter of Blue Streak.

[37] See e.g. *Economist*, 26 Jan. 1957.

[38] These changes were announced in Oct. 1955. See Eden, *Full Circle*, pp. 374–5.

of powers insufficient.[39] Sandys was of the same opinion. Within days of taking office he encountered strong service opposition to his broader interpretation of ministerial power. Convinced that the Chiefs of Staff Committee had become almost a supra-national body, Sandys approached the Prime Minister for enlarged authority. On 24 January Macmillan announced that with a view to securing 'a substantial reduction in expenditure and in manpower', he had authorized the Minister to give decisions 'on all matters of policy affecting the size, shape, organisation and disposition of the Armed Forces, their equipment and supply (including defence research and development) and their pay and conditions of service.'[40] At the same time the Chairman of the Chiefs of Staff Committee was appointed Chief of Staff to the Minister.[41]

The Sandys Doctrine

After two months of fierce debate within the defence establishment, which culminated in a series of acrimonious meetings between the Minister and the Chiefs of Staff, the service finally acquiesced in the main features of Sandys' defence plan.[42] During February and March the gist of the new Minister's proposals was leaked to the press, so that when the White Paper was published in April its contents caused little surprise. For the next five years Britain was to upgrade the priority accorded to the nuclear deterrent. Thermo-nuclear weapons would be added to the existing atomic armoury, and the V-bombers would be supplemented by ballistic rockets as they became available. Conventional forces were to be smaller but, it was claimed, better equipped and more mobile. Conscription was to be ended by 1962 and service manpower would be reduced from 690,000 to 375,000 by that year. Greater mobility, and, it was implied, the use of tactical nuclear

---

[39] See his *Riding the Storm 1956–1959* (1971), pp. 244–5.
[40] 563 HC Deb., 24 Jan. 1957, col. 396.
[41] Ibid.
[42] Evidently Sandys at first attempted to create something like a single Service of the Crown, but was restrained by his cabinet colleagues for reasons of political expediency. Macmillan, in particular, was reluctant to embark on a major re-organization. See F. A. Johnson, 'Politico-Military Organisation in the United Kingdom: Some Recent Developments', *Journal of [Politics*, 27/2 (May 1965), p. 344.

weapons would compensate for the reductions in army manpower. For the coming year defence expenditure was to amount to about £1,420 million, which represented a saving of £180 million on the programme as planned in 1956.[43]

The service reaction to the White Paper was adverse. However, service grievances perhaps turned more on the personality of the Minister and on his method of making decisions, than on the doctrinal content of his policy. A strong case can be argued that both the air force and the navy obtained the sort of forces that they wanted, and in terms of allocations each fared as well as could have been expected given the pressures for economy. The rupture between Sandys and the army was more fundamental, but the fact remains that even in that service there was an undercurrent of support for the major plank in Sandys' platform—the abolition of National Service. What earned Sandys the enmity of the services was his habit of disregarding professional advice,[44] his penchant for asking fundamental questions, and his tendency, as one senior officer put it, 'to treat the Chiefs of Staff like schoolboys'.

The White Paper was generally welcomed by the press as a sensible and coherent approach to Britain's defence problems, but from the first doubts were expressed about the government's plan for smaller conventional forces.[45] It was these forces which would have to carry the burden of defence in the Middle East and the Far East, and it was difficult to see how the increased mobility and the new equipment which were to offset the reductions in manpower could be obtained within the confines of a reduced defence budget and an even more reduced non-nuclear expenditure. That the government's scheme for overseas defence had a certain plausibility could hardly conceal the fact that it was based on a number of highly questionable assumptions and on a capability which was not yet in existence or indeed even on the immediate horizon.

[43] MoD, *Defence: Outline of Future Policy*, Cmnd 124 (1957). The White Paper made much of the need to maintain Britain's economic strength. Para. 7 noted that over the past five years defence had on average absorbed 10 per cent of the gross national product, and it emphasized the burden that this entailed. However, as was later observed, the White Paper obscured the situation in 1957 by taking the average of the five-year period 1952–1957, thereby concealing the fact that the burden of defence expenditure had been declining since 1953. A. C. L. Day, 'The Economics of Defence', *Political Quarterly*, 31/1 (Jan.–Mar. 1960), pp. 57–8.

[44] See Martin, *Amer. polit. Sci. R.*, 56/1 (Mar. 1962), p. 28.

[45] See e.g. *Manchester Guardian*, 5 Apr. 1957, and *Economist*, 6 Apr. 1957.

In view of the weaknesses shown up during the Suez operation, it was no surprise that in so far as the White Paper concerned itself with conventional forces it took mobility as its catchword. However, the government's proposals here amounted to nothing more than a restatement of earlier ideas, now outlined as part of a new and positive approach to Britain's defence problems. Overseas garrisons were to be reduced, a central reserve was to be maintained in Britain, and reinforcements were to be despatched from Britain at short notice when required. In effect, this was what the government had been saying since 1954. What mattered was the seriousness with which the government set about tackling the air transport problem, and in 1957 there was no indication that the inadequacy of Transport Command weighed any more heavily upon it than in earlier years. The government's complacency was underlined by the statement in paragraph 35 of the White Paper that a substantial fleet of transport aircraft was being built up in RAF Transport Command. Yet at the time, Transport Command's fleet consisted of 8 Comets (2 more were to be delivered shortly), 2 squadrons of Beverleys with a third in the process of formation, the old and slow Hastings and Valettas, and a handful of smaller types, such as Twin Pioneers. The Secretary of State for Air told the House that more Britannias would be ordered,[46] but the Air Estimates contained no provision for any further orders for new aircraft and the accompanying *Memorandum* referred simply to the formation of a Comet 2 squadron and an order for 13 Britannias, which in fact had been placed in 1956.[47]

When the Britannia came into service it would represent a valuable increment to Transport Command's capacity as it was capable of carrying 113 troops or a 37,000-lb. payload over 4,268 miles at 360 m.p.h. It was unsuitable, however, for lifting heavy freight and in this category Transport Command was particularly weak. The Beverley could carry most military transports up to 10-ton size (thus heavy engineering plant and tanks were excluded), but it was intended for movement within overseas theatres, not for medium- and long-range freighting. There was no British counterpart to the American

---

[46] 569 HC Deb., 9 May 1957, col. 1190.
[47] AM, *Memorandum by Secretary of State for Air to Accompany Air Estimates 1957–58*, Cmnd 149 (1957), paras 42–3.

Douglas C133 Cargomaster or the Lockheed C130 Hercules for transporting military vehicles, guns, and bulky cargoes over long distances. This was a serious gap which resulted in the Beverley often being misemployed in the strategic and medium-range role.[48]

One factor which contributed to the government's neglect of airlift capability was the absence of any strong pressure in this direction from the Air Staff. Although during 1956 there were signs that the weakness of Transport Command was causing some disquiet within the RAF, air transport was still a low priority in the eyes of the Air Staff.[49] The RAF's role was seen primarily in terms of the nuclear deterrent and the central balance, and in the struggle for resources in early 1957 it seems that the Air Staff emphasized this function at the expense of air support and transport, both because this was where it saw its *raison d'être* and because it believed that this course would secure for it the largest share of the defence budget. This situation led to some public discussion of the possibility of divorcing the provision of air transport from the problem of providing a fighting air force. One solution advocated was the establishment of an army air transport corps.[50] A speech by George Brown in the defence debate in February indicated that some parliamentarians were thinking along much the same lines.[51]

If the Air Staff continued to view the limited-war role—and by implication Britain's responsibilities in the Middle East and the Far East—as a secondary concern, the Board of Admiralty now turned to limited war as the answer to the navy's search for a strategic concept upon which to build its future. A start had in fact been made in 1956 to steer the navy away from general-war doctrines, and to emphasize the fleet's capability for handling peacetime emergencies and limited hostilities. However, at that stage the navy had not finally made its escape from the broken-backed concept, and the limited-war role sat uneasily alongside global-war theories. The turning point came in the six months following the assault on Port Said.

[48] J. W. R. Taylor, 'Military Air Transport in a Nuclear Age', *Air Power*, 4/3 (Apr. 1957), p. 183, and Kendall, *Air Power*, 7/3 (spring 1960), p. 182.
[49] See Lt Col A. Green's observations in 'Military Air Transport—Everybody's Darling: Nobody's Baby', *Air Power*, 4/2 (Jan. 1957), pp. 111–12.
[50] Ibid. pp. 114–15.
[51] 564 HC Deb., 13 Feb. 1957, col. 1298.

Suez provided the evidence, and Sandys the incentive, for a deliberate upgrading of the fleet's limited-war role to a position of precedence over its general-war responsibilities.

The Board of Admiralty viewed Sandys' appointment with considerable misgiving.[52] During his period as Minister of Supply, Sandys and the Board had seldom seen eye to eye. Shortly before his appointment as Minister of Defence, Sandys had privately indicated that the navy would have to bear a large share of the impending cuts and that the aircraft carrier would be the first candidate for retrenchment. Upon taking office, he immediately informed the Board of Admiralty that he considered carriers excessively expensive, and that he intended to phase them out unless he could be convinced of their value. In part, Sandys' challenge stemmed from his strong opposition to the broken-backed concept. In his view, the Admiralty's case for the carrier was tied to broken-backed war and it was high time that the navy did some rethinking. Initially the Board viewed Sandys' attitude with dismay, but later many naval men conceded that he had prodded the navy into formulating a viable role.

There was no question of the navy's reconsidering its commitment to carriers. For centuries the Royal Navy had been a capital-ship navy and since the demise of the battleship, the aircraft carrier had been the centrepiece of the fleet and the symbol of its strength. It remained, however, for the Board of Admiralty to determine which functions it would stress in its efforts to justify the retention of the carrier. After much discussion the Board chose to depreciate the carrier's attack capability in a nuclear war, and to stress its role in limited war and in combating the submarine menace. Of these two functions most emphasis was placed on limited war.

Here the Admiralty thought itself to be on firm ground and it proceeded to build a strong case. The part played by the four light fleet carriers in the Korean war was now put to good effect. The speed with which aircraft of the Fleet Air Arm went into action, their continuing contribution to the land battle — over 20,000 operational sorties were flown — and the mobility and detachment of their bases were all used to illustrate the value of carriers in limited conflicts in under-developed

---

[52] Crowe, pp. 180–1. Here I follow Crowe's account of the discussions between Sandys and the Board of Admiralty but also draw on material of my own.

countries. The Suez operation provided further grist for the Admiralty's mill. With the airfields in Jordan and Libya unusable, and Cyprus too distant to allow fighters and tactical support aircraft more than ten to fifteen minutes over the target areas, the assault was heavily dependent upon carrier-borne aircraft. The three British carriers employed in the operation carried a total of about 150 aircraft and in seven days of action flew some 1,600 sorties.[53] This was a telling point which the Admiralty used to good advantage. The next step was to point out that with the prospect of a further thinning out of the base chain over the next few years, Britain's dependence on carrier-borne aircraft would be greatly increased. The Board of Admiralty then went on to argue that its plan for carrier task forces accorded neatly with the government's scheme for the army. A smaller army and reduced overseas garrisons led naturally to the conclusion that the navy must assume a larger share of Britain's overseas defence responsibilities.

Parallel with this turn from general to limited war as the rationale for the navy's existence, the Admiralty began a geographical reorientation: a shift in focus from NATO and Europe to the defence of British commitments and interests in the Middle East and the Far East. During the early weeks of 1957 the navy emerged as the leading advocate of Britain's role east of Suez. To men bred in the traditions of the Royal Navy, the east of Suez role offered the promise of a future in keeping with the past, and it had an appeal altogether outweighing the comforts of a narrower role as part of a joint Western naval force which would be restricted to the waters of the Atlantic and the Mediterranean. The Board of Admiralty therefore took up the cudgels with some enthusiasm and argued that both moral obligations and commercial interest tied Britain to the area.[54] To strengthen its case it alerted those officials and policy-makers, both at home and abroad, who could be expected to concur in the need for strong naval forces east of Suez, to the government's plan to reduce the navy. According to one member of the Board, no opportunity

---

[53] Two other carriers—HMS *Theseus* and HMS *Ocean*—served as makeshift helicopter carriers and flew a further 400 sorties. Paul Garbutt, *Naval Challenge 1945–1961* (1961), p. 52.
[54] Crowe, p. 188.

was lost to press the point home. It is difficult to assess the extent to which these efforts bore immediate fruit. On Snyder's account, two senior civil servants, both in key positions in the Ministry of Defence, took up the navy's cause.[55] It is probable, however, that it was some months before the pressures generated by the Admiralty's initiatives reached the policy-making arena. Partly in response to the Admiralty's representations, both the Foreign Office and the Colonial Office took a new look at Britain's overseas responsibilities and came down in favour of stronger naval forces, but it was not until well after the publication of the 1957 White Paper that the Foreign Secretary, Selwyn Lloyd, and the Colonial Secretary, Alan Lennox-Boyd, took their arguments to the cabinet.[56] Again, although early in 1957 the Admiralty informed the Commonwealth governments east of Suez of Britain's naval weakness in the area, it was some time before Commonwealth pressure was brought to bear. During Sandys' tour of the Far East in the summer of 1957, however, he was reportedly advised by a number of his host governments of the vital role of the Royal Navy in the area.[57] At the Commonwealth Prime Ministers' Conference in August several of the delegates again expressed their dismay at the weakness of British naval and military units east of Suez.[58]

After some weeks of heated discussion and argument, the Admiralty finally won a reprieve for its carriers and a general acceptance of its plan for a leading role in meeting east of Suez defence responsibilities. Paragraphs 37 to 39 of the White Paper set out the new conception of the navy's role and they accurately reflected the views of the Admiralty. Briefly stated, the 1956 plan was now developed into a scheme for a small number of carrier groups, each consisting of one carrier, a cruiser, and a number of destroyers and frigates, which would sail as task forces in being and could be used to bring power rapidly to bear when trouble broke out. One carrier group would normally be stationed in the Indian Ocean, where its mobility and its ability to hover just beyond the horizon of any

---

[55] p. 167.
[56] 'Macmillan Faces Defence Split', *Observer*, 28 July 1957.
[57] Snyder, p. 168.
[58] Alastair Buchan, 'Weak Link in Defence Chain', Observer Foreign News Service, 8 Aug. 1957.

potential trouble centre would make it a particularly effective means of protecting Britain's interests. Although Sandys himself still had reservations about the aircraft carrier, his parliamentary colleagues warmed rapidly to its new role. Indeed, the speech of the Parliamentary and Financial Secretary to the Admiralty, Christopher Soames, developed into a positive eulogy of the carrier which delighted the naval members of the House, and became widely quoted by naval men outside.[59]

Despite the overall emphasis on air mobility, it was admitted that the navy's role as a transport service was still important. As far ahead as could be seen, Soames told the House, heavy reinforcements and logistic support would have to be by sea.[60] Very little was said about amphibious warfare. At this stage the Board of Admiralty had not established a viable method of conducting amphibious operations, and it had not yet accepted the requirement for a full range of amphibious vessels. The first steps had been taken but beyond that the Admiralty had not finalized its course of action, partly because of the preoccupation with the carrier question. Nevertheless, the Marines and certain sections in the navy were quietly pushing ahead with plans for re-equipment and expansion. The commando carrier concept was under way; the Suez operation was being examined for leads; and the American experience in this field was being carefully scanned with an eye to British needs.

In broad outline, then, by April 1957 the Admiralty had secured a measure of government approval for its new role and it was forging ahead with its own plans. Its general attitude to outside interference seemed little different from that of earlier years and emerged implicitly but clearly in the statement that 'action taken by the Board of Admiralty in recent times has led in the same direction as the Government's long-term plan for the Navy.'[61] A succinct reminder—if one were needed—that the Admiralty had its own views and plans, and that the government was expected to appropriate funds, not to determine strategic concepts.

Later in the year the various threads of naval thinking were

[59] See 568 HC Deb., 15 Apr. 1957, coll. 55–7.
[60] Ibid. col. 57.
[61] Admiralty, *Explanatory Statement on Navy Estimates 1957–58*, Cmnd 151 (1957), para. 7.

drawn together in a paper which became known as the 'Autumn Naval Rethink'. This paper contained a review of the roles of the navy and it established three things: first, the priority of the limited-war role; secondly, the fact that the aircraft carrier was essential for its fulfilment; and thirdly, the interlock between fixed-wing aircraft, commandos in special ships and helicopters, and the need for modern landing craft. In addition, it formally conferred on the Marines a commando role. Apparently, however, the amphibious operations envisaged by the Admiralty were still of more limited scope than those envisaged by Amphibious Warfare Headquarters, and the battle had still to be fought for Admiralty approval for the assault and logistic ships. The paper was accepted by the Chiefs of Staff and forwarded to the Minister. According to one report, Sandys was well pleased and considered the paper a major advance in Admiralty thinking.

The army had much less success in the struggle against the new Defence Minister. In contrast to the other two services, manpower not hardware was the army's prime concern and the end of conscription struck at the root of its strength. Notwithstanding the attraction of an all-Regular army, the Army Council was opposed to the ending of National Service if this meant a maximum strength of only 165,000 by the end of 1962. For all Sandys' reasoning and his juggling with figures, the Council firmly believed that a manpower strength of 165,000 was too small to enable the army to meet its overseas commitments. At best, army leaders were dubious about the government's plan to offset these reductions by the introduction of tactical nuclear weapons, and they were far from confident that the proposals to increase airlift capability would substantially change the situation. The CIGS, in particular, viewed Sandys' policy as something approaching a disaster and a heated dispute developed between him and the Minister. Despite strong resistance, however, the army was forced to concede defeat in the face of Sandys' determination. The ending of conscription, a smaller army, and increased reliance on nuclear weapons were the very basis of Sandys' doctrine, and, supported strongly by Macmillan, Sandys showed little hesitation in overriding the army's opposition. Apparently the CIGS discussed the possibility of resigning but the other Chiefs of Staff were not prepared to join him, and eventually he was dissuaded by the realization that such a gesture would be nothing more than an exercise in futility.[62]

The army's case hinged on a manpower assessment made in 1956. Early in that year Antony Head and Field Marshal Sir John Harding, realizing that the system of two-year National Service could not continue indefinitely, set up a War Office committee, under the chairmanship of General Sir Richard Hull, to examine the long-term manpower requirements of an all-Regular army. The committee's terms of reference were extremely wide and it was left to the committee to determine the likely extent of Britain's commitments. Working on the assumption that there would be a full civilianization of the tail and a generous supply of transport aircraft, and allowing for certain reductions in Middle Eastern commitments but not in those east of Suez, the committee concluded that about 200,000 all ranks, all Regular, was the minimum requirement.[63] This figure referred only to United Kingdom male manpower and there were some 20,000 Gurkhas and locally enlisted personnel (mainly Malays and Hong Kong Chinese), which were assumed to remain at about their existing strength. Nor did it include the German transport units in BAOR.

As it was apparent that the army was 'within narrow reach of the abolition of National Service', Head directed the War Office to reconsider its figures. After further studies and considerable ministerial pressure, the army was reconciled to a minimum strength of about 185,000. It was made clear, however, that this figure allowed no margin for safety or comfort. This left a gap of 20,000 between the absolute minimum figure acceptable to the army and the actuarial estimate of the highest possible voluntary recruitment.[64] The Suez crisis postponed further consideration but in the aftermath cabinet pressure increased to reduce the army to the level obtainable by voluntary recruiting. Head, who was now Minister of Defence, drafted a proposal to recruit as many Regulars as possible, while at the same time retaining National Service on the statute book. The idea was to maintain army numbers by selective National Service. By this time, however,

[62] Martin, *Amer. polit. Sci. R.*, 56/1 (Mar. 1962), p. 28.
[63] See Head's speech, 592 HC Deb., 28 July 1958, coll. 987–96.
[64] According to one account, the actuarial estimate of 165,000 was the mean between two widely different estimates and it was accepted simply as a convenient basis for discussion.

several cabinet ministers were committed to ending National
Service and the Treasury was strongly resisting certain proposals relating to equipment and transport aircraft. A sharp
dispute developed between Head and Macmillan, then
Chancellor of the Exchequer, and a cabinet meeting called to
resolve the issue ended without a decision, as Eden announced
his intention to resign. The issue was only settled by Head's
replacement by Sandys, who, in the face of strong opposition
from the Chiefs of Staff Committee, but firmly supported by
Macmillan, took the direct course and pushed the 1957 measures through.

No estimate was forthcoming from the government of the
number of troops which the all-Regular army would be able
to deploy in support of its overseas commitments. Certainly
the White Paper foreshadowed savings in other areas. BAOR
was to be reduced by about 13,000 men, one battalion would
be returning from Korea, and there would be small savings
because of the government's policy of reducing overseas
garrisons. On Head's later calculation, however, after allowing
for the manpower requirements of BAOR, the home base and
training, and losses in the 'pipeline', Britain would be very
lucky to have 25,000 troops available for overseas commitments. Given her existing commitments, he concluded, this
made no sense at all.[65] In the weeks following the publication
of the White Paper, it was too early for other experts to take
the army to pieces with this sort of arithmetic, but there was
general agreement that an army of 165,000 would be hard
pressed to handle Britain's overseas defence responsibilities.
As was argued by many of the government's critics, manpower
was still the main requirement for meeting these commitments.
Sir John Slessor put the point in colourful terms:

For these sorts of operations the organization of armies should be
more akin to that of the old Punjab Frontier Force, or the Frontier
Irregular Corps who went cheerfully to war on foot, with a rifle,
a couple of bandoliers, a bag of raisins, a *chupatti* or two and a
water-bottle. In other words here again the requirement above
everything else is for very mobile, very highly trained infantry.[66]

In the debate in the House, the government's manpower

---

[65] 592 HC Deb., 28 July 1958, col. 991.
[66] 'British Defense Policy', *For. Aff.*, 35/4 (July 1957), pp. 559–60, quoted in his
The Great Deterrent (1957), p. 310.

proposals met strong opposition from R. H. S. Crossman, John Strachey, and George Wigg. In Crossman's view, the government's proposals had important foreign policy implications which most parliamentarians had missed:

The provisions contained in this White Paper mean that, when they are carried out, this country will be incapable of waging any large-scale colonial war again ... once we accept the logic of this White Paper we cease to be an imperial Power.[67]

If this was a reasonable and in many ways perceptive interpretation of the 1957 White Paper, it was not one which was shared by the government. Although at no time did Sandys elaborate his scheme for overseas defence with the clarity with which he set out his home defence and nuclear measures, there is still ample evidence to show that the government clung to the traditional view of Britain as a dominant power in the Middle East and the Far East, and that it intended to adhere to its military responsibilities in these areas.

The White Paper referred to Britain's obligations to defend Aden, the Persian Gulf territories and her colonies and protectorates in South-east Asia, and to her agreement to assist in the external defence of Malaya after independence. In addition, it emphasized Britain's commitments as a member of CENTO, SEATO, and ANZAM to help preserve stability in the Middle East, and the Far East.[68] In Parliament, government spokesmen denied that the Defence Statement had in any way narrowed the scope of Britain's commitments. Sandys prefaced his speech in the Commons with the statement 'We are not contracting out of our obligations.'[69] In the House of Lords the Earl of Selkirk declared, 'We have not the slightest intention of retracting from our obligations. All that we have done is to change the nature of our contribution.'[70]

During his tour of the Far East in August, Sandys reiterated the government's wider view of its defence responsibilities. Both in Canberra and in Wellington, he made it clear that Britain regarded South-east Asia as a vital theatre in the defensive system of the free world, and that she would continue to main-

---

[67] 568 HC Deb., 16 Apr. 1957, coll. 1983–4.
[68] MoD, *Defence: Outline of Future Policy*, Cmnd 124 (1957), paras 25–8.
[69] 568 HC Deb., 16 Apr. 1957, col. 1769.
[70] 203 HL Deb., 9 May 1957, col. 550.

tain large land, sea, and air forces in the area.[71] A few months later the annual conference of the Commissioner-General for South-east Asia adopted the same position. Macmillan, who attended the final session, notes in his memoirs 'none of us at that Conference had any doubt of the importance of maintaining the authority and prestige of the United Kingdom by a substantial military presence.'[72]

In an attempt to reconcile the government's manpower reductions with its failure to cut back Britain's non-European defence commitments, Alun Gwynne Jones has argued that the 'implicit basis of the 1957 White Paper was that British commitments overseas would gradually fade away...' According to Gwynne Jones, this belief was 'based upon a mistaken reading of the strategic effects of constitutional advance in the colonies', and it 'remained an article of official faith for about five years.'[73] Although this explanation neatly resolves the paradox of the government's position, later oral evidence establishes that it had no foundation in fact. One centrally placed figure was categorical that the 1957 manpower reductions were in no way prompted by any assumption about future reductions in Britain's overseas commitments. Others concerned with policy at the time were of the same opinion and discounted the argument as a rationalization after the event. One official recalled that well after the formulation of the Sandys doctrine the Gwynne Jones view was sometimes expressed in policy-making circles, though it never approached an article of official faith and it was always strongly opposed by the Chiefs of Staff. All that can perhaps be said is that in early 1957 the government did not foresee Britain's Indian Ocean commitments becoming increasingly burdensome.

What in fact enabled the government to plan on meeting its overseas commitments with smaller all-Regular forces was certain assumptions about capability not commitments. Underlying the White Paper, and indeed the whole of the government's thinking about conventional forces, was the belief that recent scientific advances in military technology had so changed the basis of military planning that it was now

---

[71] Times, 21 and 29 Aug. 1957, and 'UK–Australian and UK–NZ Defence Discussions', in COI, The South-East Asia Treaty Organisation (1959), p. 10. (Pamphlet no. R. 4122.)

[72] Riding the Storm 1956–1959, p. 397.

[73] See M. Howard, ed., The Theory and Practice of War, p. 325.

possible to escape from the traditional dependence upon a
large army. In particular, it was assumed that the introduction
of tactical nuclear weapons and the expansion of airlift capability would enable a much smaller army to discharge the same
functions, as had earlier required some 400,000 men and a
string of garrisons from Gibraltar to Hong Kong. It was on
the basis of these two assumptions—one mistaken and the
other unduly optimistic—that the government planned to
retain its overseas commitments, if not for ever, at least for the
foreseeable future, and at ever decreasing cost.

Anthony Verrier has argued that the government's choice
of tactical nuclear weapons over men was in line with a rooted
preference, which British governments had shown over many
years, to settle for the dominant weapon, with scant regard
for the bread and butter requirements of the three services.[74]
In the present case, and this again accorded with past practice,
the government compounded its folly by staking Britain's
east of Suez policy on a dominant weapon which was neither
available nor proven. Paying little heed to the army's doubts,
Sandys and Macmillan launched themselves beyond the
detail of infantrymen and native trackers to conclude that
tactical nuclear weapons would eventually reduce the requirement for men on the ground. Although at no time was this
assumption set out explicitly in terms of tactical doctrine,
policy-making circles in Whitehall were left in no doubt that
this thinking lay behind the Sandys scheme. The basis of the
government's reasoning came out clearly in the discussion of
National Service in the 1957 debate. The Minister of Labour
and National Service told the House: 'if we refuse to rely on
the deterrent, we cannot at the same time urge the abolition
of National Service.'[75] Macmillan saw the issue in the same
terms: 'the end of conscription must depend upon the acceptance of nuclear weapons.'[76]

Hopes for manpower savings in the European theatre were
pinned on the nuclear missile Blue Water, then under development. In addition it was thought that tactical nuclear weapons
would have a direct relevance outside Europe, but how and

[74] See Verrier, *An Army for the Sixties*, ch. 4, 'Dissenting Views and Dominant
Weapons'.
[75] 568 HC Deb., 17 Apr. 1957, col. 1958.
[76] Ibid. col. 2040.

to what extent was far from clear. Lord Mancroft, Parliamentary Secretary to the Ministry of Defence, contented himself with observing that Britain contributed to the security of its SEATO and Baghdad partners 'by the very fact of our possession of nuclear deterrent forces, which could intervene with great effect in those areas'.[77] The White Paper referred to bomber squadrons based in Cyprus and capable of delivering nuclear weapons, which would be made available for Baghdad purposes in the event of a Middle Eastern emergency.[78]

During the discussion of the 1957 White Paper there was no mention of nuclear weapons for South-east Asia, but the government's policy assumed their use in this theatre also. The first public intimation that this was the case came during Sandys' visit to Australia in August. Speaking to a press conference in Canberra, Sandys announced that nuclear weapons would be available for the defence of the SEATO area. He went on to say that Canberra bombers equipped to carry atomic weapons would be going to Malaya, though he declined to reveal where the atomic weapons would be stored. 'When they are brought here, to the SEATO area,' he said, 'I don't think anything will be said about it.'[79] This brought a sharp protest from Tunku Abdul Rahman and the news that Malaya would not allow any atomic weapons to be stored on Malayan soil. Forced to choose his words with more care, Sandys explained that no decision had yet been made on what atomic weapons would be made available to British forces in the Far East, or where such weapons would be stored.[80]

The second factor which appears to have influenced the government's thinking was an unwarranted optimism over the possibilities of the airlifted strategic reserve. During 1957 both the government and many of its professional advisers seem to have accepted the scheme as a solution to the defence problems east of Suez without any full appreciation of its inherent limitations.[81] The American experience in this area offered useful leads but on the evidence available little cross-

---

[77] 203 HL Deb., 8 May 1957, col. 429.
[78] para. 27.
[79] *Times*, 21 Aug. 1957.
[80] *Times*, 24 Aug. 1957, and *Manchester Guardian*, 24 Aug. 1957. See further the *Manchester Guardian's* leader 'Atom Bombs for Asia?', 26 Aug. 1957.
[81] See further DeWitt C. Armstrong, 'The Changing Strategy of British Bases', p. 230.

fertilization took place. Certainly government statements were of a different tone from Admiral Radford's admission that

We cannot airlift a division with full equipment from one part of the world to another, and there is no prospect that we can do so in the immediate future. I think the American people have been misled in some of the statements that have been made publicly.[82]

During 1958 and 1959 the problems associated with the scheme —the number of aircraft required, the over-flying difficulties, the necessity to stockpile heavy equipment at various focal points, and the need for intermediate refuelling points—made more impact and much of the earlier enthusiasm gradually subsided.

Developments East of Suez

Before the Suez operation the question of over-flying rights never seriously troubled British strategists. At the end of the Second World War Britain still retained the 'all red' air route to the Far East, and most of the Mediterranean and Africa and the whole of the Indian Ocean area were open to British military aircraft. The first limitations to free air movement in the region came with the independence of Burma, India, Pakistan, and Ceylon. However, over-flying and staging rights were negotiated with the new governments, and these, together with the bases and staging posts that remained in British hands, enabled the RAF to move air units into and within the region with relative ease. Even the loss of the Middle East base did not seriously disrupt the flow of military aircraft as alternative routes were devised without undue difficulty.

The Suez crisis fundamentally changed this picture. During the operation Britain was severely hampered by the restrictions imposed on staging facilities and over-flying rights by Libya and Jordan, and to a less extent by Ceylon and India. Moreover, the eruption of nationalist feeling which followed the operation raised grave doubts about the reliability of any air route which passed over the Middle Eastern countries. The Suez Canal Zone was out, the Sudan and Iraq were questionable areas, and there was even doubt about Iran.[83] What was clear was

[82] Quoted by George Wigg, 569 HC Deb., 9 May 1957, col. 1229.
[83] See DeWitt C. Armstrong, 'The Changing Strategy of British Bases', pp. 234-6.

that the days when the Arab states were prepared to extend permission for general and unconditional over-flying were over. Not only were existing rights liable to be suspended in time of greatest need, but increasingly it was apparent that permission would have to be obtained for each specific occasion, a practice fraught with uncertainties for long-term planning and possibly involving serious delays in times of emergency.

With the effective closure of the Middle Eastern passage, British strategists now turned their attention to two alternative routes which could preserve the air link between the Mediterranean and the Indian Ocean. To the north there was the Turkish-Persian corridor and to the south the route over Libya and the Sudan. However, each of these routes was politically vulnerable and posed awkward logistic and technical problems. In the case of the northern route, there were doubts about how long Iran would continue to permit over-flying, particularly in view of conflicting claims in the Persian Gulf. In addition, there were practical difficulties because of the high mountain ranges, poor air traffic control, and the absence of reliable meteorological services. A further cause of concern was the close proximity of the northern route to the Soviet Union.[84] The alternative route across Africa was if anything less secure, being dependent upon the favour of the ageing King of Libya and upon the maintenance of good relations with the military rulers of the Sudan. If either or both of these countries banned British over-flying, the RAF would be forced further southward, to operate from poor runways and over long distances; and with the movement of the African states towards independence even this route seemed likely to have only a limited future.[85]

Although the full dimensions of the problem were not publicly acknowledged and perhaps not altogether seen in 1957, the emergence of the Arab barrier had certain immediate effects on British strategic planning east of Suez. If over-flying restrictions could seriously delay the movement of troops from the United Kingdom to operational areas east of Suez, it was at once apparent that the concept of a central reserve based in the United Kingdom would need substantial modification. The obvious solution was to station elements of the strategic

[84] Ibid. p. 241, and Neville Brown, *Strategic Mobility*, pp. 161–2.
[85] See further N. Brown, *Strategic Mobility*, p. 162.

reserve at points east of the air barrier. Similarly, the increasing precariousness of the air and sea links between British forces east and west of the Arab states cast considerable doubt on the ability of a command structure located in the Mediterranean to control forces operating in East Africa and in the Arabian peninsula.

It is perhaps unfair to suggest that the over-flying restrictions were not entirely unwelcome in some quarters, but there was at least the feeling that it is an ill wind that blows no good. Ever since the abandonment in late 1950 of the McKinnon Road project in Kenya there had been those, both in the army and outside, who had argued for a British base in East Africa. Their motives were mixed. For some it was really a matter of seeking to underpin white settlement in Africa, but for most it was purely a strategic concern, a desire to fill the latest and largest gap in the British defence circuit. The Middle East base had been evacuated, the Soviet threat had advanced to the Red Sea, and Soviet penetration of Africa could not be ruled out. How was the threat to be countered unless Britain established a sure footing in Africa? A deeper investigation of motives is unsafe ground for the outside observer, and yet it is hard to escape the suspicion that the allure of East Africa was not entirely a by-product of the Soviet threat in the Middle East but sprang from something more deeply rooted in the military mind. At its simplest level it was perhaps part of the soldier's conception of the broader order of things—at once a home for the military and a secure enclave from which the defence of the area could be shaped and fashioned in accordance with the traditions of an imperial past. In any event, the emergence of the air barrier gave new life to those who saw a need for a British base in East Africa and in the first half of 1957 the cause was argued with fresh vigour. In an interesting leader in March, *The Times* considered the various arguments, which by then had broadened to include acclimatization opportunities and naval facilities, and concluded that there was undoubtedly a need for some sort of half-way house in the area, although it was doubtful whether a full-scale garrison in Kenya was the answer.[86] After further argument and considerable newspaper speculation, Sandys set out on a tour of Aden, Kenya, and Libya to investigate the position for himself. From a statement

[86] 'Half-Way House', 13 Mar. 1957.

made in London on his return, it was inferred that the project for a base in Kenya would be pushed forward.[87]

Five months later Sandys announced that an element of the strategic reserve would be stationed in Kenya and would be available as reinforcements either for the Arabian Peninsula or the Far East. Dismissing speculation that something like a great new Suez base was to be erected in Kenya, he went on to say that the government's plan would not involve the creation of any new headquarters or base installations in Kenya.[88] In response to further Labour questioning, the Secretary of State for War, John Hare, explained that Sandys was thinking in terms of one or possibly two battalions in Kenya, which would pick up heavy equipment and vehicles in Aden or Singapore in the event of an emergency in those areas.[89] Despite these ministerial assurances, however, many Labour members remained unconvinced, and there was a strong feeling that the elevation of Kenya to the status of a major British base was now only a matter of time.[90] After all, the military was back on its old cycle and stop-gap proposals of this nature had a way of developing a momentum of their own.

At the same time Sandys announced new command arrangements for East Africa and the Arabian Peninsula. In July he had informed the House that the government was reviewing the command structure in the Middle East.[91] It was now clear that British forces in Arabia and East Africa could be better controlled from London than from the Middle East base in Cyprus. It had therefore been decided to create a separate integrated command at Aden responsible directly to London. The commander would control all British land and air forces in the Arabian Peninsula and in British Somaliland, and the naval forces allotted to the Persian Gulf. Similarly the government had decided to separate the East African area from Middle East Command; the troops stationed there, including those of the strategic reserve, would be administered by the

[87] *Times*, 25 June 1957.
[88] 577 HC Deb., 7 Nov. 1957, col. 334.
[89] Ibid. col. 446.
[90] In Mar. 1958 e.g. John Strachey followed up the earlier arguments of Reginald Paget and John Stonehouse. See 583 HC Deb., 6 Mar. 1958, col. 1374, and 577 HC Deb., 7 Nov. 1957, coll. 334-5, 349, and 381.
[91] 573 HC Deb., 10 July 1957, coll. 49-50.

General Officer Commanding, East Africa, and their use would be controlled from London.[92]

The eruption of nationalist feeling after the Suez crisis was not confined to the Arab states. Further east also nationalist sensitivities were aroused, with disruptive effects on Britain's air and sea links with Malaya, Hong Kong, and the Antipodes. Although since 1954 there had been considerable doubt about the future of Britain's bases in Ceylon, the Suez crisis brought the issue to a head.[93] When the Anglo-French forces landed at Suez on 31 October the bases became unusable for any purpose connected with the operation, and the Prime Minister of Ceylon stated that he would reimpose this ban in any future crisis. This was followed in December by peremptory demands for an early handing over of the bases to Ceylon, after which there would be an extension of facilities for only a strictly limited period.[94] During early 1957 negotiations took place between the two governments and in April Bandaranaike announced that the bases would be transferred to Ceylon in mid-November.[95] On 15 October Britain formally transferred the Trincomalee naval base to Ceylon, and on 1 November the Katunayake air force station.

Towards the end of 1957 the impending loss of Katunayake and increasing doubts about the reliability of the air staging facilities in India (Dum Dum) and Pakistan (Karachi), forced the government to think seriously about air communications with the Far East. Once Katunayake was lost Britain might have to depend for air facilities entirely on the goodwill of India and Pakistan, and, in view of Britain's experience in 1956, that prospect could hardly be viewed with equanimity. Moreover, Britain's staging rights in India were very limited and those in Ceylon were purely complementary to the facilities in India. The Dum Dum Agreement had to be renegotiated annually and there were restrictions on the number of troops which could be staged there each year—restrictions which would make it impossible to fly large-scale reinforcements to the Far East via India. In Pakistan, the RAF staging post at Mauripur had been abandoned at the end of 1956 and, al-

[92] 577 HC Deb., 7 Nov. 1957, col. 334.
[93] For earlier discussion see pp. 85–6 above.
[94] For a full discussion of the developments in late 1956 see *Times*, 4 Jan. 1957, and *Daily Telegraph*, 8 June 1957.
[95] *Manchester Guardian*, 4 Apr. 1957.

though an agreement was reached for the RAF's use of Karachi, the journey from Pakistan to the Far East involved flying over India.[96] The west-about route via North America was briefly considered, but this solution was rejected because of the dollar expense, the distance involved, and the weather difficulties.[97]

The Air Staff therefore turned to the island of Gan in the Maldives group. The Maldive Islands lie 500 miles south-west of Ceylon and although an independent sultanate they had been under the protection of the British crown since 1887. New agreements were signed between the Sultan and the United Kingdom in 1948 and 1953 which broadly provided that external affairs would be conducted by, or in accordance with the advice of, the British government, and that the Sultan should extend to British forces any facilities necessary for the defence of the Maldives or of the Commonwealth. A staging post on Gan therefore seemed to raise few political difficulties and it was hardly expected that the wave of Asian nationalism would even ripple the surface of this Indian Ocean backwater. Strategically also Gan had much to recommend it. The Air Ministry had surveyed the island in 1952 and concluded that the construction of a modern airfield there was a practical proposition. Although the distance from the Maldives to Penang was considerably greater than that from Ceylon or Dum Dum (2,250 miles as against 1,780 and 1,850), it could be covered by existing aircraft such as the Hastings and the Comet. Moreover, with the expected entry into service of strategic transports such as the Britannia, a staging post on Gan would make practicable a shorter direct route to the Far East and Australasia across the Indian Ocean. The development by the RAAF of a major airfield on the Cocos Islands was relevant here and The Times pondered on whether the main future air route to Australia might be via Mombasa, the Maldives, and the Cocos Islands.[98] All these considerations led the British government to negotiate an agreement with the government of the Maldive Islands which provided for the re-establishment and operation of the airfield on Gan as a United Kingdom staging post.[99]

[96] Times, 4 Jan. 1957.
[97] 'Dollars, distance and depressions', as the RAF put it.
[98] 4 Jan. 1957.
[99] For the full text of the Commonwealth Relations Office statement see Times, 4 Jan. 1957.

The loss of the Trincomalee naval base came as a serious blow to the navy because it promised to make the Indian Ocean crossing more difficult administratively, more expensive, and less pleasant. The docking, storage, and supply facilities could not be replaced by the establishment of an island base; and although Gan later became useful as a port of call and as a place where an oiler could be stationed, these benefits were outweighed by the internal security requirements of the island group which tied up frigates and destroyers for months on end. On the other hand, the loss of a mid-way naval supply base was not of the same magnitude as the loss of Katunayake, as warships had the range, which aircraft then lacked, to move between the Middle East and the Far East without refuelling in the Indian Ocean.[100]

Soon after the announcement that Trincomalee was to be vacated the Board of Admiralty set about amending the Indian Ocean command structure. In February 1958 the Admiralty announced its intention to abolish the East Indies Command and on 7 September the flag of the hundreth C in C East Indies Station was struck. The responsibilities of the Command were divided between the C in C Far East Command, the C in C South Atlantic and South American Command, and the Commander of the new Arabian Seas and Persian Gulf Station. The latter station included the Red Sea, the Persian Gulf, the Arabian Sea, and a small part of the north-western area of the Indian Ocean. The status of the Senior Naval Officer, Persian Gulf, who was resident at Bahrain, was upgraded and he assumed the new title of Commodore, Arabian Seas and Persian Gulf, and became the Naval Deputy to the Commander, British Forces, Arabian Peninsula, resident at Aden.[101]

Disaffection with the Sandys Doctrine and the Lessons of Oman

In the months following the publication of the 1957 White Paper criticism of the government's nuclear priority mounted steadily. The restlessness of the services was evidenced by a substantial increase in the number of leaks to the press and there were several reported attempts by senior officers to influence opinion both in Parliament and outside, and pre-

---

[100] *Times*, 4 Jan. 1957.
[101] *Times*, 3 Sept. 1958.

sumably many more which received no publicity.[102] Not all these efforts were aimed at securing a greater emphasis on conventional forces, and in any case pressure was usually towards more specific ends, but the main thrust was in this direction. Of the three services, the navy played the most active part. The 'Fairlead' conference, held at Greenwich in May, represented the high-water mark of the navy's endeavours.[103] Slowly, too, the Admiralty's earlier efforts to alert the Far Eastern countries and the Foreign Office and Colonial Office to the dangers inherent in the government's naval policies, began to bear fruit.[104] By July a number of responsible newspapers, most notably *The Times* and the *Observer*, were pointing to the weakness of Britain's conventional forces and to the irrelevance of nuclear weapons and air power to Britain's commitments east of Suez. In a strongly worded leader at the end of the month, the *Observer* summed up the case against the existing policy by noting that

it does nothing to allay the anxiety of the Australians, or to increase the confidence of the future Malayan nation in British good faith, or to enable Mr. Nehru gradually to edge India towards closer co-operation in Far Eastern defence, if they are told that the loss of British frigates and battalions is to be compensated by posting nuclear bombers east of Suez. The two kinds of forces cannot be equated.[105]

According to a report in the same newspaper, this line of thinking was also making considerable impact on a number of Conservative ministers, and Macmillan was faced with a split within the cabinet. A majority in the cabinet now believed that Sandys had put too much money and faith into the deterrent, and these ministers were convinced that if the present policy was continued Britain's conventional forces would be unable to sustain their world commitments. In particular, the *Observer* named Selwyn Lloyd, Sir David Eccles, and Alan

[102] See further Martin, *Amer. polit. Sci. R.*, 56/1 (Mar. 1962), pp. 31–2. The *Observer's* report, 7 Apr. 1957, set the pattern for the next few months.
[103] 'Fairlead', a one-day conference designed to show the need for a strong navy, was attended by businessmen, MPs, and journalists. See further Verrier, *An Army for the Sixties*, pp. 119–20; Crowe, p. 191, and Snyder, pp. 124–5.
[104] See pp. 112–13 below.
[105] 28 July 1957.

Lennox-Boyd as having voiced strong disagreement with the existing policy.[106]

While this reconsideration of defence priorities was taking place in the cabinet, British forces were conducting a small policing operation in central Oman which graphically illustrated some of the points under discussion. Militarily the campaign was not much more than a skirmish, but it had important lessons for policy-makers about the demands of Britain's overseas commitments and the way in which they had to be supported. In fact, this minor operation in the arid wastes of the Persian Gulf, in support of the feudal ruler of a country which had not emerged into the twentieth century, powerfully supported the hand of those ministers who argued for a greater emphasis on conventional forces, and perhaps had more effect on the cabinet's thinking about defence priorities than all the carefully balanced arguments of the preceding few months.

The revolt against the Sultan of Muscat and Oman broke out in a remote area in the interior of the Sultanate in July, under the leadership of the Imam Ghalib bin Ali. With some backing from Saudi Arabia, and a measure of tribal support, the Imam defeated the Sultan's forces in central Oman and secured the land route from Muscat to the Buraimi Oasis. On 21 July the Sultan requested British aid and two days later RAF aircraft began operations in Oman.

In a statement to the Commons on 28 July the Foreign Secretary explained that the government's decision to help the Sultan was made both because of the implicit obligations to a friendly ruler, and because direct British interests were involved, in which connection there was 'no need to emphasise the importance of the Persian Gulf'.[107] Selwyn Lloyd then went on to make an important statement about the government's interpretation of its commitments in the Persian Gulf. Although Britain's obligations to the Gulf sheikhdoms were of two kinds

the difference between a formal obligation and the obligations of a long-standing relationship of friendship is not readily apparent to the local rulers and people. If we were to fail in one area it would

---

[106] 28 July 1957.

[107] 574 HC Deb., 29 July 1957, col. 872. See also Lloyd's earlier statement, 574 HC Deb., 22 July 1957, col. 32. In his memoirs, Macmillan refers directly to the oil interest. At the time two companies were carrying out exploration in the area and major oil deposits were subsequently discovered. *Riding the Storm*, p. 270.

begin to be assumed elsewhere that perhaps the anti-British propaganda of our enemies had some basis to it, and that the Government were no longer willing or able to help their friends.[108]

In that this statement made it clear that the government took a very broad interpretation of its defence obligations in the area, it had two important implications for future British policy. First, if the government adhered to this wider view, it was probable, bearing in mind the feudal nature of the various sheikhdoms and the conflicting claims of the littoral states, that Britain would increasingly be called upon to take military action to preserve the *status quo*. Secondly, and by way of corollary, it would be necessary for some years to maintain the kind of forces—and in sufficient strength—that could intervene effectively in the area.

The course of the Oman operation was directly relevant to this second point. The basic military lesson of the campaign was that air power was no substitute for troops on the ground in maintaining stability in under-developed countries. Whatever may have been possible in Iraq and the North-West Frontier before the war, the Oman operation demonstrated that air action alone could no longer quell skirmishes and major uprisings in desert areas. Although the limitations of air action were apparent in the Aden-Yemeni border clashes in 1955 and 1956, the myth had persisted in air force circles that the RAF's air control method was an economical and successful way of dealing with local tribunal quarrels. Thus when the Oman revolt broke out the RAF asserted that it could do the job unaided, and the government, acting on this advice, authorized rocket and cannon attacks on enemy held forts, and certain other operations designed to seal off the area of disaffection.[109] In his statement to the House of Commons on 23 July, the Foreign Secretary was categorical that there was 'no question . . . of large-scale operations by British troops on the ground.'[110] Indeed, he went on to say that in view of the high temperatures in Oman at that time of year, it would be an example of military futility to seek to employ ground forces in the desert areas.[111]

[108] 574 HC Deb., 29 July 1957, col. 872.
[109] See Lloyd's statements 574 HC Deb., 22 July 1957, col. 32, and 23 July 1957, coll. 230–4; *Keesing's Contemporary Archives, 1957–1958*, 15709, and Alastair Buchan's reflections in Observer Foreign News Service, 8 Aug. 1957.
[110] 574 HC Deb., col. 231.
[111] Ibid. col. 234.

After a week of air action, however, it was clear that the air control method was not producing the desired effect and the Air Officer Commanding, Air Vice-Marshal Sir Laurence Sinclair, reluctantly announced the movement of British ground troops into the area.[112] The land attack opened on 6 August; before the rebellion collapsed ten days later, Britain had moved an armoured car regiment from Aden, a battalion from Kenya, and support elements from Cyprus to support the Trucial Oman Scouts and the Sultan's shaky forces.

The failure of the RAF's rocket and cannon attacks to eject the rebels was ascribed to the limitations of the air weapon when employed against an enemy which had some semblance of organization and cohesion. According to the pre-war theory, which was reiterated with very little change in the post-war RAF manuals, the air control method was not to kill or injure dissident tribesmen, but to interrupt the normal life of the enemy to such an extent that the continuance of hostilities became intolerable. This was all very well when dealing with a tribal society, with its principle of communal responsibility, but when the enemy was organized from outside, as in Aden or the Oman, it could hardly fail to be much less effective. Under such circumstances, air power yielded control of the ground and troops had to be brought in. Another argument advanced was that the aeroplane was no longer the unfamiliar and therefore terrifying machine of the twenties and thirties, and that its psychological effects were to a considerable extent nullified. In the opinion of an Indian doctor who was resident in a rebel-held fort during the RAF attacks, the tribesmen had never been frightened, and even the heavier attacks and shorter warnings (15 minutes instead of 48 hours) in the latter stages of the air campaign had had little effect.[113]

Looking to the future, *The Times* argued that it must now be expected that rebels would be capable of holding on to the ground in the face of the traditional type of air attack.[114] What this of course meant was less emphasis on air power and more on ground forces, and its implications for the government's defence policy were too obvious to need labouring by *The Times*. The same newspaper also noted that the Arabian

[112] See further *Times*, 3 and 5 Aug. 1957.
[113] 'Lessons of Oman', *Times*, 19 Aug. 1957.
[114] Ibid.

Peninsula was still an air force Command, and it wondered whether the structure of command ought not to be re-examined to conform with a pattern of operations which would rely more on the army and relegate the air force to a supporting role.[115]

Over the next two years army and air force commanders in the Arabian Peninsula took stock of the situation and developed a modified air control method which relied on more extensive use of troops on the ground. The land forces were used to concentrate dissidents and it was then possible to bring air action into operation. At first the Air Staff accepted this ancillary role grudgingly, but by about 1959 it had become standard procedure.

The Oman operation also had the effect of underlining a number of other points which were gaining recognition within the defence establishment. It strengthened the case for an expanded airlift capability;[116] it provided some support for the commando carrier project; it emphasized the need for acclimatized troops in Aden and Kenya which could be moved rapidly to trouble spots;[117] and it provided yet another warning that policing operations must be carried out with a minimum of delay if awkward political repercussions were to be avoided. Even in the case of Oman, American opinion was disturbed and Asian opinion hostile. In Alastair Buchan's view, the slowness of the campaign had been not only an embarrassment, but a source of real weakness.[118]

[115] Ibid. For an opposite view see Sir John Slessor's letter to *The Times*, 24 Aug. 1957.
[116] Macmillan expressed his concern about the air transport system in notes to both the Minister of Defence and the Secretary of State for Air. See *Riding the Storm*, pp. 273–4.
[117] There were seven cases of heat exhaustion at Oman.
[118] Observer Foreign News Service, 8 Aug. 1957.

CHAPTER FOUR

Role Re-examined 1958–1961

AFTER the trauma of Suez the government recovered its equanimity with surprising speed. Although it took the point about consultation, and it accepted the necessity for acting in concert with the United States in any future conflict along Suez lines, the government adhered to the wider conception of Britain's defence role, secure in the belief that the roots of her greatness were too deep to have been seriously disturbed. Paradoxically, it was not the government but the military which in the last years of the fifties constantly referred back to the Suez operation. In their endeavours to set the defence house in order, the military carefully combed the campaign for weaknesses and lessons, and it was not until 1961, when the Kuwait operation set the seal on their policies and provided the needed reassurance, that the services finally buried that unhappy chapter.

It was the military planners also who first felt a need for broader thinking about the east of Suez area as a whole. For them the return to the habit of thinking of the area in regional terms was a by-product of the uncertainty and unreliability of the air and sea links across the Middle East. Outside the defence departments, however, the regional concept had no particular significance for British policy-makers over these years. Though the bulk of Britain's remaining overseas commitments was east of Suez, and inevitably much of the thinking about the overseas role centred on Britain's obligations there, the area itself did not constitute a frame of reference. In the main, discussion was either limited to particular problems or it was conducted in terms of the overseas role in general.

At the same time, political thinking about the purposes and tasks of the deployment of overseas power moved slowly to new ground. Following the lead of the services, Britain's role was cast in terms of the maintenance of internal security and local stability. What was less clear, however, was the relationship of overseas policy to specific British interests. The one attempt to settle this issue was largely unsuccessful and thereafter attention was fixed on external developments which led naturally to the conclusion that overseas security represented Britain's most pressing military concern. As the Mediterranean declined in strategic significance and as the Middle Eastern focus of attention shifted from Egypt and the Canal to Aden and the Persian Gulf, the overseas role came to mean Britain's role east of Suez. But it was not until 1962 that the various strands of thinking were brought together and that the east of Suez role became a subject in its own right.

Co-ordination of Overseas Policy

Much of the discussion of Britain's defence role has been bedevilled by the proposition that 'defence policy is the servant of foreign policy.' Year after year politicians, senior civil servants, and military leaders have repeated this maxim until it has assumed something of the immutability of a law of nature. Whatever its usefulness as an aid in determining the direction and scope of the military component, as an account of the defence–foreign policy relationship it is altogether inadequate. Indeed, as a statement of British policy east of Suez in the years 1958 to 1961 it is actually misleading, inasmuch as it forecloses the questions which need to be asked with its assumption of the rationality of the decision-making process. Only at the most general level can British defence policy in these years be described as the servant of foreign policy—in the sense that Britain's diplomatic posture was grounded on the world role and her defence policy was still directed towards the provision of a world wide capability. And yet even here there were two conceptions—the one political and the other military—and that they met was largely because both the government and the military still saw Britain's role in the world in terms of the imperial tradition.

Although at this most general level British policies east of Suez had a measure of coherence, a closer examination reveals numerous inconsistencies and differences in approach. The heart of the problem was that there was no integrated policy during these years, but instead several lines of policy pursued independently by the various departments with interests in the area. In the absence of clear direction from the government, the pattern which emerged was one of separate and sometimes contradictory policies being pursued in accordance with different historical precepts. Each of the departments involved in overseas policy had its own interests and responsibilities, and thus tended to approach east of Suez issues along independent lines. There was very little agreement about time-scales, priorities and—on some important occasions—about the ends to be pursued. Nor was there any overall authority for co-ordinating policy in the area. In 1959 Head asked:

do not all honourable Members agree that our . . . policy in South East Asia and Africa—and within these areas what happens in one small country interacts on the other—is very bitty? We have the Commonwealth Relations Office here, the Colonial Office there, the Foreign Office there, three busy Ministers, three separate Departments, and no co-ordination for the areas as a whole.[1]

Coming from a former Minister of Defence who was widely regarded as one of the most competent and responsible occupants of that office, this was a strong indictment of the policy-making machinery.

By implication Head's statement raised doubts about the efficiency of the system for high-level planning co-ordination. The difficulty here is that although the organizational structure can be perceived in some detail, very little information is available about its day-to-day workings.[2] The system was one of co-ordination by committee. The Defence Committee was of course the central body and its responsibilities remained as outlined in the 1946 White Paper *Central Organisation for Defence*.[3] Under the reorganization of 1958, the Commonwealth Secretary and the Colonial Secretary became members of the Committee, but the relatively fixed membership of the Committee's first decade was replaced by a floating one, with atten-

[1] 600 HC Deb., 25 Feb. 1959, col. 1173.
[2] The best general survey is David Vital, *The Making of British Foreign Policy* (1968), esp. ch. 3. F. A. Johnson makes some observations about the workings of the system in *Defence by Committee* (ch. 10), but his treatment of the post-war years lacks the detail of his earlier chapters on the Committee of Imperial Defence.
[3] Cmd 6923. See p. 19 above.

dance at particular meetings being determined by the Prime Minister on an *ad hoc* basis.[4] In the field of colonial defence the Defence Committee was assisted by a subcommittee, the Overseas Defence Committee.[5] The Chiefs of Staff Committee was collectively responsible for professional advice on defence policy.[6] Supporting the work of the Chiefs of Staff Committee were a number of subcommittees, two of which—the Joint Intelligence Committee and the Joint Planning Committee—maintained links with the overseas departments, as did the Chiefs of Staff Committee. The Joint Planning Committee was composed of the service Directors of Plans and was responsible for developing military plans in the light of current events and established policies. Draft plans were produced by the Joint Planners in consultation with the Foreign, Colonial, and Commonwealth Relations Offices.[7] The Joint Intelligence Committee included the three service Directors of Intelligence and met under the chairmanship of a Foreign Office official.[8] In theory, then, even at the middle ranges of policy formulation and evaluation, the machinery for co-ordination with the overseas departments was well developed.

It is hardly necessary to labour the point that any full assessment of the workings of this system must await the opening of the archives. While some insights can be obtained through conversations with participants, the limitations of this approach are such that only a very rough and fragmented picture can be pieced together. Many of the questions to be asked are obvious. Which issues were discussed by the Defence Committee and the Overseas Defence Committee? And equally important, which were not? What scenarios were drawn up in the Foreign Office of the state of the area and the threats to be anticipated five years hence? To what extent was agreement reached at the lower levels of planning? And by compromise or by default? It is easy to pose the questions: the answers are another story. Nevertheless, even when all the problems are admitted, the picture which emerges is one of a practice which falls far short

---

[4] *Central Organisation for Defence*, Cmnd 476 (1958), para. 4.
[5] See pp. 30–1 above.
[6] Cmnd 476, para. 15.
[7] F. A. Johnson, *Defence by Committee*, p. 309, and Martin, 'The Market for Strategic Ideas in Britain: the "Sandys Era" ', *Amer. polit. Sci. R.*, 56/1 (Mar. 1962), pp. 23 and 39.
[8] F. A. Johnson, *Defence by Committee*, p. 309.

of the theory. For all the elaborate machinery for co-ordination, the performance was disappointing.

Tentatively, three weaknesses can be noted. In the first place, the Defence Committee appears to have been an ineffectual body for deciding matters of long-term policy and questions involving conflicting departmental interests. There was a wide measure of agreement on this point in Whitehall.[9] Partly it was a matter of issues not being presented squarely to the Committee, either because departmental perspectives obscured their wider significance or because they were felt to be too open to accident, and departments and ministers preferred to go along as they were. At other times the issues would be too sensitive, too divisive, or too disruptive for the collective body to act against its political instinct and settle for a declaratory course. Thus in the opinion of one minister, the Committee was little more than a 'clearing-house for short-range decisions'. He went on to say that occasionally ministers went to Chequers, with noble ideas of planning a course for five years or a decade ahead, but very little was ever achieved. According to one Chief of Staff, in the last three years of the Macmillan government the position was particularly bad and meeting after meeting would be held without a firm decision being taken. In the opinion of another, what was required was a single minister responsible for overseas policy. Among the many issues on which the Chiefs of Staff had been unable to obtain a firm decision, or at least had obtained one only with the greatest of difficulty, the base policy was invariably singled out as the services' main worry. The difficulty here was that the government was not only required to plan for some years ahead, but also to decide between the various estimates of the likely tenure of occupation and the differing interests of the departments involved. The net result, it was explained, was that the services were forced to build a strategy while 'sitting on a jelly'.

On at least some occasions this meant that, in the interval, inconsistent policies were being pursued by the Ministry of Defence and the Colonial Office. Although it cannot yet be

[9] One minister disagreed privately though he expressed the view that the presence of the service ministers reduced the effectiveness of the Committee. For more general though again favourable reflections on the system see Patrick Gordon Walker, *The Cabinet* (1970), pp. 47–8 and 131.

documented, this was clearly the case over Singapore for some years before 1956. Until the Lancaster House Conference in April 1956, the government had not settled the strategic base–self-government dilemma, with the result that the service departments were planning on the assumption of base sovereignty and control over internal security, while the Colonial Office was going ahead with its own plans for self-government.[10] A few years later a parallel case developed over Kenya, though this time with disastrous result. That here the government had a change of mind was, of course, significant, but almost equal prominence must be given to the government's earlier indecision, and to the failure not only of co-ordination but also of communication between the Ministry of Defence and the Colonial Office.[11]

Secondly, the division of responsibility for Britain's overseas relations between three separate ministries—the Foreign Office, the Commonwealth Relations Office, and the Colonial Office—greatly accentuated the inherent difficulties of formulating a coherent overseas policy.[12] It was not only that the areas of bureaucratic overlap were that much larger but also that the difficulties of adjustment were sharpened because the various ministries produced their separate and sometimes conflicting assessments on the basis of distinctive priorities and specialized administrative procedures. Although the nature of the problem was recognized, practical considerations were taken to preclude immediate unification and several years were to elapse before a reorganization was put in hand.[13] From the defence viewpoint, the main difficulty again related to co-ordination with the Colonial Office on the subject of bases. It was one thing to reach agreement with the overseas departments on the general principle that the bases must be held but it was another to secure the co-operation of the Colonial Office when it came to the process of implementation. According to one official, at various times the Ministry of Defence set out its requirements

---

[10] Apparently the government countered service doubts by informing the services that assurances had been given to the Australians and the Americans regarding the base.

[11] See pp. 205–8 below.

[12] See Committee on Representational Services Overseas, *Report* (Chairman, Lord Plowden), Cmnd 2276 (1964), p. 12.

[13] In Aug. 1966 the Colonial Office was absorbed into the renamed Commonwealth Office and in Oct. 1968 a single Foreign and Commonwealth Office was formed.

if the base structure were to be maintained. These included certain constitutional safeguards, some immunity from the civil jurisdiction, and transit and telecommunication facilities. Apparently, however, the Defence Department had considerable difficulty in securing a hearing in the Colonial Office and even when it did there was no assurance that its interests would be strenuously pressed.

Thirdly, co-ordination was hampered by the different methods and approach of the overseas departments on the one hand, and the service departments on the other. From the defence angle one difficulty was to induce the Colonial Office and the Foreign Office to broaden their conceptual horizons and to look beyond the requirements of particular countries and territories.[14] On all accounts the services had little success in this direction in the years 1958 to 1961. Another difficulty stemmed from the fact that the overseas departments approached issues in terms of the intentions of the parties whereas the service departments were more concerned with capabilities and hence possibilities than with designs. This difference in perspective was inherent in the nature of the two activities but unless the point was kept firmly in mind the resulting divergences could cause misunderstanding on both sides.

A more important source of friction arose from the fact that the Foreign Office and the service departments looked east of Suez with different conceptions of time. Whereas the services were forced to make certain assumptions about the configuration of the area five to eight years ahead, the Foreign Office was content to operate on the basis of a model which emphasized

[14] In the Foreign Office, division of responsibility between several territorial departments appears to have discouraged 'general' thinking. Six departments were responsible for advising the Secretary of State on Indian Ocean affairs: the three Middle Eastern (Levant, Arabian, Eastern), the African, Far Eastern, and South-East Asian. It appears that co-ordination between them was poor and that at times it was not even possible to speak of a common Middle Eastern policy, as each of the three departments concerned tended to pursue separate policies. As well as the territorial departments, there were others with functional responsibilities. Thus the Permanent Under-Secretary's department maintained liaison with the Ministry of Defence and with the Chiefs of Staff and represented the Foreign Office on the Joint Intelligence Committee and the Joint Planning Committee. According to departmental theory, this section collated the briefs of the territorial departments, but there are grave doubts about how effectively it discharged this function. For an account of the Foreign Office machinery see Strang, *The Diplomatic Career*, ch. 6. Lord George-Brown makes critical observations on the working of the system; *In My Way* (1971), p. 160.

the short run rather than the long run. The services' concern with the period ahead stemmed from the need to draw up contingency plans and to develop and produce the ships, aircraft, and equipment which would be required.[15] One senior official illustrated the point by explaining that military planners take only a newspaper interest in contemporary developments. This may have been an over-simplification but it does indicate the general approach of the planning sections in the service departments. The Foreign Office, on the other hand, seems to have had a deep-seated prejudice against forward planning. It was admitted on all sides that before 1957 long-term planning in the Foreign Office was seriously deficient. Indeed, on a number of occasions the Ministry of Defence was forced to carry out planning studies which were properly the responsibility of the Foreign Office.[16] The one attempt to remedy this situation—the establishment of a Permanent Under-Secretary's Committee in 1949, which was briefed to identify long-term trends—was only partially successful.[17] Although between about 1950 and 1953 the Committee produced a number of useful studies, it lacked a permanent staff and it was not integrated within the policy-making machine. With a new generation of under-secretaries interest declined. By about 1955 the Committee lapsed and long-term planning became virtually non-existent. This led to considerable pressure from the Chiefs of Staff for an overhaul of the Foreign Office machinery. Partly as a result of a personal initiative by Lord Montbatten, who was then First Sea Lord, late in 1957 the Foreign Office established a policy planning department which was specifically concerned with long-term planning.

The policy planning department was a relatively junior section of the Foreign Office, headed by a first secretary, and assisted by a small secretariat. It had no responsibility other than forward planning of a most general kind and about

---

[15] On general reckoning it takes about five years to design, develop, and produce a warship and its period of service is about twenty years. For an aircraft the developmental period is reckoned at about ten years and it is likely to be in service for another ten.

[16] On one notable occasion Ernest Bevin requested the Ministry of Defence to map out a scheme for division of the sea-bed of the Persian Gulf among the littoral states.

[17] See p. 17 above.

twelve or fourteen major papers were produced each year.[18] It is difficult to assess the department's influence but there is some evidence to suggest that, although the various papers produced were useful exercises, the department made little impact on the general thinking of the Foreign Office. After 1957 military planners were still reporting that they had the utmost difficulty in obtaining general assessments upon which contingency planning could be based.[19] The major problem appears to have been the deeply ingrained resistance to this sort of thinking in the Foreign Office. It is doubtful whether the main body of departmental opinion had changed significantly since the early fifties. In his discussion of policy planning, Lord Strang cautions against exaggerating the importance of long-term studies, and he goes on to spell out in great detail the difficulties of looking ahead.[20] Much later, another Foreign Office official explained that there is always a strong disincentive to 'crystal ball gazing' because it is so easy to appear foolish. The picture which emerges, then, is one of a department which functioned on an ad hoc basis and made little attempt to order priorities in a way which the service departments regarded as essential. Sir William Hayter, who was Deputy Under-Secretary of State at the Foreign Office in 1957 and 1958, has summed up the situation well:

The selection of the objective ... represents perhaps the greatest weakness of British diplomatic organisation. The British as a nation have never been good at long-term planning. They live from day to day, deciding questions as they come up sensibly enough, but never foreseeing what questions will come up or considering where they ultimately want to go. The Foreign Office is very like this.[21]

---

[18] To give an example of the sort of work undertaken by the department: early in 1960 a major paper on defence east of Suez was produced which anticipated, in broad outline, the Air Staff's island-base project. Taking account of the Middle Eastern air barrier and looking ahead to the time when the African air route might be closed, the paper recommended establishment of a chain of island staging posts, and a major base in Australia. It also stressed the requirement for commando carriers and suggested that Britain might need more aircraft carriers. In retrospect one official admitted that the cost of the full scheme would have been prohibitive, and he went on to reflect that the department had little sense of financial responsibility at the time.

[19] One very senior officer wrote that he had never heard of the long-term planning section nor met anyone on it.

[20] *The Diplomatic Career*, pp. 111–13.

[21] *The Diplomacy of the Great Powers* (1960), p. 46.

The Future Policy Committee

The obstacles within the executive structure both to forward planning and to determining a national policy which cut across departmental interests led Macmillan to establish a high-level inter-departmental committee to consider Britain's role in the seventies. In 1958 Macmillan expressed himself dissatisfied with the situation in which all the advice he received was loaded with the particular interest of the department concerned. Accordingly, he gave directions that a group representing the main departments of state should be set up to make some assessment of Britain's role about ten years ahead. With the strong support of Lord Normanbrook, Secretary of the Cabinet and chairman of the group, Macmillan thus launched the first major attempt to review Britain's role since the Second World War.

The Committee's report was to be in two parts: first, an appreciation of the world situation and the United Kingdom's position; secondly, and in the light of that, certain recommendations for appropriate long-term policies. Macmillan instructed that the group should be as objective as possible and not tied by departmental guide-lines. However, this departure from established practice met with the opposition of the Permanent Under-Secretaries and the Chiefs of Staff, and they were therefore interposed between the working group and the cabinet. Thus the Permanent Under-Secretaries and the Chiefs of Staff became the steering committee, and the working group became a body which submitted a draft to the Committee. Macmillan's idea was that the Committee's report should be finished in time to be presented to whichever government came to power after the 1959 general election. However, the study took longer than expected and it was not finished until well into 1960.

The working group was chaired by Sir Patrick Dean and included representatives from the service departments, the Foreign Office, the Colonial Office, the Commonwealth Relations Office, the Treasury, and the Board of Trade. Several subcommittees were set up by the working group to consider particular problems and territorial areas. In general the group was split between those who saw Britain's future in terms of the Anglo-American alliance, and who therefore argued in favour of maintaining both the world role and the nuclear role, and those who were convinced that Britain must readjust to a situation in which she was primarily a European power. All the basic issues of Britain's role east of Suez were discussed in detail and many were the object of strong controversy. Arguments about the value of the Commonwealth, Britain's obligations to developing countries, and her responsibility to assist in the containment of communism went round and round, and each service used them to justify the maintenance of forces in the area and the largest possible share of the defence budget.

Reportedly the group's recommendations included some stark proposals for limiting Britain's involvement in the area. However, these conclusions were greatly watered down by the steering committee, with the result that the Committee's final report confirmed Britain's world-wide interests and the requirement for a continued British involvement in the Indian Ocean area. The military assessment was broadly that both nuclear war and war in Europe were increasingly unlikely and that the major threat to the peace was posed by limited conflicts in Africa, the Middle East, and Asia. Hence emphasis was placed on the development of strategically mobile forces. Although there were no specific recommendations about hardware, some indication was given of the sort of forces that were likely to be required. Another section of the report dealt with Britain's economic position and the burden of defence spending. The conclusion here was that about 7 or 8 per cent of the GNP should continue to be devoted to defence.

Centrally placed ministers and officials were convinced that the Committee's report made very little impact on the government's thinking about the Indian Ocean role.[22] In the first instance, the report was considered at a weekend meeting at Chequers. However, the meeting was less useful than had been hoped, as at the last moment Macmillan was unable to attend. It is doubtful whether the report was read in full by many cabinet ministers and it certainly never became in any sense a blueprint for future policy. By 1960 the main lines of Britain's overseas defence policy had been charted and they were more firmly fixed by the various emergencies east of

---

[22] Certain sections dealing with other issues were considered separately and perhaps had more influence.

Suez over the following four years. In 1962 a major review by the Chiefs of Staff became the government's strategic text,[23] and the report of the Future Policy Committee receded further into the background.

The Politics of the Overseas Role

After the Suez débâcle interest quickened in the overseas role and it rapidly became a major issue of disagreement between the government and the opposition. It was the Labour party which first singled out the issue as a subject for full-scale debate. Sensing the government's vulnerability, Labour speakers questioned the relevance of the world-wide distribution of troops both to the realities of the world scene and to Britain's role in the post-imperial era. Their opposition to the broader interpretation of Britain's role stemmed partly from what seems to have been a genuine disagreement about Britain's interests and capabilities, and partly, one suspects, from the belief that this was the sort of issue which would make good political capital, and one, moreover, that was free from the internal ruptures which plagued the Labour party over the nuclear issue.[24]

The debate which ensued, however, was unduly polarized and therefore shallow: a sparring match between parties armed with the phrases and slogans of an earlier generation. On the Labour side, there was little attempt to investigate whether a role remained for British forces outside Europe or to distinguish between those areas where the commitment was a historical anomaly and those areas where it still seemed appropriate. The original purpose had gone: let us be done with rationalization and justification and withdraw. The government was unmoved. History was on its side and the cycle could not so quickly be ended. Indeed, from the speeches of some Conservatives it appeared that it would never be ended. The first step in the Conservative reply was to denounce the Labour party for wanting to 'welch' and 'scuttle'. Having done that, the government fell back on arguments which did little more than scratch the surface.

[23] See p. 218 below.
[24] In fact not all Labour members adhered to the party line on cutting back overseas defence responsibilities. Wigg and Paget spoke in a different vein, as to a less extent did some others.

In general, it was explained, the role of British forces was twofold: to support residual colonial commitments and to honour Britain's obligations to SEATO and CENTO. The first point was so obvious that the government saw no need to spell out its thinking in any detail. Britain was constitutionally obligated to the defence of its colonial territories. It retained certain formalized responsibilities for the defence of former colonies and protectorates. Finally, there was the unwritten but widely accepted obligation to go to the assistance of Commonwealth countries even in the absence of a specific security treaty.[25] In 1958 Sandys mentioned Kenya, Aden, the Persian Gulf, Malaya, Singapore, and Hong Kong as territories which required the assistance of Britain's conventional forces.[26] To these he might have added a score of smaller countries, ranging from the Borneo states and Mauritius to tiny island territories such as the Maldives. And in the background, though of no immediate significance, lay Britain's defence responsibilities to India and Australia, responsibilities which rested on the historical relationship and on a general sense of propriety.

Underlying the government's declaration that residual colonial commitments must be honoured were two questions which the government never answered explicitly. Could the process of clipping Britain's post-imperial commitments yet be put in hand? And were the burdens of Britain's colonial responsibilities likely to become more or less onerous? With reference to the first, the government gave no indication that the number of Britain's commitments weighed unduly heavily upon it or that it was necessary to limit their scope. On the contrary, such evidence as is available points to a surprising equanimity on the part of the government and a semi-permanent view of commitments. According to a number of reports, the Chiefs of Staff and overseas officials repeatedly approached the government with warnings that unless commitments were reduced or, alternatively, defence resources increased, the services might be unable to meet the demands placed upon them Discussions would take place—Hong Kong for example was a running sore over these years—but the government strongly

[25] See e.g. Army League, *The British Army in the Nuclear Age*, p. 16, and Alastair Buchan, 'Commonwealth Military Relations', in W. B. Hamilton and others, eds, *A Decade of the Commonwealth 1955–1964* (1966), p. 203.
[26] 583 HC Deb., 26 Feb. 1958, col. 388.

resisted adopting either course. The government's equanimity concerning the extent of Britain's commitments is amply confirmed by its public actions. In 1957 it had no hesitation in extending a defence agreement to Malaya on independence, and both in Brunei in 1958 and in Kuwait in 1961, when diplomatic and administrative considerations led to a review of existing arrangements, the government adhered to the old conception of Britain's defence responsibilities. On each occasion it is arguable that opportunities were available at least for a redefinition of Britain's responsibilities had the government inclined in that direction. Perhaps the clearest statement of the government's view came from the Minister of Defence, Harold Watkinson, in the 1961 debate on the White Paper:

We do not propose to leave the Arabian Peninsula and our treaty obligations there. We do not intend to leave places like Hong Kong defenceless or to abandon those members of the Commonwealth in whose defence we have agreed to share. . . . I have made it plain that the Government have no intention of backing out of our world obligations. I am not ashamed to stand at this Box, and say that I am proud that the nation still has some responsibilities in the world.[27]

On the question of whether colonial territories implied permanent military commitments, it seems probable that there was no single government line. Perhaps the most that can be said is that many members of the government inclined to the permanent view. It is interesting that an Army League study group composed of nineteen military leaders, parliamentarians, and defence commentators was unable to reach agreement on this issue in 1959.[28] It has been suggested that, after the Nigerian experience,[29] the government was chary of converting colonial obligations into specific defence agreements with new members of the Commonwealth.[30] However, this was denied in Whitehall and it was said that as a general rule Britain endeavoured to conclude defence agreements with newly independent countries in the hope that British influence

[27] 635 HC Deb., 28 Feb. 1961, coll. 1508–9.
[28] *The British Army in the Nuclear Age*, p. 13.
[29] The defence agreement between Britain and Nigeria, signed in Nov. 1960, was abrogated by joint decision on 21 Jan. 1962.
[30] Buchan, as cited in n. 25, p. 205.

might be maintained and British military equipment purchased.

In the absence of a clear statement at the time, it is not possible to write with any assurance about whether the government expected Britain's colonial responsibilities to become more or less onerous. It may be that the government did not see the issue in quite these terms, or if it did there is the possibility that it failed to arrive at the sort of neat conclusion for which we are searching. On the basis of discussions with policy-makers, however, it appears that the government tended to the view that overseas commitments would become more, rather than less, burdensome. The lessons of both the revolt in Central Oman in the summer of 1957 and the Aden-Yemeni conflict in 1957 and 1958 were not lost upon it. It was suggested that Britain's intervention in Jordan in 1958 lent further support to the pessimistic view. The report of the Future Policy Committee worked in the same direction. Certainly, towards the close of this period the government had no illusions that overseas commitments were going to be less onerous than in the past. In 1960 Field Marshal Lord Harding observed that the army's commitments were likely to increase rather than decrease.[31] One year later R. H. S. Crossman neatly summed up the situation with his observation that 'the defence of the scattered remains of a great Empire may be more burdensome than the defence of its earlier unity.'[32]

That the government concurred with these assessments seems to be borne out by the steady up-grading of the east of the Suez role and the strengthening of Britain's strategically mobile forces.[33]

By the close of 1961 four commitments had been renegotiated, but despite Opposition prodding and pressure from the Chiefs of Staff Britain's east of Suez responsibilities were only slightly less than they had been in 1957. In an agreement concluded in January 1957 Britain committed herself to the defence of Malaya after the territory became independent in October of that year.[34] Under Articles I and II Britain agreed to assist

---

[31] 225 HL Deb., 13 July 1960, col. 218.

[32] 'Western Defence in the 1960s', *JRUSI*, 106/623 (Aug. 1961), p. 328.

[33] See further pp. 163–4 below.

[34] MoD, *Proposed Agreement on External Defence and Mutual Assistance between the Government of the United Kingdom of Great Britain and Northern Ireland and the Government of the Federation of Malaya*, Cmnd, 263 (1957). See also the Colonial Office statement. *Times*, 11 Jan. 1957.

Malaya in the 'external defence of its territory' and with 'the training and development of the armed forces of the Federation'. In the event of an armed attack on any of the territories or forces of Malaya or any of the territories, protectorates or forces of the United Kingdom in the Far East, the two governments agreed to co-operate with each other and to take such action as each considered necessary for the purpose of meeting the situation effectively.[35] In return for British support, Malaya agreed that Britain could maintain its forces, bases, and facilities in the Federation not only for the defence of Malaya but also for the protection of Singapore, Borneo, and Hong Kong. If British forces were required for SEATO purposes it was understood that they would be withdrawn from Malaya and redeployed from Singapore.

In Singapore, Britain remained responsible for external defence after that territory attained full internal self-government on 1 August 1958. A constitutional conference met in London in March and April 1957 and on 11 April it was announced that agreement had been reached on full internal self-government for the colony, including the question of internal security, over which the previous talks had broken down in 1956. Internal security became the responsibility of the State government, assisted by an Internal Security Council chaired by the United Kingdom Commissioner. Britain remained responsible for external affairs and defence and continued to operate the Singapore base as before.[36]

Following talks in London in March and April 1959 a new defence agreement was signed between the United Kingdom government and the Sultan of Brunei, as part of the administrative separation of that territory from Sarawak. This agreement replaced the 1906 Treaty but Britain's responsibility for defence and external affairs remained unchanged.[37] For somewhat different reasons, in 1961 an agreement of sixty years' standing between the United Kingdom and Kuwait was replaced by a new agreement of 'close friendship' between the two countries.[38] Edward Heath, Lord Privy Seal, explained to the House of

[35] Article VII.
[36] *Keesing's Contemporary Archives 1957–58*, 15557.
[37] COI, *Brunei*, R (DFS), 5417/64, Apr. 1964 (Fact Sheets on the Commonwealth), and *Keesing's Contemporary Archives 1959–60*, 17066.
[38] FO, *Exchange of Notes regarding Relations between the United Kingdom of Great Britain and Northern Ireland and the State of Kuwait*, Cmnd 1518 (1961).

Commons that the 1899 agreement had been abrogated because it was inconsistent with the sovereignty and independence
of Kuwait. Nothing in the new agreement, however, affected
the readiness of the British government to assist the government
of Kuwait either in the case of external aggression or internal
subversion.[39]

The government's reluctance to reduce overseas commitments, on the one hand, and its failure substantially to increase
the allocation for conventional forces, on the other, led to a
situation of considerable strain, the extent of which will become
clear in later chapters. Criticism must attach mainly to the
government's expansive approach to commitments as there
were major financial obstacles in the way of strengthening
capability. Even so, it should be recognized that there was no
simple process by which commitments and capability could
be precisely matched. Although it is clearly necessary to relate
the size and shape of a country's military forces to the number
and extent of its defence commitments, there is a limit to how
far this kind of reasoning should be carried. Apart from the
obvious impossibility of predicting the military requirements
of a particular commitment five to eight years ahead, there is
the related difficulty of forecasting the precise attitude of the
supporting government and hence the likely extent of its
intervention. The fact is that commitments do not automatically
determine military action. The interests and obligations which
they express may wane over time – some may even be more
symbolic than real from the outset. Conversely other interests
and obligations may arise, which, although not formally
sanctioned, are none the less regarded as a sufficient basis for
military support.

The second explanation advanced by the government for
the maintenance of forces outside Europe was that they were
deployed in support of SEATO and CENTO. Each year these
alliances were brought out to justify the continued world-wide
distribution of troops in very much the same way as NATO
was used to argue the case for Europe. The uninformed observer,
reading through the defence White Papers and ministerial
speeches of these years, could hardly fail to be left with the
impression that CENTO and SEATO were to British policy
in the Middle East and South-east Asia what NATO was to

[39] 642 HC Deb., 19 June 1961, coll. 955–8.

British policy in Europe. Indeed, at the last SEATO meeting of 1957 Lord Home was reported as saying that SEATO, in British eyes, was as important as NATO.[40] That the Baghdad Pact and SEATO never had the same intrinsic importance as NATO is too obvious to need labouring here. The point was repeatedly made by Opposition speakers in Parliament and reappeared in newspaper leaders year after year.

While not denying that SEATO and CENTO had some value as planning and intelligence agencies and as forums for a limited amount of policy co-ordination, in the present context it is doubtful if they constituted anything more than a peg upon which to hang the world-wide deployment of military forces. In a nutshell, if SEATO and to a lesser extent CENTO, originally had little military significance they became important from the military viewpoint because of the feed-back. Alliance obligations could be used to justify the retention of military forces east of Suez.

Although the government's case hinged on the arguments about commitments and alliances, more shadowy explanations were suggested or implied at various times. A careful reading of government statements suggests that there was also some notion that Britain had a special responsibility for the maintenance of stability in certain parts of the world—notably the Indian Ocean area—which went beyond the maintenance of order in British territories and amounted to a somewhat more independent role than her participation in SEATO and CENTO obliged. The 1960 White Paper, for example, noted that in addition to her role in NATO, CENTO, and SEATO Great Britain 'provides a military presence to help preserve stability in politically sensitive areas for which she has a particular responsibility.'[41] This pattern of thinking applied particularly to the role of the Royal Navy. For generations the navy had been seen as much as a world police force as a warlike institution and it was natural that this conception should die hard. Its influence can be seen in paragraph 44 of the 1958 White Paper.[42] One year later Lord Home felt no embarrassment in declaring that as long as the navy was 'able to appear and be

---

[40] *Scotsman*, 17 Dec. 1957.
[41] MoD, *Report on Defence 1960*, Cmnd 952 (1960), para. 4.
[42] MoD, *Report on Defence: Britain's Contribution to Peace and Security*, Cmnd 363 (1958).

seen in these Far Eastern and Indian waters . . . and so long as these activities in peace-time continue, the Pax Britannica, although we may not use the term in its nineteenth century context, still has a meaning on the high seas.'[43]

To put the point in a different way, Britain's military presence outside Europe was regarded as an element in the existing order: an order which if not exactly viewed with veneration was understood to require only limited change. It was a British interest to minimize change, so the argument went, or at least to see that change took place in a controlled manner.[44] This line of thought was natural for conservatives but it was not uncommon for liberals to subscribe to it also. The *Observer*, for example, pointed out that

The legacy of sites, influence and interests all round the world from the days of Pax Britannica makes our potential contribution, both political and material, uniquely apt and great. Instead of either seeking to become a super-power ourselves, or retreating into being merely a corner of Europe, Britain's proper role is as a world influence in the capacity of a landlord turned bailiff.[45]

Kenneth Younger argued a similar case. In his judgement, Asia and Africa were passing through a period of rapid transition from the Pax Britannica to a new system, the eventual nature of which could not be discerned. The transition should be completed without passing through a stage in which security against aggression was altogether lacking.[46] In the last years of the period under discussion the government moved very tentatively towards shoring up the justification for the east of Suez role by referring to the Chinese threat. The 1961 White Paper pointedly stated 'nor can we ignore the rising power in China'.[47] In the debate in the Commons, the Minister of Defence stated that 'We have also rightly taken account of the growth of the industrial and military power of China.'[48] Too much significance should not be attached to these state-

[43] 214 HL Deb., 10 Mar. 1959, col. 858.
[44] See T. E. M. McKitterick. 'What are British Interests?' *Political Quarterly*, 31/1 (Jan.–Mar. 1960), pp. 9 and 10.
[45] 'The Central Question', 13 Apr. 1958.
[46] 'The Colonial Issue in World Politics', in Arthur Creech Jones, ed., *New Fabian Colonial Essays* (1959), p. 57.
[47] MoD, *Report on Defence 1961*, Cmnd 1288 (1961), para. 4.
[48] 635 HC Deb., 27 Feb. 1961, col. 1198.

ments but they at least indicate that the government considered the problem of China to be not simply an American concern but also a British one, and that British forces might have a part to play.[49]

The view that a military presence east of Suez safeguarded Britain's economic interests in the area was seldom publicly discussed over these years. The issue hardly loomed large before 1957 but at least the subject was occasionally broached in Parliament. After 1957, however, discussion began and ended with the Persian Gulf. The government's silence over the Far East was in keeping with the view in Whitehall that economic considerations were a background factor rather than an immediate determinant of British policy in that area. One official with whom the issue was discussed dwelt on the difficulties of satisfactorily costing a military presence and the impossibility, in his view, of costing economic benefit. It was pointed out that inevitably calculations of economic benefit depend on a number of assumptions which must at best be questionable and at worst misleading. Apparently neither the Ministry of Defence nor any other department attempted such calculations over these years. Where the Far East was concerned there were compelling moral and political reasons for a British presence and there was neither the need nor the incentive to resort to economic arguments or to scrutinize the trade and investment figures. Still, behind the government's planning lay the thought that Britain had a major economic stake in South-east Asia and it seems to have been widely accepted that a military presence served to underwrite it.[50]

The Persian Gulf was another story. Here the economic motive took priority. Ever since the late forties it had been understood that British troops stood guard against the effects of economic, rather than political, domination and on a number of occasions the government had had little hesitation in saying so. As in the earlier period, Britain's interest in Gulf oil was twofold.[51] In the first place, Britain had a substantial

---

[49] It is interesting that since about 1957 Lord Mountbatten and Adm Sir Charles Lambe (who succeeded Mountbatten as First Sea Lord in 1959) had been arguing for Polaris submarines for use in the China seas.

[50] A centrally placed official wrote that 'the economic effects of the French and Dutch withdrawals were after all plain to see.'

[51] For a discussion of the position in the late forties see pp. 25–6 above.

capital investment in the oil operating companies. In 1959 the gross fixed assets of British oil companies in the Middle East were estimated to be $680 million, an increase of $240 million on the 1947 figure.[52] Although the British share of the total oil assets in the Gulf had declined since the late forties, it was still more than 30 per cent. The largest single investment was a 50 per cent share in Kuwait Oil by British Petroleum, a company in which the British government had a controlling interest. If the oil companies operating the concessions were to be nationalized, it was feared Britain would lose not only the capital invested and the annual royalties but an important source of foreign exchange. Secondly, Britain was heavily dependent upon supplies of Persian Gulf oil. Between 1957 and 1961 Kuwait alone supplied about 50 per cent of Britain's oil needs. Most of Britain's remaining oil imports came from other Persian Gulf or neighbouring states.[53] Any disruption of the flow of this oil seemed likely to have serious consequences on industrial production and transportation. The crisis of 1956, when the Suez Canal was blocked and the pipelines from Iraq to the Mediterranean were cut, showed how vulnerable the British economy was to the interruption or sharp diminution of these supplies.[54]

No doubt prodded by the oil companies, the government concluded that the maintenance of the independence of the oil producing states was the surest way of protecting British interests and ensuring the flow of oil. British policy was therefore aimed at preventing the Persian Gulf states from being absorbed by or divided among the powerful adjacent Arab states. This emerged plainly during the period of violence and unrest in the Middle East which began early in 1958. The announcement in February that Egypt and Syria had agreed to form a union was seen as the first move in an Egyptian challenge to the system of Western stability in the Middle East. In the British view, Nasser was organizing an expansionist campaign which threatened not only Lebanon and Jordan but Iraq and the Gulf states as well. The union of Iraq and Jordan held out some promise but this too had its dangers because these states were anxious to enlist

[52] Charles Issawi and Mohammed Yeganeh, *The Economics of Middle Eastern Oil* (1962), p. 59.
[53] See Dept of Trade and Industry, *Digest of Energy Statistics* (London, HMSO, 1971), table 122.
[54] See further Campbell, pp. 248–53.

the membership of Kuwait—a move, in Macmillan's eyes, which was designed to enable Iraq and Jordan to draw on the oil resources of Kuwait for their own purposes.[55] The Iraqi *coup* in July faced Britain with the prospect of yet another anti-Western regime in the Middle East and it led to increased fears that violence might spread to Saudi Arabia, Kuwait, and the other oil-bearing states of the Persian Gulf. To cover this contingency, Whitehall sought from the United States a commitment that the United States would join Britain in using force, if required, to keep the Persian Gulf states separate and distinct. According to newspaper despatches, the United States was unwilling to give any blanket assurance, although the use of force was not ruled out.[56] When the situation cleared and assurances were forthcoming from Abdul Karim Kassem, the new Premier, that the oil would continue to be shipped westward, Britain decided to tread warily and in early August recognition was extended to the new regime. As events turned out, the Iraqi coup was a false alarm but the diplomatic maneouvring which it produced did show Britain's true hand.

It would be mistaken to assume that the arguments about commitments, alliances, peace-keeping, and economic interest represented the sum total of thinking about the overseas role. In fact the political understanding of Britain's role east of Suez rested more on certain well-worn and common sense propositions than on any of these attempts to develop a purely rational case. Behind the verbal superstructure which was erected to explain Britain's military presence lay three considerations which seldom found expression in policy statements but which nonetheless were at the basis of the government's policy. In the first place, British troops were already deployed east of Suez; they supported a preferred pattern of world order; and the government required very good reasons to withdraw them. In a sense it was a case of preferring the known to the unknown but mainly it was a matter of habit. As one very senior official explained, 'We were there because we were there.' Secondly, there was an ingrained sense of responsibility—an element of straight idealism. The same official went on to speak of Britain's responsibility to ensure that the final devolution from empire took place in an orderly way and that the

---

[55] *Riding the Storm 1956–1959*, pp. 503–4.
[56] *New York Times*, 23, 24, 25 July and 13 Aug. 1958, and *Economist*, 26 July 1958.

countries which she had set on the road did not stumble at the first crossing. One has only to talk to former civil servants or to glance at their writings, to realize how deeply this sense of duty to Britain's ex-colonies influenced their thinking.

Finally, there was the continuing influence of the pattern of thinking that Britain was a world power. This theme ran strongly through ministerial speeches over these years and even found diagrammatical expression in the 1961 White Paper. Viscount Watkinson best expressed the point after listening to a speech by Lord Bourne in the House of Lords in 1965, in which he had argued that Britain's duties and obligations in Asia were not yet over:

When I was Minister of Defence it was people like General Bourne, as he then was, and the noble Viscount, Lord Montgomery of Alamein, who spoke in the outside world in those terms and did not hesitate to make it plain that we were a World Power, that we had world responsibilities and that we had to have the kind of strategy that would enable us to meet our obligations—for example to Malaysia.

It was these views, which had great weight, that enabled the Conservative Government of the day to bring in the 1962 Defence White Paper, with its concept of defending our obligations east of Suez.[57]

Nature of the Military Operations Envisaged

The principal task of the defence forces was the maintenance of order and stability in British territories and protected states. In fact internal security had been Britain's main defence role east of Suez since 1947, but it was only in these years that it somewhat hesitantly became acknowledged as such in government statements.[58] In general, it was assumed that colonial operations would follow the traditional pattern and there were frequent references to the campaigns in Malaya and Kenya. The protection of territorial borders and the maintenance of the independence of the various states remained an important aspect of British policy but here there was a distinct change in emphasis. Whereas in earlier years attention had been focused on the defence of the Middle East, Africa, the Persian Gulf and,

[57] 265 HL Deb., 7 Apr. 1965, col. 115.
[58] In particular see Christopher Soames' speech, 583 HC Deb., 6 Mar. 1958, col. 1163, and that of Aubrey Jones, 583 HC Deb., 26 Feb. 1958, col. 496.

to a lesser extent, the Far East, against a Communist sweep southwards, this expansive interpretation now gave way to a more pragmatic assessment which recognized the possibilities of nationalist adventurism and placed more weight on Communist nibbling tactics than on a conventional military attack. Border skirmishes, insurgency movements, and localized emergencies were assumed to be the pattern for the future. Apparently the government was particularly influenced by the Jordan operation in 1958 and it was accepted that this sort of emergency could be expected to recur with some regularity in succeeding years.[59]

Two important assumptions underlying British policy were spelt out by the Minister of Defence during the 1959 debate. In the first place, Sandys explained, the circumstances in which Britain might have to carry out military operations on her own were extremely limited: 'In fact, apart from internal security duties and the defence of British colonies and protecting territories against local attack, I find it hard to visualise any wars which we might have to fight alone without allies.'[60]

For a major policy declaration this statement left a lot unsaid. To begin with, it implied that the defence of the colonies and other dependent territories was unlikely to involve Britain in a major military campaign. To what extent this view was actually held is unknown, but there were many in the services who took a different line and one that was subsequently confirmed both in Kuwait and in Malaysia. On the general point, senior officers were agreed that there was never any doctrine that there would be no more independent operations. One minister described the notion as 'nonsense', and he went on to say that, although attempts were made to establish certain parameters, there was never any doubt in his mind that if trouble erupted in a sphere of British influence and British lives were lost, an operation would take place, if necessary independently of allies. He concluded that no theoretical limitation could absolve Britain from that responsibility; nor could it provide a minister with a defence against resignation.

No doubt the message that Sandys intended to convey was that Britain's defence responsibilities were less onerous than many imagined, but he was forced to concede that, in honouring

---

[59] See Army League, *The British Army in the Nuclear Age*, p. 16.
[60] 600 HC Deb., 25 Feb. 1959, col. 1132.

its various colonial obligations, Britain could not expect the United States or any other Western country to underwrite it should it get into difficulties. Once this premise was accepted, however, it meant that, with the exception of tactical nuclear weapons, Britain required a complete armoury and a full range of logistic and supporting facilities as there was always the possibility that a minor colonial skirmish could develop into a major military campaign. In the final analysis, then, Sandys' statement, which at first glance seemed to offer the hope of a more limited role, went very little way towards letting Britain off the hook of military independence. Presumably what it did mean, and here we have to read between the lines as the government never made the point explicitly, was that Britain would not be committed to fighting against a major Communist power without the United States as an ally. This was the conclusion of the Army League and it was a conclusion which seemed to be very widely accepted.[61]

The second assumption spelt out by Sandys was that any colonial wars in which Britain became involved were unlikely to bring her into conflict with major military powers.[62] Translated into practical terms, what this meant was that the service departments were forced to plan on the assumption that Britain's potential enemies east of Suez were unlikely to be equipped with the latest and most sophisticated weaponry. Although Russian equipment was reaching Indonesia and Egypt in considerable quantities, much of it was about ten years old (such as the 'W' class submarines), and it was not seen as requiring Britain to deploy the advanced arms, equipment and aircraft which were needed in Europe. As one senior officer explained, Britain's opponents east of Suez were able only to field a second eleven and we therefore settled for second eleven equipment ourselves. This may have been something of an exaggeration but the fact remains that down to about 1962 the government was satisfied with equipment east of Suez which would not have been accepted in Europe. The change came during the Cuban crisis when policy-makers discovered that Cuba was equipped with the very latest Russian hardware.

The services of course campaigned strenuously for new equipment. In the Defence Committee politicians would list what

[61] Army League, *The British Army in the Nuclear Age*, pp. 15 and 61.
[62] 600 HC Deb., 25 Feb. 1959, col. 1132.

Indonesia or Egypt had today and the Chiefs of Staff would stress what these states might have tomorrow. One senior officer, then in command in an overseas theatre, recalled signing letters protesting that Whitehall was living in a 'fool's paradise'. However, these arguments were to little effect because the government's position was in part merely a rationalization of economic necessity.

It can be argued that, given the balance of forces east of Suez, the government's policy on re-equipment was not unreasonable. However, senior officers were convinced that the government placed too much reliance on the obsolescent nature of the equipment available to the indigenous states. There was some support for this view in Parliament. As early as 1958 the Parliamentary and Financial Secretary to the Admiralty emphasized the need for first-rate ships 'because an increasing number of countries are receiving up-to-date military equipment from behind the Iron Curtain'.[63] In the same debate, George Wigg doubted Britain's ability to undertake independent operations in Bahrain, the Yemen, or Malaya because of outdated equipment.[64]

East of Suez as a British Priority

In the years between 1957 and 1962 the broad level of defence expenditure was accepted without much argument. Although there was some internal questioning in Whitehall, it made little impression on general thinking.[65] Both political parties admitted the need for a large defence budget and some satisfaction was derived from the fact that defence spending, expressed as a percentage of the gross national product, showed a small decline from 8 per cent in 1957 to 7.1 per cent in 1961. Blackaby and Paige have detected a slightly more critical outlook in 1960 and 1961 but it remains true that the level of defence spending never became a major political issue.[66] The

[63] 583 HC Deb., 4 Mar. 1958, col. 986.
[64] Ibid. 26 Feb. 1958, col. 457.
[65] The Treasury made various attempts to review defence spending, especially in the Future Policy Committee, but its efforts met with very little success. Other departments sometimes suggested that resources might more effectively be devoted to economic aid than to defence, but these suggestions never got beyond the stage of preliminary studies.
[66] F. T. Blackaby and D. C. Paige, 'Defence Expenditure: Burden or Stimulus', *Survival*, 2/6 (Nov.–Dec. 1960), p. 242.

dispute arose over what the money should be spent on, and, when it was spent, where the resultant defence forces should be deployed. The debate over what proportion of the defence budget should be devoted to the nuclear element and what proportion to conventional forces will be briefly considered in the next chapter. For the moment, it is enough to realize that decisions in this area take some time to be translated into forces and hardware, and that the immediate issue of these years was to decide what proportion of the defence forces would be deployed in Europe and the Mediterranean, and what proportion should find their way east of Suez.

One factor which affected the government's thinking was the balance of payments problem. Expenditure by military forces stationed abroad, both on government account and for private purposes, constitutes a direct outflow of sterling from the domestic economy and for balance of payments purposes is counted as a deficit (the equivalent of imports into the British economy). It was recognized, of course, that defence inevitably involved some balance of payments cost and that a substantial sum had to be written off as a political necessity. But the steady increase in military expenditure abroad and the downward movement of the current account of the balance of payments during these years led the government to turn an increasingly critical eye to this outflow.

Current Account of Balance of Payments and British Military Expenditure Abroad 1957–1961

(£ million)

	Current Account of Balance of Payments	Military Expenditure in Overseas Sterling Area	Total Military Expenditure Abroad
1957	+216	109	157
1958	+342	108	180
1959	+140	115	167
1960	−272	134	208
1961	−34	139	226

Source: Central Statistical Office, *UK Balance of Payments 1963* (London, HMSO, 1963), tables 1 and 8.

There were important differences between the balance of payment costs of stationing troops in Germany and stationing troops east of Suez—which in effect meant in the sterling area—and for this reason the government adopted different policies in the two areas. Broadly speaking, in the former case the consequences were serious while in the latter they were minimal. Expenditure within the sterling area—about two-thirds of all military expenditures overseas—did not pose a major problem as Britain enjoyed a favourable balance with the rest of the sterling area and in the long run a large share of these out-flows returned to Britain in exchange for British goods. In addition, much of the remainder tended to be added to the sterling balances. For these reasons, the government was not seriously disturbed by military spending east of Suez.[67]

In Europe, however, military expenditures proved a serious problem. The difficulty here was that Britain had an adverse balance of payments with the OEEC countries and the deficit had to be financed by gold and dollars earned elsewhere. In 1957 and 1958 the foreign exchange costs of British forces in Germany ran at about £50 million and despite an annual German contribution of approximately £40 million, the balance of payment burden figured heavily in the decision taken in 1957 to reduce BAOR from about 77,000 to about 64,000, and the further reduction to 55,000 during 1958-9. In January 1958 the United Kingdom case for financial relief was endorsed by three independent experts appointed by the Secretary General of NATO, and the NATO Council subsequently accepted their conclusion that the cost of stationing troops in Germany represented a heavy additional burden on the United Kingdom balance of payments.[68] While negotiations were taking place the 1958 White Paper gave a warning that unless adequate financial assistance was forthcoming the government would have to reconsider the size of the forces retained on the Continent.[69]

However, after extensive discussions, Germany would only agree to a payment of approximately £12 million annually for the years 1959, 1960, and 1961. This led the government to plan on the basis of a strength of 45,000 for the period 1959 to March 1961 and to make certain reductions in the 2nd Tactical Air Force towards the end of the financial year

[67] See Snyder, pp. 219–22, esp. the comments of certain civil servants quoted on pp. 221–2.
[68] 589 HC Deb., 10 June 1958, coll. 11–13.
[69] MoD, *Report on Defence*, Cmnd 363 (1958), para. 43.

1960–61.[70] The possibility of further British withdrawals brought a storm of protests from the NATO countries and in particular aroused the strong opposition of SHAPE and of Dr Adenauer. General Sir Richard Gale, then Deputy Supreme Allied Commander Europe, flew to London to argue that Britain should not implement the proposed reductions. He pointed out to Macmillan that the treaty permitted temporary withdrawal of national forces for operations elsewhere and that therefore a proportion of the strategic reserve could be maintained as part of BAOR.[71] With some reluctance, Macmillan agreed to stay his hand. 'For the time being' Britain would retain seven brigade groups in BAOR and would defer the withdrawal of certain fighter squadrons from RAF Germany.[72] Despite the increasing pressure on the balance of payments as foreign exchange costs rose to about £75 million annually, the government adhered to the figure of seven brigade groups. However, by 1960 BAOR was two battalions short and many of the units were considerably under strength.[73]

The European withdrawals in 1957 and 1958 had the effect of easing the pressure on British deployments east of Suez. The reduction in force levels necessitated by the ending of National Service in 1962 had led many to anticipate wholesale withdrawals from the Indian Ocean area and a serious cut in British capability. However, these fears proved groundless. One important factor, no doubt, was that British troops were still involved in anti-terrorist operations in Malaya and were continually being called upon to put down some tribal revolt or border skirmish in the Arabian Peninsula and the Persian Gulf. For these and other reasons the 1958 White Paper was able to announce that Britain still maintained armed forces of over 100,000 men in the Far East and the Middle East.[74] A month later the First Lord of the Admiralty told the House of Lords that in general terms Britain's position in the Indian Ocean was not greatly dissimilar to what it had been before. Looking to the future, the army and the air force would be broadly on the same basis, while the navy would if anything

---

[70] 589 HC Deb., 10 June 1958 coll. 11–13.
[71] MoD, *Report on Defence 1960*, Cmnd 952, para. 5.
[72] Gen Sir Richard Gale, *Call to Arms* (1968), p. 209.
[73] See further *Times*, 28 July 1960, and F. W. Mulley, *The Politics of Western Defence* (1962), p. 133.
[74] Cmnd 363, para. 39.

be a little stronger, because of the addition of an aircraft carrier and a commando carrier.[75]

Until about 1960 force levels in the Indian Ocean remained much the same as during the mid-fifties, and proportionately the area fared better than ever. Official figures are not available, but according to one informed estimate the Indian Ocean had gained slightly since 1958 at the expense of Europe and the Mediterranean. In terms of army manpower, while BAOR was reduced by a further two battalions between 1958 and 1960, and the number of battalions stationed in the Mediterranean had been cut from twenty-two to seven, three and a half additional battalions were stationed in Africa, the garrisons in the Arabian Peninsula had been reduced by only half a battalion (the number of troops deployed there was actually greater because armoured units and a Royal Marine Commando had been added), and those in the Far East had been reduced by one battalion.[76] The defence White Papers and ministerial speeches told much the same story. The government gave little indication that the military importance of the commitment of troops to Germany weighed at all heavily upon it; the Mediterranean was seen as an area of decreased strategic importance; the Indian Ocean commitment retained its old hold.

If anything, 1960 saw an increasing emphasis on Britain's role east of Suez. It is difficult to document the slight sharpening of focus, as it rested more on decisions taken regarding hardware and force structures than on any changed appreciation of the risks of conflict in the Indian Ocean area *vis-à-vis* Europe. However, the gist of military thinking, the strengthening of Britain's strategically mobile capability, and the movement of some additional forces into the region all indicate the government's tendency to upgrade the east of Suez role. In an article entitled 'Britain's Defence Emphasis Shifts East', *The Times* defence correspondent noted that the navy's Amphibious Warfare Squadron, which was then based on Malta, was to be moved to the Arabian Peninsula in the summer.[77] More armour was also being stationed east of Suez. One

[75] 207 HL Deb., 6 Mar. 1958, coll. 1205–6.
[76] *Times*, 28 July 1960. These figures give a slightly misleading impression as some troops previously stationed in the Mediterranean and available for east of Suez duties had to be moved into the area because of the emergence of the Middle East air barrier.
[77] 15 Mar. 1960.

squadron of the Queen's Own Hussars, equipped with Centurion tanks, sailed for Aden in February and the rest of the regiment moved to Kenya later in the year. In the spring 45 Royal Marine Commando, with a strength of about 600 men, moved to Aden. These developments aroused considerable misgivings in the Labour party which was more than ever concerned to give Britain's conventional contribution to NATO a far higher priority.

The trend of 1960 was confirmed in 1961. Harold Watkinson, Minister of Defence, declared that 'the risk of an incident which might lead to limited or unlimited war is perhaps more likely outside the NATO area than within it.[78] He went on to state in unmistakable terms the government's intention of retaining its overseas commitments and of ensuring that Britain had sufficient power of the right kind to meet these obligations. The opposition was equally unequivocal: NATO must be Britain's number one priority; the world-wide distribution of troops did not belong to the 1960s; Britain should gradually withdraw from its onerous commitments east of Suez. A number of influential newspapers took up the cry. The *Observer* likened Britain to a man whose umbrella had been torn to shreds by the wind but who still insisted on carrying the spokes.[79] *The Times* adopted a more restrained line but it agreed that Europe must take precedence over the Middle East and the Far East: '. . . the first claim must be for Europe. It is here, apparently, that Britain's political and economic future lies, and it is here in the North Atlantic Treaty Organisation, that its main military strength should be applied.'[80]

On the Labour side, only George Wigg, in words which were often to be repeated in succeeding years, firmly defended the east of Suez emphasis.[81] Wigg took strong exception to Christopher Mayhew's remarks about nineteenth century ideas and deployments and by implication he rebuked R. H. S. Crossman for his description of many of Britain's African and

---

[78] 635 HC Deb., 27 Feb. 1961, col. 1202.
[79] 12 Nov. 1961.
[80] 27 Oct. 1961. See also *Times*, 22 and 23 Aug. 1961; *Observer*, 17 Sept. 1961 (Anthony Verrier), and 10 Dec. 1961 (Sir William Hayter). For a contrary view see *Daily Telegraph*, 15 Nov. 1961 (Brig W. F. K. Thompson).
[81] See 635 HC Deb., 27 Feb. 1961, coll. 1286–7 and 636 HC Deb., 7 Mar. 1961, coll. 317–20. There were some Labour members such as F. J. Bellenger and Reginald Paget who adopted a mid-way position.

Indian Ocean obligations as the 'fag end' of imperial commitments. Referring to the despatch of British troops to the Southern
Cameroons in August 1960, he declared:

It ought not to be suggested to those officers and men that they are
the last vestige of imperialism. They should be told that they are
discharging a duty in accordance with the noblest traditions of our
race. There is no-one who can stand up in the House of Commons
and say that Britain has sent those men out there either in her own
interests or in those of her friends. They are discharging a most
uncomfortable United Nations job and they are doing it in the most
difficult of conditions.[82]

[82] 636 HC Deb., 7 Mar. 1961, col. 320.

CHAPTER FIVE

Development of Strategic Mobility
1958–1961

By 1958 the broad guide-lines of Britain's overseas defence policy were clearly established but it remained to examine more closely their implications and inter-relationships, to modify or develop various aspects as required, and to invest the new policies with the substance which previously they had lacked. Of the three services, the navy did most during these years to push forward the boundaries of its limited-war role, partly because its scheme for overseas security emerged later and was not so fully developed as that of the airlifted strategic reserve, and partly because this was where it saw its *raison d'être*. The air force too made progress, more rapidly at the beginning of the sixties than in 1958 and 1959. Increasingly it came to regard the east of Suez role as a back-stop which would strengthen its financial hand, give it some hardware, and help preserve its separate identity. By the very nature of its role, the army had less scope for strategic theorizing. Although still deeply committed to the east of Suez venture, its efforts to adapt to the deepening British involvement were restricted to lower-level considerations such as air portability, helicopters, and light aviation.

The manpower and matériel limitations imposed by the Sandys formula presented service chiefs with a formidable problem: to maintain the same capability for operations east of Suez with very much smaller forces and only marginally increased allocations for weapons and equipment. Nor did the situation substantially improve in succeeding years. As the hardware budget steadily rose, so the demands of Britain's east of Suez commitments became greater. The problem took on a different shape according to the perspective of the viewer and each of the services tended to settle for an approach which accorded with its own particular interests. But behind these different conceptions lay certain lines of thinking which were common to all three services. Very early and very clearly it emerged that the key to success was greater mobility and increased co-ordination between the various arms.

Mobility is in many ways an unsatisfactory word. All too often it has been bandied about as a vague but acceptable military objective and it has frequently served as a substitute for detailed thinking or at least detailed explanation. On the one hand, it is sufficiently anodyne to allay suspicion that nothing is being done and, on the other, sufficiently general not to require precise information about projects and developments actually under way. Again as an objective it can readily be accepted as an end in itself, thus diverting attention from the problem in hand and serving to avoid what could be embarrassing disclosures about capability, and perhaps the admission that capability is in no way commensurate with commitments. Nevertheless, admitting all the dangers, it is a useful shorthand way of referring to the ability to move men and matériel rapidly from one location to another. In the present context the basic point was that if forces could be transported quickly and redeployed from one theatre to another as circumstance required, they could be smaller, because of the consequent savings in the pipeline and in garrisons, training depots, administrative headquarters, and so on. It was scarcely an exaggeration when the Army League declared that 'the essence of this country's overseas military problem is mobility.'[1]

Three factors worked to increase the importance of close co-ordination between the various fighting arms. The changes in weaponry and in the composition of forces meant that by 1958 operations had become joint-service affairs, even if this had not always been the case in past years. The strain imposed by manpower and financial ceilings provided a new incentive to eliminate or at least to minimize overlapping roles and duplicated efforts. And the development of greater mobility brought in its trail new problems of co-ordination in command,

[1] *The British Army in the Nuclear Age*, p. 29.

organization, and supply which became increasingly difficult to ignore. Repeatedly ministers, senior officers, and independent commentators stressed these points and the solutions canvassed varied from proposals to improve co-ordination at the 'sharp end' to integration in Whitehall. The approach adopted, however, was to aim at something less than integration and to work from the grass-roots upwards – that is, from formations in the field. Although some improvement took place, the conclusion can hardly be avoided that in this area the performance of the services was disappointing.

The Shifting Balance Between Nuclear and Conventional Forces

Service endeavours to strengthen their respective stakes in the east of Suez enterprise took place against a background of continued struggle between the nuclear and conventional components for resources from a defence budget with a relatively fixed ceiling. Broadly, 1958 saw very little change in the priorities established in 1957, but thereafter a cautious and by no means fully explicit shift of emphasis took place. Although the government adhered to the basic principles of the Sandys doctrine, it gradually moved away from its reliance on an over-simplified interpretation of the potentialities of nuclear power and the disproportionate resource allocation which it involved. It is not possible to argue this case in any precise way as no figures are available to show the breakdown of the defence budget as between nuclear and conventional allocations. Nonetheless the trend emerges plainly both from government statements and from actual hardware procurements.

The 1958 White Paper restated the doctrine of massive retaliation in much the same terms as one year earlier and in a way which appeared even to go beyond American policy.[2] The text gave no indication that the government was concerned to upgrade the priority of the conventional component, and the few proposals relating to conventional defence preparations were barely sufficient to maintain the 1957 balance. In 1959 the first steps were taken to redress the balance between nuclear

[2] See MoD, *Report on Defence*, Cmnd 363. Already the Pentagon was moving towards a more narrowly defined nuclear role. See *New York Times*, 15 Feb. 1958.

and conventional forces with the decision to allow the army to recruit up to a ceiling of 180,000 men instead of 165,000, and the approval of a number of important projects and procurements relating to weapons and equipment. At this stage, however, the government was content to operate on the basis of the 1957 model and no doctrinal adjustments were forthcoming. The White Paper was strictly a summary of work in progress and developments planned, and nothing was said about the balance between nuclear and conventional forces. *The Economist* concluded that policy was 'unchanged and unexplained'.[3] According to *The Times*: 'This year's Defence White Paper, except for the change of policy over the strength of the army, is last year's writ quietly.'[4]

If the White Paper was taken in isolation these comments were by no means unreasonable, but they lightly passed over the government's weapons and equipment policies, and in any event they tended to over-emphasize the importance of the annual statement on defence. Already there were signs that the government was adapting its strategic thinking to the needs of limited war. In the subsequent debate in the Commons it was noticeable that ministers placed more emphasis on plans to strengthen conventional capability than on the government's nuclear programme. Sandys himself declared that in reshaping the navy and replanning the distribution of its ships and bases, 'especial weight' had been given to its task in peace and limited war.[5] The Secretary of State for War spoke at length about the re-equipment of the Regular army and made a point of stressing that the decision to raise the army's recruiting target was in line with recent experience, notably in Cyprus, which had shown that a higher strength was desirable.[6] The same pattern was apparent in the government's treatment of the air force. Apart from the now customary recitation that Transport Command's capacity was increasing by leaps and bounds, three ministers successively told the House that the TSR2 was primarily designed for the non-nuclear role and that it would be able to intervene decisively in local

---

[3] 14 Feb. 1959.
[4] 25 Feb. 1959.
[5] 600 HC Deb., 25 Feb. 1959, col. 1134.
[6] 601 HC Deb., 3 Mar. 1959, coll. 228–50 and esp. col. 229. But compare the reasoning of MoD, *Progress of the Five-Year Defence Plan*, Cmnd 662 (1959), para. 27.

conflicts in the strike, reconnaissance, and ground support roles.[7]

At the same time but behind the scenes, military planners were going ahead with projects which, when they materialized, would substantially increase Britain's conventional capability. Each of the services was coming to view the nuclear priority with more dissatisfaction and there seems to have been a widespread feeling that before too long there would be a renewed emphasis on conventional forces and weaponry. Service opposition stemmed partly from the belief that each arm represented a particular form of power and that nuclear rockets cut across the traditional boundaries and threatened service identities. It was also linked with the preference for mobile power, and if atomic weapons and guided missiles were not exactly synonymous with continental power, they at least represented a very different form of mobility from that to which the services were accustomed. In short, all three services saw their roles and their hardware threatened by weapons which, on the one hand, had little service allegiance, and on the other, were so expensive that there was not much left over for conventional arms.[8] Moreover, particularly in the case of the army, there were compelling practical reasons to resist the government's nuclear obsession. Whatever the politicians might say, overseas commitments seemed likely to be as onerous as ever and there were few in the services who saw nuclear weapons as a substitute for well-equipped conventional forces. General Sir John Cowley's much publicized criticism of the government's nuclear philosophy, although primarily directed towards the European role, was merely the tip of the iceberg and came near the end of a period of growing service discontent.[9] There were many factors, therefore, which in-

[7] Aubrey Jones, 600 HC Deb., 26 Feb. 1959, coll. 1321–2; George Ward, 601 HC Deb., 5 Mar. 1959, col. 635; Airey Neave, ibid. col. 735. According to Jones, Minister of Supply, for the first time in the RAF's history it was to have 'an aircraft designed from the beginning to make use of rudimentary airfields overseas, in other words, to cope with limited war'.

[8] The RAF's enthusiasm for the deterrent waned in face of the planned replacement of the V-bomber force by missiles. In the eyes of the Air Staff, Sandys' conviction that Britain was in the last generation of manned aircraft, except for the transport and tactical roles, jeopardized the RAF's future as a balanced force.

[9] In a speech at the Royal United Service Institution on 4 Nov. 1959. See 'Future Trends in Warfare', *JRUSI*, 105/617 (Feb. 1960), pp. 4–16.

fluenced the Chiefs of Staff to prod the government about conventional forces and in the interval the services pushed forward with plans for new aircraft, ships, and equipment which could be submitted for government approval as the political climate became more favourable.

The steady shift in emphasis of the weapons and equipment programmes continued during the last months of the Sandys regime and even Sandys himself appeared to be having second thoughts about the wisdom of too much reliance on the nuclear deterrent. By the time he changed portfolios in September, therefore, there had been a significant change in the government's attitude to conventional forces and weapons. Even so, there were still many in the services who thought that the government was spending too much on nuclear preparations. It would be mistaken to dismiss service objections simply on the grounds that they represented vested interests. Although the desire to maintain service identities undoubtedly influenced their stand, the military case rested on much the same reading of the international scene as the government's. The disagreement was not so much about what kinds of conflict were likely as about the usefulness of nuclear weapons in situations short of general war. Here the services had the strong support of such responsible newspapers as *The Times*, the *Guardian*, and the *Observer* as well as most of the professional defence commentators.

The appointment of Harold Watkinson as Minister of Defence in the new cabinet which took office in September 1959 brought no sudden change in Britain's overall military policy, but it served to accelerate the trend to strengthen conventional forces. In contrast to Sandys, the new Minister was an administrator rather than a theorist, and he was more impressed with the usefulness of conventional forces east of Suez than he was interested in speculation about nuclear forces and the central balance. Subscribing to the philosophy that the main threat was limited war, and less prepared than Sandys to stand out against determined military pressure, over the next three years Watkinson steadily upgraded Britain's conventional forces and their ancillary and supporting organizations. Speaking at Greenwich in January 1960, he set the tone of the new regime: 'It would be wrong for us to seek to shelter in our defence policy too much under the shadow of the major nuclear deterrent. This means that we must see that we have well-balanced forces, equipped with the best and most modern weapons that are available.'[10]

In line with this pronouncement, the 1960 White Paper further emphasized the importance of mobile forces and announced that steps were being taken to increase the tactical and short-range air transport force and to develop amphibious capability and 'afloat support'. At this stage the government was still engaged on a detailed review of the defence effort and the White Paper therefore attempted no general re-appraisal. For the meantime, it endorsed the five-year plan, subject to the pointed reminder that not everything laid down in 1957 was to be taken as gospel.[11] In the view of *The Times* and *The Economist* this was a satisfactory start for the new Minister, and both drew comfort from the fact that generally the White Paper showed a flexibility which had been little enough in evidence over the past three years.[12] Even more promising was Watkinson's statement, by way of general comment on the government's plans, that the defence review seemed likely to lead to 'greater emphasis on mobility'.[13]

For all the encouraging signs, however, there was a strict limit to the resources available for strengthening Britain's conventional forces. As long as the deterrent remained at the centre of Britain's defence preparations, the more ambitious schemes of the military planners—a new generation of aircraft carriers, a massive increase in the capacity of Transport Command such as envisaged by a number of politicians in the mid-fifties—had scant hope of fulfilment. For a start, routine expenses took up about half the annual defence budget. In 1960, for example, 49 per cent of total defence expenditure went on paying the forces and looking after them.[14] Add to this the cost of the deterrent, variously estimated at between 10 and 20 per cent, and with the best will in the world and regardless of how much nibbling was done around the edges of the nuclear component, the development of conventional capability was inevitably a piece-meal affair.

[10] *Times*, 9 Jan. 1960. Editorially, *The Times* described Watkinson's statement as 'refreshing'.
[11] MoD, *Report on Defence 1960*, Cmnd 952, para. 2.
[12] *Times*, 17 Feb. 1960. *Economist*, 20 Feb. 1960.
[13] 618 HC Deb., 29 Feb. 1960, col. 847.
[14] Watkinson, 618 HC Deb., 29 Feb. 1960, col. 849.

For this reason the 1961 White Paper, although it carried the conventional emphasis further, could hardly live up to the more sanguine hopes of some of the government's critics. According to the White Paper, the nuclear deterrent cost about 10 per cent of the defence budget. But as *The Times* pointed out, this figure was misleading as it covered only bombers and offensive weapons; nothing was said about the cost of the fighters and missiles used to protect the deterrent bases nor about the cost of the early warning system necessary to get the bombers off the ground in time. In past years the government had admitted that these took up a further 10 per cent.[15] Nevertheless, the White Paper acknowledged the limitations of nuclear deterrence and its thrust was directed to strengthening strategically mobile forces. Therefore it was generally conceded that the report was the most heartening issued since the arrival of Duncan Sandys on the defence scene.[16] *The Times* even went so far as to comment, 'This year, for the first time, the Government's defence policy has been written in the light of the nuclear stalemate.'[17]

Command and Co-ordination

Among other factors the development of the policies of strategic mobility gave a new edge to the problems of co-ordinating the planning and force structures of the three services and of the various geographical commands. In accordance with traditional practice, the conduct of defence east of Suez still rested with the individual services and the various command headquarters. For some years this system had produced its difficulties inasmuch as the services no longer represented functional units, and the command headquarters reflected the heritage of empire rather than the needs of contemporary strategy. But it had been possible to make certain adjustments and modifications and to pass lightly over the anomalous nature of the division of responsibility and the framework of command, communication, and co-ordination. So long as National Service remained on the statute book, manpower was adequate for the tasks in hand, and there were

[15] 15 Feb. 1961.
[16] See e.g. FM Lord Harding's comments, 229 HL Deb., 15 Mar. 1961, col. 912.
[17] 27 Feb. 1961.

few forces or pieces of hardware that could not be fitted into the existing structure without too much straining of traditional boundaries.[18] By the early sixties the problems had become more obvious and more pressing but still little systematic progress was made in the way in which they were tackled.

One development which impinged directly on east of Suez policy could hardly escape attention. The emergence of the Middle Eastern air barrier had the effect of dividing the area of Britain's overseas responsibilities into two parts. No longer was it possible to rely on airlifting troops from Britain to points east of Suez in an emergency. At the very least, delays were involved because of the circuitous routes. During the Jordan operation in 1958 both Israel and the Sudan suspended over-flying rights and for a period British aircraft had to be diverted over the Congo.[19] By 1960 the southern route had been pushed deeper into Africa and ran from Malta to Kano in Nigeria and thence across Central Africa to Nairobi in Kenya.[20] Under these conditions, *The Times* estimated that it would take about eight days to move a brigade group by air from Britain to east of Suez.[21] At worst, strategists feared that the events in the Congo and the impending change in the political status of Nigeria, and later of Kenya, might close the African route altogether. The Middle Eastern sea passage was equally uncertain. Once control of the Suez Canal passed to the Egyptian government naval strategists could no longer assume that warships would be free to pass through the canal to take part in operations in the Indian Ocean.[22]

One result of these developments was to give the east of Suez area a strategic coherence for British planners which it had not had since the days when Britain had been responsible for the defence of India. If forces could not be moved eastward as circumstance required, and if developments in the Arabian Peninsula, for example, could no longer be controlled from a

[18] The Marines were, of course, most immediately concerned with the inter-service problem and it was this corps which was worst served by the continuance of the tri-service mentality. It is relevant that two of the foremost advocates of service integration – Lord Mountbatten and Maj Gen J. L. Moulton – had both been concerned with amphibious operations, respectively as Chief of Combined Operations and Chief of Amphibious Warfare.

[19] DeWitt C. Armstrong, 'The Changing Strategy of British Bases', p. 239.

[20] Army League, *The British Army in the Nuclear Age*, p. 37.

[21] 15 Mar. 1960.

[22] V Adm Sir Peter Gretton, *Maritime Strategy* (1965), p. 50.

headquarters in Cyrpus, what was needed, and was recognized as needed, was a defence establishment east of Suez which would be self-sufficient, at least for the early stages of an emergency. This reasoning lay behind many of the strategic developments of the years 1958–61: the establishment of elements of the strategic reserve in Kenya and Singapore, the pre-positioning of heavy equipment and supplies at select points in the area, the maintenance of a balanced fleet based on Singapore, the stationing of the Amphibious Warfare Squadron at Aden, and the reorganization of Middle East and East Africa Commands at the end of 1957.[23]

Important as these new measures were, it is not too far from the truth to say they were forced upon the defence establishment by developments over which it had no control. In a sense, they were the minimum adjustment that had to be made if the old power structure was to pass down into the sixties. As each year passed, however, the performance of the new defence sub-system came more and more to depend on the degree of co-ordination between the services operating within the area and the commands which were responsible for ordering defence effort. Here the pressure of external developments lost most of its momentum, and initiative had to come from within the defence establishment. And it was here in fact that very little progress was made.

To turn first to the command arrangements: the services appear to have shown the utmost resistance to any serious tampering with the systems inherited from empire; with the exception of a very small number of senior planners, the continued utility of control by geographical commands seems to have been accepted without thought or inquiry. Without access to the service reports, it is impossible to avoid the conclusion that changes in the command systems followed changes in the base structure and had very little to do with current strategic concepts. As bases were abandoned, command headquarters were shifted, seemingly as a matter of course, to the next foothold in the line, and the boundaries of responsibility were redrawn with the least possible dislocation to the existing arrangements.

Broadly, the command structure as amended in late 1957 and early 1958 following the reorganization of Middle East

[23] For discussion of this reorganization see pp. 125–6 above.

Command and the abolition of East Indies Command, continued down to 1962 with only slight modification. The only important development was the establishment of a unified command in Aden on 1 April 1958 and reportedly this was secured against determined service opposition. Although it was some time before integration worked its way downwards, by 1959 the new organization was claimed to be working smoothly and to have proved its worth.[24] In 1959 the command was upgraded to conform with the growing strategic importance of the Arabian Peninsula and the western half of the Indian Ocean generally.[25]

Both the unification and the upgrading of the command represented important advances but there remained considerable doubt about whether such a large and unwieldy parish was a manageable proposition. Irrespective of almost any organizational rationalization, the problems of controlling British forces from the Persian Gulf to East Africa seemed to some to be too complex and too disparate to be handled from one headquarters. Shortly after relinquishing the command of British Forces, Arabian Peninsula, Air Vice-Marshal M. L. Heath suggested that a commissioner general might be appointed for the area; on the analogy of South-east Asia, this official could be responsible for co-ordinating the political authorities throughout the area.[26] This interesting suggestion carried with it a hint that, at least in terms of politico-military co-ordination, the new arrangements still left much to be desired.[27] *The Times* stated that Heath's proposal would clearly reduce the burden on the Commander-in-Chief, but it favoured separating East Africa from the Arabian Peninsula Command.[28] Neither of these suggestions made any headway in Whitehall, although in the former case recommendations were forwarded to the Ministry of Defence.

In the Far East the existing command arrangements continued without much change until November 1962. The area

---

[24] MoD, *Progress of the Five-Year Defence Plan*, Cmnd 662, para. 24.

[25] See *Times*, 16 Apr. 1959, and *Observer*, 13 Sept. 1959.

[26] Speaking at the Royal United Service Institution, *Times*, 14 Jan. 1960.

[27] The C in C had to concert his actions with the requirements of the Governors of Aden, Kenya, Somaliland, Tanganyika, and Uganda, and the Political Resident, Persian Gulf. Apparently, therefore, he was often absorbed in diplomatic duties, to the neglect of military ones.

[28] *Times*, 14 Jan. 1960.

of the service commands was widened as a result of the abolition of the naval and air East Indies Commands in late 1957
and the disbandment of the army's Malaya Command in
1958. In addition, there were increased burdens of responsibility which flowed from the development of strategically
mobile forces in the area and from the general policy of increased centralization of control, communications, and supply
on the Singapore base. The three service commanders were
informed about political and diplomatic correspondence,
and at regular intervals met in committee together with the
Commissioner General to decide matters of general policy and
to consider high-level problems of co-ordination. Reportedly,
it was often difficult to reach decisions and there were times
when service commanders left meetings with quite different
conceptions of the policies to be pursued.

Early in 1959 it was announced that the possibility of setting
up a unified command in the Far East was under examination.[29]
A number of senior officers were strongly opposed to the proposal and Field Marshal Sir Francis Festing and Air Vice-
Marshal Heath were sent to Singapore to investigate the problems and to persuade the local commanders of the advantages
of the system. In May 1962 it was announced that the proposal
would be pushed forward.[30] Partly as a result of Mountbatten's
initiative, on 28 November 1962 the unified command was
finally inaugurated—sixteen years after the dissolution of
Mountbatten's wartime unified command and his personal
recommendation that a supreme commander with a small
staff be left in Singapore, to co-ordinate planning and to conduct inter-service exercises.[31] Only when the files are opened
can the record of those sixteen years be told. However, remem-
bering the inter-service difficulties recorded by Mountbatten
and the occasional glimpses of friction which appeared publicly,
it will be surprising indeed if it is not a somewhat sorry tale.

The establishment of the unified command brought no immediate improvement. In the field of policy co-ordination it
merely replaced the British Defence Forces Co-ordinating
Committee, its scope in administrative matters was very limited,

[29] MoD, *Progress of the Five-Year Defence Plan*, Cmnd 662, para. 24.
[30] *Times*, 19 Sept. 1962.
[31] *Report to the Combined Chiefs of Staff by the Supreme Allied Commander South-East Asia 1943–45*, para. 30.

B.D.P.—7

and it involved a considerable increase in staff and cost.[32] More than ten months after its inception the Commander-in-Chief admitted to members of an Estimates subcommittee that the unified command had not achieved the success of the organization in Aden.[33] It was suggested that this might partly be explained by the difference between the situation in Aden, which remained essentially an RAF command to which army and navy units had been attached, and that in Singapore, where each service had built up its own substantial headquarters organization operating autonomously.[34] Equally relevant, the diversity of service interests and requirements and the geographical separation of the three service headquarters placed formidable obstacles in the way of closer co-operation.

The state of co-ordination between the various geographical commands is rather less clear. The difficulty here is that because forces and hardware were in short supply it is far from easy to assess the extent to which planning difficulties resulted from over-commitment or from poor co-ordination. However, it would seem that co-ordination between commands, particularly between Middle Eastern and Far Eastern, was often unsatisfactory. By way of illustration, one senior officer spoke at length about the complications which in 1960 surrounded contingency planning for the defence of Kuwait. Both the commando carrier and the aircraft carrier stationed in the Indian Ocean came under Far East Command, and Middle East Command was unable to rely on their availability in time of need. The ships were therefore regarded as a 'useful bonus' but could not be made the basis of Persian Gulf planning.[35] Similar arguments took place about aircraft dispositions. In the case of the army, it was said there was less requirement for close liaison and one army commander admitted that he had little contact with his opposite number.

The independence of the services emerged relatively unscathed from the battle for unification in 1957 and 1958.

[32] See HC, *Ninth Report from Estimates Committee ... Session 1963–64: Military Expenditure Overseas* (1964), pp. xix–xx, paras 49–52, and pp. 156–7, paras 2 and 3.
[33] Ibid. p. xix, para. 50.
[34] Ibid.
[35] There was an additional factor here as Admiralty policy was opposed to committing carriers and commando ships to contingency plans, except in a most provisional way. In retrospect, opinions varied about the wisdom of this policy and its implications.

Macmillan sided with the services in the major engagement before the publication of the 1957 White Paper and Sandys was forced to abandon his plans for complete integration. However, still hopeful that something might be achieved, in April 1957 Sandys announced a Defence Administration Committee to investigate the problems of service unification. Little more was publicly heard of this committee, but for some months a fierce debate raged in Whitehall over both the unification issue and proposals for further centralization of authority. The outcome of the debate was recorded in the White Paper *Central Organization for Defence* in July 1958. This paper represented a major victory for the service departments. Despite the assertion of the overall authority of the Minister and certain improvements in the decision-making apparatus, Sandys' unification proposals were blocked at every point.[36] For the remainder of the period, unification and stronger central control over the service departments were dead issues in Whitehall. There is no question that the existing machinery for co-ordinating the planning and programmes of the three services failed to prevent serious duplication of effort and frequent inter-service conflict.[37] The government admitted as much when it introduced new machinery for central control in 1963: 'The arrangements set out in the 1958 White Paper (Command 476) have not in practice secured the degree of central control over defence policy which is necessary in the national interest.[38]

At the lower levels some improvement in co-ordination between the various arms took place. In large part this was forced upon the services, but it was also the opinion of some senior officers that this was the correct way to approach the whole question of integration. It was Mountbatten's idea, for example, that the establishment of unified commands overseas would help to force integration at home. With a unified command at Aden, it was argued, difficulties of communication would eventually lead to the creation of a combined unit in London. In fact that is what happened and a small operational executive was formed at the centre.

Among other relatively modest advances, these years saw

[36] For comment see Martin, 'The Market for Strategic Ideas in Britain', *Amer. polit. Sci. R.*, 56/1 (Mar. 1962), p. 30; and D. Divine, *The Blunted Sword* (1964), p. 14.
[37] See M. Howard, *The Central Organisation of Defence*, pp. 10–13.
[38] MoD, *Central Organisation for Defence*, Cmnd 2097 (1963), para. 5.

the re-activation of No. 38 Group RAF with responsibility for providing tactical and short-range air transport and air support for the army, a substantial increase in the number of airborne exercises, and systematic experiments to modify army equipment to make it air-portable.[39]

Establishments such as the School of Land/Sea Warfare at Old Sarum, near Salisbury, the Amphibious Warfare Training Centre at Poole, and bodies like the Joint Services Staff College continued to develop inter-service techniques and habits of co-operation, within the limits of their competence and resources. But much remained to be done. The problem of standardizing service stores and their code numbers, accountancy practices, and transfer procedures remained largely untouched. There were still no combined training centres overseas. The establishment of the Army Air Corps in September 1957 was a monument to the failure of army-air force co-operation. The Army League drew attention to the unsatisfactory nature of the navy's approach to amphibious operations and to the embarrassment which attended the army's dependence on the other services for support logistics. Particular difficulty, it claimed, stemmed from not having LSTs under army command.[40] In its later report the League claimed that integration still had a long way to go and it cited administration and communications as fields where there was much scope for further integration.[41]

Air Mobility

Between 1957 and 1962 the long-awaited and much heralded expansion of Transport Command at last got under way. Some twelve years after the idea of an air-lifted strategic reserve had first gained currency in defence circles, and about four years after the scheme had become government policy, the provision of transport aircraft began to obtain the firm backing of the government and of the Air Staff. Expenditure on transport types of aircraft and spares for the period from 1958–59 to 1961–62 totalled £80 million, as compared with an expendi-

---

[39] These developments are discussed on pp. 188–9 below.
[40] *The British Army in the Nuclear Age*, p. 44.
[41] *The Army Britain Needs* (1964), pp. 34–5.

ture of £52·5 million for the period 1954–55 to 1957–58.[42] Even so, the expansion of the transport fleet proceeded in a piecemeal fashion. Initial orders for a particular aircraft were usually small and they were then increased year by year. In many cases the RAF did not participate in civil projects until late stages of development. Generally transport requirements were broadened more in 1960 and 1961 than in 1958 and 1959. The Assistant Under-Secretary of State (Supply) explained to an Estimates sub-committee that the 1957 forward-look costing had projected a total transport force (including helicopters) of about 130 aircraft by the spring of 1963, whereas in fact in 1963 it was about 260.[43] However, the Estimates Committee considered even the 1963 figure inadequate and it noted that only two of the ten types of transport aircraft then in service could be described as modern aircraft. Not altogether unfairly, it concluded that 'the present number and age of the transport aircraft possessed by the RAF is an adequate commentary on the efficacy of the Air Ministry's advance planning.'[44]

Various factors lay behind the Air Staff's reluctance to plan more boldly, but the fact remains that the expansion of Transport Command was the product of a distinct change in RAF outlook. Two factors seem to have contributed to this change of heart on the part of the Air Staff. First, a genuine recognition of the necessity for an adequate transport fleet if Britain's overseas commitments were to be met with smaller ground forces. Senior air force officers were perhaps influenced on this point by political pressure and representations from the army. Secondly, the run-down of Fighter Command and the growing doubts about the viability of the bomber force meant that the Air Staff was casting around for a new role and some means of maintaining aircraft numbers at a respectable level.

The broad lines of the Command's expansion can be sketched from the orders and procurements somewhat haphazardly outlined in the Defence White Papers, Air Estimates, and ministerial speeches. Earlier orders for additional Beverleys meant that considerable numbers of these aircraft came into

[42] HC, *Second Report from Estimates Committee . . . Session 1963–64: Transport Aircraft*, p. 119.
[43] Ibid. p. 126, para. 926.
[44] Ibid. p. xv, para. 40.

service in 1957 and 1958. In 1958 the order for 13 Britannias
was increased to 20, and later to 23, and the first of these aircraft appeared in early 1959.[45] The arrival of the Britannias
was a more important development than even its extra payload would indicate, for the important calculations were the
distance the aircraft could fly, its speed and capacity, and the
rate of turn-round at the distant point and at base. Looked
at in this way, when all the Britannias came into service they
would be able to carry a greater number of troops to a given
destination in a given period of days than the rest of the fleet
put together.[46] The most serious gap in the transport force
remained the lack of an aircraft for moving heavy or bulky
cargoes over long distances.[47] In 1959 the Secretary of State
for Air announced that the Belfast had been selected as a strategic freighter.[48] Developmental work continued during 1960
but it was not until February 1961 that it was announced that
a contract had been placed for 10 aircraft.[49] It has been suggested that the Belfast, a turbo-prop aircraft with a cruising
speed of 346 m.p.h., represented a compromise between
RAF specifications and the employment requirements of
Northern Ireland.[50] Apparently the RAF campaigned for a jet
freighter, but an aircraft with a payload of over 35 tons and a
maximum range of some 5,300 miles was acceptable as a useful
stop-gap. The first aircraft did not come into service until
1964.

For the medium-range role—which included the carrying
of troops and supplies within overseas theatres and the dropping
of parachutists—a decision was taken in 1959 to procure the
Argosy.[51] This aircraft could carry 69 troops or 54 paratroops
over a range of 345 miles. Its maximum cruising speed was
268 m.p.h. and its fully loaded range was 345 miles. By early
1960, 20 Argosies were on order and a further 20 were to be

[45] AM, *Memorandum by Secretary of State for Air to Accompany Air Estimates 1958–59*,
Cmnd 373, para. 53, and Kendall, *Air Power*, 7/3 (spring 1960), p. 182.
[46] Army League, *The British Army in the Nuclear Age*, p. 34.
[47] See de Freitas' criticisms, 618 HC Deb., 3 Mar. 1960, col. 1454.
[48] 601 HC Deb., 5 Mar. 1959, col. 634.
[49] AM, *Memorandum by Secretary of State for Air to Accompany Air Estimates 1961–62*
(1961) Cmnd 1292, para. 39.
[50] J. W. R. Taylor, 'No Second Deal Thoughts on Tactical Transport for British
Army Units', *RAF Quarterly*, 2/1 (spring 1962), p. 3.
[51] MoD, *Progress of the Five-Year Defence Plan*, Cmnd 662, para. 13.

ordered shortly.[52] The first deliveries took place in early 1962.

Short-range tactical aircraft, particularly helicopters, had always been a low priority in the eyes of the Air Staff, and despite continued prodding from the army comparatively few machines were available in the period down to 1958. After a visit to Southern Arabia at the beginning of 1959, Lord Harding drew attention to the absence of helicopters in an area where they would have been immensely useful.[53] Lord Shackleton criticized the serious gap in the medium-range helicopter force revealed during an exercise in March 1960.[54] Generally, however, by the late fifties attitudes were changing and new machines slowly became available in reasonable numbers.

To sum up the position it is perhaps useful to reproduce the 1961 figures for transport aircraft.

The RAF Transport Force 1961

Strategic Aircraft
| Britannia | 23 |
| Comet | 10 |

Medium-range Aircraft
Hastings	48
Beverley	32
Valetta	12
Argosy	(5)*

Short-range Aircraft
Pioneer	15
Twin Pioneer	27
Pembroke	4

Transport Support Helicopters
Whirlwind 2/4/10	6 + (17)*
Sycamore 14	15
Belvedere	3 + (9)*

* Numbers in brackets refer to aircraft to be brought into service between April 1961 and March 1962.

Source: AM, *Memorandum by Secretary of State for Air to Accompany Air Estimates 1961–62*, Cmnd 1292, Appendix.

[52] Statement by Under-Secretary of State for Air, 618 HC Deb., 3 Mar. 1960, col. 1566.

[53] 222 HL Deb., 6 Apr. 1960, col. 771. In fact there was a flight of air/sea rescue helicopters but none available for army support. On occasions the ASR helicopters were used in operations. It was said that no military helicopters then available could hover in high temperatures and at high altitudes.

[54] 222 HL Deb., 6 Apr. 1960, col. 737.

By stretching his figures a little, the Secretary of State for Air was able to claim a three-fold increase in carrying capacity since Suez. At the time of the Suez operation, the Command's capacity was about 55 million passenger miles a month. In February 1961 the figure was just short of 150 million passenger miles a month and in an emergency could be doubled. The introduction of the Britannias was the major factor responsible for this increase, but since 1957 the Beverley force had been doubled and the number of Hastings had been greatly increased.[55] Expressed in another way, although for different years, in 1955 Transport Command had an airlift equivalent to 78 Hastings loads. By 1960 it represented the equivalent of some 190 Hastings loads. The introduction of the Argosies would push the figure up to 245, and later with the Belfast freighters to 320.[56]

The development of British air-lift did not prove as fruitful as had been expected by many earlier enthusiasts. The emergence of the air barrier posed an immediate and awkward problem and one that could hardly fail to modify the original conception, with its promise of much lessened reliance on overseas deployments and bases. In addition, a number of difficulties which previously had been overlooked or at least minimized now became apparent as serious limitations. In partial explanation, one very senior RAF officer pointed out that until the transport fleet was expanded there was little opportunity to carry out realistic exercises that could enable planning to go ahead on a practical basis. Even in the late fifties planning was still woolly. In 1960, for example, the Air Staff produced a Chiefs of Staff paper which failed to distinguish between an infantry brigade and a brigade group. Gradually, however, it became apparent that the scale of the east of Suez role and the inevitable restrictions on the development of a massive air transport fleet, the number of air crew required, the need for intermediate refuelling points or flight-refuelling aircraft, and the delays involved in turn-round and re-supply meant that air mobility could be only a partial solution to Britain's problems.[57]

[55] 635 HC Deb., 28 Feb. 1961, col. 1418.
[56] MRAF Sir Dermot Boyle, 'The Next 10 Years', *Air Power*, 7/2 (winter 1959–60), p. 95. For similar extrapolations, though for more limited periods, see the Earl of Selkirk's speech, 207 HL Deb., 6 Mar. 1958, col. 1205, and that of the Earl of Home, 214 HL Deb., 10 Mar. 1959, col. 857.
[57] See generally DeWitt C. Armstrong, 'The Changing Strategy of British Bases', pp. 229–37; Snyder, pp. 12 and 14; and N. Brown, *Strategic Mobility*, ch. 6.

The most important modification to the original scheme was the decision to station elements of the strategic reserve in Kenya and Malaya. The immediate motive was to counter the emergence of the Middle Eastern air barrier but the need to acclimatize troops, psychologically and politically as well as physically, and to familiarize them with jungle and desert conditions, strengthened the case for overseas reserves. Another consideration was the deterrent effect of visible power. The decision announced in November 1957 to station an element of the strategic reserve in Kenya was followed by considerable speculation in the press about the number of troops likely to be garrisoned there. When the 1958 Army Estimates were published, it was understood that only one battalion would be moved, but in August the War Office announced that two battalions would be permanently stationed in Kenya.[58] By March 1959 a company of a third battalion had been added, and one year later the reserve had increased by an additional battalion, plus a headquarters and some engineers.[59] Less publicity attended the formation of the Malayan reserve – no doubt because this was largely a matter of changing the label on troops already there. The 1961 White Paper said simply that a reserve of forces was also maintained in Malaya.[60] Presumably this referred to the Commonwealth Brigade group but no government confirmation was forthcoming.

Considerable doubt surrounded the strength of the main part of the reserve stationed in the United Kingdom. As already noted, it was not War Office policy to release the size of the reserve, and the constant movement of units between the United Kingdom and overseas theatres made it difficult for unofficial observers to write with any degree of certainty. In March 1959 the 3rd Division was earmarked as part of the strategic reserve and its training programme was adjusted to the requirements of limited war. In theory it was to be kept as a 'larger combat force'; in practice, units would be despatched at short notice and others designated to replace them. According to a *Guardian* report in 1960, although elements of

---

[58] *Manchester Guardian*, 17 Mar. 1958; *Times*, 27 Aug. 1958.
[59] *Manchester Guardian*, 25 Mar. 1959; *Guardian*, 23 Feb. 1960; *Times*, 28 July 1960. According to reports in the *Daily Telegraph*, 2 Mar. 1960 and 19 July 1960, the government intended to station a brigade group in Kenya as part of the strategic reserve.
[60] MoD, *Report on Defence 1961*, Cmnd 1288, para. 13.

the 1st and 3rd Divisions were stationed in Britain, and units in Colchester and on Salisbury Plain were assigned sometimes to one and sometimes to the other, there was no evidence of any substantial force. Two brigades seemed about the likely figure.[61] In 1961 *The Times* listed the Parachute Brigade (less 1 battalion in Cyprus), 51st Infantry Brigade, and 19th Infantry Brigade as in theory constituting the central reserve. However, it emphasized that the reserve was simply a loose organization of brigade groups and implied that it would be unrealistic to attach too much significance to its formal composition.[62]

The establishment of elements of the strategic reserve in Kenya and Malaya carried with it the need to deploy sections of the transport fleet in both these places. This was not entirely a new problem as it had always been necessary to maintain transport aircraft in overseas theatres. The number of aircraft required was now considerably greater, however, not only for actual operations, but for exercises and intensive training. In 1959 the Far Eastern Air Force included Beverleys, Hastings, and small numbers of Pembrokes, Pioneers, Twin Pioneers, and Sycamore and Whirlwind helicopters.[63] Headquarters, British Forces, Arabian Peninsula, had at its disposal a few Beverleys, a number of Pembroke, Pioneer and Twin Pioneer light aircraft, and some recently arrived Sycamore helicopters.[64] Early in 1959 No. 21 Squadron RAF—with four Twin Pioneers— was formed and flew to Kenya shortly afterwards.[65] Beverleys arrived later in the year.[66]

In view of certain disclosures which followed Lord Merrivale's visit to Aden in September 1959, there is some doubt about the efficacy of the overseas transport forces. Speaking in the House of Lords in December, Lord Merrivale drew attention to problems relating to the Beverley, the Sycamore helicopter, and the twin-engine Pioneer. Replying for the government, the Earl of Onslow admitted that difficulties had

[61] 23 Feb. 1960.
[62] 18 Aug. 1961. The details given relate to the period before the Kuwait operation in July.
[63] AM, *Memorandum by Secretary of State for Air to Accompany Air Estimates 1959–60* (1959), Cmnd 673, appendix 3.
[64] Ibid.
[65] *Manchester Guardian*, 25 Mar. 1959.
[66] AM, *Memorandum by Secretary of State for Air to Accompany Air Estimates 1960–61*, Cmnd 950, para. 37.

been experienced with the supply of spare parts for the Beverley with consequent unserviceability. The original provisioning of spares had been based on the assumption that all Beverleys would be based in the United Kingdom. The subsequent decision to deploy some squadrons overseas had led to a temporary shortage of spares and the problem had been aggravated by the climatic conditions of the Arabian Peninsula. With reference to Lord Merrivale's claim that the Sycamore helicopters were grounded during his visit and 'had been so for several months', Onslow explained that these machines had been temporarily withdrawn owing to difficulties that were found to affect the rotor blades in tropical conditions. In the case of the Pioneers, Onslow admitted that it had been found necessary slightly to reduce their total load because of the very hot conditions.[67]

The second modification to the original conception related to equipment and supplies. Although no one had imagined that all equipment could be moved by air, for some years there was little recognition of the limitations of air freighting or of the implications of the re-supply problem.[68] In an attempt to overcome some of these difficulties, the 1958 White Paper announced that heavy equipment, vehicles, and supplies would be stored at focal points such as Singapore.[69] Apart from the renewed dependence on a number of major bases, such a policy had important limitations. Some idea of the stockpiles required, if overseas depots were to correspond with those in the United Kingdom, is apparent from the fact that it took about 200,000 separate items to maintain an army in the field.[70] Obviously stocks had to be limited because duplication on such a vast scale would have been prohibitively expensive. As the Army League pointed out, once this was decided, it was always a gamble on having the right equipment at the right place at the right time. Moreover, all equipment needed men to keep it serviceable and it was often necessary to test and adjust individual items before use.[71] Then there remained the problem of moving equipment into the battle area. Still, confronted with very little choice, the Ministry of Defence pushed ahead

[67] 220 HL Deb., 7 Dec. 1959, col. 71.
[68] DeWitt C. Armstrong, 'The Changing Strategy of British Bases', p. 230.
[69] MoD, *Report on Defence*, Cmnd 363, para. 40.
[70] *Times*, 27 Aug. 1958.
[71] *The British Army in the Nuclear Age*, pp. 31–2.

with the scheme and major depots were established at Singapore, Aden, and Kenya.

Notwithstanding the diminished optimism about the airlifted strategic reserve, these years saw a considerable improvement in army-air force co-operation. Once the initial enthusiasm had subsided, defence planners turned to consider the practical problems associated with the scheme, and policy became more realistic as a result. By 1960 a general change was apparent in the army's attitude to air mobility. As one writer observed, 'air mindedness' had been slow in coming but the army now began to tackle seriously the matter of closer co-operation with the air force.[72] A similar change of heart was evident in the RAF. Perhaps the most important development was the substantial increase in the number and scope of airborne exercises. In 1959 there were forty-five such exercises, as compared with three in 1956.[73] In 1960 there were three major exercises, including exercise 'Starlight' in the spring which involved the movement of a brigade group to North Africa. In all, 4,800 troops, nearly 300 vehicles, 175 tons of equipment, and 14 helicopters were flown from the United Kingdom to Libya.[74] The move of a battalion of the strategic reserve to Kenya in August was, however, less impressive. Five days were taken for the assembly and despatch of the unit. The *Daily Telegraph* commented that 'the fire-brigade is being kept on the basis which assumes there will be very few fires.'[75] The training programme for 1961–62 included more than 100 air mobility exercises, of which about 50 involved the movement of at least one battalion.[76] Commenting generally on the exercises in these years, one senior army officer spoke of the optimistic assumptions upon which they proceeded. Heavy equipment was always carefully pre-positioned and the shortage of helicopters was often ignored.[77]

[72] Kendall, *Air Power*, 7/3 (spring 1960), p. 183.
[73] AM, *Memorandum by Secretary of State for Air to Accompany Air Estimates 1960–61*, Cmnd 950, para. 26.
[74] AM, *Memorandum by Secretary of State for Air to Accompany Air Estimates 1961–62*, Cmnd 1292, para. 43.
[75] 3 Aug. 1960.
[76] Cmnd 1292, para. 44, and *Memorandum by Secretary of State for Air to Accompany Air Estimates 1962–63* (1962), Cmnd 1630, para. 42.
[77] The shortage of helicopters meant that the army required two systems of movement into the battle area, one based on helicopters and the other on wheeled vehicles.

In 1959 it was disclosed that experiments were being conducted to lighten the load of an infantry battalion (which was then of the order of 56 tons excluding vehicles).[78] Some progress was made over the following years but there was a strict limit to how far weight could be reduced without affecting capability, and taken all round not very much was achieved.[79] More significance must attach to the re-establishment of No. 38 Group in January 1960, for this marked a notable step forward in army-air force co-ordination. The Group was first formed in November 1943 to control war-time airborne forces but in the run-down after 1945 many of the Group's support squadrons were disbanded and the Group itself finally disappeared in 1951. In 1959 the Air Ministry decided to re-activate the Group to organize and co-ordinate land-air operations. Over the next few years it was developed as a self-contained force, equipped with a variety of transport aircraft including helicopters, and eventually fighter and ground attack squadrons.[80]

Seaborne Task Forces

The increased recognition of the limitations of air mobility strengthened the navy's case for seaborne task forces. Indeed, with restricted funds available for defence spending and strong competition between the services, the Admiralty lost no opportunity to point out the shortcomings of the RAF scheme and the advantages attaching to the maritime solution. The Navy League gave prominence to this theme in its monthly journal.[81] Retired admirals spoke out in the press while serving officers discreetly canvassed support within the Ministry of Defence and in other overseas departments.[82] In the Commons the naval lobby adopted the east of Suez role with an enthusiasm which

[78] Statement by Soames, Secretary of State for War, 601 HC Deb., 3 Mar. 1959, col. 240.
[79] E. C. Shepherd, 'Air Support for the Army', *Brassey's Annual 1962*, p. 140.
[80] Gp Capt N. Cameron, 'The 38 Group Concept', *RAF Quarterly*, 2/2 (summer 1962), pp. 101–4, and J. W. R. Taylor, *RAF Quarterly*, 2/1 (spring 1962), p. 5. For later developments see Gp Capt A. R. Gordon-Cumming, 'Fighters in Transport Command', *RAF Quarterly*, 4/4 (winter 1964), pp. 263–6.
[81] See esp. the League's statement to the press, 18 Jan. 1960, emphasizing the need for stronger naval forces east of Suez; *Navy*, 65/2 (Feb. 1960), pp. 46–7.
[82] Crowe, p. 330. Generally see Martin, *Amer. polit. Sci. R.*, 56/1 (Mar. 1962), p. 32.

contrasted sharply with the relative lack of interest in the early fifties. Public reaction was generally favourable. The quality press gave its approval to the naval scheme—indeed the *Observer* and to some extent the *Guardian* tended to promote the Admiralty's cause. Independent commentators accepted it without much question as a sensible complement to the airlifted strategic reserve. B. H. Liddell Hart expressed a decided preference for the marine force. While he recognized that it was essential to have both seaborne and airborne forces, he thought it better that the former be the bigger of the two.[83] In parliament an increasing number of MPs, especially on the government side, were won over to the naval scheme.

In 1959 changes in the top level of the defence hierarchy worked to the navy's advantage. In July Mountbatten, who had served as First Sea Lord from early 1955 and who had steered the navy on to its new limited-war role, became Chief of the Defence Staff. His successor as First Sea Lord was Admiral Sir Charles Lambe, an old friend and collaborator of Mountbatten's, and the two men co-operated closely. The return of Sir Solly Zuckerman to the Ministry of Defence as Chief Scientific Adviser completed the team.[84] Zuckerman had served during the war on Mountbatten's Combined Operations Headquarters, and, despite his RAF background, was known in the Admiralty and outside to be sympathetic towards the naval role. Finally, the appointment of Harold Watkinson as Minister of Defence in September 1959 brought to the political helm a man well disposed towards the navy. Watkinson had served as a lieutenant commander in the RNVR during the Second World War and he was receptive to the Admiralty's plans for seaborne task forces.[85]

It must not go unremarked that the development of the naval scheme met with opposition in certain quarters. Within the Admiralty itself the shift from global to limited war, and from the Atlantic and the Mediterranean to the Indian Ocean, was opposed by a number of more traditionally minded officers. It is difficult to gauge the strength of this group, but there are some reasons for believing that it was considerable and that

[83] *Deterrent or Defence*, p. 127.
[84] Mountbatten and Zuckerman worked hand in glove and in later years it became common to speak of the Mountbatten-Zuckerman axis.
[85] Crowe, p. 214.

certain proposals were pushed through only after a stern fight.[86] Hardly surprisingly, opposition was stronger among retired officers and the old guard of the naval lobby, and the pages of *Navy* contain numerous warnings of the consequences of too great an emphasis on the limited-war role to the neglect of the traditional anti-submarine and anti-mine roles associated with global war. Generally the army favoured the development of amphibious capability and it supported the commando carrier projects, but there was disagreement about command arrangements and friction on certain points of detail.[87] Initially the Air Staff viewed the navy's entry into the limited-war field with some suspicion but it supported the conversion of the commando carrier and it was prepared to accept some expansion of amphibious capability. The plan for a new generation of aircraft carriers brought the RAF into determined opposition and thenceforward the Air Staff regarded the naval scheme as a direct competitor to RAF attempts to secure a larger share of the limited-war budget. Throughout the period the Treasury maintained a close watch over the financial aspects of the Admiralty's proposals and it could be relied upon to oppose any plan which involved a large expenditure on a single weapons system. During the carrier debate, for example, the Treasury emerged as a powerful ally of the Air Council and its economic arguments were marshalled alongside those of the RAF relating to the inferior performance of carrier-borne aircraft.[88]

By the close of 1957, it will be recalled, the Admiralty had settled on the limited-war role as the chief concern of the fleet and it had secured a measure of government support for its changed priorities, including Sandys' acquiescence in the continuance of the aircraft carrier.[89] Despite dissenting views and despite the Admiralty's insistence that the navy still had an anti-submarine role in the event of general war, the limited-war priority was henceforward the basis of naval planning.

---

[86] For a start, one member of the Board of Admiralty was unsympathetic to the limited-war priority. A picture of the diversity of naval views about this time is sketched by a senior naval officer writing under the nom-de-plume 'Blake'; see 'The Modern Navy', *Blackwood's Magazine*, 290/1751 (Sept. 1961), pp. 193–4.

[87] See Crowe, pp. 200–1, and Army League, *The British Army in the Nuclear Age*, p. 44.

[88] Crowe, p. 219.

[89] See pp. 110–14 above.

The 1958 *Explanatory Statement on the Navy Estimates* declared flatly: 'It will be quite clear that there is no intention to maintain a fleet, or any part of it, purely for global war.'[90] One year later the Minister of Supply set the seal of government approval on Admiralty planning when he told the House:

The main role of the Navy at present, whatever the future may hold, is the limited war role. . . . The air role of the Navy is to provide air strike support and air cover for ground forces from mobile bases at sea, pending the establishment of bases on land—a limited war role.[91]

In summary, then, 1958 to 1961 saw the consolidation of a limited-war doctrine, the development of limited-war capability, and the strengthening of naval deployments east of Suez at the expense of the Atlantic and the Mediterranean.

The first important step in the development of limited-war capability was the decision to proceed with the commando carrier project. Shortly after the end of the Second World War the United States Marine Corps began to study new techniques for amphibious operations in the belief that the Second World War concept, with its great concentrations of troops and shipping, could not be employed against an enemy armed with atomic weapons. After experimenting with a number of schemes, the Americans developed the idea of landing marines from a converted aircraft carrier by means of helicopters. Their first marine helicopter ship, the *Thetis Bay* (8,000 tons), came into service in 1956 and was adapted to carry up to 1,600 marines in her landing force. This was shortly followed by the conversion of the *Boxer*, a 27,000-ton Essex class carrier.[92] For some time the Royal Marines had been watching American developments closely and design work for a British helicopter carrier was already in hand when the Suez crisis intervened. Rather to their horror, Amphibious Headquarters were forced to put some of their ideas into practice and there was considerable worry lest the equipment fail and hence kill the whole project. However, the success of the improvised helicopter force landed from HMS *Ocean* and *Theseus* gave a fillip to the scheme, and on 20 May 1957 it was announced that the govern-

[90] Admiralty, Cmnd 371, para. 13.
[91] 600 HC Deb., 26 Feb. 1959, coll. 1320–1.
[92] Capt T. M. P. Stevens, 'The Helicopter Carrier', *Navy*, 62/10 (Oct. 1957), pp. 322–3, and Maj Gen J. L. Moulton, 'Mobility in Amphibious Warfare', *Brassey's Annual 1962*, p. 166.

ment was considering the conversion of an aircraft carrier into a commando ship.[93] The project was approved in July 1957 and subsequently HMS *Bulwark* was selected for conversion. After a refit costing about £4 million, *Bulwark* was recommissioned on 19 January 1960. In addition to a ship's company of about 1,000 and a helicopter squadron of something less than 200 men and about 20 Westland Whirlwinds (an obsolescent machine which could take only 4 or 5 men with equipment), she carried a Royal Marines Commando (then about 600 men), and 4 LCAs. The normal load of vehicles was about 100, including 20 three-ton trucks. For short journeys an additional infantry battalion could be carried.[94] *Bulwark* retained her original radar gear and was therefore capable of directing fighter aircraft. The success of this first venture led to a decision in 1960 to convert a second carrier—HMS *Albion*—to the commando role. Carrying Westland Wessex helicopters (each taking about 12 men) and incorpating a number of improvements, Britain's second commando carrier was commissioned in 1962.

The second stage in the programme to replace the Amphibious Warfare Squadron was the assault ship. At first there was some doubt about whether the Board of Admiralty would support the project, as it went beyond the Board's conception of amphibious warfare within the naval context. However, after prodding by Amphibious Warfare Headquarters, design studies were authorized for a 12,000-ton assault ship which could keep pace with the commando ship over oceanic distances and which could support an initial landing by a lightly armed commando group. Amphibious Warfare Headquarters maintained close touch with the Americans on this project and the design adopted was broadly similar to the American Thomaston class landing-ship dock, although it incorporated certain improvements. The first ship (HMS *Fearless*) was ordered in 1961. Basically a floating dock, it carried its own landing craft, the LCMs, which could float in and out through the stern. To support a commando landing, it carried armour, guns and heavy equipment, and 111 Royal Marines and army personnel.

[93] *Times*, 27 May 1957.
[94] In the early sixties a small Royal Artillery battery equipped with howitzers was added. After *Bulwark's* first exercise in the Mediterranean, Amphibious Warfare Headquarters pressed the Admiralty to include an armoured unit but it was some time before the Board was convinced.

A second assault ship (HMS *Intrepid*) was approved in 1961 and ordered in 1962. Construction proceeded slowly, however, and these ships were not commissioned until 1965 and 1967.[95]

At the same time steps were taken to modernize the supply ships maintained by the army. In August 1960, after recommendations from Amphibious Warfare Headquarters, the Chiefs of Staff approved the building of the first of six new logistic ships (LSL). *Sir Lancelot* and others of the class were designed to replace the old LSTs and were primarily intended for transporting tanks, heavy equipment, and troops. Built on the roll-on-roll-off principle which facilitated quick loading and unloading, the ships were capable of landing troops and equipment directly on to a beach. They came under the army's budget and control, and were built and operated by the Ministry of Transport on behalf of the army. *Sir Lancelot* was completed in January 1964 and the remainder followed at regular intervals later.[96]

Among other developments of these years, the expansion and modernization of the 'afloat support' fleet had a particular relevance to the navy's limited-war role east of Suez. Afloat support ships were of two main kinds. First there were repair, maintenance, and depot ships which were manned by Royal Navy personnel and whose function was to increase the operational availability of warships. Secondly, there were replenishment-at-sea ships with civilian crews, which supplied fuel, ammunition, and provisions at sea. Until the end of the fifties very little progress was made in this field and the fleet consisted almost entirely of those Second World War ships of the Pacific fleet train which had been kept in commission. Indeed, until well into the sixties only four oilers had the necessary speed to operate with other naval forces, and dry store and ammunition ships were still 12-knot wartime standard design merchant ship conversions.[97] With the shift in naval deployments from the Mediterranean to the Indian Ocean, however, the great

[95] See further Orr-Ewing's statement, 635 HC Deb., 2 Mar. 1961, coll. 1769–75; Moulton, 'Amphibious Warfare in the Late 1960s: Seaborne/Airborne Operations', *JRUSI*, 107/625 (Feb. 1962), p. 21; Gretton, *Maritime Strategy*, p. 103; Cdr T. S. Sampson, 'The Assault Ship—HMS *Fearless*', *Brassey's Annual 1964*, pp. 162–4; Cdr N. E. Whitestone, 'HMS *Fearless*', *Navy*, 71/1 (Jan. 1966), pp. 16–17. Also Crowe, pp. 202 and 231–2.

[96] See further Gretton, *Maritime Strategy*, p. 103; Crowe, p. 232; D. MacIver Robinson, 'The Logistic Ship Sir Lancelot', *Brassey's Annual 1964*, pp. 165–71.

[97] Desmond Wettern, 'Far Eastern Fleet', *Navy*, 71/1 (Jan. 1966), p. 19.

distances involved, the lack of supply and repair facilities, and the need to keep ships in commission for the longest possible period led the Admiralty to embark on a major programme of modernization and later of new construction. In 1958 the Admiralty announced that a fast fleet replenishment ship (*Retainer*) had completed conversion, a second ship (*Resurgent*) was then undergoing conversion, and a fast freighter had been acquired for conversion.[98] By 1960 a maintenance ship (HMS *Hartland Point*) had been modernized and plans were afoot to modernize several more.[99] Although progress was slower than some naval officers thought desirable, fuel supplied at sea increased from 10 per cent of the total used by Royal Navy ships in 1949 to a third in 1959, and over half in 1963.[100]

The one grievous gap in the naval construction programme was the aircraft carrier. Despite the strongest pressure from the Admiralty, by the close of 1961 the government still had not approved the construction of a new generation of aircraft carriers. Modernization of existing carriers went ahead almost as a matter of course but the proposals for new construction provoked fierce disagreement to which no end was yet in sight. In 1958 there were four operational aircraft carriers: by 1962 there were still only four, although *Hermes* (27,500 tons deep displacement) had come into service late in 1959, the *Victorious* (35,500 tons) had completed a seven-year modernization in 1958, *Ark Royal* (53,340 tons) had been modernized in 1959, and *Eagle* (53,000 tons) in 1960. While these refits were an acceptable—indeed essential—stop-gap measure there was no question in the Board of Admiralty that the older generation of aircraft carriers, all of whose hulls had been laid during the Second World War, would soon need replacing.

After the reprieve of the aircraft carrier in early 1957 the issue lay fallow for some two years. No approach for a new type of carrier was made to the government during this period as it was not technically necessary to start design work. Early in 1959, however, a committee was set up to investigate the carrier position. The committee reported that the *Victorious* (launched in 1939) should be replaced about 1970–2, and that the remaining carriers should be systematically phased out

[98] *Explanatory Statement on Navy Estimates 1958–59*, Cmnd 371, para. 39.
[99] *Explanatory Statement on Navy Estimates 1960–61*, Cmnd 949 (1960), para. 66.
[100] Ibid.; and *Naval Review*, Jan. 1963, p. 83.

and replaced at the rate of about one every two years. After considerable argument about requirements and design, the Board decided to ask for four large carriers. It was accepted that this number had to be regarded as a bargaining figure. The important thing, in the Admiralty's view, was to obtain approval for one new ship, and it believed that once this had been secured the project might go forward of its own accord. Accordingly, early in 1960 the Admiralty approached the Chiefs of Staff and the Minister of Defence with its plans. As expected, the Air Staff was bitterly opposed to the project, all the more since it was at that stage making preliminary investigations into the island base project which was later to become an alternative to carrier air power. Clearly the defence budget could not support both. Moreover, it was becoming increasingly apparent that the future of the RAF might come to rest on its east of Suez limited-war role. Equally predictably, the Treasury strongly resisted the carrier project. At this stage the cost of a new aircraft carrier was estimated at about £50 million, without aircraft, and such a large single slice of the defence budget was too much for Treasury officials to swallow. Already, too, the Treasury doubted the figure itself. [101]

Although Watkinson was sympathetic to the navy's case, other issues intervened before any final decision could be taken. Thought had to be given to a successor to the Sea Vixen, the Fleet Air Arm's all-weather fighter, and to the Hunter, the RAF's tactical support aircraft.[102] Watkinson instructed the two services to attempt to co-ordinate their requirements and develop a single aircraft for both roles. Countering Admiralty objections, he said that only on this basis would he be prepared to fight for the carrier in the Defence Committee. Neither service was happy with this directive but studies were put in motion to see what could be achieved. At the same time the Air Council hurriedly pushed ahead with its plan for island bases. For about eighteen months a fierce inter-service debate raged in Whitehall, accompanied by a variety of proposals being shunted backwards and forwards between the two services, the Chiefs of Staff, and the Minister, for renewed con-

[101] See *The Times*, 26 Oct. 1960.
[102] Although the Sea Vixen was expected to come into service only in 1961, it would be obsolescent by the mid-sixties. The aircraft under common consideration was the P1154.

sideration, costing, and appreciation. By the end of 1961 no agreement had been reached and none was in sight. However, the Admiralty had secured one important concession in that design work for a new carrier was allowed to go forward.[103]

The naval deployment pattern over these years reflected the Admiralty's limited-war theme. By 1958 the idea airily voiced in 1956 and 1957 of a number of task forces roaming the high seas had given way to two main groupings—in the Atlantic and the Mediterranean, and east of Suez. Responsibilities in the Atlantic and the Mediterranean tended to be linked together, thus enabling certain reductions west of Suez to be more easily made.[104] East of Suez the policy was a balanced all-purpose fleet based on Singapore and including an aircraft carrier, a commando ship, and a cruiser. Supporting the main fleet were a number of frigates permanently stationed in the Persian Gulf (usually about four) and at Simonstown (at least two).[105] The Far Eastern fleet was steadily strengthened over these years by additional destroyers and frigates and by 1961 there were more operational ships east than west of Suez.[106]

At the same time the main elements of the amphibious force moved from the Mediterranean to the Arabian Peninsula and the Far East. In October 1959 the Admiralty announced that 45 Royal Marine Commando, with a strength of about 600 men, would move to Aden during 1960.[107] In February 1961 a decision was taken to station the Headquarters of the 3rd Commando Brigade, then based on Malta, at Singapore in April.[108] This move involved about 200 men and was followed one year later by the movement of a second Royal Marine Commando from Malta to Singapore.[109]

Even more important was the movement of the Amphibious

---

[103] *Explanatory Statement on the Navy Estimates 1962–63*, Cmnd 1629 (1962), para. 4. See further Orr-Ewing's comments 655 HC Deb., 14 Mar. 1962, coll. 1341–2.

[104] Donald Barry, 'The Navy Today', *Navy*, 63/5 (May 1958), p. 108, and Crowe, p. 196.

[105] Speech by Mountbatten, *Times*, 1 May 1958. See also MoD, *Report on Defence*, Cmnd 363, paras 47–9.

[106] See the deployment table in 'Reactor', 'Where is the Royal Navy?', *Navy* 66/1 (Feb. 1961), pp. 28–30.

[107] *Daily Telegraph*, 30 Oct. 1959.

[108] *Times*, 8 Feb. 1961.

[109] *Guardian* 26 Jan. 1962. It was announced in 1961 that a fifth commando was to be raised, presumably because of the strain imposed by the commando ship requirements and the expanded amphibious role east of Suez.

Warfare Squadron to Aden in the summer of 1960.[110] This decision was taken by the Chiefs of Staff largely because of the Centurion tanks (perhaps about 100) in the Iraqi army, and the realization that if an emergency developed over Kuwait, Britain would not be able to move armour into the area in time. The first stage of the plan was to send some 16 Centurions together with technical advisers to the Ruler of Kuwait. Doubts about Kuwaiti ability to handle the Centurions led to the second element—the decision to send a squadron of British Centurions to Aden and to move the recently refitted Amphibious Warfare Squadron out to Aden to handle transport. The third stage was to institute the Gulf patrol. Recognizing that the Centurions would be required within a couple of days of the outbreak of an emergency, and that the Amphibious Squadron could not travel from Aden to the Persian Gulf in anything like that time (the ships of the squadron had a speed of only about 9 knots and the distance was about 2,000 miles), a ship loaded with half a squadron of Centurions was kept permanently patrolling the Gulf waters. The ship did a three-month tour between Sharjah and Bahrain and was poised to move into Kuwait at short notice.[111]

Army Developments[112]

The most important decision taken in these years was to raise the army's recruiting ceiling from 165,000 to 180,000. Announcing the change, the 1959 White Paper explained that although the government was satisfied that the 1957 plan was soundly conceived, it was desirable to aim at an army of 180,000 'to ensure that its strength shall not fall below the planned figure of 165,000.'[113] As The Times observed, this was a remarkably silly statement for a White Paper: 'If it were really necessary to safeguard the lower figure by aiming at a

[110] Times, 15 Mar. 1960. These ships had been stationed in Malta since 1952. In 1959 they returned to the UK to be overhauled and air-conditioned. Carrington, 221 HL Deb., 10 Mar. 1960, col. 1063.
[111] This explains the rapid movement of Centurions into Kuwait during the emergency in July 1961.
[112] As reference has already been made to the army's part in the development of air and sea mobility I have restricted myself here to a consideration of those other aspects of army policy which had an important bearing on the east of Suez role.
[113] MoD, Progress of the Five-Year Defence Plan, Cmnd 662, para. 27.

higher one, then it was just as necessary in 1957, when the plan was first announced.'[114]

What of course was important was that in 1959 recruiting was going well, whereas in 1957 it was not.[115] As earlier predicted, the government's manpower policy was in fact following the curves of the recruiting graph.[116]

Both in Parliament and in the press there was considerable speculation about whether voluntary recruiting would enable the 180,000 figure to be reached. According to one estimate, the change from National Service to an all-Regular army would draw in an additional 40,000 men and, on this basis, the Army League concluded that there was every prospect that the 180,000 target would be reached by 1963.[117] Other observers were more doubtful.[118] Assuming that recruiting went well, however, there remained the question of whether an army of 180,000 would be adequate for its tasks. The various lines of thought may be summarized thus: the army was resigned to, but also unhappy with, the 180,000 ceiling; Lord Harding spoke for many informed observers when he declared: 'My guess is that those who have put the figure at 220,000 are likely to be proved much nearer the mark than those who have thought or hoped that 165,000 would be sufficient.'[119]

On Sandys' reckoning an army of 180,000 men would mean that 70,000 would be available for service in the strategic reserve and overseas—as against a figure of 75,000 in 1959—and he contended that the difference would be more than offset by the higher state of training of all-Regular forces and the much greater air mobility.[120] According to Wigg's arithmetic, however, even with only 45,000 in Germany, it was dubious whether an army of 180,000 could produce 70,000 men for limited-war operations. Once pressure from Konrad

---

[114] 11 Feb. 1959.
[115] One relevant factor was the report of the Grigg Committee in Oct. 1958 recommending improvements in pay, pensions and conditions, and its general acceptance by the government the following month. See MoD, Advisory Committee on Recruiting, *Report*, Cmnd 545 (1958).
[116] *Times*, 11 Feb. 1959.
[117] *The British Army in the Nuclear Age*, p. 53.
[118] See esp. Wigg's statements: 601 HC Deb., 10 Mar. 1959, coll. 1091–2, and 618 HC Deb., 29 Feb. 1960, coll. 909–10.
[119] 215 HL Deb., 18 Mar. 1959, col. 37.
[120] 600 HC Deb., 25 Feb. 1959, col. 1133.

Adenauer and from SHAPE had stabilized the BAOR figure at 55,000, it seemed impossible. Indeed, on Wigg's reckoning, in order to produce 70,000 men for overseas operations, Britain needed an army of 220,000.[121] What was feared in some quarters was that the same commitments and a smaller army would mean that all units would be kept just a little under strength. And in fact this was already happening in 1961, although there were still considerably more than 200,000 men in the army.[122]

Until the early sixties a very large part of the army's equipment was of Second World War origin or was drawn from stocks built up during the Korean War. In 1959 the Minister of Supply explained: 'There is something here which is deeply embedded in tradition. The weapons of the Army, by tradition, change but slowly.'[123]

More to the point, until that year re-equipment of the army had been deliberately postponed because of the large accumulated stocks and the need to economize. The Director of Ammunition and Stores at the War Office, Brigadier H. E. Fernyhough, left no doubt about the seriousness of the position when he wrote in an official document that:

the means to fight a limited war are confined to what can be retained from the residue of an incomplete re-equipment programme which was stopped several years ago. This process is officially known as 'living on our fat'. . . . All operations including Suez have had to be equipped by improvisation using out-of-date, incomplete mobilisation packs and feverishly making scale issues from stores left over from the last war. In relation to its small size and large commitments, the British Army must be one of the worst equipped in the world.[124]

Starting in 1959, however, a major re-equipment programme was put in motion, which was officially described as the most concentrated ever undertaken by the British army in peacetime.[125] It was some time before new equipment came into

---

[121] His figures were BAOR: 55,000; staff, workshops, and home commands (Head's figure of 28 July 1958): 70,000; in the pipeline: 25,000. 618 HC Deb., 29 Feb. 1960, coll. 910–11.

[122] Sir F. Maclean, 636 HC Deb., 7 Mar. 1961, col. 347.

[123] 600 HC Deb., 26 Feb. 1959, col. 1317.

[124] Quoted by Wigg, 618 HC Deb., 29 Feb. 1960, coll. 916–17.

[125] Aubrey Jones, 600 HC Deb., 26 Feb. 1959, coll. 1317–18.

service and longer before it reached all units but generally there was steady improvement over the next few years.[126]

Another significant development was the inauguration of the Army Air Corps in September 1957. Under the terms of an agreement signed on 21 February 1957 the army assumed responsibility for operating light unarmed aircraft, of an all-up weight not exceeding 4,000 pounds, employed in the reconnaissance, aerial observation, and liaison role. The Corps took over full operational responsibility on 1 April 1958.[127] The weight restriction proved less burdensome than at first expected as the air force agreed that this limitation should not be rigidly applied. In 1957 the Corps had only Auster aircraft, mostly of an obsolete mark, but over the next five years new Austers, Beavers, and Skeeters came into operation, as did a small number of Westland Scout and Alouette helicopters.[128]

The abolition of National Service and the consequent manpower reductions forced the army to embark on a major reorganization. In July 1957 plans were announced for reducing the 'teeth arm' units by about 50, including infantry reductions of about 17 battalions.[129] The new infantry strength was to be of the order of 60 battalions—3 parachute, 8 foot-guards, and 49 infantry of the line. By mid-1962 most of the disbandments and amalgamations had been completed. Parallel with this reorganization and beginning in 1958, a change was made from the divisional organization to a system of brigade groups, though smaller divisional headquarters were retained capable of commanding from 2 to 4 brigade groups.[130]

It is difficult for the outside observer—and perhaps for the expert—to assess the consequences of these changes for the army's role east of Suez. However, three aspects may be briefly mentioned. First, it seems clear that the brigade group organiza-

---

[126] For details see MoD, *Progress of the Five-Year Defence Plan*, Cmnd 662, paras 7–9, and *Report on Defence 1960*, Cmnd 952, paras 24–9; and Brig. W. F. K. Thompson, 'Progress towards an All-Regular, Long-Service Army', *Brassey's Annual 1960*, pp. 225–6.

[127] Statement by the Earl of Gosford, 209 HL Deb., 7 May 1958, coll. 51–2.

[128] WO, *Memorandum on Army Estimates 1961–62*, Cmnd 1280 (1961), para. 27, and Brig. P W. Mead, 'Army Aviation', *RAF Quarterly*, 2/3 (autumn 1962), pp. 189–93.

[129] See further MoD, *Report on Defence*, Cmnd 363, para. 56, and MoD, *Progress of the Five-Year Defence Plan*, Cmnd 662, paras 37 and 38.

[130] See further the statement by the Secretary of State for War, 583 HC Deb., 6 Mar. 1958, coll. 1361–2.

tion was well suited to the requirements of counter-insurgency campaigning and limited conflicts. It was very unusual for more than one brigade group to be committed to policing operations and the new organization made it easier to send off small self-contained units than had been the case with the larger grouping.[131] Secondly, the maintenance of a fixed number of units meant that in times of manpower shortage the army was faced with the alternatives of spreading its men evenly throughout the 60 battalions, and thus keeping them all below strength, or establishing a system of priorities which might clash with powerful traditional and territorial associations.[132] The former approach was the one mainly adopted, and in the post-1962 period it created very considerable problems. Finally, Gwynne Jones has argued that the new organization left the army with a disproportionate balance of arms.[133] That is to say, the number of teeth arms was greater than the communications, intelligence, and support units available for proper backing. The Army League briefly referred to this problem but expressed no opinion as the group was divided.[134]

Turning to doctrine and training, it appears that in the post-Suez years the army began to develop a coherent theory of anti-guerrilla warfare and to adjust its training programmes accordingly. One important step was the publication in 1957 of *Keeping the Peace*, a revised handbook of duties in aid of the civil power. Later a team of officers from the Commonwealth Brigade Group in Malaya, working in close co-operation with an American unit, undertook a careful study of the campaigns in Malaya, Indo-China, Kenya, and Cyprus. Partly as a result of their efforts, the new doctrine was consolidated and much of the old imperial policing theory was rejected, as were the more extreme proposals for specialized forces.[135] By 1962 the War Office was preparing new training manuals which upgraded the limited-war role and incorporated much of the new thinking.[136] In broad outline, army strategists reaffirmed the traditional conception of an all-purpose army, but new tech-

---

[131] 'Tarbrook', 'Britain's Future Strategic Reserve', *Brassey's Annual 1958*, pp. 78–9.
[132] Gwynne Jones, 'Training and Doctrine in the British Army since 1945', in M. Howard, ed., *The Theory and Practice of War*, pp. 330–1.
[133] Ibid. pp. 329–30.
[134] *The British Army in the Nuclear Age*, p. 51.
[135] Gwynne Jones, as in n. 132, pp. 325–6.
[136] *Times*, 13 June 1962.

niques were grafted on to existing principles and it was admitted that specialized training would have to be superimposed on a common basic programme.

The Base Strategy

The early hopes that the policies of strategic mobility would offer an escape from the traditional dependence on the chain of overseas bases were soon dashed. Despite the optimistic forecasts about the airlifted strategic reserve, it was not long before the realization set in that instead of lessening the value of overseas bases, the very success of the policy depended on their continuance—or at least on the continuance of Britain's major bases east of Suez. The naval scheme, it is true, was less dependent upon overseas bases. In theory it could have been made almost entirely independent, but the cost would probably have been prohibitive.[137] No full costing of such a scheme was ever carried out, however, because total dependence on seaborne task forces was never a practical possibility. The government's reluctance to commit itself to a course of action that would tie its hands for a decade or more ahead and the dominance of separate service interests effectively ruled out any such major shift in policy. For this reason, the Admiralty refrained from urging an early withdrawal from Kenya and Singapore. It did, however, oppose major expenditure on those bases. Moreover, with an eye to the future, the Board pointed out that the base policy could not survive indefinitely, and it floated the idea of putting more troops to sea and back-basing the naval force at Cockburn Sound in Western Australia.

As things stood, therefore, the combination of air reserves, seaborne forces, and troops on the ground left policy-makers with no opportunity to abandon all Britain's strategic footholds east of Suez, though it was open to them to reduce their number, to some extent to scale down the establishments maintained, and arguably to change their location. Not very much was said about base requirements or policy over these years, but the pattern which emerged was one of increased dependence on three major bases, Kenya, Aden, and Singapore.

[137] See further V Adm Sir Peter Gretton's observations in *Maritime Strategy*, pp. 49–50 and 148–50. There is also relevant material in L. W. Martin, *The Sea in Modern Strategy* (1967), esp. pp. 66–8.

Singapore was a case on its own as it represented an investment in being. Kenya, and to a lesser extent, Aden were new ventures and the build-up which occurred in both places was the result of deliberate government policy.

In November 1957 when Sandys announced that an element of the strategic reserve was to be stationed in Kenya he was at pains to point out that this plan did not involve the setting up of a great base organization.[138] Three months later the Secretary of State's *Memorandum* stated that permanent barracks would be built in Kenya.[139] Over the following months design work went ahead for the construction of air-conditioned accommodation and married quarters for two battalions. Work was to begin in 1959 and barracks for the first battalion were expected to be completed early in 1961 and for the second about a year later. The cantonment was expected to cost between £2 million and £2.5 million, the whole expense being borne by the British government which would also pay the costs of maintenance.[140] By July 1959 when the contract was awarded, the cost had risen to £3.5 million.[141] As the number of troops stationed in Kenya steadily rose, reports appeared in the British press of new projects about to be undertaken in Kenya. According to one report in early 1960, about £10 million was to be spent on accommodation over the next two years.[142] A few months later, Major General Sir Nigel Tapp, General Officer Commanding, East Africa, admitted that in addition to the Kahawa project the army was spending a considerable sum, between £500,000 and £1.5 million, refurnishing its old camps at Gilgil and elsewhere.[143] At the same time the RAF was developing its two airfields at Eastleigh and Embakasi, near Nairobi, and was undertaking a general construction programme of its own.[144] Expenditure on works in East Africa amounted to nearly £3 million in 1960–61.[145]

[138] 577 HC Deb., 7 Nov. 1957, coll. 334–5.
[139] WO, Cmnd 372 (1958), para. 29.
[140] *Times*, 10 Apr. 1958 and 27 Aug. 1958.
[141] *Times*, 20 July 1959.
[142] *Daily Telegraph*, 2 Mar. 1960.
[143] *Times*, 20 July 1960.
[144] *Daily Telegraph*, 19 Nov. 1960.
[145] HC, *Tenth Report from Estimates Committee . . . Session 1962–63: Military Expenditure Overseas* (1963), p. 4, para. 28.

Despite increasing doubts about the viability of the base, work proceeded as planned during 1961. In September of that year a Ministry of Defence spokesman said that about £7.5 million had been or was being invested in defence facilities in Kenya.[146]

One important factor underlying the building programme was the policy that wherever possible the married officer or man posted for service overseas should be accompanied by his wife and family.[147] For some years before 1958 recruiting pressures and the higher proportion of married men in the services had led to an increase in accompanied postings. The report of the Grigg Committee led to a further development of this policy.[148] By the late fifties it was accepted that a period of one year was the normal maximum for unaccompanied service in the army. In the case of Kenya it was considered that optimum operational efficiency could not be achieved in this period and accompanied postings therefore became the rule. As a result, the army saw no alternative to the construction of a major cantonment.

That Kenya attained full internal self-government less than six years after the decision was made to proceed with the cantonment, and that the last British troops left Kenya little more than five years after work first began on the major construction project, is now common knowledge.[149] What is not so clear is how the defence establishment came to undertake building the base in the light of the territory's uncertain future as a colony. The answer seems to lie in changed political objectives and lack of co-ordination within the government machine.

In 1957 when the Ministry of Defence decided to go ahead with the scheme to station troops in Kenya, independence for the East African territories seemed several generations away. Despite Ghana's independence in 1957, and Nigeria's approach to self-government already gathering momentum, the belief in Whitehall was that the East African situation was so different—because of general backwardness and the complication of the white colonists—that events in the west of the continent

---

[146] *Sunday Telegraph*, 19 Nov. 1960.
[147] See HC, *Tenth Report . . . 1962–63* (cited fully in n. 145), p. 149, para. 11, and generally pp. vii–xi, paras 10–23.
[148] MoD, Advisory Committee on Recruiting, *Report*, Cmnd 545, para. 72.
[149] The final stage in the Kenya story is related in ch. 7 below.

had little relevance.[150] Indeed new recruits then entering the
Overseas Civil Service were assured that Kenya's colonial
future could be measured in decades.[151] As late as January
1959, when a conference was held at Chequers on the future
of the East African territories, the British government apparently
had no firm plans for the grant of independence to any of the
three territories. At this conference, however, a tentative time-
table was suggested according to which Tanganyika might
obtain independence in 1970, with Uganda following her lead,
and Kenya much later, probably after 1975. Reportedly the
British government accepted this overall pattern and certain
steps were taken to enable the government to adhere to it.[152]
However, there must be doubts about how far the government
in fact considered itself committed and even more about the
extent to which the various departments and officials were
informed of the government's thinking. One piece of evidence
here is particularly interesting. In the months before the British
general election the Governor of Kenya, Sir Evelyn Baring,
toured the colony delivering the message 'Kenya can't go
independent because it is a fortress colony.'

In this atmosphere of uncertainty and conflicting views, but
with official policy directed towards a slow and unspectacular
advance to self-government, the service departments pushed
ahead with plans for the cantonment. According to a War
Office memorandum of 1963, in July 1959 when a major
contract for the cantonment at Kahawa was let, 'a virtually
indefinite tenure in Kenya was envisaged'.[153]

After the general election in October there was a dramatic
change in British colonial policy. Iain Macleod, the new
Secretary of State for the Colonies, was convinced that a
sweeping transfer of power was necessary in Africa, and he
set in motion a revision of Colonial Office plans.[154] Events in
Africa—the Mau Mau rebellion, the return of Dr Hastings
Banda to Nyasaland and the subsequent riots and shootings, the

[150] Perham, *African Outline*, pp. 38–9, and W. P. Kirkman, *Unscrambling an Empire*
(1966), pp. 47–9.
[151] Kirkman, pp. 47–8.
[152] This account was given by Sir Michael Blundell in his revealing and moving
autobiography, *So Rough a Wind* (1964), pp. 261–2. Blundell was the Kenyan
Minister of Agriculture 1955–9 and then leader of the New Kenya party.
[153] See *Tenth Report . . . 1962–63* (cited fully in n. 145), p. 64, para. 7.
[154] See his own account of the factors behind the 'change of tempo'. *Weekend
Telegraph* (suppl. to *Daily Telegraph*), 12 Mar. 1965.

report of the Devlin Commission, the Belgian decision to give independence to the Congo in 1960—hastened the pace. Macmillan, for some time anxious to withdraw from Africa, set the seal on the new policy with his famous 'winds of change' speech delivered in South Africa in February 1960. At the same time a constitutional conference met at Lancaster House and the way was opened for a transfer of power in Kenya. The compromise constitution signified not simply a change of emphasis but a major reversal of policy. The Kenya base was dead.

Again, however, communication through the machinery of government in Whitehall and in Nairobi was deficient. More to the point, the government was unable to adapt the various strands of its policy to the new objective. Writing of the post-Lancaster House period, W. P. Kirkman has described British government policy as 'a dismal hotch-potch of unkeepable promises, irreconcilable objectives, right to the end'.[155] The base, the future of the white settlers, the fate of Kenyatta—all disrupted the announced and now inevitable movement to independence. Sir Patrick Renison's description of Kenyatta as 'the African leader of darkness and death' symbolized the tragic inconsistency of British policy, all the more since it was made on the authority of the Colonial Secretary.[156]

The services adjusted slowly to the new situation. It was not until the autumn of 1960 that the War Office had serious doubts about tenure in Kenya.[157] By this time work had begun on the Kahawa cantonment and the project was allowed to continue without any substantial change in scope. At Gilgil planning did not begin until 1959 and the actual contracts were let in the course of 1960. The provision of living accommodation went ahead as originally planned, but once it became clear that the army's tenure of occupation was likely to be very limited, certain amenities buildings were abandoned and substantial economies were effected in others.[158]

A number of factors worked to discourage the services from substantially modifying the original plans. In the first place, once decisions had been taken and contracts let, it was a matter of great difficulty to reverse the process. There was also the

[155] *Unscrambling an Empire*, p. 54.
[156] *Guardian*, 10 May 1960. Renison succeeded Baring as Governor of Kenya on 23 Oct. 1959.
[157] HC, *Tenth Report . . . 1962–63* (cited fully in n. 145), p. 64, para. 7.
[158] See further ibid. paras 6 and 7.

point that any major change in the building programme was likely to be interpreted as an indication of early withdrawal and therefore had to be avoided. More important, for some time after the reversal of Colonial Office policy, the service departments clung to the hope that progress towards self-government would be slower than Macleod expected, and that some special arrangement might be negotiated to protect Britain's defence interests. In autumn 1960 the War Office thought the army would remain in Kenya for at least seven years.[159] This view seems to have continued throughout 1961.[160]

However, the writing was on the wall and the chances of salvaging much from the defence wreck after independence seemed slim indeed. As early as April 1959 Tom Mboya, then Secretary of the Kenyan Federation of Labour and a member of the Legislative Council, had come out against the British base.[161] In August Mboya and five other leading African MPs issued a statement opposing 'unreservedly' foreign military bases.[162] From that time on Kenyan nationalists made it abundantly clear that the British base had no future once independence was achieved.[163] Late in August 1961 Macleod admitted to a meeting of Conservative back-benchers that Britain must face the prospect of losing the Kenya base. He went on to say that the policy of setting up or retaining bases in colonial or newly independent countries did not work.[164]

Macleod's comment was almost equally applicable to Aden although there the problem was of a somewhat different nature and the time-span longer. The crunch did not come in Aden until after 1962, but already the ground was being laid with the development of a major building programme in apparent disregard of the colony's future and of nationalist sentiments. Again the pattern was a step-by-step movement into the colony

[159] Ibid. para. 7.
[160] There is some evidence that the government may have encouraged the services on this point. At the end of Aug. 1961, Macleod told a meeting of some fifty Conservative back-benchers that the government would make every effort to negotiate a treaty with whatever government was formed in Kenya. *Sunday Telegraph*, 3 Sept. 1961.
[161] *Daily Worker*, 14 Apr. 1959.
[162] *Manchester Guardian*, 5 Aug. 1959.
[163] See reports in the *Guardian*, 27 Feb. 1960; *Daily Telegraph*, 27 Feb. and 1 Oct. 1960; *Times*, 24 Oct. and 19 Nov. 1960.
[164] *Sunday Telegraph*, 3 Sept. 1961.

until the project acquired a momentum of its own and eventually received official sanction as a major British base.

Although a garrison had long been maintained in Aden, the military establishment before 1957 was on a small scale. After the Suez crisis the build-up of forces and the creation of an independent command led to a four-fold increase in the service population in three years.[165] The result was a grave shortage of accommodation, serious overcrowding, and poor conditions. On 7 December 1959 a debate in the House of Lords focused public attention on service problems in Aden. A number of speakers strongly criticized the general lack of facilities and what were described as 'slum conditions.'[166] In reply, the government spokesman admitted that 700 troops were living in tented accommodation and the permanent quarters available were badly overcrowded. The position was broadly similar in other stations in the Arabian Peninsula and the Persian Gulf.[167] On 8 December 1959 Lady Tedder, wife of Marshal of the Royal Air Force Lord Tedder, added further fuel to the fire and suggested that three ships should be sent to Aden as floating barracks.[168] The *Daily Telegraph* commended Lady Tedder's plan, with the warning:

Nevertheless it is only reasonable, before sinking great sums in Aden to recall a few precedents where bases have been vastly improved, new barracks and married quarters built, only to be evacuated a few months later. . . . It would be foolish to make the same mistakes about Aden.[169]

The seriousness of the situation in Aden led to important decisions to provide extensive permanent accommodation and generally to expand military facilities and stockpiles of weapons and equipment. On 7 December 1959 it was announced that work had started on the first of five air-conditioned blocks, each for about 150 airmen, at Khormaksar. A new school was also under construction. In addition, the RAF building programme included new messes, a club, and 66 married-quarter flats at Steamer Point. A proposal was under consideration to erect some 200 additional married quarters at an estimated

---

[165] *Daily Telegraph*, 17 Dec. 1959.
[166] Lord Merrivale, 220 HL Deb., 7 Dec. 1959, coll. 53–6; Lord Shackleton, ibid. coll. 57–8; Lord Tedder, ibid. coll. 59–64.
[167] Earl of Onslow, 220 HL Deb., coll. 70 and 76.
[168] *Daily Telegraph*. 9 Dec. 1959.   [169] 'Aden Amenities', 19 Dec. 1959.

cost of £1 million. For the army, plans were also going ahead for long-term accommodation. A contract had been let for 240 married quarters and for air-conditioned barracks for an infantry battalion. Sixteen new barrack huts, providing air-conditioned accommodation for 640 men, were nearly complete. Another contract, worth about £850,000, for messes and offices, was to be let in the spring.[170] An accelerated building programme was announced ten days later.[171] Work pushed ahead during 1960, and the White Paper of that year mentioned single accommodation for nearly 1,500 men, some 270 new houses, and 2 new schools as major projects due to be completed shortly.[172] In 1961, with the loss of Kenya on the horizon, a decision was taken to develop Little Aden, an area some 20 miles away from the main town. This project, the biggest single military building scheme ever undertaken by the British government, included a £5 million cantonment for 2,500 soldiers and 1,000 women and children, workshops and store, a church, a cinema, and a sportsground.[173]

The political background to these developments was broadly similar to that in Kenya. The two main elements of the Kenyan situation—the belief that independence was perhaps decades away and the rising tide of nationalist opposition—played their part in this colony also. As in Kenya, the defence establishment chose to put its faith in the first and to shut its eyes to the second. In 1956 the moderate pro-Commonwealth party, the Aden Alliance, presented certain proposals for further advance to self-government, including an entirely elected legislature and an elected ministry. Lord Lloyd, Under-Secretary of State for the Colonies, left no doubt about the British government's position when he spoke in the Legislative Council later that month:

I should like you to understand that for the foreseeable future it would not be reasonable or sensible, or indeed in the interests of the colony's inhabitants, for them to aspire to any aim beyond that of a considerable degree of internal self-government.

... Her Majesty's Government wish to make it clear that the

---

[170] Earl of Onslow, 220 HL Deb., 7 Dec 1969, col. 75–6.
[171] *Daily Telegraph*, 17 Dec. 1959, *Times*, 18 Dec. 1959.
[172] MoD, *Report on Defence 1960*, Cmnd 952, para. 17.
[173] WO, *Memorandum on Army Estimates 1961–62*, Cmnd 1280, para. 66. For a general discussion of the project see *Times*, 9 Oct. 1961.

importance of Aden both strategically and economically within the Commonwealth is such that they cannot foresee the possibility of any fundamental relaxation of their responsibilities for the colony.[174]

Aden, then, was a strategic colony and independence was not a possibility. It need hardly be said that this was unacceptable to the nationalist leaders. Opposition to the slow rate of constitutional development led 73 per cent of Aden voters to observe a boycott of the election held in January 1959. Thereafter Arab opposition steadily mounted. Political strikes became a characteristic feature of the Aden scene and outbreaks of violence occurred from time to time.[175] By 1961 the British government was moving towards closer links between the colony and the Federation of Arab Amirates, in the belief that this represented the best hope of safeguarding Britain's defence investment in the colony.[176]

There was never any doubt about the government's position on the Singapore base. During 1957 both Duncan Sandys and George Ward, Secretary of State for Air, made it clear that Singapore was a long-term investment and that Britain required uninhibited freedom of movement.[177] According to *The Times* military correspondent, the services were equally emphatic and they were convinced that there was no alternative to the existing base—a view later confirmed by General Hull.[178] Even the navy did not oppose works expenditure here.

During the emergency troops were living in the jungle on active service conditions. As the emergency came to an end it was necessary to provide proper accommodation and facilities. The years 1958 and 1959 therefore saw extensive building of new barracks and married quarters and other projects both on the island and on the mainland. Preliminary work also went ahead on the construction of a new cantonment near Malacca to house the Commonwealth Brigade. When completed in the spring of 1964 it would house between 7,000 and 9,000 men. The overall cost was expected to be between £8 million and £9 million.[179] In October 1959 it was announced

---

[174] *Times*, 21 May 1956.
[175] For a full discussion see Gillian King, *Imperial Outpost—Aden* (1964), ch. 4.
[176] See Kirkman, p. 149.
[177] *Times*, 2 Oct. 1957.
[178] *Times*, 17 Jan. 1958 and 16 June 1959.
[179] WO, *Memorandum of Secretary of State for War Relating to Army Estimates 1959–60*, Cmnd 669 (1959), para. 66; *Times*, 16 June 1959; *Daily Telegraph*, 13 Jan. 1960.

that Britain would spend between £2 million and £3 million developing the RAF base at Tengah on Singapore Island.[180] In 1960 and 1961 a number of additional new projects were begun or approved including churches, schools, swimming pools, a hospital and a cinema on the mainland, and barracks, married quarters, and a depot for training Gurkha soldiers in Singapore.[181]

Despite occasional disturbances and demonstrations on the island and some nationalist opposition to the base arrangements, Britain's defence facilities in Singapore seemed reasonably secure. Indeed, if we remember the troubled conditions existing in other parts of the Indian Ocean where Britain had defence interests, Singapore was almost the brightest dot on the British defence map.[182] Still, the colony's approach to independence posed problems and it was a matter of considerable relief when Tunku Abdul Rahman took the initiative in proposing the Malaysian Federation. Without at this stage going into the various manoeuvres and negotiations, suffice it to say that the Malaysian scheme provided an ideal formula by which Britain's defence investment could be protected.[183] After merger talks in London in November 1961, a joint statement issued on behalf of the three governments made it clear that the Singapore base would remain in British hands and that Britain would not be any more restricted in its use than she was then.[184]

Generally during 1958 and 1959 there were few who questioned the increased expenditure on Britain's three major bases east of Suez. Nor was there much discussion about the viability of these bases in the light of the growth of nationalist feeling in Africa and Asia. In the debate on the 1960 White Paper, however, by which time the Kenyan venture seemed likely to have a short run, a number of speakers stressed the futility of trying to hold on to bases in colonial or ex-colonial territories. Several times the question was asked, was the

---

[180] *Daily Telegraph*, 13 Oct. 1959.
[181] WO, *Memorandum on Army Estimates 1961–62*, Cmnd 1280, para. 64.
[182] An exception must be made for the small British base at Simonstown. In Mar. 1961 South African ministers said there would be no change in existing defence arrangements with Britain when South Africa left the Commonwealth.
[183] See pp. 281–2 below.
[184] *Times*, 23 Nov. 1961. On 24 Nov., however, Tunku Abdul Rahman expressed a slightly more qualified interpretation. *Times*, 25 Nov. 1961.

government clinging to the imperial strategy of overseas bases?
In a sense it was. Neither the government nor the military had
finally discarded the Victorian conception of *places d'armes*,
secure British enclosures from which the military could maintain an area of stability, or at least from which they could
venture forth to stamp out such violence as from time to time
inevitably occurred. There were suggestions for more limited
projects. Geoffrey de Freitas asked, 'Is it not refuelling bases
that we need?'[185] Other speakers were quick to point out that
the differences between traditional bases and refuelling bases
was not so great as might be supposed.[186] The point was well
taken. Indeed, once it was decided to garrison troops of the
strategic reserve, the difference was more a matter of theory
than of substance.

The controversy continued into 1961 by which time doubts
were growing, not only in Parliament but also in the press,
as to the worth of overseas bases in the world of the sixties. In
an article entitled, 'Is Showing the Flag Worth the Cost?', *The
Times* defence correspondent drew attention to the 'mystique
of pins', and questioned how much longer Britain could afford
to support a strategy dependent upon a network of overseas
bases.[187] The following day *The Times* reflected that it might
be better to rely more fully on strategically mobile forces,
which in any case would accord with the developing European
outlook. Either way, however, what was clear was that world
strategy was not available in an economy size.[188]

[185] 618 HC Deb., 29 Feb. 1960, col. 951.
[186] e.g. Lt Cdr Maydon, 618 HC Deb., col. 957.
[187] 22 Aug. 1961. See also 'Britain's Outposts a Wasting Asset', *Times*, 23 Aug.
1961. For a contrary view see *Daily Telegraph*, 15 Nov 1961.
[188] Britain's Outposts a Wasting Asset'.

CHAPTER SIX

Role Defined 1962–1964

SPEAKING in the House of Lords in March 1962, Viscount Montgomery summed up the strategic scene with characteristic pungency: 'The Atlantic is safe; Europe is safe; the Mediterranean is safe: the potential danger spots lie elsewhere, in the Near East, the Middle East and the Far East and in Africa. It is to those areas that we should direct our gaze . . .'[1]

Broadly the government agreed, and for the next four years its strategic gaze was firmly fixed outside Europe and especially east of Suez. This was not entirely a new development as for some years there had already been considerable rethinking about the world balance. However, 1962 was the year in which the balance swung decisively eastward, and if any one statement had to be selected as illustrative of the change it would be the White Paper of that year.

Clearly the 1962 re-weighting of the European and overseas roles flowed from a changed appreciation of the most likely threats to the peace, the accent being placed on the instabilities of Africa and Asia as compared with the stabilizing situation in Europe. The *détente* in Europe taken together with the probability that the rimlands of China would be the scene of impending conflict had the effect of shifting the central balance eastwards. It would be too much to say that China was about to replace the Soviet Union as the major threat to the peace, but the movement was in this direction, and the world view of British policy-makers ensured that this development had its impact on strategic thinking in Whitehall. Not unrelated, though by no means simply a product of the rise of China either, was the growing recognition that conditions in Southeast Asia, the Middle East, and to a lesser extent Africa were

[1] 238 HL Deb., 21 Mar. 1962, col. 579.

too precarious to enable indigenous power balances to be constructed without the involvement, either active or in a guarantor role, of the external powers.

The events of the following three years strongly confirmed the government's strategic assessment. East of Suez one crisis succeeded another. British forces saw action in Malaya, in Arabia, and in Africa. British support was extended to India and Thailand. In Whitehall and in the Far East, policy-makers carefully watched the situation in Laos and in Vietnam, and planning and force dispositions were altered as assessments changed. At the same time, the risk in Europe receded into the background. If doubts remained about the long-term prospects, and if many were concerned about the diplomatic implications of the priority of the overseas role, the immediate requirement in these years was to draw on European forces to support Britain's overseas commitments, but in a way which would cause least concern to Britain's European allies and which would maintain the NATO barrier.

As events crowded in, Labour policy underwent a profound change. At first the party held firmly to the priority of the European role, which had been a major plank in its defence platform throughout the fifties. Its disagreement with the government was not so much about which conflicts were likely as which were Britain's concern. Europe was Britain's business: Asia was a part-time commitment, and one, moreover, which could not continue indefinitely. In the year before the general election, however, the Labour front bench re-examined Britain's position in the world and saw a mission in *staying* in Asia where before it had seen a mission in *leaving*. Thus the shadow cabinet adopted the world role, injected it with a stronger moral content, and the stage was set for the empire's swansong.

At the same time as this broadening of the political conception of Britain's role, the military position on which it was based was becoming less secure. During these years the demands upon Britain's military resources imposed a considerable strain on the defence establishment. Although it was possible to argue about the extent of this strain, as each year passed the military burdens became more onerous. Paradoxically as the political case for staying east of Suez became stronger so the military costs became higher. So long as the calls for British assistance were limited the military establishment was capable of handling them. But as these calls increased it became apparent, at least within the Ministry of Defence (though it was not altogether admitted even there), that the outlay required would soon be beyond the capacity of what was fundamentally a modest military investment.[2]

Diplomatic and Strategic Background

By the beginning of the sixties the belief that regional power balances were unnecessary in South-east Asia and the Middle East had died a natural death. In the early fifties it had been fashionable for nationalist leaders to decry the power balance theories as European importations and to argue that the newly independent countries had certain common interests which would enable them to establish a more harmonious pattern of inter-state relationships.[3] The Bandung Conference in 1955 represented the high-water mark of this thinking. The conference was attended by delgates from twenty-three Asian and six African countries and at the time it was hailed as the beginning of a new era of Afro-Asian solidarity. But the significance of Bandung lies in the divergence of views it uncovered. It showed how precarious and how fragile was the façade of common interest. It failed to establish any guarantee of continued co-operation. And none was possible because a good proportion of the participants were even then involved in disputes amongst themselves or were already committed in the East–West struggle.

Events after Bandung confirmed the disunity of the Afro-Asian states. The existence of actual and potential sources of friction and conflict largely overshadowed the shared problems, fears, and interests. The pulls and pressures from the Soviet Union and the United States created new disagreements and exacerbated old ones. Later the declining intensity of the cold war weakened the sense of Afro-Asian identity and mission.

---

[2] The manpower difficulties attracted considerable public attention in these years and became an important consideration in the discussion about Britain's role. For this reason the manpower position is considered in this chapter. Other aspects of the strain are discussed in ch. 7 below.

[3] Jawaharlal Nehru was the leading exponent of this doctrine and it lay behind India's opposition to CENTO and SEATO.

By the time of the Belgrade Conference in 1961, despite a convergence of views on anti-colonial questions, there was little to suggest that habits of co-operation were being acquired. Almost all that the new states had in common was a lack of national power and by itself that was hardly an adequate basis for concerted action.

Nor was there much progress to report in the development of regional power balances. In South-east Asia many of the regional states were preoccupied with the more immediate problems of internal security; others were already looking to the United States to provide some countervailing power to the shadow cast by the emergence of China as a major military power. In the Arabian Peninsula and the Persian Gulf an indigenous balance seemed scarcely further advanced than fifty years earlier. In Africa the problem was seen in a rather different light. With the number of independent states rapidly increasing, that continent was unhappily poised between the euphoria of racial unity and the fear of the sort of fragmentation posed by the Congo episode and the movement of the French-speaking and some other states away from, and perhaps against, the remainder. To the outside observer there were still few encouraging signs that either unity or a power balance was in the process of emerging.

The reasons for this Balkanized pattern were complex. Probably the most important factor was the domestic instability and disunity of many of the individual countries. Ethnic, linguistic, religious, and cultural differences inhibited the development of national solidarity on the Western model and meant that the threat of internal disorder was seldom far from the minds of national leaders. Further, external conflicts frequently had internal repercussions, thus increasing the difficulty of constructing indigenous balances. One such source of tension was the presence of racial minorities in many countries of Asia and Africa. Another was the artificiality and uncertainty of national boundaries, which were more often attributable to the accident of colonial control than to any geographical, cultural, or ethnic division. A second factor was the low level of national power both in absolute and relative terms. The resultant sense of insecurity, heightened by the realization that any power balance could be easily upset by the injection of even small numbers of outside arms into the system, led many of the Afro-Asian states to maintain their existing defence links with external powers or to develop new ones.

It was against this background that late in 1961 the Chiefs of Staff addressed themselves to the likely burden of Britain's defence responsibilities over the next ten years. In a series of meetings the Chiefs of Staff considered in turn Britain's various defence commitments throughout the world, with the object of determining the sort of operations which Britain might be expected to undertake over the next decade. Their conclusions were set out in a paper produced in January 1962. The gist of the paper was that the main threat had shifted from Europe to Africa and Asia. Among other factors, the preponderance of atomic power of the West and the emergence of the Sino-Soviet split made war in Europe very unlikely. Outside Europe, however, the rise of nationalism had increased the likelihood of minor disturbances and the Communists could be expected to exploit every opportunity to their own advantage. The Chiefs of Staff therefore concluded that Britain must increasingly be prepared to intervene in Asia and Africa and that this would be her major military role over the next decade.

However, given the existing size and shape of the armed forces, there were certain general limitations to the range of operations which could be carried out. In the first place, Britain could undertake only one major operation at a time. Secondly, not more than one major operation could be conducted each year. Thirdly, there was a limit to the number of minor operations which could be carried out in a given period of time. This third limitation derived from the size of Britain's reserves of equipment and manpower, whereas the first and second followed from the size of the front line. Apparently by setting down these limitations the Chiefs of Staff hoped to focus the Defence Committee's attention on the imbalance between the extent of Britain's existing commitments and the forces then available.

The paper was carefully argued and it was well received by the Minister of Defence and by the Defence Committee. Its general tenor accorded neatly with the government's own thinking and it became something of a strategic blueprint for the next few years. As events turned out, it identified fairly accurately the sort of emergencies which in fact occurred, although it failed to foresee the conflicts in Malaysia and Southern Arabia.

One factor which influenced the thinking of the Chiefs of Staff and even more the government was the circumstances and the success of the Kuwait operation in July 1961. Less than a week after the abrogation of the Anglo-Kuwaiti Agreement of 1899 and its replacement by a new agreement of 'close friendship' between the two countries, General Kassem, the Iraqi Prime Minister, revived an old claim that Kuwait was an inseparable part of Iraq. After rejecting Kuwait's new independence, he went on to announce that a decree would shortly be issued appointing the Ruler of Kuwait as Qaimaqam (district governor) of Kuwait under the Basra province of Iraq.[4] Over the next few days evidence derived from a number of sources, including an important report channelled through the War Office, indicated that reinforcements—especially of armour—were making towards Basra, close to the border with Kuwait.[5] The Iraqi forces were thus in a position to invade Kuwait in a matter of hours. In these circumstances the Ruler of Kuwait made a formal request for British assistance on the morning of 30 June.

The British reaction was prompt and businesslike. Within twenty-four hours 42 Commando, Royal Marines, had landed at Kuwait from HMS *Bulwark* and the first of a squadron of Centurion tanks had disembarked from HMS *Striker*. By 7 July the British force had been substantially reinforced and included the Headquarters 24th Infantry Brigade plus two battalions, the 2nd Parachute Battalion Group, 42 and 45 Commandos, Royal Marines, one squadron of the 11th Hussars with armoured cars, and two batteries of the 29th Field Regiment, Royal Artillery. Air support on station consisted of two Hunter squadrons (one ground attack and the other fighter reconnaissance), eight Canberra bombers, and a number of Beverleys for short-range transport. In addition, other Hunter and Canberra squadrons and V-bomber squadrons with high-explosive bombs were alerted and positioned to intervene if necessary. On the naval side HMS *Bulwark* and the Amphibious Warfare Squadron were initially supported by only one frigate. The other two frigates assigned to the Persian Gulf made hurried

[4] *Times*, 26 June 1961.
[5] *New Statesman*, 14 July 1961. But see Ralph Hewins, *A Golden Dream* (1963), pp. 282–9 for a contrary account.

returns from Karachi and Mombasa. The fleet carrier HMS *Victorious* with her escort of one destroyer and three frigates, proceeded at full speed from the Hong Kong area and reached Kuwait on 9 July. HMS *Centaur*, accompanied by three destroyers and a tanker, sailed through the Suez Canal on 5 July and could have reached Kuwait seven days later, but on Admiralty instructions was held at Aden. By 10 July a total of 45 ships was under the command of the Flag Officer, Middle East.[6]

Three days after the arrival of the first British troops their commander declared that he was satisfied he could deal with any Iraqi attack.[7] Independent observers were not so complacent but there was general agreement that at least by 9 July, when the arrival of HMS *Victorious* ensured British air supremacy, an Iraqi attack would have been defeated. As things turned out, however, the British force was never put to the test and the war clouds disappeared almost as quickly as they had gathered. In the space of a few weeks British troops withdrew and Kuwait's admission to the Arab League on 20 August brought an Arab agreement to support her independence. By mid-October an Arab force of about 2,400 men was on duty within her territory.[8]

Briefly summarized, the British reaction to the operation was one of profound satisfaction. At the very least, it was regarded as finally burying the Suez episode and to some extent it gave rise to a new feeling of confidence, not only in the strategic apparatus constructed since 1957, but also in Britain's ability to play a major role in shaping events outside Europe. In succeeding months the operation was held up in official circles as an example of the speed and efficiency with which British forces could counter limited threats to the peace east of Suez. Without too much questioning, both the government and the press accepted that the rapid deployment of British forces had prevented, or at least had been an important element in deter-

---

[6] The daily press gave a fairly complete account of force movements, and the approximate strength of the British forces at various stages in the build-up can be gauged without undue difficulty. Useful summaries are also available in N. Brown, *Strategic Mobility*, pp. 88–9; Moulton, *Defence in a Changing World*, pp. 107–8; and Verrier, *An Army for the Sixties*, pp. 225–7.

[7] As reported in *The Economist*, 8 July 1961.

[8] But see *Times* leader 'After the Withdrawal', 16 Oct. 1961.

ring, an Iraqi attack.[9] Nor was it forgotten that the British troops had promptly withdrawn once the threat had receded—a crucial factor, it was believed, in enabling other new states to call for British assistance with some equanimity.

Much of the discussion about Kuwait has concentrated on the military lessons of the operation,[10] but its importance for future planning extended to the political framework within which the military appreciation was structured. Underlying all the discussion of the military aspects was the assumption that this was the sort of threat which could be expected anywhere in Britain's area of interest. Especially to the point, the Iraqi threat provided the Chiefs of Staff with a concrete example to which they could point. In much the same way, ministers used the incident to help sell the government's strategic assessment to the House of Commons. Moreover, the actual operation was taken to show that British forces could now handle such a threat with smoothness and despatch. This theme ran clearly through the 1962 White Paper and it came out explicitly in the subsequent debate. Watkinson, for example, told the House that the Kuwait operation was the basis of 'much of our future planning'.[11] In the debate on the Army Estimates, the Secretary of State for War confidently declared: 'Outside Europe, the Army is prepared to intervene to keep the peace in all parts of the world where our interests or those of our allies are directly involved, and we have proved our ability in Kuwait.'[12]

Thus far our analysis has postulated the elevation of military over political considerations in the upgrading of the priority of the defence role east of Suez. That is to say, the shift in the strategic balance took precedence over the political significance of the European commitment, despite the 1962 negotiations for British entry into the Common Market. There was one diplomatic consideration, however, which worked to reinforce the

[9] Several writers have argued that this was not so. According to Hewins a traditional Iraq-Kuwait understanding was the real reason why the attack did not take place; see *A Golden Dream*, pp. 292 f. Neville Brown has suggested that the prospective hazards involved in aggravating simultaneously the oil companies, the other Arab states, and Persia were probably a sufficient deterrent in themselves. *Strategic Mobility*, p. 95.
[10] The military side of the operation is discussed in ch. 7 below.
[11] 655 HC Deb., 5 Mar. 1962, col. 44.
[12] Ibid. 8 Mar 1962, col. 618.

strategic assessment and that was the change in the American attitude to the east of Suez role. Until late in 1961 American diplomacy was primarily directed towards increasing the British contribution to NATO, and the east of Suez role attracted little attention or serious support. The first recorded indication of a change in policy was given by Paul Nitze, then Assistant Secretary of Defence for International Security Affairs, in an address to the Institute for Strategic Studies on 11 December 1961. The new administration had then been in office eleven months, and in line with McNamara's policy of a conventional build-up in Europe, Nitze attacked the notion that the strengthening of NATO's non-nuclear forces was defeatist or lessened the credibility of the nuclear deterrent.[13] However, in reply to a question by Sir John Slessor, Nitze startled his audience by saying that the adminstration was more concerned that Britain maintain the present number of troops east of Suez than in Germany. Nitze's disclosure led to some re-thinking in the press. *The Times*, for example, in a leader later that month argued that Britain should bear her share of the defence of Europe 'without defaulting on commitments to the other regional alliances'—a considerable change from the stance it had held for some months previously.[14] What impact Nitze's visit had on official thinking is unknown, but certainly the government was aware of the new administration's position and it was regarded as a matter of some significance.

By February 1962 it was clear that the United States was exerting considerable pressure to keep Britain east of Suez. On 15 February Robert McNamara was reported to have testified at a closed session of the Senate Military Appropriations Sub-Committee that the administration strongly favoured the continued deployment of British forces in a broad area of Asia, and that he had so informed the British government. Both McNamara and General Lemnitzer, Chairman of the Joint Chiefs of Staff, told the sub-committee that British withdrawals from Asia would constitute a virtual invitation to the Sino-Soviet bloc to move into what would then be a power vacuum. According to those present, McNamara illustrated the value of the British deployment in the area by citing the

[13] This part of Nitze's speech is quoted in Kaufmann, *The McNamara Strategy*, pp. 108–10.
[14] 'Defence in 1962', 28 Dec. 1961.

operation in Kuwait.[15] Later reports told much the same story.[16]

The 1962 White Paper

Although the 1962 White Paper heralded no drastic change in objectives or strategic doctrine, Britain was firmly set on the road to an expanded conception of the world role. This emerged clearly from the key sections considering Britain's military commitments in the light of contemporary trends. After a perfunctory acknowledgement of Britain's obligations to NATO, the White Paper hastened to add that here Britain had a particular problem. Account must be taken, it argued, of the tasks which Britain had to perform in other parts of the world, 'tasks which contribute to the containment of Communism and the maintenance of peace and order in areas whose stability is vital to the West'.[17] Paragraph 15 then went on to note the heavy balance of payments burden imposed by the European deployment, and to hint that forces in Germany might have to be cut in the interests of foreign exchange. *The Times* commented that 'on the evidence of the White Paper the government looks upon this (the European commitment) as the least of its responsibilities.'[18] In the Mediterranean Britain had no longer to discharge her obligations alone and therefore there could be some adjustment of forces. The White Paper was more equivocal about Africa. For the moment Britain would maintain the military means for the support of the civil power in various African countries, but during the sixties this requirement would have to be re-examined in the light of its continuing need. On the British role in Arabia, the Persian Gulf, and South-east Asia the White Paper left no doubt. Britain was vitally interested in the preservation of peace and stability in these areas and the forces there would have to be maintained. Indeed, in later sections the White Paper went on to emphasize the require-

---

[15] *Times*, 16 Feb. 1962.
[16] See e.g. *Sunday Times*, 25 Feb. 1962. Apparently in 1962 the US Naval War College analysed whether or not the navy's rebuilding programme should assume strategic responsibility for the Indian Ocean area. The report recommended that the Indian Ocean should remain a charge upon Britain. Verrier, *An Army for the Sixties*, p. 262, n. 10. See also *Christian Science Monitor*, 22 Dec. 1962.
[17] MoD, *Statement on Defence 1962*, Cmnd 1639 (1962), para 15.
[18] 5 Mar. 1962.

ment for strategically mobile forces to support these commitments, and to outline plans for strengthening Britain's capability in this sphere.

The process of inter-regional adjustment—the retraction in Europe and the Mediterranean because of the upgrading of the east of Suez role—resulted directly from the arbitrary allocation of defence resources. The Chiefs of Staff paper of Janaury 1962 had assumed a growth rate of about 4 per cent a year, and a defence expenditure of about 7 per cent of the GNP. This apportionment was written into the 1962 White Paper, paragraph 12 of which explained that the government's aim was not to cut defence expenditure but to contain it. Taken in conjunction with the earlier decision that compulsory military service was politically unacceptable, this meant a defence budget of about £1,700 million to £1,800 million a year (at 1962 prices) and armed forces of rather less than 400,000. The years 1963 and 1964 saw no change in this general framework. Both the political parties and the responsible press accepted the need for an arbitrary limit on defence resources, and 7 per cent was broadly accepted as a reasonable compromise. Nor did the nuclear budget provide much scope for argument about reallocation of resources. About 10 per cent of the defence vote was still devoted directly to the nuclear deterrent, and given that Britain was to remain a nuclear power, it was accepted that this figure was relatively fixed.[19] Thus the problem facing defence planners was to allocate conventional defence resources in a way which would minimize risk.

Notwithstanding the decided shift in emphasis east of Suez, the justification for the deployment of power in the area remained very much a mixed bag of bilateral obligations, treaty commitments, and a general interest in the peace and stability of the area. Compared with previous years, rather more stress was placed on those responsibilities which were Britain's alone. At the same time, however, the government did its best to elevate CENTO and SEATO to the level of NATO. Harold Watkinson solemnly told the House of Commons that Britain was equally committed to all three, and he later went on to explain that 'these three alliances are absolutely interdependent, and the failure of one is the failure of all.'[20]

[19] See Thorneycroft, 673 HC Deb., 4 Mar. 1963, col. 31.
[20] 655 HC Deb., 5 Mar. 1962, col. 46, and ibid. 6 Mar. col. 324.

Despite the repeated statement of Britain's interest in peace and stability, the White Paper made no attempt to spell out any more general role for British forces east of Suez. Nor was there any suggestion that Britain would act independently, apart from operations in support of states which were under British protection or to which Britain was bound by bilateral agreement. In the Commons debate, however, John Profumo's use of the word 'interests' instead of 'commitments' or 'obligations', and his reference to keeping the peace, suggested a rather broader role.[21] Perhaps the most that can be said is that both in alliance planning and in bilateral commitment much depends upon construction and circumstance, and the general impression conveyed was that henceforward the government would be more likely to adopt an expansive interpretation than would have been the case a few years earlier.

In Parliament the government's analysis was received with mixed feelings. To many on the Conservative side it was heartening that the most recent swing in the strategic balance emphasized the old beats of empire rather than the grey political realities of Germany and the Rhine. Few doubted that troops could be more profitably employed east of Suez than in NATO and there was almost a sense of relief to be discussing once more external lines of communication and sea mobility rather than trip wires and continental threats. Labour speakers adopted a very different line. NATO was Britain's first responsibility and it could not be lumped together with SEATO and CENTO. What mattered above all was that BAOR be brought up to strength—only Shinwell on the Labour side could see no purpose in having 55,000 and not 45,000 troops in Germany.[22] Yet for all the accent on Europe, it was noticeable that Labour front-bench speakers adopted a more moderate position on the east of Suez role than a year earlier. Patrick Gordon Walker, for example, admitted that Britain's responsibilities must continue, and George Brown accepted the need for seaborne forces to carry out Britain's world obligations, especially in the Far East—though, it seemed, without very much idea of the cost involved.[23]

[21] See the quotation from his speech on p. 221 above.
[22] Indeed he went on to advocate withdrawing British troops from Germany altogether and injecting them into the strategic reserve. 655 HC Deb., 6 Mar. 1962, coll. 257-8.
[23] Ibid. 5 Mar. 1962, col. 70, and 6 Mar. 1962, col. 324.

Underlying much of the parliamentary discussion of the White Paper were certain assumptions about the nature of Britain's relations with the new states of Asia and Africa, and about her role in the world, which were shortly to become the basis of a more coherent theory which could underpin the deployment of power east of Suez. It was obvious enough that British forces were organized and equipped to provide military support for the new states. What was perhaps not so obvious was that for reasons of history and circumstance, British influence in the area remained very substantial and that a British presence was likely to be acceptable when that of other Western powers would not.[24] There was therefore a sense of responsibility: for some Labour MPs primarily a duty to the new states of Africa and Asia; for others, like Viscount Montgomery, an opportunity and a requirement to lead Europe into the broader field of international security.[25] There was a second aspect here: Britain's role was not seen simply in terms of national interest narrowly defined. The maintenance of stability in Africa and Asia was fundamentally an international interest, and although it was true that Britain had a much stronger motive for involvement—for political, moral, and economic reasons—than the European countries, it was a difference of degree and not of kind.[26]

In a sense the 1962 White Paper and the subsequent debate mark a half-way point between the justification of the main overseas deployments of British power in terms of specific commitments and regional alliances, and that comprehended by the notion of peacekeeping. It would be unwise to make too much of this point, since in 1957 and 1958, for example, general considerations of overseas security tended to be subsumed under particular headings, while in 1964 and 1965 the pattern was reversed. Moreover, it must be remembered that what we are contrasting is largely the method by which the same problems

[24] See e.g. Lord Carrington's reflections, 238 HL Deb., 21 Mar. 1962, col. 535.
[25] According to Montgomery, NATO 'must cease now to look inwards at its own affairs and look outwards. Those nations which have world-wide commitments and world-wide responsibilities outside the NATO area must be given freedom to handle them. In fact, one can say that the time has come, after twelve years of NATO, to redeploy our NATO forces'. 238 HL Deb., 21 Mar. 1962, col. 580.
[26] For a critical analysis of the concept of stability as an end of policy see the author's 'The West, Military Intervention and the Third World', *Brassey's Annual 1971*, pp. 65–79.

were analysed and to some extent the language in which they
were discussed. Still, there were some important differences
between the two approaches, if only by implication. It can
hardly be denied, for example, that the peacekeeping role was
of broader ambit than that based on alliance and bilateral
commitment. Of scarcely less importance, it suggested a more
independent role and even a sense of mission. To go beyond
this, however, is to tread on shaky ground. No canonic formulation of the concept of peacekeeping is possible, for the simple
reason that it meant different things to different people. In
one context it could be interpreted as referring mainly to local
stability—that is, keeping the Queen's peace rather in the old
Indian tradition. This was certainly what many soldiers understood by the term. In part this merely reflected the soldier's
proper concern with his immediate environment. It was not
so much a disregard for the wider setting as a recognition that
in the last resort the stability of the area depended upon the
stability of the individual states. Sailors and airmen, on the
other hand, tended to adopt a loftier view in keeping with
their more general responsibilities and the nature of their
weaponry. To them peacekeeping meant maintaining the
status quo in the area generally. Similarly peacekeeping could
be viewed from either a national or an international standpoint.
While some saw Britain's east of Suez role as a kind of nuclear-
age Pax Britannica, others saw it as part of a world security
system still in embryonic form.[27] Again the concept had strong
emotional overtones which tended to differ according to the
particular perspective of the individual. For many conservatives it was seen as a link with the imperial past; for others it
was associated with a new conception of a multiracial Commonwealth; for some it was a role held in trust for the United Nations.

The Strategic Assessment Confirmed

The twelve months following the defence review provided a
striking vindication of the government's strategic assessment.
Against a background of almost continuous international

---

[27] The latter viewpoint was well put by Peter Calvocoressi in 'No Time to Retire',
Survival, 6/3 (May–June 1964), pp. 142–5, and by Leonard Beaton in 'Strategy:
East or West?', *JRUSI*, 111/644 (Nov. 1966), pp. 281–90, esp. pp. 286–7.

tension in Asia one emergency after another dominated Whitehall's attention. At the same time the task of maintaining internal security in the various colonies and protected states imposed its recurrent demands.[28] The events of these months were important in that they drew Britain more firmly into the elaborate tangle of Third-World tensions. Once an issue reached crisis point the government was faced with the prospect of demonstrating in a practical way that it took its security responsibilities seriously, or of allowing its role as a military principal in Asia and Africa to lapse by default. And a military involvement, however limited, represented a more positive commitment than any formal obligation or general pronouncement and one, moreover, which had a way of snowballing of its own accord.

The government's response to the various emergencies of the period sheds light on the extent to which British policy was a mixture of certain long-term lines of approach and specific reactions to particular crises. When the government was confronted by the requirement to act or at least to declare its position publicly, some of the assumptions in the background of policy-making came to the surface. This was true of the three major crises of 1962—Thailand in May, India in October and November, and Brunei in December—each of which gives some insight into the government's understanding of the east of Suez role.

The Thai emergency arose out of the rout of the Royal Laotian army by the Pathet Lao in the Plain of Jars in Laos. Following the Pathet Lao capture of Nam Tha, an important town not far from the Thai border, on 6 May, many of the right-wing forces retreated into Thailand. Communist troops were believed to have followed them for some forty miles, and this led to Thai and American fears that in the confused situation then prevailing, the Pathet Lao might embark on a major offensive behind the Thai border.[29] The United States immediately ordered a military build-up and on 16 May the

---

[28] In the internal security role, British forces undertook some minor operations in East Africa and carried out routine policing tasks in the Aden Colony and Protectorate. In June the navy resumed guardship duties at Gan.

[29] For the government's understanding of the situation see Edward Heath's statement, 659 HC Deb., 15 May 1962, coll. 1147–51.

first elements of an additional 4,000 American troops began to arrive in Thailand.[30] In Bangkok the SEATO Council of Representatives issued a warning that any Communist aggression would be resisted but apparently it was left to individual members to take such independent action as they deemed appropriate, under a newly formulated doctrine that the member states had an independent at well as a collective responsibility.[31] At the same time the United States requested Britain together with certain other SEATO allies to send token forces to Thailand.[32]

The following day the Prime Minister told the House of Commons that the government had not received a formal request from the government of Thailand but, should one be received, Britain would be prepared to send a contingent.[33] Macmillan was at first evasive about Britain's responsibility under the Treaty, but when pressed he went on to say that each government must decide for itself what to do: 'This is a question where an ally—although this is not a formal action on the part of the SEATO Powers as a whole—is involved; and an ally has a right to call upon all her other allies.'[34]

This interpretation represented an important policy statement for it in fact broadened Britain's obligations under the treaty. In effect what the government was saying was that it accepted the United States view that SEATO obligations were individual as well as collective.

The prospect of Britain's involvement in the Thai-Laotian situation was not to the liking of the Labour left-wing and Macmillan's statement was followed by a motion urging an immediate debate. This was resisted by Hugh Gaitskell and his colleagues on the Labour front bench on the ground that it might create abroad the impression that the opposition funda-

---

[30] *New York Herald Tribune*, 17 May 1962.
[31] Until 1962 it had been understood that any action under SEATO would be unanimous. However, the unreliability of France, Pakistan, and, to some extent, the Philippines forced re-thinking on this issue and during the Laotian crisis bilateral action replaced joint action as the means of implementing the treaty. The first formalization of this change was contained in a joint statement by the Foreign Minister of Thailand and the American Secretary of State on 6 Mar. 1962. (For text see *New York Times*, 7 Mar. 1962.) Several other SEATO countries followed suit.
[32] *Times*, 17 May 1962.
[33] 659 HC Deb., 17 May 1962, col. 1530.
[34] Ibid. coll. 1534–5.

mentally opposed the government's decision. The front-bench position was that so long as it was clear that British forces were solely for the purpose of defending Thailand—with which the government agreed—it accepted the need for Britain and other SEATO powers to reassure Thailand of allied support. A division was taken and the motion was defeated by 173 votes to 36.[35] A few days later Thailand made a formal request for a British force and on 25 May six Hunters and a Canberra took off from Singapore for Bangkok. They were followed by some 200 ground crew and a few additional aircraft. The force withdrew on 16 November.

As tension eased in Thailand the Sino-Indian conflict erupted in the Himalayas. The immediate incident which triggered off the war concerned a frontier post established by the Indians in June 1962 in disputed territory on the border of the North-East Frontier Agency. On 8 September the Chinese advanced into the area and established positions near the post. Exchanges of notes between India and China proved fruitless and in the following weeks India publicly committed itself to use force if necessary to expel the Chinese and made military preparations accordingly. The major Chinese offensive began on 20 October when Chinese troops moved simultaneously into the North-East Frontier Agency and Ladakh, securing control of much of the frontier area. On 16 November China advanced again and by 21st, when Peking announced a cease-fire, Chinese forces had penetrated more than 150 miles into Indian territory.

The Chinese assault brought an immediate response from Britain. Macmillan promised: 'What they [the Indians] ask us to do to help them, we will do.'[36] Arrangements were made for a continuous supply of small arms and ammunition to India, the first consignments reaching Delhi on the 29 October. *The Times* echoed the general satisfaction when it noted that: 'Britain, first with an offer to help, has also been the first to supply it.'[37] Further consignments were flown to India in RAF Britannias and the remainder was sent by sea. It was later

---

[35] Ibid. coll. 1542–51. At a private meeting of the Parliamentary Labour party that night, Gaitskell was reported to have said that the party was not prepared to see South-east Asia go Communist, and that it would therefore support sending a token British force to Thailand. *Times*, 18 May 1962.

[36] 666 HC Deb., 30 Oct. 1962, col. 34.

[37] 30 Oct. 1962.

announced that Britain had offered to supply these items as a gift, and after some hesitation India accepted.[38]

On 10 November Major-General E. S. Lindsay, Assistant Master-General of Ordnance, arrived in Delhi for talks with Indian defence officials about the immediate requirements of the Indian army.[39] Later that month a high-ranking British mission which included the CIGS visited India to discuss long-range needs.[40] It was joined two days later by Duncan Sandys. Very little is known of the results of these discussions beyond the fact that they figured in the Macmillan-Kennedy agreement reached at Nassau in December, to extend a £42 million military aid programme to India. Under the terms of this agreement, Britain and other Commonwealth countries would contribute aid up to a financial limit of about £21 million, with the United States providing a similar amount. The United Kingdom contribution was expected to be of the order of £15–17 million for the army. The final figure would depend upon the amount devoted to air force supplies, and upon other Commonwealth contributions.[41]

Notwithstanding a number of high-level exchanges between the British and Indian governments, no attempt was made publicly to spell out the nature or extent of Britain's commitment to the defence of India. The reason for this would seem to rest largely with Britain's anxiety not to cause unnecessary alarm in Pakistan and India's political sensitivity to any public acknowledgement of military dependence. Britain's ready response to Indian requests and the various ministerial statements did, however, give substance to the long-assumed moral obligation to the defence of India. The *New York Times* reported that the British government would carefully and sympathetically consider any Indian request for British troops as reinforcements against any further aggression by China.[42] This was confirmed by Peter Thorneycroft in a speech on 21 November.[43] However, General Hull's statement that there are many Indians in

[38] Sandys, 667 HC Deb., 13 Nov. 1962, col. 36, and *Times*, 28 Nov. 1962.
[39] *Hindu*, 10 Nov. 1962.
[40] *Hindu*, 22 Nov. 1962.
[41] HC, *Fourth Report ... Session 1962–63: Spring Supplementary Estimates* (1963), p. 56, para. 232.
[42] 2 Nov. 1962.
[43] *Hindu*, 23 Nov. 1962.

India and 'not an awful lot of men over here', indicated that aid in other directions was both more useful and more likely.[44]

A further indication that some responsibility for the defence of India was regarded as a continuing commitment was given by the despatch of a joint Commonwealth–United States air defence mission in January 1963. According to newspaper reports, soon after the fall of Se La and Bomdi La in the North-East Frontier Agency on 18 and 19 November, Jawaharlal Nehru made an urgent request to the United States for an 'air umbrella' to guard Indian cities against possible attack by the Chinese air force. An American aircraft carrier began the voyage from the Pacific to the Bay of Bengal but the an-nouncement of the cease-fire led to its recall before it reached Indian waters. No further action was taken until early in January when President Kennedy wrote to ask the Indian Prime Minister whether India wished to proceed with the scheme.[45] Nehru reiterated his request and on 30 January a fifteen-man Commonwealth–United States mission arrived in Delhi with the task, among other things, of assessing the feasibility of providing air cover for Indian cities and other targets, should China move south again.[46] Although at first Nehru denied reports that an air umbrella was under considera-tion, he later explained to the Lok Sabha that plans were afoot to improve India's airfields and communications facilities, and that these steps would make it possible for the West to lend air support in an emergency.[47] Early in July a Western plan for the air defence of India received the tacit approval of Nehru's government, and on the 22 July it announced accep-tance of the scheme, stoutly maintaining that it was nothing of the sort.[48] In November 12 RAF Javelins, supported by some 250 ground crew, took part in air defence exercises over Delhi and Calcutta.

Compared with the Sino-Indian conflict, the Azahari rebellion in Brunei was a minuscule affair but it none the less had important implications for the development of Britain's

[44] *Times*, 22 Nov. 1962.

[45] *Times*, 24 Jan. 1963; *New York Times*, 25 Jan. 1963; *Hindu*, 25 Jan. 1963.

[46] See esp. Dean Rusk's statement, *Hindu*, 29 Jan. 1963. Also *Times* and *Daily Telegraph*, 31 Jan. 1963.

[47] See *Daily Telegraph*, 11 Feb. 1963; *Times*, 18 Feb. 1963; and *Guardian*, 22 Feb. 1963.

[48] *New York Times*, 13 July 1963. *Times*, 23 July 1963.

overseas defence policy. The rebellion was linked to a dispute between the Sultan of Brunei and Azahari, a minor nationalist leader, over the Malaysian issue. In July 1962 the Sultan announced that he accepted in principle Brunei's entry into the Malaysian Federation. This was opposed by Azahari and his party, which held all sixteen elected seats in the Legislative Council, and an illegal para-military body was formed to take direct action. The rebels claimed to be opposing Brunei's entry into Malaysia even though no final decision had been taken at that stage.[49] In fact, however, it seems that the real origins of the revolt lay in dissatisfaction with the rate of political progress and in local schemes for a united Borneo under Brunei leadership. The fighting began in the early hours of 8 December. An attack on the palace was quickly repulsed by the Sultan's forces but in the oil town of Seria the rebels gained control of the oil installations and held about 400 Europeans hostage. In these circumstances the Sultan requested British assistance in putting down the rebels.

Britain's rapid and successful intevention followed the pattern established at Kuwait.[50] The first Gurkha company arrived from Singapore at 8 p.m. on the 8th, and the remainder of the 1st Battalion, 2nd Gurkha Rifles, flew in later that night and the following day. Brunei town was swiftly cleared and the arrival of further reinforcements enabled troops to move up country. By 10 December nearly 2,000 men had been moved into the state, Pioneer aircraft were operating and Hunters standing by, and three of the twelve warships and auxiliaries diverted to the scene had arrived. The following day saw Seria retaken and the hostages released. Thereafter army and Marine units advanced steadily through Brunei and parts of Sarawak and North Borneo clearing up rebel pockets. By the 15th organized resistance had collapsed, but for some months anti-insurgency operations continued in the jungle and coastal swamps. According to a Ministry of Defence estimate more than

---

[49] The Sultan later declined to join the Federation.
[50] This account is based on the daily press reports and subsequent articles in the strategic journals. Of the latter see esp. V Adm B. B. Schofield, 'Maritime Aspects of the Brunei Operation', *Army Quarterly*, 86/1 (Apr. 1963), pp. 14–18; Maj Gen J. L. Moulton, 'Brush-Fire Operation – Brunei, December 1962', *Brassey's Annual 1963*, pp. 77–84; Brig C N. Barclay, 'East of Suez', *Marine Corps Gazette* (US), Feb. 1965, pp. 45–9.

2,000 rebels were put out of action during the campaign, the majority being captured.[51]

Although it was agreed that the operation was prompt and effective, different views were held about the lessons to be derived from the emergency. In the government's view the incident reinforced the case for a strong military presence. However, it was now prepared to admit that the world role imposed a very heavy strain on Britain's resources.[52] In other quarters attention was primarily focused on the planning relating to reinforcement had the campaign been prolonged. Although the rebel forces were small and poorly organized, the government was forced to detach an essential component of signals from BAOR, to alert half the strategic reserve in the United Kingdom, and to plan to employ the 5th Field Regiment, Royal Artillery, without its guns, in an infantry role.[53] In some sections of Parliament and the press this was taken to demonstrate what many defence commentators had long been saying, namely, that an army of 175,000 was seriously overstretched supporting existing commitments and that one unexpected crisis could bring down the whole system.[54]

Senior commanders appear to have steered a midway course. Although the manpower strain was already causing some concern, few military men thought the situation as grave as depicted by Denis Healey or *The Times*. It was sometimes suggested in Whitehall that many senior officers, particularly in the army, were reluctant to admit the extent of the problem because of their commitment to all-Regular forces (and therefore smaller forces). This consideration may well have influenced military thinking but it can scarcely have been a central factor. Of much greater importance was the fact that British forces in Europe were regarded as a manpower reserve for the world role and few senior officers saw anything imprudent in withdrawing certain of these units in an emergency. Indeed, given the policy of a general-purpose army, this was accepted as an inevitable—and sensible—course. The Treaty permitted temporary withdrawal of troops and aircraft from Germany for operations elsewhere, and, particularly since the *détente*

---

[51] MoD, *Statement on Defence 1963*, Cmnd 1936 (1963), p. 45, para. 12.

[52] Thorneycroft, 673 HC Deb., 5 Mar. 1963, col. 330.

[53] Denis Healey, 673 HC Deb., 4 Mar. 1963, col. 46, and Raymond Fletcher, £60 a Second on Defence (1963), p. 90.

[54] e.g. Healey, as cited in n. 53, and Sir Fitzroy Maclean, ibid. coll. 302–3.

with Russia, this practice was acceptable to the Supreme Allied Commander, Europe. Moreover, it was becoming increasingly apparent that Royal Armoured Corps and Royal Artillery units were unlikely to get active service experience in Europe. For this reason, the Director of the Royal Artillery actually volunteered gunner regiments for active service overseas in an infantry role.[55]

The emergence of Indonesia's hostility to the plan for a federation of Malaya, Singapore, and the Borneo territories had the effect of demonstrating even more clearly than the Brunei revolt both the benefits and the burdens of the world role. When the Malaysian scheme was first publicly proposed in May 1961 Indonesia voiced no objection, professing to regard the proposed federation as a matter for the countries concerned. This view was reiterated by the Indonesian Foreign Minister, Subandrio, when he addressed the United Nations General Assembly on 20 November 1961.[56] One month later, however, the Indonesian Communist Party (the PKI) denounced Malaysia as a 'form of neo-colonialism', and with the growth of PKI influence in 1962, this outlook gained currency in government circles.[57] The Azahari revolt provided the occasion for Indonesia to adopt a posture of hostility to the new federation. The week following the revolt both Soekarno and the Indonesian Parliament declared their support for the revolutionaries, and a National Committee of Solidarity with the struggle in North Borneo was formed. On 20 January 1963 Subandrio announced that Indonesia would begin a policy of 'confrontation' towards Malaya. He accused Malaya of being accomplice of 'neo-imperialists' and said that Malaysia was an extension of 'neo-colonialism'.[58]

The threat of Indonesian action over Malaysia, coming on top of clearing operations in Borneo which continued to tie up British troops, led Far East Headquarters to press for reinforcements from the United Kingdom. Reportedly both

[55] The general feeling of army commanders at the time was that east of Suez service was a 'shot in the arm' for forces stationed in Europe.
[56] See Australia, Dept of External Affairs, *Malaysia* (Canberra, 1963), p. 10. (Select Docs on Int. Aff., no. 1 of 1963.)
[57] See further H. F. Armstrong, 'The Troubled Birth of Malaysia', *Foreign Affairs*, 41/4 (July 1963), pp. 673–93.
[58] For Indonesian statements see *Malaysia*, cited in n. 56, p. 11. For a discussion see G. P. Means, 'Malaysia—a New Federation in South East Asia', *Pacific Affairs*, 36/2 (summer 1963), pp. 138–59.

Admiral Sir David Luce, C in C Far East, and Lieutenant-General Sir Nigel Poett, C in C Far East Land Forces, were agreed that the existing theatre forces were inadequate should it become necessary to send further troops to Borneo.[59] As a result of Admiral Luce's representations, late in January an infantry brigade of the United Kingdom strategic reserve was put at 72 hours' notice to move.[60] After two weeks at alert the brigade was stood down, apparently because of the reluctance of the Minister and the Chiefs of Staff to authorize a move which seemed likely to be in the nature of a semi-permanent Far Eastern reinforcement. *The Times* commented: 'To lose 51st Brigade now would leave the Chiefs of Staff virtually without an effective reserve.'[61]

The 1963 White Paper did little more than restate the previous year's policy. Peter Thorneycroft, Minister of Defence since July 1962, admitted as much in his explanatory speech in the Commons.[62] Defence continued to take about 7 per cent of the GNP and direct spending on the deterrent remained at about 10 per cent of the defence budget.[63] The White Paper contained the usual references to the need to maintain peace and stability in Asia and Africa, and the service programmes emphasized the new weapons and equipment which would still enable conventional military force to be brought to bear wherever required. Neither the White Paper nor the responsible ministers took up the notion of peacekeeping, though it was implied in all that was said. The House split broadly on party lines: Labour members stressing NATO, and Conservatives paying most attention to Britain's overseas responsibilities. If anything, the exigencies in the east strengthened the government's case for the world role; the shutting of the European door in January 1963 temporarily dampened the ardour of its critics.

New Advocates and Sharper Critics

By February 1963 there was little doubt that Britain's remaining overseas commitments were likely to become more

---

[59] *Times*, 28 Jan. 1963, and 4 Feb. 1963.
[60] See Thorneycroft's statement 670 HC Deb., 28 Jan. 1963, coll. 580–3.
[61] 4 Feb. 1963.   [62] 673 HC Deb., 4 Mar. 1963, col. 31.
[63] Ibid. However, the form of the deterrent was to change when the V-bombers became obsolete. At Nassau in Dec. 1962 an agreement had been signed for the purchase of Polaris missiles from the United States to replace the cancelled Skybolt.

rather than less burdensome, but the next eighteen months drove the point home with a vengeance. Indonesia's confrontation of Malaysia, disturbance in Aden and fighting in the Radfan, the mutinies in East Africa, and the continuing demands of Cyprus and British Guiana all placed severe strains on British forces and set many critics wondering how much longer the defence establishment could continue to carry such a range of world responsibilities before it collapsed under the load. In South-east Asia the period of quiescence which followed the success of the Borneo operation gave way in April to a number of 'hit and run' raids by Indonesian guerrillas across the 970-mile jungle border of Sarawak and Sabah. From about the beginning of August, guerrilla raids became more frequent and necessitated an increasingly strong build-up of British and Gurkha forces.[64] The proclamation of Malaysia on 16 September brought more serious clashes with terrorist bands, and by the end of that month over 6,000 troops were under Major General Walker's Borneo command.[65] Guerrilla action, including attempted espionage and sabotage in Malaya and Singapore, continued unabated over the next six months. After several attempts at mediation had failed, Indonesia declared a cease-fire on 23 January 1964. However, this declaration was qualified by an announcement that the 'confrontation' policy would continue as before. On 25 March it was officially announced in Kuching that there had been five major Indonesian incursions across the border since President Soekarno had announced the cease-fire.[66]

On the other side of the Indian Ocean trouble followed in the wake of Aden's accession to the South Arabian Federation on 18 January 1963.[67] Out-manoeuvred by the British government, various elements opposed to the Federation resorted

---

[64] The *Guardian*, 20 Nov. 1963, reported that since Aug. there had been 69 armed incursions from Indonesia, four of them major ones.

[65] *Straits Times*, 28 Sept. 1963.

[66] *Keesing's Contemporary Archives 1963–64*, 20183.

[67] The Federation was set up with British encouragement in 1959. The circumstances surrounding Aden's accession are complicated but there can be little doubt that the UK government rushed the merger through, at least partly because it was seen as a way of safeguarding the base facilities. Under the agreement, Britain retained power to administer the base areas separately if she so wished. See further King, *Imperial Outpost—Aden*, pp. 64-73; Kirkman, pp. 149-62, and Monroe, pp. 213-14. There is also an interesting personal account by Sir Charles Johnston, Governor of Aden 1960-3, *The View from Steamer Point* (1964).

to violence, which in December 1963 culminated in a grenade attack directed against the United Kingdom High Commissioner, Sir Kennedy Trevaskis.[68] A state of emergency was immediately declared, and from that time on terrorist activity tied down a substantial part of the resident British force. At the same time unrest increased in the hinterland of the Federation. During the republican *coup* in the Yemen in September 1962, Egyptian troops had established themselves in the towns of Taiz and Sana, and over the following year they proceeded to incite the hill tribes along the frontier to violence. In order to put down dissident tribesmen, a large-scale security operation was launched on 4 January 1964 in the Radfan region, north of Aden. Some resistance was encountered, but Federal troops with British air, artillery, and armoured car support succeeded in establishing a measure of temporary stability.[69]

While fighting continued in South-east Asia and South Arabia violence broke out in East Africa which threatened the area with a repetition of the Congo disaster. A *coup* in Zanzibar on 12 January 1964, and the transfer of a small police contingent from Tanganyika to the island in support of the new regime, sparked off a chain of mutinies in the small armies of Kenya, Tanganyika, and Uganda. British forces were quickly redeployed in such a way that they were able to take action within minutes of requests being received from the three governments on 23 and 24 January.[70] Forces of all three services, including Marines landed from HMS *Centaur* which served as an improvised commando carrier, carried off a *coup de main* characterized by careful organization and great restraint.[71] That the East African territories had been in need of external assistance, and that they had requested British help, had a profound effect on liberal thinking in Britain.

[68] These elements later coalesced in the rival Front for the Liberation of South Yemen (FLOSY) and the National Liberation Front (NLF).

[69] For a full account of the South Arabian campaign see Lt Col Julian Paget, *Last Post: Aden 1964–67* (1969).

[70] See *The Economist*, 1 Feb. 1964, and esp. the excellent map on p. 395 showing British deployments.

[71] The daily press gave full coverage of the operation and expressed great satisfaction with the way in which the mutinies were suppressed. See also Lt Col T. M. P. Stevens, 'A Joint Operation in Tanganyika', *JRUSI*, 110/637 (Feb. 1965), pp. 48–55 and Lt Col W. E. Burr (US) 'On Quelling Mutinies', *Navy*, 70/12 (Dec. 1965), pp. 398–9.

Since 1961 it had been fashionable in certain quarters to argue that there would be no more 'Kuwaits'—meaning that independent states in Asia and Africa were unlikely again to call for British assistance. For some time after January 1964 this line of argument was seldom heard.

Although 1963 had seen British forces over-stretched, January 1964 was the crisis month. *The Times* commented:

So long as the demands upon Britain's armed forces were made at the decorous rate of one military emergency at a time it was possible for the Government, by adroit use of the stage army technique, to create an illusion that the most serious gaps in the defences were being filled. Suddenly the stage has grown too big.[72]

At least some senior officers considered this an exaggerated assessment, but within the Ministry of Defence a number of officials were increasingly thinking along these lines. To some extent the difference between senior officers and those outside the services may be explained by different perspectives in time. As a statement of the existing position, *The Times* leader perhaps over-dramatized the problem but the long-term trend was undeniable. The position adopted was also partly a reflection of the attitude to drawing on European forces for the world role, and outside the services there had long been a marked reluctance to merge the two roles. Now, however, several commentators suggested that Rhine Army troops should be used to bridge the gap.[73] Healey, a recent convert to the east of Suez role, hinted that he would favour such a course.[74] The following day a Rhine Army brigade—less its armoured regiment—was put at seven days' notice to move and one of its battalions at 72 hours' notice. According to the *Sunday Telegraph*, the strategic reserve was now down to one battalion.[75] Another solution was to draw on territorial reserves, and later that month it was reported that preparations were being made to

[72] 'At Full Stretch', 3 Jan. 1964.
[73] See e.g. Chapman Pincher in the *Daily Express*, 3 Jan. 1964.
[74] Answering questions about the possible withdrawal of British troops from Germany to serve in the Far East, Healey admitted that Britain would damage its political reputation in Europe by such a move. But he added: 'The immediate need for British forces is obviously greater overseas than in Western Europe'. *Guardian*, 4 Jan. 1964.
[75] 5 Jan. 1964.

call out the 'Ever-readies'.[76] In the view of the *Daily Telegraph*, these were merely palliatives and what was really needed was what the army leaders had always wanted, namely, an army of 220,000.[77] On 16 January a Labour motion expressing concern at the over-stretch provided the occasion for these various arguments to be discussed in the House of Commons. Harold Wilson led the way with a suggestion that Britain's commitment to BAOR and to NATO might have to be reduced. In his view, if Britain was to deploy its full influence in the world, 1,000 men east of Suez were preferable to another 1,000 in Germany.[78]

Given this background, it was no surprise to find the 1964 White Paper and parliamentary debate more meaty than in 1963. More surprising was the fact that attention was concentrated on the need to maintain the world role rather than on the problems to which it gave rise. The *Statement* itself was a straightforward document which expanded on three important aspects of the Indian Ocean commitment that had been rather glossed over in previous years. In the first place, the elaborate rationalization based on CENTO and SEATO obligations was replaced by a plain statement of Britain's interest in the stability of Africa and Asia. What this meant was that the concept of peacekeeping was spelt out in fuller form and emerged as the primary justification for the British presence east of Suez: 'In Asia and in Africa, in all the under-developed regions, there are powerful pressures for change, and it is for us both an interest and a responsibility to help it to take place with a minimum of violence.'[79]

The White Paper then went on to declare that no immediate reduction in commitments could be expected in the Middle East and the Far East; nor was any immediate relief likely in Africa, as 'new demands of a delicate and difficult kind have been placed upon us.'[80] Finally, paragraph 19 contained the blunt statement that although the burdens of the east of Suez role were heavy, the government intended to maintain it

---

[76] *Times*, 25 Jan. 1964. The 'Ever-readies' were members of the Territorial Army who were liable for service at short notice and without the embodiment of the Territorial Army as a whole.
[77] 6 Jan. 1964
[78] 687 HC Deb., 16 Jan. 1964, coll. 449-50.
[79] MoD, *Statement on Defence 1964*, Cmnd 2270 (1964), p.8.
[80] Ibid.

'for as long as circumstances in these areas, and the vital interests of our friends and allies, demand.'

The most striking feature of the parliamentary discussion was the support for the east of Suez role from the Labour benches. The days when the opposition front bench had called for a gradual withdrawal from Asia and Africa in order to concentrate on Europe seemed far behind as Healey, Paget, and other Labour speakers supported the peacekeeping role with an enthusiasm that even the government could not equal. Almost overnight Britain had become not only a world power again, but the midwife to Africa and Asia and the vanguard of an international police force:

... overwhelmingly our most important and worth-while job in the 10 or 20 years we can foresee ... will be not so much the protection of specific national interests overseas as the prevention of anarchy and war in those areas of the world, many of them newly independent, in Asia, the Middle East and Africa and perhaps in Central America, where we and we alone have at present the political right and the physical capacity to intervene effectively.[81]

Not all Labour members were prepared to go along with Healey's expanded conception of Britain's role. Doubts remained that men like Philip Noel-Baker, Wayland Young (Lord Kennet), and Professor P. M. S. Blackett might convince Harold Wilson to adopt a more narrowly European role should Labour come to power.[82] Patrick Gordon Walker attempted to allay international fears on this score in an article published in *Foreign Affairs* in April.[83]

The next few months provided strong evidence that the east of Suez role, as then defined, might soon overtax the defence resources available. In the Far East operations in support of Malaysia continued to tie down the bulk of the strategically mobile forces of the three services. Clashes with Indonesian raiders were still numerous and no respite was yet in sight. In South Arabia terrorism in Aden and the guerrilla campaign in the mountains to the north imposed new and heavy demands on British forces. In May the insurrection in the Radfan area

[81] Healey, 690 HC Deb., 26 Feb. 1964, coll. 469–70.
[82] See Anthony Verrier, 'British Defense Policy Under Labor', *For. Aff.*, 42/2 (Jan. 1964), pp. 282–92.
[83] 'The Labor Party's Defense and Foreign Policy', *For. Aff.*, 42/3 (1964), pp. 391–8 esp. pp. 392–3.

and the increasing intensity of Yemeni attacks across the Dhala border made it necessary to fly out substantial reinforcements from the United Kingdom. The following month HMS *Centaur* returned to the Aden area to lend air support. By the end of the summer the Radfan operation had dampened dissident activity up-country but the terrorist campaign in Aden was gathering force. Farther afield, outside the region, the situation in British Guiana led the government to send army and naval reinforcements in May and June. The manpower strain was most acute in June. In a leader entitled 'A Perilous Gamble', *The Times* noted the speed and skill with which troops were despatched from one side of the world to the other, but likened the government's situation to that of a juggler at the climax of his performance, admiration for whose skill was tempered by the fear that at any moment his apparatus might collapse in irretrievable confusion. *The Times* concluded that the choice was clear: 'If the number of tasks entrusted to the armed forces cannot be reduced, the number of men to fulfil them must be increased.'[84]

The Chiefs of Staff did not adopt such an uncompromising position. For one thing, they did not see the situation in such grave terms as did *The Times* defence correspondent. For another they accepted that some strain was an inevitable consequence of the government's policies. For these reasons the Chiefs of Staff simply warned the government that no further commitments could be undertaken. Reportedly the CIGS described his position as akin to that of a trumpeter with five stops and only two fingers, but apparently neither he nor other senior officers felt it necessary to make strong representations. At one level this may be regarded as a recognition of the facts of political life. At another, it can be argued that when faced with the alternatives of pressing for a return to some form of National Service or a retreat from the world role, the army preferred to go along as it was.

Political thinking about the east of Suez role remained largely untroubled by the private doubts in Whitehall and the questioning in the press. By now the priority and scale of the east of Suez role was a fact of political life and as the 1964 general election approached it seemed likely to remain so. The previous two and a half years had established that from time to

[84] 2 June 1964.

time the new states of Asia and Africa would require military assistance and that Britain could provide it. The Conservative government had underlined the point and the Labour opposition had been converted. Stability, it was agreed, was the end of policy and there was a sufficient consensus to avoid searching questions about the weighting to be attached to hard national interests, moral values, and considerations of international order. For the moment it was a case of political leaders seeing only what they wished to see: this was the calm before the storm.

CHAPTER SEVEN

A Strategy for Crises 1962–1964

ALTHOUGH the annual White Papers and service memoranda set out the system for defence east of Suez and revealed in broad outline the forces available, it was difficult—purely on the basis of this information—to gauge whether the military establishment was adequate to handle the various emergencies that might be expected. Even the strategic planner with access to specialist sources was to some extent dependent on assumption and conjecture. The Kuwait operation of 1961 represented a landmark in the development of a strategy for crises. By providing an opportunity to test, under emergency conditions, the mobile forces and strategic concepts developed since 1956 it served to underline the strengths of post-Suez policies and to pinpoint the weaknesses. Gaps shown up during the course of the operation stimulated military thinking and encouraged a fuller development of amphibious capability, air mobility, and inter-service co-ordination.

The Kuwait Operation

The first reaction to the operation was one of satisfaction, even complacency. Britain had assembled land forces of something more than brigade strength, transported them by sea and air to the threatened state, and deployed them in defensive positions with considerable speed and organizational skill.[1] The operation showed that the mobile forces developed since Suez were of the appropriate kind. The commando ship in particular

[1] It should be pointed out that military planners had visualized an Iraqi attack on Kuwait for some two years and the contingency planning was therefore detailed and appropriate to the situation in July 1961. In this respect, Kuwait differed from the subsequent operations in Brunei, Southern Arabia, and East Africa.

was proved a worthwhile investment. As the evidence came in, however, it became clear that there were debits also. Some shortcomings were of a straightforward military or administrative character and, once over their initial satisfaction, planners set to work to iron them out. Although doubts remain about how effectively certain of the larger issues were tackled, generally it must be admitted that procurement policies over the next few years attempted to fill a number of gaps revealed in hardware and that subsequent operations gave evidence of improved co-ordination and administrative arrangements. In this respect, therefore, Watkinson's claim that 'there were lessons to be learned, and they have been learned' was hardly an over-statement.[2]

More generally, the Kuwait operation gave the first substantive indication that the east of Suez role was likely to extend fully, and perhaps to over-extend, the forces and hardware available. Given the extent of Britain's east of Suez commitments and the forces at the Ministry's disposal, it suggested that even answering one major call would be a matter of marshalling such forces as were not already committed, relying to some extent on fortuitous factors (as for example the availability of a carrier or commando ship), and accepting that an element of risk could hardly be avoided. There were a few flickers of awareness in the press and in Parliament, but the government gave no indication that it saw the situation in this way. It was perhaps too much to expect that an operation which at least militarily helped to erase the memory of the Suez débâcle, and which set the seal on the policies of strategic mobility, should be seen also as disclosing trends which would make Britain's new military posture much less tenable in the not too distant future.

The first thing to be said about the debit side of the operation is that to land and maintain what was a comparatively small force had necessitated drawing troops, aircraft, and naval units from British establishments all over the world. Not only did the operation absorb the entire theatre forces of the Middle East, but it disrupted dispositions in Germany, Cyprus, Kenya, and Singapore and drew heavily on the strategic reserve and other units in the United Kingdom. Behind the force deployed lay a tenuous reserve consisting only of the Parachute Brigade

[2] 655 HC Deb., 5 Mar. 1962, col. 45.

and one infantry brigade, the latter of limited utility because of its large Gurkha component. In the circumstances of mid-1961 the situation was acceptable if vexatious, but it was easy to envisage occasions when it could be disastrous. *The Times* commented: 'One inference is that Britain would find it difficult, if not impossible, to deal with more than one emergency of this sort without either taking away forces from Germany or calling on her allies for help.'[3]

Of more immediate concern, the mixture of units from so many different quarters resulted in a combat force of extreme diversity. Infantry, for example, came from three different brigades, each with a different internal organization. Armour and artillery came from other quarters again. To provide reconnaissance, close support of ground forces, and air defence at least five different types of RAF and RN aircraft were in use. Had the Iraqi threat materialized, the difficulties of organization and standardization might well have proved a major factor. As it was, it appears that the Joint Administrative Headquarters at Bahrain was somewhat overwhelmed by the problems of controlling and co-ordinating small administrative units and personnel, to the detriment of its proper duties. At the very least, there was a measure of agreement that a special administrative headquarters should have been provided.[4] A more penetrating critic went further and questioned the functional efficiency of an organization which had to be 'torn apart and reconstructed to do the sort of job for which it should have been designed'.[5]

Closely related to this first point, there were obvious and serious gaps in the composition and equipment of the British force deployed at Kuwait. The gravest weakness was its defence against armour. The tank ratio was 4:1 in Iraq's favour. Nor was the air situation very satisfactory. Ground arrangements at Kuwait airport were primitive and it was often closed because of sandstorms. On one account, a rather light-hearted approach was taken to radar warning and direction. Until 9 July, when HMS *Victorious* arrived in the Gulf, the adequacy

---

[3] 11 July 1962.
[4] See Brig C. N. Barclay's articles, 'Britain's Strategic Reserve and Sea-borne Task Forces in Action', *Brassey's Annual 1962*, pp. 36–8, and 'East of Suez', *Marine Corps Gazette* (US), p. 48.
[5] Maj Gen Moulton, *Defence in a Changing World*, p. 109. We shall return to this point on p. 255 below.

of the air cover available was open to question.[6] This was a fundamental issue because British planning and deployment proceeded on the assumption that RAF fighter and ground attack aircraft could stop the Iraqi armour.[7] Communications were another problem, particularly between the Brigade Headquarters and the RAF at Kuwait New Airport. On the naval side, a considerable risk attended taking an unguarded commando ship up the narrow waters of the Persian Gulf, and it was several days before the arrival of reinforcements ensured adequate anti-aircraft, anti-submarine, and anti-mine defences.

The air movement of some 7,000 men to Aden and the Persian Gulf in the first six days of the operation showed that Britain's capacity to fly troops over long distances had greatly increased since the exercises of 1958 and 1959.[8] However, several problems associated with the airlift highlighted the drawbacks of air mobility and led some strategists to conclude that a greater concentration on seaborne forces was desirable. When the air contingency plan was first activated it at once ran into the difficulty of obtaining over-flying permission from the Sudan, Saudi Arabia, and even from Turkey, a NATO ally.[9] Consequently the first troops to arrive were 42 Commando, Royal Marines, from HMS *Bulwark*. Although the airlift figure of 7,000 in six days was satisfactory, it imposed a considerable strain on Transport Command and was achieved only by chartering seventeen civil aircraft and employing three transports of the Royal Rhodesian Air Force.[10] Over the same period about 70 tons of equipment and supplies were moved by air, the remainder being carried by sea and motor transport.[11] The obvious inadequacy of the airlift figure seems to have put an end to any lingering thoughts that in operations of this kind supply could be maintained by air.

[6] See Neville Brown, *Strategic Mobility*, p. 95.

[7] The day fighter/ground attack squadrons were armed and trained to attack armour but doubts remain about how effective such tactics would have been, particularly if an advance had taken place at night or in sandstorm conditions. However, it was said that one wider consideration which influenced planners was the Canberra force in Cyprus, which posed a potential threat to Iraq and especially to Iraqi airfields.

[8] Figures from statement by Under-Secretary of State for Air, 644 HC Deb., 19 July 1961, col. 1224.

[9] Donald Macintyre, 'Soldiers at Sea: a Study in Strategic Mobility', *Navy*, 70/ (Apr. 1965), p. 104.

[10] 644 HC Deb., col. 1224.

[11] Supplies and equipment came mainly from stockpiles at Aden and Bahrain.

Most important of all, the airlift demonstrated in practical terms what many soldiers and medical advisers had long argued —that troops could not be flown from one part of the world to another regardless of climatic conditions and without a full programme of acclimatization. A report subsequently prepared by the army's Operational Research Establishment showed that although heat casualties were negligible among the men already stationed in Aden and the Persian Gulf, they were higher among those units from Kenya and Cyprus, and some 10 per cent of those flown direct from the United Kingdom were out of action from heat disorders in the first five days.[12] Part of the problem, it was admitted, lay in the failure to follow instructions in heat discipline, and in the inadequacy of food, equipment, and clothing for desert conditions. According to one line of thought, had troops been engaged in active operations, heat casualties might have been substantially higher. These disturbing conclusions led the army to carry out a controlled experiment in Aden, comparing the reactions to exercises of a platoon flown direct from Aldershot with those of a platoon stationed in Bahrain for the previous nine months. The results showed that none of the troops from Bahrain suffered from severe heat illness and only a few from minor complaints; but one quarter of the men from the United Kingdom were ineffective after a few hours and over the twelve-day period that platoon became, for practical pruposes, ineffective.[13]

In summary then, although the Kuwait operation was taken to confirm the policies of strategic mobility it also had the effect of demonstrating their inherent limitations. To some extent interpretation varied according to service perspective. For the sailors and airmen the lessons of Kuwait were largely, though not exclusively, concerned with developing and refining the concepts and hardware appropriate to their particular forms of mobility. In their view, Kuwait showed that the post-Suez policies were in the right direction and it provided a key to their fuller development. The army, however, was more dubious. Granted the need for mobility and the satis-

---

[12] *Times*, 23 July 1962. The government at first denied that heat casualties were serious. See Watkinson's statement, 644 HC Deb., 11 July 1961, col. 26. The Operational Research Establishment's report was never officially released.
[13] *Times*, 23 July 1962.

faction about Kuwait on this score, the soldiers tended to adhere to their traditional view that it was not enough to put men down at the scene of trouble. Heat exhaustion was only one aspect of a larger problem—the problem of adaptation. In contrast to the navy and the air force, where weapons and equipment tended to produce certain standardized procedures, the army had to adapt to the conditions of the area—the terrain, the customs, the language, and so on—and this could not be accomplished overnight. A second consideration was that the size of a force which could be quickly moved into a combat area was severely limited. In any subsequent operation it seems that the army would have wanted a rather larger force and more armour. For these reasons the army was less inclined than either of the other services to see overseas defence primarily in terms of strategic mobility.

Sailing into the Wind

Before examining the strategic concepts and service programmes in the three years following the Kuwait operation, it is useful to consider some of the general problems confronting military planners in their efforts to sustain the east of Suez role. A number of aspects have already been mentioned but it remains to draw the various threads together in an attempt to sketch the background of technological and political change and rising costs—the background against which the defence establishment had to translate the government's strategic policy into hardware and contingency planning.

The unprecedented exploitation of technology for military purposes in the two decades following the Second World War had the effect of greatly increasing the complexity and sophistication of weapons systems, their rate of obsolescence, and their cost. A few examples will illustrate the magnitude of the financial problem. The destroyer of 1938 had radio equipment[14] costing a little more than £5,000. For the 'Leander' frigate of the sixties the figure was over £250,000. Similarly the radio equipment of the old *Ark Royal*, built in 1938, cost just over £10,000; that of the post-war *Ark Royal*, in 1962, cost over £500,000; in 1964, on completion of her modernization, the

---

[14] This term covers radio, radar, sonar, and the like as appropriate.

corresponding figure for *Eagle* was £2.5 million.[15] Looking at naval costs generally, it is indicative that the pre-war *Ark Royal* cost £3,216,000; that of 1955, £21,500,000; and *Eagle's* extensive refit in 1964 came to more than £30 million, more than twice her original price of £14 million some eighteen years earlier.[16] Much the same was true of aircraft. The cost of a Mark-3 Lightning was about five times that of a Mark-6 Hunter and over thirty times that a of wartime Spitfire. In the Fleet Air Arm, a Sea Vixen of 1965 cost approximately seven times as much as its predecessor, the Sea Venom.[17] Even the small items of army equipment rose sharply in price. The FN rifle cost £35 as against £16 for the .303. The new general-purpose machine-gun cost £400 as compared with £62.10s. for the Bren gun which it replaced.[18] The price of 'walkie-talkie' sets rose from £80 in 1944 to about £600 in 1963.[19] To make matters worse, by the mid-sixties it was clear that the upward trend was rising still more steeply, with the result that the capital cost of equipping an infantry battalion was estimated to increase six-fold between 1963 and 1968.[20]

To some extent it was possible to stave off the full impact of cost inflation by postponing re-equipment programmes and allowing obsolescent and even obsolete weapons systems to remain in service for much longer periods than the forces considered prudent. This expedient became almost the standard procedure during the fifties, particularly in relation to the overseas role where the limited military resources and outdated equipment of Britain's actual and potential enemies made the risk much less than in the European theatre. Many examples immediately spring to mind—the Valettas and Hastings in Transport Command, the Sea Furies and Firefly IIs and later the Sea Hawks and Sea Venoms in the Fleet Air Arm, almost the complete range of army equipment and weapons, the ships of the Amphibious Warfare Squadron, and arguably the Second World War generation of aircraft carriers.

---

[15] Statement by the Civil Lord of the Admiralty, 690 HC Deb., 2 Mar. 1964, col. 939.

[16] Fletcher, *£60 a Second on Defence*, p. 96.

[17] MoD, *Statement on the Defence Estimates 1965*, Cmnd 2592 (1965), para. 6.

[18] The comparison is not exact because the general-purpose machine-gun also replaced the Vickers machine-gun.

[19] Fletcher, p. 96.

[20] MoD, Cmnd 2592, para. 6.

A second approach lay in improving the machinery and techniques which could enable a choice to be made between competing weapons projects. In a limited way the individual services had long been forced to choose between one weapon and another. Centrally, the Defence Research Policy Committee attempted to harmonize the various service programmes. Under the chairmanship of Sir Frederick Brundrett this committee met regularly and made some headway with the problem of competing weapons projects.[21] However, attempts to choose between competing roles and competing services met with very little success. The strengthening of the central machinery and the establishment of an Operational Requirements Staff in 1963, and the somewhat reluctant acceptance of cost effectiveness techniques soon after, led to some improvement here, but there remains a strong suspicion that even by 1966 the process was by no means a smooth one.[22] In any case the development of systems analysis, however necessary, hardly went to the root of the problem. No rationalization could alter the hard fact that a given amount of money—or as earlier expressed a given percentage of the GNP—could produce only a progressively smaller armoury. Ironically but inevitably the services' quest to tap the benefits of modern technology was eroding their ability to maintain Britain's world role.

Yet it was scarcely open to the services to stand aside from the world-wide process, especially since many of the new countries of Asia, Africa, and the Middle East were acquiring modern weapons and equipment from the Soviet Union and to a lesser extent from the West. By the early sixties this had become a problem in its own right. The Kuwait emergency provided a warning not to be lightly disregarded. The volume of extra equipment acquired by Iraq in the late fifties meant that that country had to be taken as a potentially serious threat. By 1961 the Iraqi army had been re-equipped with Soviet T54 tanks as well as Centurions and American M24s, and the air force had MiG17s, MiG19s, and IL28 bombers in the front line supported by Hunters, Venoms, and Vampires.[23] The

---

[21] On one account, after Brundrett retired as chairman of the committee in Dec. 1959 it hardly ever met and failed to do its job.

[22] For a description and assessment of the machinery for central control see Howard, *The Central Organisation of Defence*, pp. 17–19 and 28–33.

[23] See N. Brown, *Strategic Mobility*, pp. 91–2.

position worsened over the next few years as the Soviet Union began supplying up-to-date weapons in place of the obsolescent ones supplied in the fifties. During the confrontation of Malaysia, for example, Indonesia was equipped with a range of advanced missiles, including Guide Line and air-to-sea, air-to-air, and surface-to-surface varieties.[24] On his return from the Far East in May 1965, Christopher Mayhew, then Minister of Defence for the Navy, felt constrained to write to Denis Healey that he left:

> with the uneasy feeling that in our operational calculations we are having to place a great deal of weight on the superiority of our men in morale, training and the ability to maintain and man their hardware, over the Indonesians. . . . the balance of numbers and material left me uneasy.[25]

The matériel and manpower difficulties of the British services took on a new urgency as east of Suez commitments were increasingly tested in the years after Kuwait. So long as Britain's defence responsibilities remained quiescent—as in the last years of the fifties – it was possible for the government to resist or severely prune the services' claims for more men and new equipment and to play the part of a world power with some sleight of hand and a good deal of military inadequacy. It is perhaps not too much of an exaggeration to suggest that in these years the government was more concerned with the symbolism of the diplomatist than the military requirements of the strategist. But once commitments became operational, what had been academic problems became matters of great practical concern. The defence establishment coped by tightening the screws—extracting more hours and more mileage from men and equipment. However, the screws could not be tightened indefinitely; the costs were high both in terms of wear and recruitment, and the risks were considerable. The overall picture emerges plainly in the table opposite.

Short of a major overhaul of existing commitments and the revision of the various contingency plans or a significant in-

---

[24] David Divine, *The Broken Wing: a Study in the British Exercise of Air Power* (1966), pp. 361–2.
[25] *Britain's Role Tomorrow* (1967) pp. 27–8.

NAVY   AVERAGE EMPLOYMENT OF DESTROYERS/FRIGATES

	Annual Mileage	Annual Hours Underway	Days of 24 hours Underway	Ratio Sea: Harbour
1956–57	27,600	1,950	81	1 :4
1963–64	33,450	2,430	142	1 :1.5

ARMY   NUMBERS OF UNITS AND MEN SENT OVERSEAS ON
EMERGENCY OR UNACCOMPANIED TOURS

	Major Units	Numbers in Units	Individual Postings	Total
1963	8	4,000	600	4,600
1964	16	8,000	1,200	9,200
1965	17	8,500	1,400	9,900

RAF   EMERGENCY MOVES OF OPERATIONAL FORMATIONS
TO OVERSEAS THEATRES (INCLUDING AIRCRAFT DETACHMENTS
AND RAF REGIMENT UNITS)

	Formations	Aircraft Numbers
1963	13	58
1964	22	91
1965	26	157

Source: MoD, *Statement on Defence Estimates 1966*, Pt 1: *The Defence Review*, Cmnd 2901 (1966), p. 2.

crease in the resources devoted to defence, neither of which was under consideration, the opportunities for redressing the balance were strictly limited. Certainly there was scope for rationalization in several quarters and there were some obvious cases of duplicated effort, but by and large the unwieldy stretch of the defence establishment was a product of the breadth of Britain's involvement in the area and the interdependence of the various points of the system. On the political side, for example, even striking a number of lesser commitments off the British defence books might not have resulted in any substantial saving.[26] The argument here was that the strategically mobile forces maintained for Southern Arabia and Malaysia could comfortably

[26] Indeed, Healey said at a press conference in Aug. 1965 that it would be possible for Britain to contract out of ninety commitments without making any saving. *Times*, 5 Aug. 1965.

handle emergencies such as East Africa and Brunei. It was all a matter of timing: if that was favourable they could be handled; if not, they would have to be passed over. Nor on the military side was it possible to limit substantially the range of weapons and equipment. To take confrontation as an example, although that conflict was pre-eminently a matter of patrolling land and sea borders, a war for infantrymen and frigates, part of the explanation for the British success must lie in the escalation threat.[27] Senior officers stressed this aspect and mentioned particularly the three V-bombers stationed at Penang and the passage of HMS *Victorious* through the Lombok Straits.[28] To make a somewhat different point, no less than in earlier years, the east of Suez role required what was known in the services as a 'world-wide capability'. Although it was necessary to maintain some specialized equipment for certain terrains, the diversity of conditions—tropical and temperate, desert and jungle—required that equipment and weapons be designed with many purposes in mind, with all that this entailed in terms of cost and loss of performance in any one role. Add to these difficulties the fact that the services were engaged in operations and that long-run savings almost inevitably involve increased costs in the short run, and a picture emerges of very limited scope for maneouvrability.

Finally, and this is a crucial point, operations and even major strategic redeployments involved a considerable additional expense which had to be borne on the defence vote. With a military budget already gravely strained in meeting the day-to-day costs of running the armed services and providing weapons and equipment, the margin left over for these extra expenses was very small indeed. A clear illustration was provided by the Kuwait operation. A statement by Harold Watkinson in the House of Commons on 25 July 1961 gave the cost of the build-up and partial withdrawal at about £1 million.[29] As Neville Brown subsequently pointed out, Britain could not afford to shoulder this sort of burden every

[27] See N. Brown, 'Disengaging in South East Asia', *Survival*, 8/8 (Aug. 1966), p. 256.
[28] There were plans to meet various forms of escalation which included bombing Indonesian targets. It was widely believed in the services that the parachute raid on Malaya in 1963 was not repeated because Indonesia feared that a second attempt might attract a British air attack.
[29] 645 HC Deb., col. 40.

time a few T54s went careering across the desert; this was perhaps one reason why Iraq's redeployment in December produced such a limited response.[30] As the financial strings tightened, the reluctance to become committed increased. In February 1965 the cost of the Malaysian operations, over and above the cost of the normal deployment of British forces, was about £90,000 a week.[31] With expenditure running at this level there was very great resistance within the Ministry of Defence to becoming involved elsewhere.[32] The point was driven home by a consideration of the American experience in Vietnam which was taken to provide an object lesson for middle powers. The peacekeeping fist might still be clenched, then, but more and more the economics of defence was keeping it firmly in the British pocket.

Command and Co-ordination

As the first example of the new type of emergency, Kuwait focused attention on the need for greatly increased co-operation between the three services and their various arms. In the view of some, it also demonstrated the command and organizational shortcomings of a system which involved the movement of a large number of separate units from various points of the British defence arc and then attempted to fuse them under a resident commander-in-chief.[33] In earlier years British forces had usually been on the spot when trouble flared and it was a comparatively simple matter to bring in reinforcements and incorporate them under existing arrangements. Now, however, the main forces had to be rapidly moved to the trouble spots, integrated and brought under some kind of centralized control, perhaps immediately to be faced with experienced and well-armed antagonists.

The 1962 White Paper indicated a measure of recognition and the first steps were taken to adjust to the new situation.

[30] *Strategic Mobility*, pp. 95–6.
[31] Statement by Healey, 705 HC Deb., 1 Feb. 1965, col. 200.
[32] Reportedly in the first two and a half years of the Labour government's period of office 'quite a lot' of requests for military assistance were received but Britain acceded to only two of them.
[33] Maj Gen J. L. Moulton has argued this point cogently. See *Defence in a Changing World*, pp. 109–11; 'Mobility in Amphibious Warfare', *Brassey's Annual 1962*, p. 171, and 'Bases or Fighting Forces?', *Brassey's Annual 1964*, pp. 144–9.

The services were to retain their separate identities, but in order to facilitate inter-service co-ordination in the development of equipment, doctrine, and techniques a new Joint-Service Staff was established, which was charged with advising the Chiefs of Staff on all aspects of joint-service operations including training. This body replaced the Land/Air Warfare Committee and the Amphibious Warfare Headquarters.[34] Paragraph 25 went on to explain that, outside Europe, British forces would become essentially joint-service task forces. However, the label 'joint-service task forces' had been bandied around for some years previously and no attempt was made to elaborate how the new policy differed from the pre-Kuwait policy. The only concrete proposal was that joint exercises along the lines of those in North Africa in 1959 and 1960, and the Arabian Peninsula and Borneo in 1960 and 1961, would continue on an increased scale. Further measures for harmonizing service planning and operational activities were outlined in the *Central Organisation for Defence* White Paper of July 1963.[35] Four new organizations—the Defence Operations Executive, the Defence Operational Requirements Staff, the Defence Signals Staff, and the Defence Intelligence Staff—were set up to work in conjunction with existing staffs such as the Joint Planning and Joint Warfare Staffs. For present purposes the key organization was the Defence Operations Executive which became responsible for co-ordination and control of the activities of the individual services and was charged with handling any sudden emergency.[36]

Despite these improvements in Whitehall, arrangements in the field continued broadly on the old pattern. As before, forces had to be drawn from various points around the Indian Ocean when a crisis developed. Inevitably the opportunities for

[34] MoD, *Statement on Defence 1962*, Cmnd 1639, para. 24.

[35] MoD, Cmnd 2097 (1963). Mountbatten was the moving force behind the 1963 reorganization. In his view, clearly and forcefully expressed, only a radical reorganization of the three service ministries and the centralization of power and responsibility within a new Ministry of Defence would enable a government to formulate and execute an effective defence policy. See Peter Thorneycroft, 'Defence Reforms that would check Service Rivalries', *Times*, 23 June 1966. Also F. A. Johnson, 'Politico-Military Organization in the United Kingdom: Some Recent Developments', *Journal of Politics*, 27/2 (May 1965), p. 346. According to Watkinson, now a back-bencher, one of the main considerations behind the government's proposals was the need for an integrated effort in the Indian Ocean area. 682 HC Deb., 31 July 1963, coll. 506–7.

[36] See MoD, Cmnd 2097, section IX, esp. paras 35–6.

training between units of different services and forces attached to different commands were limited. There was still no provision for central control of the task forces, and command continued to be exercised by the various territorial headquarters. On the face of it, the decision to graft functional forces on to a system of territorial commands seemed an unhappy compromize. Not only did it guarantee the continued fragmentation of the mobile forces available, but it divorced the preparation and training of forces from operational control, and introduced an unnecessary link in the chain of command from Whitehall to the field. Writing at the end of 1962, Major General Moulton strongly criticized the existing arrangements:

Our forces are still organised to fight an imaginary war, in which large parts of each service will go about their business quite independent of the other services and somewhere, along the fringes, link up with them, mostly at high levels or in jolly parties.[37]

On the information available there is no evidence that the Ministry of Defence seriously considered maintaining a joint-service task force as a formation in being. A number of officers saw such a force as the ideal, but in general it seems to have been regarded more as a distant goal than as a practical possibility to which an advance could slowly be made. In fact, the most that was done was to build up some sort of a task force about three or four times a year for exercises and training. More than this was not possible, it was said, because operational commitments, contingency plans, and general duties left few ships and units available for such a force.

Quite apart from the practical difficulties of assembling such a force, many officers had reservations about the value of maintaining it as a formation in being. One argument advanced was that given the ships and equipment then available, this would have meant that everything would be in one place, with all the dangers that that involved. It is debatable whether this was a serious objection, for come what may British forces could undertake only one major operation at a time. Again, a number of officers contended that inevitably such a task force would have been tailored to meet certain strategic requirements, and that with the range of Britain's responsibilities east of Suez, this was too limited an answer. In any

[37] 'Mobility in Amphibious Warfare', *Brassey's Annual 1962*, p. 171.

case, it was said with conviction if no great logic, the notion of an ideal force made little sense because circumstances differ so much that a measure of improvisation could not be avoided.[38]

After Kuwait the limited reforms and the generally sharpened awareness of the need for closer co-operation led to some improvement in service performance. In both the Brunei and East African operations the organization and integration of the various units was markedly superior to that at Kuwait, and the main body of press and journal reports suggests that in both operations the forces meshed together well. However, little headway had been made in solving the problems of movement into the combat area; and improvisation, poor communications, and gaps in hardware (especially the shortage of helicopters) could easily have prejudiced success. Writing in 1964 Moulton argued, 'It is for this critical stage that the practised integrated team is needed, and is at present invariably lacking.'[39]

Confrontation was a rather special case. That operation followed the pattern of the earlier Malayan Emergency and British troops were therefore fighting along familiar lines. According to officers then in Malaya and Borneo, the various arms co-operated closely. Moreover, the problems posed by the different rules of engagement were successfully overcome.[40] In partial explanation it was said that the command structure evolved in Singapore was carefully attuned to the needs of confrontation. For this reason, however, it was not well suited to handling SEATO requirements or to controlling the reduction in forces. For example, the Operational Air Command was a great immobile structure with very large headquarters which handled the Indonesian situation well because there was no requirement for mobile control and no need to deploy air power over long distances. As the Malaysian situation eased it was pruned and rendered more mobile.

Air Mobility

By 1962 Transport Command was over the hump. The next four years saw steady if unspectacular progress. By now

[38] Maj Gen Moulton considers and rejects other arguments in *Defence in a Changing World*, p. 110.
[39] 'Bases or Fighting Forces', *Brassey's Annual 1964*, p. 150.
[40] The various national forces had different rules of engagement and there were even differences between individual services of national forces.

the principle of twin approaches—air and sea—to the problems of overseas security was accepted on all sides, and although inevitably there were differences about the relative priority to be accorded to each, the build-up of Transport Command went forward with wide support. One important factor was that after the substitution of Polaris for Skybolt in December 1962, the deterrent days of the RAF were numbered and that service therefore devoted itself more and more to the strategically mobile role. The lift capacity was substantially increased as new aircraft came into service and a continued improvement in techniques and an expansion of training and joint-service exercises can be recorded.[41] Transport Command's operational performance over these years evoked wide satisfaction, and if the airlift was not as large as some desired it was at least a far cry from the mid-fifties when capability and government policy were so much at variance.

A short account of the expansion of the transport fleet will prove the point. In 1962 5 Comet 4Cs came into service, bringing the Comet fleet to 15.[42] In the same year, orders were placed for 5 VC10s—a long-range, high-speed aircraft which could carry 150 troops for 3,670 miles without refuelling.[43] The order was increased to 11 in 1963 and later to 14. The first of these aircraft and also the first of the 10 Belfast strategic freighters ordered in 1961 were due to come into service in 1965. In fact both aircraft were late. The first Belfast entered service in January 1966 and the first VC10 followed six months later. In the medium-range role, the first squadron of Argosies was formed in the United Kingdom in March 1962 and another was operational in Aden later in the year. By March 1963, 30 Argosies had come into service and a squadron was being built up in Singapore. Deliveries of this aircraft were completed in April 1964.[44] To replace the Beverleys and Hastings, it was announced early in 1963 that a decision had been taken to

---

[41] On the latter point see MoD, *Statement on Defence 1963* . . . , Cmnd 1936, p. 71, paras 38–9; *Statement on Defence 1964*, Cmnd 2270, para. 191; and A Mshl Sir Kenneth Cross, 'Transport Command 1943–1964', *RAF Quarterly*, 4/2 (summer 1964), p. 91.

[42] The Comet 4C accommodated 94 passengers instead of the 44 of the Comet 2C.

[43] AM, *Memorandum by Secretary of State for Air to accompany Air Estimates, 1962–63*, Cmnd 1630, para. 39.

[44] Ibid. para. 40; Cmnd 1936, p. 70, para. 36; MoD, Cmnd 2270, para. 189.

develop a VTOL aircraft based on the AW681.[45] The short-range transport fleet was augmented by deliveries of the gas-turbine engine version of the Whirlwind, the twin-rotor Belvedere, and the twin-engined Wessex. In addition, a number of light planes for communications and tactical transport came into service during these years and others were placed on order.[46]

The average time for getting a medium-range airlift under way was said to be about 24 hours, though in certain circum-stances this could be considerably reduced.[47] Indeed, during the Azahari revolt the first aircraft touched down at Brunei 18 hours after the alert had been given in Singapore.[48] For a long-range lift, Britannias and a Comet had taken four days to fly the 1st Battalion, the Royal Welch Fusiliers from the United Kingdom to Singapore, to take over duties from units that had been posted to Brunei.[49] The same operation illus-trated the Command's much increased capacity. Using medium-range aircraft only, 2,000 troops and 100 tons of freight were lifted 850 miles in three and a half days.[50] Over the following year, some 18,000 passengers, 1,500 tons of freight, and many vehicles, light aircraft, and helicopters were airlifted between Singapore and Borneo.[51]

In mid-1965 Air Marshal Sir Kenneth Cross estimated that the Command could fly a brigade group (roughly 3,860 troops, 56 vehicles, and 170 tons of freight) to Aden in four and a half days and to the Far East in nine days.[52] When asked what was

---

[45] See further the statement by Secretary of State for Air, 673 HC Deb., 7 Mar. 1963, col. 660, and Cmnd 1936, p. 70, para. 36. The projected AW681 transport was cancelled soon after the Labour government took office and a decision was made to purchase the American Hercules C130E. This aircraft could carry 92 troops or 64 paratroops at a normal cruising speed of 340 m.p.h. over a distance of 2,430 miles. The first of 66 Hercules ordered for the RAF arrived in the UK in Dec. 1966.

[46] See further Cmnd 2270, para. 189, and MoD, *Statement on Defence Estimates 1965*, Cmnd 2592 (1965), paras 151, 154, and 155.

[47] E. C. Shepherd, 'Implications of Strategic Mobility', *Brassey's Annual 1964*, p. 181.

[48] Moulton, 'A Brush-fire Operation—Brunei, December 1962', *Brassey's Annual 1963*, p. 78.

[49] *Times*, 11 Dec. 1962, and Cmnd 1936, p. 71, para. 40.

[50] Shepherd, *Brassey's Annual 1964*, p. 181.

[51] Cmnd 2270, para. 198.

[52] These times would of course vary according to the routes on which the Command was forced to operate.

the limiting factor, the availability of aircraft or crews, he replied that it was neither. The limiting factor, in his view, was the capacity of the staging posts en route.[53]

Even more important than the capacity of the staging posts was their reliability. This had been a preoccupation of Transport Command since about 1960, at least. The fear here was that many of the newly independent states would deny Britain staging rights in an emergency. Already the Middle Eastern air passage and a large part of northern Africa had been effectively closed to British military aircraft and it seemed likely that over the next decade the air routes to the Indian Ocean would be pushed farther and farther southward. One solution was seen in a chain of island staging posts which would enable the RAF either to secure a route across Africa about 9° south of the equator, or alternatively to fly round the Cape. Strategic transports could then land and refuel at these islands, or tanker aircraft could take off from short landing strips to refuel medium-range transports, thus freeing them from the need to land on foreign soil. By such means it was thought, an 'all red' air route could be re-established to the Far East and Australia.

This concept was first proposed about 1960 by Air Chief Marshal Sir Edmund Hudleston, then Vice-Chief of the Air Staff.[54] One factor which influenced the Air Marshal and other senior RAF officers was that by the early sixties the increased range of transport aircraft, their greater reliability because of engineering advances, and the development of in-flight refuelling techniques had reduced the need for frequent landings. It was therefore possible to plan on the basis of aircraft flying very long distances between stops. Moreover, it was clear that aircraft range and radius of action would increase even more markedly over the next few years. The original idea seems to have been primarily concerned with enabling transport aircraft to circumvent the air barrier but it was later broadened to include bomber/reconnaissance and fighter/ground attack aircraft. As the navy's plans for a new generation of capital ships moved into full swing, the Air Staff saw further possibilities and certain islands were projected as minor bases

---

[53] 'Transport Command Today', *JRUSI*, 110/639 (Aug. 1965), p. 215.
[54] In his later appointment as Air Officer Commanding-in-Chief, Transport Command (1962–3), Hudleston remained the chief advocate of the island staging-post scheme. See *Times*, 4 Nov. 1963, and *Guardian*, 4 Nov. 1963.

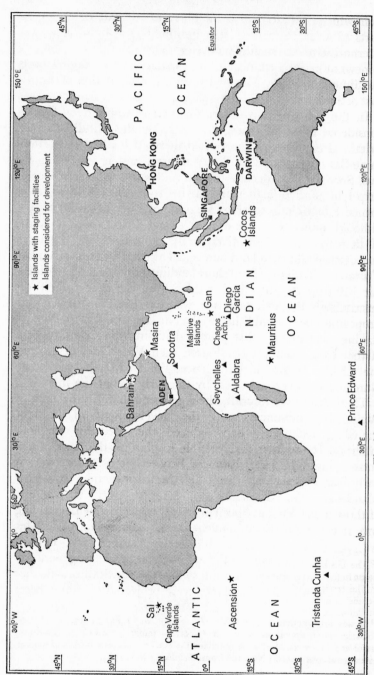

The island staging-post scheme of the early sixties

from which combat aircraft could operate in Africa and various parts of Asia. The island-base scheme thus developed into an alternative to carrier air power. In that form, it represented a somewhat belated attempt on the part of the RAF to move into the limited-war role and to carve for itself a major share in the east of Suez venture.[55]

In the preliminary stages of planning, many islands were considered as candidates for development. On certain islands Britain already had facilities and installations. In this category came Sal in the Cape Verde Islands, Ascension,[56] and Mauritius. Socotra was another possibility, particularly since an airstrip had been built there during the war. Tristan da Cunha, Prince Edward Island, and Aldabra were obvious candidates, although none had been developed and very little was known of their potential. Prince Edward Island was reconnoitred and discussions took place with the South African government. Tristan da Cunha and Aldabra were both surveyed by the Air Ministry. Prince Edward and Tristan da Cunha proved unsuitable,[57] but Aldabra was thought to be a manageable proposition and preliminary plans for the development of a staging post there went ahead.[58] Gan and Masira, much farther to the north and already developed, would complete the chain. Other islands—including the Seychelles, Diego Garcia, and the Cocos—were considered at later stages.

The Air Staff's proposals and the subsequent debate in Whitehall remain clouded. In part this may be attributed to the uncertainty within the Air Ministry about island sites and differing conceptions about how the scheme should be developed. Indeed, one minister went so far as to say that, at least in the early years, the Air Staff 'never had a consistent policy on island bases.' In 1961 the Air Staff submitted a broad outline of the scheme to the Chiefs of Staff. At this stage no approach was made for finance or for approval of specific projects.

[55] See Crowe, p. 221.
[56] The US had built an airstrip on this island and had certain installations. A clause in the lease restricted Britain's use, but this was subsequently changed.
[57] The topography of Prince Edward Island posed enormous difficulties and the weather conditions were unfavourable. A volcanic explosion took place on Tristan da Cunha and in any case it was decided that the island was 500 miles too far west.
[58] It was thought that long-range transport aircraft would soon be able to fly non-stop round the Cape from Ascension to Aldabra. The island would also be useful as a forward mounting base for African operations and for maritime reconnaissance aircraft to patrol the naval route round South Africa.

The motive was primarily to get 'official blessing' for the general scheme. In addition, it was believed that by producing an alternative to carrier air power, the Air Staff would strengthen its case against a new generation of aircraft carriers. On one account the reaction of the Chiefs of Staff was described as 'polite interest'. That was perhaps a fair statement of the army's response but the First Sea Lord was strongly opposed and the Chief of the Defence Staff offered little encouragement. The Minister of Defence also was decidedly cool about the project. Nevertheless the Air Ministry pushed ahead with its planning. In March 1962 the Minister of Defence said simply that the government was investigating the feasibility of the scheme.[59] Investigations and single service studies continued over the next eighteen months but no major decisions were taken. By late 1963 the climate of opinion in Whitehall remained unfavourable to the broader scheme and the Air Staff therefore concentrated on securing government approval for an airstrip and certain installations on Aldabra. In November 1963 it became known that plans had been submitted to the Chiefs of Staff and it was understood that they were being examined with rather more than the polite interest that had been shown earlier.[60] However, no decision was taken by the Minister, though it seems that thereafter Air Staff planning about the development of Aldabra went forward with some official approval.

From the outset, the island staging-post scheme was viewed as a competitor to the navy's plans for a new generation of aircraft carriers. The outcome of the issue was therefore a matter of vital concern to both the air force and the navy. Passions ran high and the debate in Whitehall developed into a bitter exchange between these two services. Both services produced their own studies and costings, and there was little common ground between them.[61] The Board of Admiralty opposed the project on the grounds that one set of bases was

[59] 655 HC Deb., 5 Mar. 1962, col. 48.

[60] *Times*, 4 Nov. 1963.

[61] In 1962 or early 1963, for example, the Air Staff produced a fully detailed exercise comparing the deployment of troops and supplies by air and sea. In the opinion of the Chief of the Air Staff, this exercise proved convincingly that the air method was more economical than the naval. The Chief of the Naval Staff, on the other hand, dismissed it as a starry-eyed exercise, drawn up with everything in the air force's favour. On this occasion the army sided with the air force, although not strongly. Eventually the exercise was put in the Ministry of Defence library.

merely being exchanged for another, that the aircraft deployed would have only a limited operational range, and that the cost would be excessive—the rationale for the latter being that money spent on island bases was money lost to carrier task forces. The Air Staff replied in kind, pointing to the advantages of the air scheme and to the weaknesses and cost of carrier task forces. The army remained broadly neutral. Although it saw merit in both schemes, its main concern was to ensure that the army did not bear the financial brunt of these gradiose conceptions.

In 1964 the United States entered the picture. Early in that year discussions took place with American defence officials about the feasibility of jointly establishing a small number of staging posts in the Indian Ocean. It was understood that any new facilities would be complementary to the British bases at Aden and Singapore, which the United States continued to regard as essential for the security of the area.[62] During July and August an Anglo-American group undertook a survey of prospective island sites and it was reported that Diego Garcia and Aldabra were possible candidates.[63]

There is some doubt about which country took the initiative but a joint arrangement was clearly in the interests of both parties. For Britain it held the promise of diplomatic support and an opportunity to reduce the financial burden through a cost-sharing arrangement with the United States; to the American administration it seemed a means of satisfying the services without embarking on a major new commitment. American interest in some form of strategic presence in the area had been growing since the Chinese attack on India in October 1962, and by 1964 there was strong pressure from the American services, particularly the navy, for action by the administration. The State Department favoured an American presence as a political stabilizer, all the more as it would help to keep Britain in the area. Robert McNamara was initially opposed to the project on the ground that it would be disastrous if the navy got hold of another ocean. However, he was prepared to support a small-scale undertaking once it became clear that the Indian Ocean would remain primarily a British

---

[62] See further *Guardian*, 3 Aug. 1964, *Observer* and *Washington Post*, 30 Aug. 1964.
[63] *Observer* and *Sunday Express*, 30 Aug. 1964.

responsibility and that the arrangement could not serve as a ticket of entry for an American fleet.[64]

Apart from the possibility of American involvement, the last nine months of the Conservative government's period of office saw little change in the general scheme. Although doubts remained about the extent to which the RAF's plans would be implemented Sal, Ascension, and Mauritius were still seen to secure the route to the Indian Ocean; Aldabra was projected for development; and other islands would be raised for consideration as opinion in Whitehall became more favourable. In addition, developmental work continued on a trilogy of aircraft—the TSR2, the P1154, and the HS681—which the Air Staff considered relevant to the east of Suez role. On the information available, it seems there was considerable vagueness about the shape of the eventual scheme. It may be that the Air Staff was reluctant to be too specific or to press for firm decisions —as apparently the Minister of Defence, Peter Thorneycroft, was no more enthusiastic about island bases than his predecessor Harold Watkinson had been, and with an election not far off things might shortly take a turn for the better.

Seaborne Task Forces

The year 1962 opened hopefully for the navy. The Kuwait operation had confirmed the main lines of the Admiralty's approach to limited conflicts east of Suez and in some respects it had demonstrated that money spent on seaborne forces was a better investment than money devoted to the airlifted strategic reserve. The various projects undertaken or authorized in the preceding four years promised to streamline the shape of the task force by the mid-sixties and to increase substantially its capability and staying power. One vital programme remained to be secured—a new generation of aircraft carriers. For the next year and a half, the Board of Admiralty devoted its efforts to selling the project to the government.

During the last months of Watkinson's period of office the pendulum swung in the navy's favour.[65] In March it was

---

[64] Some published material is to be found in *Washington Post*, 30 Aug. and 7 Nov. 1964.

[65] This account again follows Crowe (pp. 222–9) but it has been modified in certain respects in the light of later material.

announced that design work for a new carrier to replace HMS *Victorious* had been put in hand. Although this decision did not imply the rejection of the Air Staff's proposals, increasingly the Minister of Defence appeared to regard the air scheme as unrealistic. Still, however, no final decision had been made. When Thorneycroft assumed office in July, therefore, the issue had taken on some urgency. Although the new Minister was not unsympathetic to the Admiralty's case, he required clear evidence that the carrier was a necessary investment. By this time the First Sea Lord was 'word perfect'. A committee headed by J. C. Kendrew, a part-time scientific adviser to the Ministry of Defence, was appointed to make a dispassionate examination of the issue and it reported in favour of the carrier. The project then went before the Chiefs of Staff Committee, but the opposition of the Chief of the Air Staff forced the navy to carry its case direct to the Minister without the support of the Chiefs of Staff Committee. After considering various papers produced by the Admiralty, Thorneycroft informed the Board that he would support the project but he advised that the submission be scaled down from four to two.[66] At this stage the First Lord of the Admiralty, Lord Carrington, privately approached the Treasury to take soundings there. In the light of strong Treasury opposition to two new carriers, the Board settled for one new carrier and two modernizations in the late sixties. Approval of even one carrier, the Board felt, would mean that the Admiralty had 'its toe in the door' and others could follow later. Despite the Air Staff's vigorous arguments the Prime Minister and the Chancellor of the Exchequer were converted and the Defence Committee decided in the navy's favour. On 30 July 1963 Thorneycroft announced the government's decision to build a new 50,000 ton carrier. Together with HMS *Eagle* and *Hermes* suitably modernized, this would give Britain a force of three carriers until about 1980.[67]

The other aspects of the navy's limited-war programme followed the lines laid down between 1958 and 1961 and aroused little opposition. Beginning in February 1963 the Fleet Air Arm was re-equipped with Buccaneer strike aircraft, and deliveries of the Mark-2 version of the Sea Vixen began early

[66] Crowe, p. 227.
[67] 682 HC Deb., col. 237.

in 1964.[68] In February 1964 it was announced that plans for a common replacement for the Sea Vixen and the Hunter had been abandoned and that a decision had been taken to purchase the American Phantom for the navy.[69] A number of changes in existing ships and formations promised to strengthen the capability of task forces to intervene on land. In 1962 it was stated that the strength of a Royal Marine Commando was being increased from 600 to 750, which would give it greater hitting-power and increase its ability to operate independently at greater distances from a commando ship.[70] It was also decided to include detachments of Marines in the complements of a number of frigates.[71] In 1963 plans were drawn up for adapting the three Tiger class cruisers to the needs of amphibious assault.[72] The after six-inch gun turret was to be removed and replaced by a deck for four Wessex helicopters. In the event of an opposed landing their remaining six-inch guns would afford heavy support. In addition, berths were to be made available for about 450 troops. These plans were readily approved by the Chiefs of Staff Committee but at a later stage the Board decided against making provision for troops. The project was announced in March 1964 and HMS *Blake* was selected for the first conversion in 1965.[73] Another development of significance for the east of Suez role was the expansion of afloat support. The appropriation for new supply ships was increased from £3 million in 1961 to £6 million in 1962.[74] In 1963 orders were placed for two fleet replenishment ships of about 19,000 tons gross.[75] By 1964 both these ships plus three fleet replenishment tankers and a number of smaller vessels were under construction.[76]

During these years both commando ships returned to the United Kingdom for refits – *Bulwark* in 1963 and *Albion* in 1964.

[68] MoD, *Statement on Defence 1963*, Cmnd 1936, p. 17, para. 12, and MoD, *Statement on Defence 1964*, Cmnd 2270, paras 39 and 41.

[69] Statement by Thorneycroft, 690 HC Deb., 26 Feb. 1964, coll. 451–2.

[70] Admiralty, *Explanatory Statement on Navy Estimates 1962–63*, Cmnd 1629, para. 4.

[71] Statement by the Civil Lord of the Admiralty, 673 HC Deb., 11 Mar. 1963, col. 968.

[72] At least some members of the Board doubted the value of keeping these ships in commission but for political reasons they could not be scrapped.

[73] 690 HC Deb., 2 Mar. 1964, col. 935.

[74] Statement by Civil Lord of the Admiralty, 655 HC Deb., 14 Mar. 1962, col. 1333.

[75] D. Nap, 'Afloat Support', *Navy*, 69/8 (Aug. 1964), p. 268.

[76] MoD, *Statement on Defence 1964*, Cmnd 2270, para. 36.

Increased accommodation was provided for embarked troops and a number of minor modifications were carried out.[77] The introduction of Wessex Mark 5 helicopters (with a capacity of about 12 men) in *Albion* in 1964 and later in *Bulwark* marked another step forward. Notwithstanding these improvements, however, the British ships compared poorly with their American counterparts, the *Boxer* and the *Princeton*. The American ships were also converted carriers (tonnage, 27,100 tons light and 38,500 loaded), but each carried a landing force of 1,650, nearly twice the British figure of 900 (840 Commandos and 60 Royal Artillery).[78] As the American specially designed helicopter ships came into service, the comparison was even more unfavourable. With a displacement of 17,000 tons (full load), ships of the Iwo Jima class carried a landing force of 2,090 and 24 helicopters, each with a capacity of about 25 men.[79]

With the limited funds available for defence spending and the fierce inter-service competition, the Admiralty's construction and re-equipment programme represented an inventive and balanced attempt further to adapt the navy to the requirements of the east of Suez role. Few naval men questioned that the programme was aimed in the right direction and the Admiralty succeeded in attracting considerable support from the army, independent commentators, and many parliamentarians. Viewed against the background of the navy's struggle to meet east of Suez calls in the years after 1961, however, there were grave doubts about its adequacy.

Despite the continued redeployment of forces from the Atlantic and the Mediterranean to the Indian Ocean and the entry into service of a number of inshore minesweepers previously held in reserve, the sudden demands of Britain's commitments in the area created a situation of considerable strain. In part the navy's difficulties, particularly those relating to the lack of adequate tactical amphibious capability, could be attributed to the time-lag between ordering and commissioning, which meant that the construction programmes undertaken in the late fifties and early sixties afforded no immediate relief. For example, the first of the army's new logistic ships,

---

[77] See D. Barry, 'The Thin Blue Line', *Navy*, 69/5 (May 1964), p. 133.
[78] Moulton, 'Mobility in Amphibious Warfare', *Brassey's Annual 1962*, p. 166.
[79] Id. 'The Role of British Forces in a Strategy of Flexible Response', *Brassey's Annual 1965*, p. 31.

Sir Lancelot, did not come into service until late 1964; the assault ship *Fearless* until 1965; and her sister ship *Intrepid* until 1967.

The root of the problem, however, went much deeper. Maritime task forces were expensive both in ships and manpower and a strong case can be argued that the naval vote was too small to support a programme commensurate with the tasks in hand. According to one estimate in 1962, the maintenance of even one task force in being would require about 30 per cent of the total number of major types then in the operational fleet (excluding submarines and minesweepers), and taking only the estimated number of ships at immediate readiness for service at any given time, this figure would be increased to about 50 per cent.[80] Moreover several writers argued forcefully that to police an area as extensive as the Indian Ocean, two task forces were really required (which meant roughly two and a half task forces if two were to be kept operational).[81] These arguments remained academic, however, because the existing naval building programme left no slack for a further expansion of the limited-war fleet—all the more since in 1962 the navy had been saddled with the Polaris programme. There was also the fear that any additional claims might prejudice the carrier project.

The strain was heaviest on the carriers and commando ships. During most of 1962, only one carrier and one commando ship were deployed east of Suez. For the next two years the Admiralty succeeded in keeping two carriers in the Indian Ocean out of an operational fleet of three (four aircraft carriers were in fact on the operational list but one was normally working up). In addition, one commando ship remained east of Suez at all times. In 1965, as the pressure in the area eased, the formula was changed to three carriers or commando ships, to be made up of either two carriers and one commando ship or one carrier and two commando ships.[82]

A glance at some of the emergencies over these years indicates the risk involved in relying on such a small number of essential

[80] 'Reactor', 'The New Defence Policy', *Navy*, 67/5 (May 1962), p. 108.
[81] See e.g. Gretton, *Maritime Strategy*, p. 84; Patrick Wall, 'The Navy We Need', *Brassey's Annual 1965*, pp. 226-7; Editor's Notes, *JRUSI*, 110/640 (Nov. 1965), p. 297.
[82] Statement by Minister of Defence for the Navy, 708 HC Deb., 11 Mar. 1965, coll. 658-9.

units. When the Kuwait emergency developed, by happy chance *Bulwark* was on a goodwill visit to Karachi, only 1,200 miles away or under two days' steaming. However, the one carrier stationed east of Suez, HMS *Victorious*, was in the Hong Kong area and although she proceeded at full speed it was nine days before she reached Kuwait. HMS *Centaur* sailed from Gibraltar but could not have reached the area until three days after the *Victorious*—that is, twelve days after orders had been received.[83] The outbreak of the Azahari rebellion found the commando ship *Albion* in the west of the Indian Ocean. On receipt of orders early on 8 December she put on full speed, but it was not until the 13th that she arrived at Singapore and a further day before troops were disembarked at Kuching.[84] In the East African operation in January 1964 the Admiralty was forced to employ a strike carrier—HMS *Centaur*—in what was a commando carrier's role. When the revolt broke out *Centaur* was near Aden and after embarking 45 Commando, Royal Marines, which in fact had been trained for an air-transported role, she sailed for Kenya arriving four days later. The congestion on board was said to be indescribable and the shortage of helicopters made it necessary for *Centaur* to steam close inshore to launch the assault.[85] In the circumstances, such improvisation involved little risk and it certainly showed a commendable flexibility, but it was easy to envisage a situation in which a similar venture might be costly.

Manpower was another problem. Mayhew records that it became quite common for ships to operate without their full complement and with some of their less essential equipment unmanned.[86] A commando ship captain wrote of the extreme difficulty of maintaining a proper readiness for landing and supporting a Royal Marine Commando because the three Commandos east of Suez were frequently fully committed to an infantry role and had little time to practise from the commando ship.[87] Inevitably working conditions deteriorated and

[83] V Adm B. B. Schofield, 'Maritime Affairs: Britain: the Naval Side of the Kuwait Question', *Army Quarterly*, 83/1 (Oct. 1961), pp. 11–12.
[84] Id. 'Maritime Affairs: Britain: the Revolt in Brunei', *Army Quarterly*, 86/1 (Apr. 1963), p. 15.
[85] Lt Col T. M. P. Stevens, 'A Joint Operation in Tanganyika', *JRUSI*, 110/637, pp. 48 and 52.
[86] Mayhew, *Britain's Role Tomorrow*, p. 37.
[87] Capt J. H. Adams, 'Commando Ship. Her Qualities and Uses', *Navy*, 70/10 (Oct. 1965), p. 327.

men were separated from their families for longer periods.[88] No doubt partly as a result, recruiting slackened and the rate of re-engagement fell sharply.[89]

Army Developments

In August 1962 the army reached its minimum target of 165,000 regular, adult males. Confounding the sceptics, recruiting during 1962 showed a 19.3 per cent increase over 1961 and 49.6 per cent over 1960.[90] It was not, however, to reach its upper figure of 180,000. After 1962 recruiting slackened, and the army's strength rose only slowly if erratically from 169,817 at the end of 1962, to 171,588 in February 1964, and to 176,382 by the end of January 1965.

Before 1962 there had been much speculation about whether an army of 180,000 would be adequate for its tasks. By now almost all observers were convinced that it would not. During 1963 and 1964 when Britain's east of Suez commitments imposed a heavy strain on the army, it was in sight of its ceiling of 180,000 and it was apparent that an additional 4,000 to 8,000 men would have filled only some of the worst gaps. Even if voluntary recruitment had made up the deficiency, the army would still have been without the reserves of manpower so necessary for effective operation over the long term.[91] The government stoutly maintained the reverse. Indeed to compound its earlier folly of committing the army to the mercy of the recruiting graphs, in 1963 it moved to cut the one independent source of the army's strength east of Suez—the Gurkhas. In March the Secretary of State for War announced that the government had decided that the Gurkha Brigade, which then had a strength of about 14,600, should revert to an establishment of 10,000 by 1966.[92] Eight months later, however, the

[88] See further Mayhew, *Britain's Role Tomorrow*, pp. 36–7, and Desmond Wettern, 'Far Eastern Fleet', *Navy*, 71/1 (Jan. 1966), p. 19.
[89] See MoD, *Statement on Defence Estimates 1965*, Cmnd 2592, paras 109–11, and *Statement on Defence Estimates 1966*, Pt 2: *Defence Estimates 1966–67*, Cmnd 2902, (1966), p. 70, para. 18, and p. 72, para. 29.
[90] MoD, *Statement on Defence 1963*, Cmnd 1936, p. 51, paras 36–8.
[91] See e.g. *Times* leaders, 3 Jan. and 2 June 1964, quoted above on pp. 239 and 242, resp.
[92] 673 HC Deb., 14 Mar. 1963, coll. 1559–60.

government conceded that it had miscalculated and the planned run-down was halted.[93]

A general picture of the strain imposed upon the army by the succession of emergencies following Kuwait has been sketched in chapter 6. Three aspects were especially significant and require discussion here. In the first place, no amount of rationalization could conceal the fact that on several occasions east of Suez commitments had drained the United Kingdom strategic reserve and compelled reinforcements to be drawn from such uncommitted units as happened to be available.[94] In practice what this usually meant was calling on units on home service between overseas tours, and at times employing artillery regiments in an infantry role.[95] On this issue, as with many others, serious discussion in Parliament and in the press was hamstrung by lack of precise information. Broadly summarized the government's case was that reserves existed to be used: its critics contended that a reserve was needed for the reserve.

Secondly, the manpower shortage against authorized establishment mainly hit certain arms, of which the infantry was the most important.[96] As a result, many of the infantry battalions serving overseas were seriously below their established strength of between 600 and 700 men. On 1 January 1963, for example, eighteen battalions of the line were between 50 and 100 short of establishment and twelve were over 100 short of establishment.[97] This issue produced some stormy exchanges in the House of Commons the following year when the position appears to have worsened. The government managed to rebut George Brown's allegation that some units were being sent abroad at a little more than half strength, but the margin was obviously narrow.[98] No reply was forthcoming to George Wigg's disclosure that the Staffords went into Uganda 480 strong, minus a company and plus a company of Scots Guards, and that the Devons and Dorsets when

[93] Statement by Minister of Defence, 684 HC Deb., 20 Nov. 1963, col. 98.
[94] Army League, *The Army Britain Needs*, pp. 41–2. Also Mayhew, *Britain's Role Tomorrow*, p. 36.
[95] e.g. in June 1964 a battery of 20 Medium Regiment, Royal Artillery, was flown to British Guiana in an infantry role.
[96] Army League, *The Army Britain Needs*, pp. 40–1.
[97] Answer by Secretary of State for War to a question from George Wigg, 670 HC Deb., 31 Jan. 1963, col. 234.
[98] Speech by Under-Secretary of State and Financial Secretary for War, 690 HC Deb., 5 Mar. 1964, col. 1675–6.

B.D.P.—10

brought to the alert were only 300 strong and that it had been proposed to take a company of the Coldstream Guards to bring them up to establishment.[99] Even by March 1965, when the overall manpower shortage had been reduced to about 2 per cent, some infantry battalions were 15 per cent short of establishment.[100]

In the view of most army men, the real infantry shortage was even greater because the standard authorized establishment of 635 was inadequate for the counter-insurgency and peace-keeping roles.[101] In 1959 the Secretary of State for War admitted that experience in working with this figure had shown that in certain circumstances a higher strength was desirable and he cited the case of Cyprus where it had been necessary to keep battalions at a strength of over 700.[102] Lord Harding went further and argued that for maximum operational efficiency an infantry battalion in the field needed a strength of the order of 750.[103] A study of the emergencies in 1963 and 1964 convinced the Army League that even this figure was too low. In a report published in September 1964 the League recommended that the battalions forming the normal garrison in Aden and Singapore and those in the 3rd Division in the United Kingdom be permanently maintained as battalion groups on a four-rifle-company basis at an established strength of around 900.[104]

Finally, the strain involved in answering east of Suez calls while at the same time attempting to maintain a standing army of about 55,000 in Europe led to a blurring of the distinction between the forces for the two roles. The 1962 White Paper abandoned the original conception of the strategic reserve as a force solely for overseas emergencies when it redefined its role to include a reinforcement of BAOR.[105] In a leader in May, *The Times* drew attention to the dangers implied by this policy of 'double accounting', and concluded that the govern-

[99] Ibid., col. 1544.
[100] Statement by Under-Secretary of State for Defence for the Army, 708 HC Deb., 8 Mar. 1965, col. 189.
[101] The plan for the 165,000 army was drawn up on the basis of most infantry battalions having a strength of 635. See Soames' speech, 601 HC Deb., 3 Mar. 1959, col 229.
[102] Ibid.
[103] 215 HL Deb., 18 Mar. 1959, col. 36.
[104] *The Army Britain Needs*, p. 41.
[105] MoD, *Statement on Defence 1962*, Cmnd 1639, para. 29.

ment was preoccupied with the technique of maintaining a stage army instead of facing up to the fact that more men were required.[106] Then there was the expedient of withdrawing units from BAOR for east of Suez requirements and the increasing tendency of army leaders to look upon BAOR as a manpower reserve for the overseas role. On military grounds the efficacy of this course of action was debatable. It was a matter of weighing the disruption to BAOR and the loss of some immediate fighting capacity in Europe[107] against the value of active service experience gained outside Europe.[108] There was also room for argument on diplomatic grounds. Although the practice of drawing on BAOR units could be supported in terms of maintaining Britain's world influence, opponents argued that it provided the European states with another illustration of Britain's lack of commitment to Europe.[109]

Outside the Ministry of Defence the most detailed study of the army's manpower requirements was that undertaken by the Army League in September 1964. Under the chairmanship of General Sir Richard Gale the League concluded that the establishment figure of 180,000 should be increased to 195,000 This would make it possible for the battalions employed on peacekeeping duties to be brought up to about 900, an additional brigade to be attached to the central reserve, and a holding organization provided which could absorb the stresses and strains which then fell on units. Taking account of the existing shortage on establishment of some 5,000, an additional 20,000 men were required. The answer was seen in selective National Service.[110] This solution was not taken seriously by the Army Council. A return to any form of National Service had little appeal to senior army officers and the principle of selectivity was believed to be ruled out on political grounds. As a result, no approach was made to the government along these lines.

---

[106] 28 May 1962.
[107] One possibility considered by the Army League was that units withdrawn from BAOR in a crisis might be replaced by units of the Territorial Army. However, this policy would have required a radical change in accepted ideas about the employment and availability of the TA. See *The Army Britain Needs*, p. 42.
[108] One senior commander contrasted the British army's situation with that of the German army, which lacked active service experience.
[109] For Verrier's reflections on this problem see *An Army for the Sixties*, p. 196.
[110] *The Army Britain Needs*, chs 5 and 6.

The Base Strategy

On 5 March 1962 Harold Watkinson outlined to the Commons the government's policy on overseas bases and garrisons:

Here is really in the long term a fundamental change in policy. It is no longer a concept of British forces dispersed round the world in small pockets, but a concentration on three main bases from which to fan out by air and sea. These bases are Britain, Aden and Singapore.[111]

If the statement contributed little to existing knowledge, it was at least in keeping with the utterances of earlier ministers. The first point had been government policy since 1954. The second was a reaction to circumstance and not a considered change in policy.

Despite the development of air and sea mobility, the continuance of the base strategy was never seriously in doubt. For one thing, the issue was deeply entwined with service politics. Bases represented the army's stake in the overseas role. A change in policy would require an immediate reallocation of the defence vote. In the long run, to withdraw from overseas bases could only mean a smaller army and a larger navy and a corresponding adjustment of tasks and senior appointments. It was therefore necessary to tread warily: care had to be taken not to upset the delicate balance of service roles, hardware, and manpower. Again, opinion in the other two services was by no means united and to judge from the public statements of ministers, the government was readily open to conviction. Although the issue developed into something of a feud in late 1961 and early 1962, nothing eventuated and policy continued along existing lines.[112]

During the deliberations which led to the Chiefs of Staff paper of January 1962 the service chiefs received an assessment from the Foreign Office that Britain's tenure in Singapore was likely to be about seven years and in Aden about three or four years. Although more optimistic assessments were received from the Colonial Office, the navy dwelt on the uncertainties surrounding Aden and Singapore and urged a further develop-

---

[111] 655 HC Deb., coll. 46–7.
[112] See *Times*, 8 Feb. 1962.

ment of seaborne forces and the establishment of a major base in Australia. The latter point aroused considerable interest in Whitehall, and with the support of the Minister of Defence and the Defence Committee certain informal approaches were made to Canberra. Little encouragement was received, however, and the idea lapsed.[113] Two considerations appear to have influenced Australian thinking. On the one hand, the government was not prepared to commit itself to any additional military expenditure. On the other, it was reluctant to do anything that might hasten Britain's withdrawal from Singapore, the rationale here being that the front line of Australia's defence should be as far to the north as possible.

For the remainder of the period the future of the bases at Aden and Singapore was secure. The navy and the air force continued to press for a fuller development of strategically mobile forces but their respective schemes were presented more as a complement to the base strategy than as a substitute. The army's case was clear. All the old arguments still held good and if practical confirmation was required Kuwait provided it. That operation was taken to show that for all the advantage of the new mobility Britain could not dispense entirely with theatre and forward bases.[114] Acclimatization and training were strong arguments.[115] Another was the need for air staging posts and terminal facilities.[116] A more dubious proposition was that bases were required for the forward supply of equipment and stores. The Commander of the Parachute Brigade Group pointed out, for example, that about 400 to 500 tons of stores a day were needed for a parachute brigade and a commando brigade on the ground.[117] To this General Moulton could reply that such a commitment could be handled by one 5,000 ton store ship every ten days. The issue was there-

---

[113] Verrier throws some light on this subject in *An Army for the Sixties*, pp. 261–2. In 1962 Verrier was asked to write an appreciation for the West Australian government on the likelihood of Britain's considering an Australian base as a replacement for Singapore.

[114] See further Verrier, 'Strategically Mobile Forces—US Theory and British Practice', *JRUSI*, 106/624 (Nov. 1961), p. 484.

[115] These arguments are developed in Army League, *The Army Britain Needs*, pp. 28–9.

[116] See Maj Gen J. L. Moulton, 'The Real Cost: a Study of the Effectiveness of Overseas Forces', *Navy*, 69/11 (Nov. 1964), p. 360.

[117] In discussion after Moulton's lecture on 'Amphibious Warfare in the late 1960s: Seaborne/Airborne Operations', *JRUSI*, 107/625, p. 27.

fore one to be resolved on cost effectiveness grounds but it is doubtful how far the services saw it in those terms.

Within the Ministry of Defence the door to serious analysis of the different courses of action overseas was barred by existing forms of costing. The Ministry's position appears to have been an amalgam of mistrust of the methods of functional costing and indifference to the results which might be obtained. No figures were normally available of the overall expenditure at a particular base or garrison. Nor could the Ministry compute what might be saved by closing down these establishments.[118] One senior official told the Estimates Committee in February 1963 that these figures were not of any particular interest because a base was maintained for strategic reasons and not on financial grounds.[119]

Scarcely a matter of surprise, the Estimates Committee was decidedly unhappy about the Ministry's costing procedure, but it appears to have accepted the argument that there was no alternative to land bases. The Committee therefore contented itself with observing that 'while abandoning a base merely on financial grounds may be inconceivable, overall figures of the complete cost of a base would seem to be of the greatest importance.'[120] In its second report on overseas military expenditure, the Committee went much further and recommended that the Ministry of Defence undertake a review of the cost of overseas bases and garrisons with the object of reducing land establishments and taking fuller advantage of the development of strategically mobile forces.[121] *The Times* took the Committee to task for a somewhat oversimplified assessment of Britain's strategic requirements and claimed that the Committee's recommendation was superfluous as the subject was under constant study.[122] But surely

[118] HC, *Tenth Report from Estimates Committee . . . Session 1962–63: Military Expenditure Overseas*, p. xi, paras 24 and 25. See also, p. 1, replies by Min. of Defence representative to Questions 1 and 4.

[119] Ibid. p. xi, para. 25.

[120] Ibid. p. xii, para. 26. A year earlier, when considering the form of the Defence Estimates, members of the Estimates Committee had expressed concern with costing procedures that made it impossible to give a statement of military expenditure at overseas bases. See HC, *Fifth Report from Estimates Committee . . . Session 1961–62: Form of the Estimates of the Defence Departments* (1962), pp. 22–3, Questions 21–31.

[121] HC, *Ninth Report from Estimates Committee . . . Session 1963–64: Military Expenditure Overseas*, pp. xviii–xix, paras 48–9.

[122] 25 Aug. 1964.

this was shaky ground. The evidence taken before both Committees disclosed few signs of re-thinking in the Ministry. Similarly the Ministry's subsequent observations on the Committee's second report were mainly notable for their emphasis on the difficulties attending any policy of greater reliance on strategic reserves.[123]

In both reports the Estimates Committee severely criticized the services for lavish building programmes and general extravagance, thus highlighting the tendency for overseas bases to develop out of all proportion to their original strategic function.[124] On one account, at times the responsibility for elaborate building projects rested with the Foreign Office rather than the services. Frequently in Defence Committee meetings the Treasury advocated prefabricated structures in place of buildings designed to last a generation and the Ministry of Defence would be in agreement. On some occasions, however, the Foreign Office countered successfully that if a building could be seen to be temporary, it would be taken as an indication that withdrawal was imminent, and Britain would then find it impossible to hold on.

By 1962 the end of the road was in sight for the Kenya base. The White Paper *Statement on Defence 1962* admitted as much when it outlined alternative arrangements to support operations in the Middle Eastern theatre.[125] The most that could be hoped for now was some limited staging facilities, and perhaps training rights for British troops. General Hull fished for an offer during his visit to Kenya in May 1962. Further feelers were put out in 1963, and on 6 March 1964 Kenya agreed to grant certain training facilities for the army, overflying and staging rights for the RAF, and port maintenance facilities for the Royal Navy.[126] At the same time the withdrawal of some 6,000 British troops began. Over the next nine months the Headquarters, 24th Infantry Brigade Group, and most of the administrative units of the brigade were redeployed at Aden and the remaining troops returned to Britain. On 10

---

[123] HC, *Second Special Report from Estimates Committee, Session 1964–65: Military Expenditure Overseas* (1964), pp. 3–4.
[124] Recruiting was undoubtedly a factor here. Dependence of the services on voluntary recruiting necessitated an improvement in the conditions of overseas service.
[125] MoD, Cmnd 1639, para. 17.
[126] *Times*, 7 Mar. 1964.

December 1964 the last British troops left Kenya and another chapter closed in the army's search for secure footholds around the Indian Ocean. £7.5 million poorer the army moved on to Aden. There surely it could make a stand.

By 1962 the development of Aden was already well under way.[127] However, the rapid movement of Kenya towards independence gave a boost to the scale of the whole enterprise. A complete picture of the build-up cannot be made but a few figures relating to specific projects will illustrate the trend. In March 1962 Harold Watkinson inaugurated a £5 million communications centre.[128] Nine months later a £3.5 million contract was awarded for building married quarters and army workshops.[129] Further contracts for construction at Little Aden were signed early in 1963.[130] In March 1963 Geoffrey Rippon, Minister of Public Building and Works, announced that about £20 million would be spent on building projects in Aden over the next three years.[131]

Along with the development of defence facilities at Aden came an increased enthusiasm to secure the future of the territory by linking it to the Federation of South Arabia. Preparatory talks took place in Aden and London during 1961 and early 1962. Aden acceded to the Federation on 18 January 1963.[132] British sovereignty continued as before and the United Kingdom reserved the right to withdraw any part of Aden from the Federation, 'if it considers this desirable for the purpose of its world-wide defence responsibilities'.[133] By this formula, so indelicately imposed upon the colony, Britain sought to prevent a repetition of the Kenya disaster. The price of constitutional security, however, was violence in Aden and insurgency in the Federation. From the time of Aden's accession, terrorist activity became endemic. More and more British forces were tied down maintaining local security. Month by month the argument grew stronger that the British presence was encouraging

---

[127] See pp. 204–8 above.
[128] *Times*, 30 Mar. 1962.
[129] *Guardian*, 12 Dec. 1962.
[130] MoD, *Statement on Defence 1963*, Cmnd 1936, p. 57, para. 68.
[131] *Daily Telegraph*, 20 Mar. 1963.
[132] See also pp. 211 and 237–8 above.
[133] CO, *Accession of Aden to the Federation of South Arabia: Exchange of Letters between Federal and Aden Ministers and the Secretary of State for the Colonies*, Cmnd 1814, p. 8, Art. IX.

tensions rather than bringing added stability to the area.[134] The government, however, was unmoved. History was not to repeat itself.

Parallel with the development of Aden, the services embarked on smaller expansion projects at Bahrain and Sharjah in the Persian Gulf. Since the Kuwait operation a battalion group had been stationed at Bahrain and in 1962 work started on the provision of permanent accommodation and other facilities there.[135] Similarly at Sharjah permanent accommodation was being built for the British garrison.[136] At the same time, the RAF pushed ahead with schemes of its own which included airfield construction, additional quarters, and amenity services. The immediate objective was to establish forward facilities for operations in the Persian Gulf but the ground was being laid, perhaps unwittingly, for yet another redeployment should Aden prove untenable.

Singapore was a rather different case. For one thing, it represented an investment in being, and although large sums continued to be spent during these years, there was no requirement for the enormous construction programmes such as in Kenya or Aden. For another, the political climate was distinctly more favourable, especially after Indonesia embarked on its policy of confrontation. It can be argued, of course, that the Malaysian Federation was simply a device by which Britain could relinquish residual authority in Singapore within the context of a wider political stability and so ensure the continued use of the military facilities on the island. Further, that therefore confrontaion itself must be debited against the base. This line of reasoning, however, involves an exceedingly oversimplified interpretation of the events of 1961–4. Although Britain took up the Malaysian scheme with enthusiasm, partly for strategic reasons but also because of genuine concern about the future of the Borneo territories, the initiative came largely from the Tunku and the original inspiration was almost

---

[134] Moulton argued this case strongly in 'The Real Cost', *Navy*, 69/11, pp. 360–1, and 'Bases or Fighting Forces?', *Brassey's Annual 1964*, pp. 147–8. The Army League, on the other hand, contended that Aden should be retained 'at all costs'. *The Army Britain Needs*, p. 29.

[135] WO, *Memorandum on Army Estimates 1962–63*, Cmnd 1631 (1962), para. 80; *Daily Telegraph*, 28 Feb. 1962.

[136] MoD, *Statement on Defence 1963*, Cmnd 1936, p. 57, para 69.

certainly Lee Kuan Yew's.[137] Moreover, it can hardly be
denied that the project had widespread support in all the
territories concerned.[138] Indonesia's motives are outside the
scope of this book, but it can at least be said that it is a naïve
view which seeks to pin confrontation simply on the fact of a
British military presence.

[137] For a full discussion see H. F. Armstrong, 'The Troubled Birth of Malaysia',
For. Aff., 41/4, pp. 673–93; G. P. Means, 'Malaysia—a New Federation in South-
East Asia', *Pacific Affairs*, 36/2, pp. 138–59; and Kirkman, pp. 162–6.
[138] See Australia, Dept of External Affairs, *Malaysia*, p. 6 (Cobbold Commission);
p. 8 (merger referendum in Singapore); p. 61 (extracts from Report of Commission
of Enquiry, North Borneo and Sarawak).

CHAPTER EIGHT

The Critics and the Compromise

By one of the ironies of history, the task of dismantling the final pieces of the apparatus of imperial defence fell upon a government which more than any other since the Second World War had been committed to their maintenance. For all Harold Wilson's romantic conception of Britain's world role and his determination to preserve it, economic and political pressures forced his hand. Yet it was Wilson who had dealt the cards. Once the new economic lines had been drawn the fate of the world role was sealed. Again, much of the political pressure stemmed from the government's own presentation of the case for remaining east of Suez.

Within a matter of months of Labour's return to office in October 1964 the ranks of the east of Suez opponents swelled dramatically: what during the last years of the Conservative government had been little more than a general concern about the extent of Britain's defence responsibilities and a recognition that the services were overstretched, developed into a powerful case for withdrawal from Arabia, the Persian Gulf, and the Far East. The result was an impassioned and highly polarized debate about Britain's role in the world. During 1965 the government maintained its world power posture but behind the scenes the Treasury removed the substance. The 1966 Defence Review recorded the unhappy compromise. Over the next two years the east of Suez critics weakened the government's resolve. The final blows were struck by economic circumstance. Scarcely more than three years after returning to power, the party which had given India its independence completed the withdrawal from empire. It was not, however, a matter of ideological continuity. Whatever may be said of the policies of the Attlee government in the late forties, that of Harold

Wilson in the mid-sixties beat its retreat reluctantly and under pressure of immediate events.

Setting the Stage: First Months of the Labour Government

Very shortly after taking office the Labour government reached two fundamental decisions which established the parameters of British defence policy for the next eighteen months and to some extent beyond. The first, entirely consistent with the Labour front-bench view in the debate on the Defence Estimates earlier that year, was to maintain the peacekeeping role east of Suez. Wilson left the House of Commons in no doubt about this aspect of the government's policy when he spoke in the foreign affairs debate on 16 December.

I want to make it quite clear that whatever we may do in the field of cost effectiveness, value for money and a stringent review of expenditure, we cannot afford to relinquish our world role—our role which, for shorthand purposes, is sometimes called our 'east of Suez' role . . .[1]

All the factors which had earlier influenced the Conservatives —the sense of duty to the new states of Africa and Asia, the conception of Britain as a world power, the American notion of a world security system with tacit lines of responsibility, the east of Suez role as a continuing justification for Britain's special relationship with the United States—now showed their impact on the Prime Minister's thinking. Speaking of Britain's role as a world power, he went on to declare that while Britain must always be a second class contributor to NATO, no other country could compete in the range of the contribution Britain could make outside Europe. This, he said, was recognized by Britain's allies, particularly the United States.[2] Addressing himself to Sir Alec Douglas-Home, he explained in expansive terms:

. . . our American allies are not so impressed with our claims to be a world power or to have a seat at the top table if we base those claims on matching our nuclear policy with theirs. They are perfectly capable of doing the arithmetic of megatons. What does

---

[1] 704 HC Deb., 16 Dec. 1964, coll. 423-4.
[2] Ibid. coll. 424-5.

impress them is our ability to mount peace-keeping operations that no one else can mount.[3]

Thus far, it could be argued, Wilson had not substantially broadened the Conservative conception of the overseas role. However, one new ingredient and two clear hints that the government was thinking in a bolder vein combined to give the Prime Minister's speech a quite different tone from any delivered by Conservative ministers. The first point relates to Wilson's historical perspective and sense of mission. It is possible to interpret the whole speech as a clash between Wilson the economist and the pragmatist and Wilson the romantic conservative. On Europe and on the deterrent the pragmatist is uppermost: on east of Suez the conservative takes over.[4] To take the point further, both in this speech and in others, Wilson introduced a new emotional content to discussions about the east of Suez role. Partly this was a matter of political style: an instinct for the extravagant phrase.[5] But it also went deeper and when Wilson and other Labour ministers used language with a remarkable similarity to that of the later imperialists they drew on a fund of imperial romance, of enthusiasm for the Commonwealth, and a deep-seated paternalism which reflected their alienation from Europe and from America. Such language at once disturbed the rank and file and made grist for the critics' mill. As Neville Brown has aptly commented, it was not long before the evocative content was drawn from the phrases of empire and they became weapons of irony.[6]

Of more substance, Wilson warned the House that to fulfil the world role it might be necessary to develop Britain's strength in certain respects.[7] He then went on to argue that

[3] Ibid. coll. 425–6. It was significant that the previous week Wilson had had long discussions with President Johnson and the two leaders were reported to be in complete agreement about the value of Britain's role east of Suez. *Times*, 8, 9, 10 Dec. 1964.

[4] Wilson later admitted that he clung to the east of Suez role when facts were dictating a recessional. He was, he said, one of the last to be converted. See his *The Labour Government 1964–1970: a Personal Record* (1971), p. 243.

[5] Phrases such as 'our frontiers are on the Himalayas' and Britain's role in preventing an 'eyeball-to-eyeball' confrontation between the Americans and the Chinese will long be associated with Wilson's presentation of the case for remaining east of Suez.

[6] *Arms Without Empire* (1967), p. 27.

[7] 704 HC Deb., 16 Dec. 1964, col. 422.

the balance between Britain's three roles must be re-examined, the implication of his analysis being that the European role required pruning and that the highly expensive and intricate weapons which were suitable only for Europe would have to give way to more and simpler weapons which were relevant to the kind of wars Britain was likely to fight.[8]

Wilson's final offering concerned Britain's nuclear role and here he broke new ground. Confirming speculation in Washington the previous week, he made it plain that the government was considering carving a role for Britain in the nuclear balance in Asia. Replying to questions, he hinted that part of the V-bomber force reserved for use outside Europe might be used for guaranteeing non-nuclear powers against nuclear attack.[9]

The government's second decision was to cut back on defence expenditure, and this was the undoing of the first. Before the Labour government took office, the Treasury had prepared a detailed paper arguing the case for a major reduction in defence spending. Shortly after the election, this document was presented to the government and the new ministers accepted its broad conclusions and the need for a review of the defence effort. The matter was then considered by the cabinet in the context of the government's overall economic plans and in November a provisional decision was taken to reduce the defence budget planned for 1969–70 from £2,400 million to £2,000 million at constant prices.[10] At this stage, however, no public announcement was made of the £2,000 million objective and in the debate in December the Prime Minister spoke simply of the need for 'reappraisal and retrenchment.'[11]

The process of reviewing the defence programme now got under way. Pursuant to a decision in November, the first stage of the review consisted of pruning weapons programmes and reserve forces in an attempt to cut defence spending. For the moment it was assumed that commitments would continue as before. It was not until later, at the second stage, that the

[8] Ibid. coll. 423 and 426. *The Times* accepted this reasoning in a leader on 17 Dec. 1964. The gist of Wilson's remarks suggests that at this stage he had a somewhat naïve view of the weapons and equipment required for the east of Suez role.
[9] Ibid. coll. 434, 441–2. *The Times* gave this proposal its blessing in a leader on 23 Dec. 1964.
[10] Mayhew, *Britain's Role Tomorrow*, p. 131.
[11] 704 HC Deb., 16 Dec. 1964, coll. 419–21.

commitments themselves would be reappraised.[12] The major part of the review was undertaken by the Official Committee which met about once a week for the next two months. At a lower level working committees were set up to determine where the cuts should fall. The most important development of these months was that the £2,000 million figure gradually changed from a provisional target to an absolete ceiling. In meetings of the Official Committee, the Treasury and the Department of Economic Affairs vigorously opposed all items of defence expenditure which might conceivably threaten the new target. After a disappointing start, the economic departments had won a major success and they were determined to hold their ground.[13] According to Christopher Mayhew, who then held the navy portfolio, although at the outset he was continually assured that the £2,000 million limit was conditional on a reduction in commitments, as the National Economic Plan began to take concrete shape the reduction in commitments proviso receded into the background and the ceiling became immutable.[14]

Predictably the 1965 White Paper was something of a holding operation. Long-range decisions about Britain's role and about the eventual shape of the defence forces were to await the findings of the studies which had just been set in motion. In the meantime, the government confirmed the need to reduce defence spending but it stressed the requirement to maintain the world role. On the first point, a start had been made in pruning defence expenditure by cutting certain weapons projects. The P1154 Hunter replacement and the HS681 medium transport aircraft had been cancelled, as had the fifth Polaris submarine, and the government gave notice that

[12] Mayhew, *Britain's Role Tomorrow*, p. 134. In practice the two stages of the review tended to overlap. A senior official explained that exploratory discussions about reducing Britain's commitments began before review of the hardware programme had been completed. He went on to argue that Mayhew's account invested the two stages of the review with a rigidity they did not have.

[13] Apparently the creation of the Department of Economic Affairs greatly strengthened the Treasury's hand in forcing cuts in defence spending as it now spoke with two voices instead of one.

[14] Mayhew, *Britain's Role Tomorrow*, p. 133. The 1965 White Paper (MoD, *Statement on Defence Estimates 1965*, Cmnd 2592), para. 2, stated the government's financial aim in general terms. Healey put it specifically at a press conference on 4 Aug. 1965 (see *Times*, 5 Aug. 1965). Together with other aspects of the government's policy on defence expenditure, it was set out fully in DEA, *The National Plan*, Cmnd 2764 (1965), Pt I, pp. 182–3.

the TSR2 and the new carrier were under review. On Denis Healey's own admission, however, there was a limit to the degree to which the problem of defence expenditure could be solved by savings on equipment programmes.[15] In the long run it was clear that what was required was a major reduction in commitments but on this score the White Paper held out little hope of early relief.[16]

On the second point the White Paper was categorical. Outside Europe instability was likely to continue and perhaps increase. Many of the newly independent countries were threatened by unrest and armed conflict, and if help were required Britain must be ready to give it where she could. In the Far East the Chinese nuclear explosion raised new problems for regional stability; pending some international agreement, Britain's nuclear policy must help to provide reassurance to non-nuclear powers.[17] To justify the translation of what were strategic facts of life into diplomatic objectives, the White Paper argued that national and international interests coincided to tie Britain to the wider military role. On the one hand, Britain had treaty relations and commitments east of Suez which must be honoured and a major interest in the stability of the area and in its economic prosperity. On the other, the prevention of violence and chaos in this part of the world was a fundamental international interest, and Britain, because of her special situation, was able to make a contribution to international peacekeeping which no other country could equal.[18] Under such circumstances, paragraph 20 concluded, it would be 'politically irresponsible and economically wasteful' for Britain unnecessarily to abandon her bases at Aden and Singapore.

Having established the government's intention to maintain the east of Suez role, the White Paper went on to make a claim for allied assistance in carrying out the peacekeeping tasks since the interests at stake were common to the West and not Britain's alone. It continued, 'If some of our burdens can be assumed or shared by our allies, we may not need the full

---

[15] 707 HC Deb., 3 Mar. 1965, col. 1342.
[16] The *Guardian* and *Financial Times* made pertinent observations on this subject in leaders on 24 Feb. 1965.
[17] MoD, *Statement on Defence Estimates 1965*, Cmnd 2592, paras 11 and 12.
[18] Ibid. para. 19. See also Healey's speech, 707 HC Deb., 3 Mar. 1965, coll. 1337-9.

range of military power we should require to carry them all alone.'[19]

Such a solution would accord nicely with the government's aim of halting the upward trend in defence expenditure, but as the *Financial Times* was quick to point out, it seemed over optimistic to expect much support from Britain's allies at a time when even the United States was seeking to cut down defence costs by every means possible.[20] As it stood, therefore, this line of approach represented little more than a pious hope.

Leaving aside the possibility of substantial allied assistance the problem of holding the defence budget at £2,000 million while maintaining the world role resolved itself into one of scaling down Britain's military involvement in Europe. That is to say, the savings resulting from sharpened techniques for judging cost-effectiveness and improved cost control would need to be supplemented by savings on at least one major role. With the fifth Polaris submarine already cancelled, and the government committed to an Atlantic nuclear strategy and talking broadly about another east of Suez, there was little hope of further economies in the strategic nuclear role. For the moment, the door seemed closed east of Suez as well. Indeed Harold Wilson admitted this in a speech on 4 March. Having restated the government's intention to maintain east of Suez commitments, he went on: 'I would be wrong, I say it again, to raise the hopes of the House by any suggestion that we can do what we have to do cheaply and at a diminishing cost in terms of our defence effort'.[21]

The one remaining role was Europe, and the clear implication of the White Paper was that this was where the reduction in commitment must fall. In assessing likely threats, the possibility of deliberate aggression in Europe was specifically discounted. The development of mutual deterrence had greatly reduced the likelihood of war between the Soviet and Western alliances and there were grounds for hoping that the central balance might become yet more stable and that some limitation and control of arms could be achieved.[22] In later sections the

[19] para. 21.
[20] 24 Feb. 1965.
[21] 707 HC Deb., 4 Mar. 1965. col. 1569.
[22] paras 9 and 10.

White Paper went on to argue that the time had come to revise the existing NATO strategy which tied up resources against a risk which was almost inconceivable.[23] It also drew attention to the heavy balance of payments burden imposed by stationing forces in Germany and contended that this must be reviewed against the background of Britain's total defence burden and the nature of the military threats in Europe and overseas.[24] On military grounds, the government's case was unarguable. Nor could its economic reasoning be faulted. But viewed in the broader light of Britain's diplomatic interests and of the government's stated objective of joining the Common Market, proposals to reduce the European commitment lost much of their persuasiveness. Moreover, there were good grounds for thinking that, when it came to the point, the government would be reluctant to let go of a valuable lever in Europe in favour of such a shadowy conception as the world role.

The Commitment Stands

The twelve months following the publication of the 1965 White Paper produced strong cross-currents of opinion and pressure about the Indian Ocean commitment. Within the Labour party, the government's conception of the world role came under hard attack from the left wing and it aroused considerable misgivings among large sections of the parliamentary party. In the other two parties and in the press opinion was changing also and at various times the case for withdrawing from east of Suez was presented forcefully by advocates who made strange bed-fellows for Konni Zilliacus, Sydney Silverman, and other left-wingers. Disturbing as these voices were, however, and admitting that on occasions they forced the government to indulge in dubious verbal acrobatics, there is no evidence that the government seriously reconsidered its position. Although the government admitted that certain commitments would have to be revised, it left no doubt that Britain would retain a major role east of Suez for many years to come. Moreover, despite the difficulties of these months,

[23] para. 18.
[24] para. 17. See also Healey's strong remarks on this subject in his Commons speech on 3 Mar., 707 HC Deb., col. 1336.

the government adhered to its view that final decisions about revising Britain's east of Suez commitments could not be taken for some time and that in the interim they would continue as before.

Before 1964 had come to a close the first murmurings of Labour back-bench discontent could be heard but the debate on the 1965 White Paper brought opposition into the open. On 2 March Silverman and more than twenty other Labour back-benchers tabled an amendment congratulating the government on its decision to review its commitments, but, among other things, calling for 'greatly accelerated progress in the reduction of Great Britain's overseas commitments.'[25] Despite a number of strongly critical speeches in the House, however, when it came to a division all the Labour members voted with the government. With a majority of only three, the will to survive as a government overrode even the deep-seated objections of men like Silverman and Zilliacus to the government's defence policy. The same debate gave evidence that opposition to the east of Suez role was not confined to the left wing. Several speakers of rather different political complexions questioned the extent of Britain's commitments, either on the ground of economy or on the ground that Britain was basically a European nation and that the retention of a major role in the East merely delayed the inevitable process of adjustment. Reginald Paget led the moderates with a carefully reasoned argument against the government's proposal for a nuclear guarantee for India, which he dismissed as a fantastic piece of nonsense, and its case for conventional forces, which he described as entirely obsolete.[26] When he puzzled over how the Labour party's defence policy had been abandoned and the Conservative policy adopted in its stead, he echoed the words of a number of members on both sides of the House.[27]

Two weeks later three Labour back-benchers, who had not up to that time been linked with the conflict over the government's defence policy, tabled a stiffly worded motion urging a rundown in Britain's defence effort east of Suez.[28] Further rumblings led Healey to assure back-benchers at a private

[25] *Times*, 3 Mar. 1965.
[26] 707 HC Deb., 3 Mar. 1965, coll. 1369–70.
[27] Ibid. col. 1367.
[28] *Guardian*, 19 Mar. 1965.

meeting on 31 March that the scale of Britain's east of Suez role had been greatly exaggerated. Reportedly, however, he reminded MPs that Britain was, for good or ill, heavily involved in the area and that, irrespective of the government's wishes, she could not evade her obligations there.[29] A more general censure came in August when a full meeting of the Parliamentary Labour party adopted a motion calling on the government to speed up cuts in defence expenditure.[30] This development marked a substantial victory for the 77 left-wing MPs who had just signed a statement urging a 25 per cent cut in defence spending.[31] Late in September, at the annual conference of the Labour party, members of the same group pressed home their advantage and secured the adoption of a resolution calling for a drastic reduction in military expenditure. The resolution drew particular attention to the 'heavy burden on the national income involved by maintenance of outmoded military bases abroad'.[32]

By this time opposition to the extent of Britain's commitments east of Suez was growing rapidly outside the Labour party, particularly in European oriented circles. At the Liberal party conference at Scarborough from 22 to 25 September, Lord Gladwyn and Jo Grimond roused the Liberal assembly to cheers by attacking the peacekeeping role. Although Grimond's speech struck an unfortunate note, the Liberal stand was perhaps unexceptional enough, for the party had long shown a marked lack of enthusiasm for the British presence east of Suez.[33] Of an altogether different character was Enoch Powell's challenging address to the Conservative conference on 14 October. The burden of the shadow defence minister's analysis was that in the seventies Britain should withdraw entirely from the east of Suez arena. It may have been that few of the delegates realized what was happening, but Powell's attempt to lead the Tories away from their traditional stamping

---

[29] *Guardian*, 1 Apr. 1965.
[30] *Times*, 3 Aug. 1965.
[31] *Guardian*, 3 Aug. 1965.
[32] Sixty-fourth Annual Conference ... Sept. 27–Oct. 1 1965, *Report* (1965), pp. 186–201.
[33] In the course of his speech, Grimond said that if Britain's peacekeeping role east of Suez had led to two major wars and a revolution in Aden, the sooner it was stopped the better. This brought a spirited reply from Leonard Beaton, 'Mr. Grimond Misfires', in the *Guardian*, 29 Sept. 1965.

ground earned him a standing ovation.[34] In the press, also, a hardening of attitude was evident. Liberal publications such as the *Guardian* and the *Observer* had for some time criticized the burden east of Suez. Now, however, their leaders became stronger and more frequent and on 25 October they were joined by the *Times*.[35]

Many factors no doubt contributed to the government's resolve to maintain the world role and to resist the critics' demands for an immediate withdrawal from constitutional commitments and larger savings in defence expenditure. For one thing, the military case for deploying British forces east of Suez was as strong as ever and the government could at least draw heart from the fact that no critic could argue that the present dangers were elsewhere. For another, the emotional ties and the sense of history which succoured the commitment were not things that could be immediately discarded as political expedience—or arguably economic circumstance—required. Indeed, it could be said that nothing had happened to weaken the force of any of the arguments or influences which some two or three years earlier had converted Labour leaders from their narrowly European policy. A more debatable consideration was the pressure of American diplomacy and the feeling in London that the east of Suez role represented a continuing justification for Britain's special relationship with the United States.

For some years Labour party defence policy had been strongly influenced by thinking in Washington, and after the party was returned to office this stream of authority remained persuasive.[36] Wilson's visit to the United States in December 1964 provided the occasion for a frank exchange of views. The Johnson administration stressed the importance it attached to Britain's role east of Suez: Wilson in return assured the Americans that the government intended to maintain the commitment but emphasized Britain's financial difficulties and the need for American support during a transitional period in which the British house would be put in order.[37] The December meeting may therefore be regarded as having established an awareness

---

[34] See *Times* and *Guardian*, 15 Oct. 1965.
[35] On that day *The Times* ran a leader entitled 'Burden Beyond Suez'.
[36] See Leonard Beaton, 'The Price of Security', *Guardian*, 9 June 1965.
[37] *Times*, 8, 9, and 10 Dec. 1964.

on the part of both governments of the other's wants, thus providing a basis for the close working relationship over the next eighteen months.

It will be useful to examine the position of the two governments. The American stand was an amalgam of strategic, diplomatic, and financial considerations.[38] Robert McNamara was determined to keep the British flag flying east of Suez because he saw it as the one way of resisting US service demands for an American military presence. In his view, forcefully expressed, Britain could maintain both the east of Suez and the European commitments on her current military budget if only the Ministry of Defence rigorously applied cost-effectiveness techniques. As a result, the argument advanced by some American officials and academics that if America wanted a British presence it should pay for it, never made any headway in the Pentagon.[39] Dean Rusk, on the other hand, supported a British presence primarily for diplomatic and domestic reasons. On his reading of the scene, Britain had to be 'kept in the world' because it was vitally important for the United States to have at least one major ally in its global undertaking.

On the British side the evidence about the government's thinking is incomplete but it seems likely that United States representations were to some effect. Apart from the fact that there was almost continuous cross-fertilization of thought which in itself was significant, there were certain practical considerations which appear to have made Labour ministers particularly responsive to American pressure. In the first place, with the European door firmly closed and the Prime Minister and certain of his lieutenants, notably Healey and Callaghan, by no means zealous Europeans, Britain's role in the world was seen as hinging on the Anglo-American partnership.[40] Secondly, there was the government's need to have its economic measures underwritten by the United States.[41] Those concerned with policy negotiations in Whitehall were convinced that this

[38] See also pp. 265–6 above.

[39] Put bluntly, the argument was that America should hire the British flag. It became known as the Hessian argument.

[40] Aubrey Jones argued a similar case in the House of Commons on 3 Mar. 1965. 707 HC Deb., coll. 1375–6.

[41] For a somewhat crude statement of the argument see 'Why is Labour so Reluctant to Govern?' by 'C', *Times*, 10 June 1968. Christopher Mayhew has advanced a more reasonable interpretation of the same line of thinking and by implication suggests that it had some influence. *Britain's Role Tomorrow*, pp. 47 and 131.

consideration had some influence though the process was seen as a subtle one, in no sense constituting a kind of diplomatic bargain. On all counts Patrick Gordon Walker disagrees. In his view American pressure was not a factor in the cabinet's resolve to stay east of Suez though he recalls that occasionally the argument that a continued military presence strengthened Britain's influence in Washington was 'prayed in aid'.[42] It is difficult for the outside observer to question this assessment but even if we accept that collectively the cabinet was not swayed by American pressure there are reasonable grounds for believing that individual ministers were influenced by the nature of the Anglo-American relationship and the force of United States arguments.

During the first half of 1965 there were few signs of American diplomatic pressure. The United States view was well known and the administration seemed satisfied with the December talks and with the British government's subsequent approach to its east of Suez commitments.[43] At a lower level discussions continued about the island base scheme.[44] Thereafter, however, as the world role came under increasing attack in Britain, the United States government lost no opportunity to restate its case and to remind Whitehall of its responsibilities east of Suez. In June officials indicated that although there would be no objection to reductions in BAOR, cuts east of Suez would be viewed with concern.[45] Later that month when Callaghan, Chancellor of the Exchequer, visited the United States, McNamara was reported to have said that he 'fervently hoped' the British government would not attempt to solve its economic problems by abandoning its responsibilities east of Suez.[46] In October the Powell exposition produced a minor storm in Washington. James Reston writing in the *New York Times*, pointed out that however popular a policy of withdrawal might be in Britain, 'it would certainly not be popular in Washington.'[47]

United States pressure intensified during the three months

---

[42] *The Cabinet*, p. 125.
[43] See *Daily Telegraph*, 9 Apr. 1965.
[44] See further *Observer*, 18 Apr. 1965; *Times*, 20 Apr. 1965; and *New York Herald Tribune*, 6 May 1965.
[45] *Times*, 18 June 1965.
[46] *Guardian*, 1 July 1965, *Sunday Times*, 18 July 1965.
[47] 20 Oct. 1965.

before the publication of the 1966 White Paper. According to one report, in November Britain was frankly informed that the current American drive to buy British military and aircraft equipment was heavily dependent upon the maintenance of Britain's world role.[48] This was followed by strong representations to Harold Wilson during his visit to Washington in December and to Denis Healey and Michael Stewart who made the trek a month later. It seems probable that American pressure, coupled with the vigorous initiatives of Commonwealth countries in the Far East, had considerable impact upon British ministers and led the cabinet to place more emphasis on Anglo-American military co-operation and contributed to the postponement of a final decision about withdrawal from the Singapore base.[49] In turn, Healey and Stewart appear to have satisfied American and Australian leaders that, despite economic difficulties, Britain would maintain the world role.[50] Indeed, before returning to the United Kingdom, Healey gave a public assurance that Britain would not shrink back into Europe. Addressing the National Press Club in Canberra on 2 February he said:

We have no intention of ratting on any of our commitments. We intend to remain and shall remain fully capable of carrying out all the commitments we have at the present time, including those in the Far East, the Middle East and in Africa and other parts of the world. We do intend to remain in a military sense a world power.[51]

Notwithstanding the government's re-affirmation of the world role, it was accepted that the scale of Britain's commitments east of Suez would have to be revised. To some extent this had been recognized from the outset but it became increasingly clear as the review wore on. Speaking at a press conference in August, Healey confirmed that it was only by revising commitments that the government could achieve its aim of reducing defence spending to £2,000 million.[52] However, little progress

[48] *Financial Times*, 1 Dec. 1965.
[49] See pp. 297–8 below.
[50] See *Times*, 28 Jan. 1966, and *Statist*, 11 Feb. 1966. For a report of Lee Kuan Yew's impressions see *Straits Times*, 14 Feb. 1966. On Healey's return to the UK several Labour party critics accused him of saying one thing to the Americans and Australians and another to Labour back-benchers. *Sunday Telegraph*, 6 Feb. 1966.
[51] *Times*, 3 Feb. 1966.
[52] *Times*, 5 Aug. 1965.

was made in this sphere before the publication of the 1966 White Paper. Indeed, until late in 1965 the government was almost exclusively concerned with reviewing the force structure for the seventies and virtually no thought appears to have been given to revising commitments.

Christopher Mayhew has recorded that on 4 May and later on 6 August he wrote to Healey expressing misgivings about the government's leisurely approach to this side of the review.[53] Despite reassuring words from Healey, the cabinet took no action and the Defence Committee remained preoccupied with the search for economies. On Mayhew's account, part of the problem derived from the initial decision to fix a ceiling for defence expenditure. Once that decision had been taken and the economic departments had ensured that it was adhered to, the reduction in commitments ceased to be of interest to any department other than the Ministry of Defence.[54] Here Mayhew's argument has a familiar and convincing ring about it, as does his assertion that defence officials were unable to stir the interest of the economic and overseas departments.[55]

Towards the end of 1965 and in January and February 1966 the cabinet began preliminary thinking about revising the scale of Britain's east of Suez commitments. Although very little headway was in fact made, the government at least raised certain possibilities and took soundings on others. One senior official described the government's approach over these months as 'a groping after some more realistic policy regarding commitments', and he went on to stress the difficulties about spelling out proposals explicitly. In the Middle East the government regarded a withdrawal from Aden and a refusal to enter into a defence agreement with the Federation of South Arabia as necessary first steps in the process of cutting back commitments. In the Far East, the government had thoughts about a withdrawal from the Singapore base in the mid-seventies and the development of alternative defence facilities in Australia.[56] Such a policy would have been followed by a reduction in commitments both there and in the Far East generally. However, these ideas were checked by allied pressure

[53] *Britain's Role Tomorrow*, pp. 135–8.
[54] Ibid. p. 134.
[55] Ibid. p. 139.
[56] For a published report see *Observer*, 19 June 1966.

during the overseas tour of Healey and Stewart in January and February 1966.[57] By the time of the publication of the 1966 White Paper, therefore, the government was able to offer only a limited reduction in commitments in the Middle East and to hold out the dubious hope of closer allied co-operation in the area.

The Struggle for a Strategy

While the debate about Britain's role east of Suez raged in Parliament and the press, the Chiefs of Staff and their political associates struggled to devise a strategy which could combine a world military capability with a defence budget of £2,000 million. It was an exercise carried out under the critical eye of the Treasury and accompanied by fierce inter-service rivalry. Elaborate studies were drawn up in the Ministry of Defence and in the service departments. In a series of long and often heated meetings, the Defence Committee considered the various military proposals. When all was said and done, however, it was in the offices of the Treasury that the shape of the review was determined and the retreat from the world role began. At the political level it was possible to argue endlessly and without apparent result about commitments and Britain's role. On the strategic front, on the other hand, the lines were firmly drawn by the £2,000 million ceiling and the sharp edge of the Treasury knife. Once it became clear that the cost of both the carrier and the F111s could not be met within a £2,000 million budget, the crucial battle was lost. The government soldiered on, but deprived of the carrier—at once the hub and the symbol of British power east of Suez—its strategic scheme lacked conviction, the political super-structure began to crumble, and the withdrawal to Europe seemed assured.

[57] Australia's opposition to British withdrawal from Singapore was one reason for her limited response to Healey's exploratory proposals for developing base facilities in Australia. The Australian government agreed to set up a working party to consider the scheme's feasibility. However, Harold Holt, barely a week in office as Prime Minister, offered slight encouragement. Old arguments about defence spending and economic development were brought out. A related difficulty the Australians claimed, was lack of building labour. This was confirmed by studies in the UK Ministry of Defence, and discussions took place about prefabricated buildings and the possibility of using outside labour. The prospect of tension if British troops were in Australia while Australian troops were fighting in Vietnam also influenced the Australian government.

Following the cancellation of the P1154 and the HS681 projects and the fifth Polaris submarine, the cabinet turned to consider the case of the TSR2. Opinion was strongly divided but in the early hours of 1 April a decision was taken against the aircraft primarily on the ground of its mounting cost.[58] Five days later Parliament was informed of the cancellation and of an option which had been obtained from the United States government on the F111A, which was seen as the appropriate aircraft to bridge the gap until the Anglo-French variable-geometry aircraft became available.[59] Having thus secured a further saving of £35 million on the projected expenditure for 1965–66 the Treasury settled down to the fight for the major prize, the projected carrier CVA01.

The basis of the navy's case was that the carrier force was essential for the east of Suez role. Further, it was argued that there was no alternative to the larger carrier on the grounds of cost-effectiveness and the possibility of conflict with a major power.[60] In accordance with earlier plans, the Admiralty sought approval to place an order for CVA01 late in 1965. The new carrier together with HMS *Eagle* and HMS *Hermes* suitably modernized would give Britain a three-carrier fleet through the seventies.[61] Contrary to certain reports, no approach was made for a second new carrier, the Board being convinced that it would be a tactical error to press for CVA02 before CVA01 was on the slipway. However, Healey was well aware that a minumum of three new carriers would be required, and at least one Commander-in-Chief told him so openly.

About the same time as the Navy made its bid for the carrier,

[58] Harold Wilson, pp. 89–90.
[59] See Callaghan's budget statement, 710 HC Deb., 6 Apr. 1965, coll. 279–80, and Healey's statement, ibid. coll. 318–41. On 13 Apr. Soames moved a motion deploring cancellation of the TSR2, HS681, and P1154. The ensuing debate highlighted problems facing Britain in the development and production of military aircraft. Ibid. coll. 1171–1298.
[60] The Board maintained this position until the eleventh hour, but refusal to consider a smaller ship was subsequently regretted.
[61] In the Defence Committee the RAF capitalized on the fact that *Hermes* could carry only 17 Buccaneer strike aircraft, in addition to her 12 fighters. Healey and Lord Shackleton, later making the same point in Parliament, claimed on this basis that *Hermes* would have the capability of only about 3 land-based F111s. 725 HC Deb., 7 Mar. 1966, coll. 1791 and 2043, and 273 HL Deb., 8 Mar. 1966, col. 965. According to *The Times* defence correspondent (18 Nov. 1965), CVA01 would accommodate four times as many strike aircraft as *Hermes*.

the RAF presented its submission for 75 F111s. The Air Staff contended that the F111 was required as an interim replacement for the Canberra which would have to be phased out by 1970.[62] The aircraft's primary tasks would be long-range reconnaissance and long-range bombing. Although the case for the F111 stood independently, the Air Staff went on to argue that such a force, together with certain other aircraft,[63] operating from Aldabra, Mauritius, Masira, Bahrain, Gan, possibly Diego Garcia,[64] and—for working with the Australians —Darwin and the Cocos Islands, could replace the aircraft carrier system in the Indian Ocean. From a purely military standpoint there was much to be said for the proposition that the two forces were complementary, but because of the financial ceiling the air scheme increasingly came to be regarded as an alternative to carrier air power.

In April or May the Secretary of State issued a directive to the Ministry of Defence to determine whether land-based aircraft could carry out the major tasks of carrier-based aircraft. This now became the central issue of the review. A working party was set up under the chairmanship of Vice-Admiral Sir Frank Hopkins, Deputy Chief of the Naval Staff, to consider the matter in detail.[65] In the light of certain politically given assumptions, various scenarios were drawn up and attempts were made to determine the relative effectiveness of land-based/seaborne aircraft.[66] Although no agreement could

[62] The Air Staff had earlier planned on the basis of 120 TSR2s but it was believed that 75 F111s would bridge the gap until the Anglo-French variable-geometry aircraft came into service about 1976. The planned deployment of both the TSR2 and F111 was broadly that 25 per cent would be stationed east of Suez and the remaining 75 per cent in the UK. The latter were for NATO and for reinforcement east of Suez. Of the 50 F111s eventually ordered, 12 were to be stationed east of Suez.

[63] The Phantom for air cover for the fleet and fighter defence; the Buccaneer for strike at sea; the Nimrod for maritime patrol.

[64] Diego Garcia was intended primarily as a naval signalling station but when the Americans expressed interest the Air Staff saw marginal advantages in having installations there. However, Gan was adequate for the RAF's requirements and the idea was rejected.

[65] The working party consisted of six naval representatives, four or five scientists, two civil servants, and one RAF representative. As a matter of policy, the Air Staff decided against multiple representation and chose AVM P. C. Fletcher, Assistant Chief of the Air Staff, to present its case.

[66] One study supposed a Malayan request for British assistance which involved flying in troops and following up the air movement with a sea-tail. According to a senior RAF officer, the report concluded that land-based aircraft could provide

be reached about the capability of land-based aircraft between a certain maximum range and a certain minimum range, the burden of these studies was to show that many of the required tasks could be satisfactorily performed by land-based aircraft.[67]

In the absence of any agreed conclusions, however, the debate continued throughout 1965. Repeatedly the Air Staff and the Board of Admiralty returned to the various scenarios to take issue on specific points. There was also much argument about the relevance of these studies to the 'real world' situation and inevitably the debate developed into a general exchange about the value of the aircraft carrier, one side relying on sea power theories and the other on air power theories. As in the earlier period, feelings ran high, and very little common ground was established between the two services.[68]

The air force case was carefully attuned to the cost-effectiveness theme and it was presented with great force.[69] The Air Staff conceded that land-based aircraft could not duplicate every function of carrier aircraft, but it was argued that taking into account the political presuppositions and the fact that some areas required very little air protection (convoys could be re-routed near island bases, for example), the air scheme was adequate for the task in hand. At the same time, it was contended that the carrier represented poor value for money. Particular stress was placed on its vulnerability, its slowness, and the fact that the radius of action of carrier aircraft was substantially less than that of land-based aircraft.

The Admiralty's task was more difficult because the case for the carrier rested partly on various factors which were not easily fitted into the cost-effective mould. Account had to be taken, the Board argued, of the carrier's flexibility of function,

the protection required but with several major reservations. The study was later repeated at the Defence Operational Analysis Establishment because of naval doubts. The earlier conclusion was confirmed, except that the number of tanker aircraft required was increased.

[67] See Mayhew, *Britain's Role Tomorrow*, pp. 139–40.

[68] At one stage there was considerable misunderstanding about an air force map which showed Australia about 200 miles out of position. The scenario in question was comparing the radii of action of the F111 and the Buccaneer, but apparently the main point at issue was not affected.

[69] The main part of the RAF case was presented by Air Chf Mshl Sir Charles Elworthy, Chief of the Air Staff, and AVM Fletcher, both of whom had been educated as lawyers. Commenting on the air force case, one airman explained that because the RAF had been under attack since birth, the Air Staff had long ago identified the positions vital to it in the Whitehall battle.

its deterrent effect, and the savings in foreign exchange and political embarrassment. Throughout the review the Board insisted that the carrier's fate should not be determined simply on the basis of the effectiveness studies. In the first place, the Board would not accept certain of the Air Staff's assertions relating to aircraft range, pilot endurance, training, the number of aircraft needed, the suitability of the island bases, and the nature and size of the installations which would be required. The Board then went on to argue that many of the political assumptions laid down were either so questionable or so imprecise that the Ministry's sophisticated studies were open to serious doubt.[70] As Mayhew put it, without much clearer directives about the operations in which aircraft were likely to be engaged, the navy was being asked to phase out its carriers in a 'political vacuum'.[71]

Strong as these arguments were, however, they could not outweigh the financial considerations. As a result of earlier studies certain cost projections were available which greatly strengthened the case against the carrier. The total cost of the three-carrier force over a ten-year period was assessed at about £1,400 million.[72] With the navy's agreement, some forty different programme elements went into this calculation. Broadly it included the cost of the new carrier, running and refitting expenses, the cost of the aircraft and helicopters, and a proportion of the expenses of the extra supply ships and escort vessels required. No dockyard costs were included. In addition, account had to be taken of the cost of the F111 force which, it was agreed, was required irrespective of the outcome of the carrier debate. The programme cost of a force of 50 F111s was assessed at £280 million. This figure was derived by adding the unit cost of the RAF version of the aircraft (about £2.5 million) to the running costs over a ten-year period.[73] It thus became clear that if a decision was taken to proceed with CVA01 and to purchase the F111, the defence budget would exceed the £2,000 million ceiling.

---

[70] Indeed, in the view of at least one member of the Board, the political assumptions were deliberately weighted against the carrier.

[71] Britain's Role Tomorrow, p. 140.

[72] MoD, Statement on Defence Estimates 1966, Pt 1: Defence Review, Cmnd 2901, p. 10, para. 5.

[73] Lord Shackleton, 273 HL Deb., 8 Mar. 1966, col. 958.

With the Admiralty's plans running counter to the government's financial objectives and with opinion in the Ministry of Defence and in the Defence Committee increasingly sceptical about the value of the carrier, the Board of Admiralty was forced to reconsider its position. One possibility was to purchase a second-hand carrier from the United States but after much consideration the Board decided that in view of the time scale, the expense of refitting the ship, and the problem of maintenance this was not a practical proposition.[74] Another possibility was to submit a defence structure within the £2,000 million ceiling which included carriers but excluded the F111 and involved large cuts in the army. This course was strongly pressed by a group of young officers but it was rejected by the Board.[75] After a number of long and anxious meetings, the Board decided simply to make certain economies in the non-carrier elements of the naval building programme, and vigorously to argue the point that an acceptance of the revised carrier project would push defence expenditure only marginally above the £2,000 million ceiling.[76]

The Admiralty's submission was unsuccessful. Eventually the Minister of Defence and the Chief of the Defence Staff accepted the RAF's arguments and recommended that the air scheme was adequate for the requirements envisaged beyond the mid-seventies.[77]

From there it was a short step to decide against the CVA project and to adopt instead a second-string proposal to prolong the life of HMS *Ark Royal* with a £30 million refit and to keep the existing carrier force running until about 1975. With £500 million in the balance, even the resignation of the Chief of the Naval Staff and the Minister of Defence for the Navy could not tip the scales.[78] In mid-February the cancellation of CVA01 was formally approved by the government.

[74] See statement by Mayhew, *Times*, 16 Oct. 1965.
[75] Mayhew, *Britain's Role Tomorrow*, pp. 141–2.
[76] Ibid. pp. 142–5.
[77] See *Observer*, 16 Jan. 1966.
[78] According to Healey, £500m. was the net saving over the next ten years. The revised carrier programme would save £650m., but against this had to be set £150m.—the additional cost of reproducing the carrier's capability by other means. 725 HC Deb., 7 Mar. 1966, col. 1793. Mayhew resigned on 20 Feb. and Adm Sir David Luce's resignation was announced two days later.

The 1966 White Paper

Viewed sympathetically the 1966 White Paper may be regarded as a reasonable compromise between political exigency and economic necessity. Less charitably it might be described as the final monument to the inability of post-war British governments to bring commitments into line with capability. The White Paper began with a statement of the financial target and the manpower stretch. In accordance with customary procedure, it then outlined Britain's military role and subsequently went on to consider the equipment of the forces. In point of logic that sequence might more appropriately have been reversed inasmuch as the decisions about equipment necessarily determined the formulation of the nature and extent of the east of Suez role. In particular, the decision to phase out the carrier force lay behind two of the three general limitations on military action outside Europe set out in paragraph 19.[79]

Outside Europe and especially in the Indian Ocean area the White Paper projected a substantial and enduring role. In ascending order of priority economic interests, obligations which could not be relinquished unilaterally or at short notice, and a general interest in the maintenance of peace and stability justified a British military presence. Henceforward, however, although Britain would retain a major military capability outside Europe, it would be subject to three general limitations. In the first place, Britain would not undertake major operations of war except in co-operation with allies. For a fundamental policy declaration, this statement was extraordinarily vague. Would Kuwait or Malaysia come within the category of major operations of war? What of a minor operation that subsequently developed into a major campaign?[80] Did 'allies' refer simply to the United States or would some support from, say, Australia as during confrontation, be sufficient to invoke British intervention? With these questions unanswered, the statement did little more than repeat what had been the message of the Sandys White Paper and indeed had remained a pious hope ever since.

[79] MoD, *Statement on Defence Estimates 1966*, Pt 1: *Defence Review*, Cmnd 2901, p. 7.
[80] On this point *The Times* asked who could have predicted that the Brunei revolt would have sucked in over 50,000 British troops within two years. 'Making Do on Less', 23 Feb. 1966.

The government's second proposition was that Britain would not accept a defence obligation to another country unless that country was prepared to provide appropriate facilities. Under cover of an expression of unwillingness to allow the Asian and African states to cash freely on the British military bank without making any deposits, this limitation was merely a recognition of the fact that, without the aircraft carrier, Britain's ability to provide military assistance was dependent upon base facilities being made available by the recipient country. On the face of it, this seemed a reasonable arrangement but if interpreted to the letter it could easily become an absolute bar. For example, it was one thing to insist on ports and airfields but there would still be a need for associated facilities which were complex, specialized, and expensive and there was little likelihood that these could be provided by many of the Asian states.[81]

Finally, there would be no attempt to maintain defence facilities in an independent country against its wishes. As it stood, there was nothing very new about this statement. Paragraph 20 of the 1965 White Paper had expressed much the same position and insofar as it related to the wishes of the government of a host country, there had been no such attempt for many years. Healey later explained, however, that the point of the statement was that there would be no attempt to maintain base facilities in a country where the government was agreeable but the population hostile.

Having thus established the new parameters of Britain's military role, the 1966 White Paper set out the three major decisions around which the east of Suez strategy for the seventies had been constructed. The base at Aden was to be abandoned when South Arabia became independent in 1967 or 1968, and a decision had been taken not to extend a defence agreement to the Federation. A small increase in the forces stationed in the Persian Gulf would enable Britain to fulfil her remaining Middle Eastern obligations.[82] The base at Singapore

---

[81] See further Maj Gen J. L. Moulton, 'The 1966 Defence White Paper and Debate', *Brassey's Annual 1966*, p. 8.

[82] See p. 8, para. 23, and Healey, 725 HC Deb., 7 Mar. 1966, coll. 1782–6. The decision to withdraw from South Arabia without extending a defence agreement to the Federation provoked a major storm, for in July 1964 Sandys, then Secretary of State for Commonwealth Relations and the Colonies, had promised a defence treaty after independence. See especially Sandys' statements, 725 HC Deb.,

would be retained for as long as it was possible to use it freely, but as a precautionary measure discussions had begun with the Australian government about the possibility of obtaining military facilities there.[83] The existing carrier force would continue until well into the seventies, and thereafter the major tasks woud be performed by aircraft operating from land bases.[84] In the longer term the Anglo-French variable-geometry aircraft would fill this role. Until that aircraft became available in the mid-seventies, the F111A would bridge the gap. Fifty of these aircraft were to be ordered from the United States government.[85]

In the half-light of the information provided about the nature of Britain's east of Suez commitments and their potential military significance, it was difficult to assess the adequacy of the government's military programme. However, except on the narrowest interpretation of that role, and the most sanguine assessment of the outlook east of Suez, the decision to run down the carrier force was questionable on both political and military grounds. Without the carrier the range of operations which Britain unaided could carry out east of Suez would be greatly limited. Despite the provisos of the 1966 White Paper there could be no categorical assurance that, by force of circumstance, Britain would not become involved in situations in which carrier-based air power was essential. To cover this contingency, the government apparently looked to operations in conjunction with the United States, or at the very least action only with the agreement and support of the United States. The practical difficulties inherent in this situation were formidable but the political implications were perhaps more serious still. Here there was

22 Feb. 1966, coll. 250–1; 23 Feb. 1966, coll. 418–19; and 7 Mar. 1966, col. 1784. See also letter to *The Times*, 28 Feb. 1966, by the former High Commissioner, Sir Kennedy Trevaskis; and Sultan Saleh Bin Husein Al-Audhali's speech reported in the *Sunday Times*, 15 May 1966.

[83] MoD, *Statement on Defence Estimates 1966*, Pt 1: *Defence Review*, Cmnd 2901, p. 8, para. 24.

[84] Although no final decision had been taken about Aldabra, in Nov. 1965 the Secretary of State for the Colonies announced that the island, together with the Chagos archipelago (which includes Diego Garcia) and certain other islands in the western Indian Ocean, would be linked to form a new colony, preparatory to the construction of defence facilities by the UK and the US. 720 HC Deb., 10 Nov. 1965, col. 2.

[85] MoD, Cmnd 2901, pp. 9–13.

much force in Mayhew's contention that there was not a firm enough political basis for the degree of military co-operation proposed.[86]

On purely military grounds there were widespread doubts about whether the air scheme offered a viable method of maintaining the sort of general capability to which the government was committed. In the first place, the suitability of the F111 for the peacekeeping role had never been established. A number of writers asked whether a highly sophisticated aircraft which was designed almost solely for strike and reconnaissance in the enemy's deep rear would prove appropriate for east of Suez requirements.[87] The White Paper envisaged its use in support of amphibious operations, but except for those occasions when theatre and base were relatively close, it was difficult to see how the need for unremitting air cover and co-ordination in command could be met. Then there was the problem of the protection of the task force at sea to which the F111 seemed only a very limited answer. A further source of concern was the size of the F111 force envisaged. It was by no means clear that a force of 50 aircraft, of which only 12 would be based east of Suez, would be adequate for the tasks they would be called upon to perform. Finally, there was considerable uncertainty about the suitability and tenure of the island bases and about the costs and complexity of the installations required.

In wider perspective it can reasonably be argued that the selection of the F111 to replace the aircraft carrier went against the whole development of Britain's strategically mobile forces since 1957. Deprived of the carrier, the future of the amphibious task forces was thrown into the air. Nor was it simply a matter of substituting one instrument of power for another as the carrier task force represented a very different form of strength from that of strike bombers, and one, moreover, much better attuned to acceptable political aims east of Suez. Although the F111 represented one form of strategic mobility, there were

[86] See his personal statement to the House of Commons, 725 HC Deb., 22 Feb. 1966, coll. 254–65, esp. 261–2. See also *New York Times*, 25 Feb. 1966.
[87] See e.g. Moulton, as cited in n.81, p.8; Neville Brown, 'Reviewing Defence Policy', *New Statesman*, 4 Feb. 1966; V Adm Sir Richard Smeeton, 'Maritime Air Power', *Navy*, 71/9 (Sept. 1966), p. 289. See also AM Sir Maurice Heath's letter to the *Daily Telegraph*, 19 Jan. 1966.

good grounds for wondering if the end of the road was in sight and if the 1966 Defence Review might come to be regarded as the first step in a change from strategically mobile forces to a continental system.

CHAPTER NINE

Role Relinquished

By March 1966 the main arguments for and against the east of Suez commitment had been developed and presented. The next two years produced little that was new, although increasingly the debate reached a wider audience with the inevitable simplification which this involved. By now it was accepted that the issue was not the protection of economic interests nor was it a matter of playing an independent role in world affairs for its own sake. Essentially it was a matter of maintaining stability in the area during a transitional period, and thus ensuring the viability of the successor states of empire and strengthening Britain's ties with the older dominions. As the debate wore on the disagreement came to centre not on withdrawal as an aim, but on how it should be carried out and at what rate, and what would be left at the end.

For some time the case against an early withdrawal from east of Suez had been losing ground but in the post-CVA01 period a number of developments quickened the pace. The most important was the deterioration in the balance of payments position and this increased the government's particular concern to reduce the level of overseas defence expenditure, in addition to its earlier concern with the level of overall defence spending. Then there was the ending of Indonesian confrontation earlier than expected, with more immediate prospects for disengagement. At the same time there was increasing support within the cabinet for British entry into the Common Market and a concomitant shift in opinion away from the world role. A more marginal consideration was the easing of United States pressure on Whitehall to maintain the east of Suez role. To point to these factors is not to absolve the government from responsibility for the dismal trail of shifting targets and broken pledges. A strong case can be argued that although the eventual abandonment of a major and unilateral role east of Suez was inevitable, there remained the possibility of more limited options for an interim period.

To Stand but not so Firm

The 1966 White Paper was soon overtaken by events. Within a matter of weeks interest shifted from what the White Paper meant to the cuts that were to succeed it. The next twelve months was therefore a period of debate at home and uncertainty overseas. On the one hand, the government made it clear that there would be further reductions and larger savings. On the other, the critics called for a decision to withdraw and its speedy implementation. Only for the Admiralty did the 1966 White Paper mark the end of the road. In other quarters it was seen as but round one in a tussle which might continue for years.

Until July the government's stand and its response to the pressures upon it do not appear to have differed substantially from the situation at the end of 1965. Despite agitation from sections of the Labour party, the government was firm that although there would be further cuts east of Suez there would be no withdrawal. Back-bench discontent increased after the election lull and late in May a direct challenge was issued at a special meeting of the Parliamentary Labour party. At this stage the government secured a tactical victory when Emanuel Shinwell, Chairman of the Parliamentary Labour party's liaison committee, refused to accept on procedural grounds a motion signed by a cross-section of Labour MPs which called for a decisive reduction in Britain's military commitments east of Suez by 1969–70, including withdrawal from Malaysia, Singapore, and the Persian Gulf.[1] However, reports that at the meeting Healey and Stewart had made it clear that the government did not disagree with its critics about the principle of withdrawal but only about timing caused concern overseas. To clarify the issue a meeting was held between the Prime Minister and the Australian High Commissioner. At a press conference after the meeting, Harold Holt described the discussions as 'thoroughly satisfying', and he said the British Prime Minister had reaffirmed that there had been no change in policy since

[1] *Guardian*, 26 May 1966.

the publication of the White Paper in February.[2] At the same time the British High Commission in Canberra issued a statement confirming that withdrawal from Singapore was not one of the budget savings under consideration.[3] A week later Lord Shackleton on a tour of the Far East delivered the same message. Certainly there would be reductions in Malaysia but the bases would remain as long as they were wanted, despite the approaching end of confrontation.[4]

These reassurances sharpened the critics' case when the withdrawal motion was put to a vote at a meeting of the Parliamentary Labour party on 15 June. It was therefore a matter of some surprise that the motion was rejected overwhelmingly (225 votes to 54). However, the government's show of strength hardly reflected the true state of opinion in the party. As the meeting was crowded with ministers and peers brought along for the occasion, the Prime Minister ensured that the issue and the vote were seen as much in terms of party loyalty as in terms of defence particulars, and in any case there were perhaps fifty unexplained abstentions.[5] So that there should be no misunderstanding of the government's position, the unusual course was taken of releasing the text of the Prime Minister's speech. To disarm the critics there was a long piece about the value of support for the United Nations, there was the promise of massive cuts in the Far East following the end of confrontation, and there were some familiar generalities about an increasing emphasis on mobile forces. But generally the Prime Minister stood his ground: Britain had a duty to assert its influence east of Suez and the government would not default.[6]

Further assurances along the same lines were given by Labour ministers over the next month. Addressing the Australian Institute of International Affairs in Canberra on 29 June, Michael Stewart declared 'we have neither the wish nor the intention to abandon the world east of Suez.'[7] Denis Healey was equally emphatic during his tour of the Far East in early July. Indeed, speaking to journalists in Hong Kong, he said

[2] *Times*, 3 June 1966.
[3] Melbourne *Age*, 3 June 1966.
[4] *Sunday Telegraph*, 12 June 1966.
[5] *Times*, 16 June 1966; *Economist*, 18 June 1966.
[6] For text see *Times*, 16 June 1966.
[7] *Times*, 1 July 1966.

Britain would stay in Singapore and Malaysia as long as she was wanted on acceptable conditions.[8]

Given the various pressures upon the government and the sensitivity of the issue, the public record could hardly convey the element of doubt which lay in the background of ministerial thinking. Apparently even at this time there were thoughts about withdrawal. Although there was nothing specific, there was a feeling in some quarters that it would be unprofitable to remain in Singapore and Malaysia after the end of confrontation. In particular the separation of Singapore from Malaysia in August 1965 and the widening rift between the two states led to considerable rethinking about the future security of the area. A related line of thought was that Britain might well be asked to leave, and that it would be desirable to have gone before that happened. This applied especially to the future of the base complex now that Singapore had become an independent state. One official explained that a strategy of Indian Ocean islands and a presence in Australia was becoming increasingly persuasive but the lock on a full examination of the project was confrontation. Whatever weight is attached to this undercurrent of opinion, it can at least be said that the pressure to curb government expenditure and the mounting discontent within the Labour party weighed more heavily on the government that it was prepared to concede.

Overseas also there were doubts about how long the British government would be able to hold on. In Singapore it was said that from the end of 1965 defence planning proceeded on the assumption that Britain would withdraw from the Far East by the mid-seventies. Equally in Canberra policy-makers were decidedly sceptical about the prospects for a continued British involvement east of Suez. In both countries this assessment was not derived from any specific evidence but was an impression formed from the political and economic drift in the United Kingdom.

Uncertainty and scepticism were a long way from actual policy, however, and the fact remains that in the period to July 1966 there was no official consideration of the possibility of a British withdrawal from the Far East. As one very senior officer put it, the word at this time was reduction or perhaps rationalization but withdrawal was a non-starter. Little was

[8] *Times*, 13 July 1966.

said publicly about the commitment in the Persian Gulf and apparently rethinking about the area did not loom large in Whitehall either. The expansion of facilities and accommodation at Bahrain and Sharjah went ahead as planned and new financial arrangements were negotiated with both these states.[9] Although the diplomatic arguments in favour of a continued British presence in the Persian Gulf were not felt to be as compelling as those for the Far East, the requirement for transit facilities thwarted reconsideration. In any event, it was said, the practical problem of withdrawing British forces was scarcely significant in that it was a small task and the economic implications for the Gulf states were negligible.

A new phase in defence planning began late in July as a result of the continued deterioration in the economic position. Throughout the first half of 1966 the government had not succeeded in bringing expenditure under control and in July the pressure on liquidity in the world's financial centres put sterling under heavy pressure. On 20 July the Prime Minister announced steps designed to curb expenditure, particularly overseas. Public investment in 1967–68 would be substantially reduced including a cut in military and civil expenditure overseas of at least £100 million.[10] Wilson went on to say that given an end to confrontation, the plans made by Healey during his visit to the Far East earlier that month would secure a major contribution to that saving.[11] As *The Economist* observed, this did not necessarily imply much larger reductions than had seemed likely earlier.[12]

In fact, however, the search for economies now began in earnest and the formal acknowledgement that confrontation was over opened the way for a major reconsideration of Britain's role east of Suez.[13] Within the Ministry of Defence a new review was launched and in the autumn the department began working with a smaller target than the £2,000 million ceiling at 1964 prices which had been the basis of defence planning since the early days of the Labour administration. The result was

[9] See *Daily Telegraph*, 3 June 1966, and *Times*, 18 July 1966.
[10] 732 HC Deb., 20 July 1966, coll. 631–2.
[11] Ibid. col. 623.
[12] 23 July 1966.
[13] An agreement between Malaysia and Indonesia ending the three-year confrontation had been signed in Bangkok on 1 June and this was ratified by the two governments on 11 Aug.

that military planners were now forced to consider a shorter time-table and smaller forces, and for the first time withdrawal was on the official agenda. Although no declaratory statement of long-term policy could be expected from the government until the review was completed, almost immediately an accelerated programme of reductions was put into operation. In August Healey stated that about 10,000 troops would be withdrawn from Borneo, though on the matter of timing he said simply as soon after the ratification of the Bangkok Agreement as Malaysian forces were able to assume full responsibility for the defence of eastern Malaysia.[14] Six weeks later he was able to announce that most of these men would be home by April 1967 and that he was considering the possibility of further withdrawals.[15] Privately Healey informed the Prime Minister that he was ready to propose an approximate terminal date for east of Suez deployments, though this would have to be worked out in terms of its diplomatic, military, and economic implications.[16]

While within the Ministry of Defence the search for economies was in process of being translated into plans and figures, the cabinet was prodded to move with greater speed. At the Labour party Conference in October the government's critics mounted a concerted attack. George Brown reminded the conference not to assume that there was nothing between the traditional east of Suez role and complete abandonment.[17] But the majority was not interested in transitional arrangements. The government was on the run, larger savings were in the air, and Mayhew was roundly applauded for dismissing the role as a 'sure road to bankruptcy'.[18] Thus a resolution was carried calling upon the government to make a decisive reduction in military commitments east of Suez including withdrawal from Malaysia, Singapore, and the Persian Gulf by 1969–70— despite its description by Brown as not a plan but a scuttle.

Predictably the 1967 White Paper confirmed the decreasing emphasis on the east of Suez role and it gave details of the run-down of forces then in progress. There was, however, little indication of where and when a line would be drawn. *The Times*

[14] 733 HC Deb., 3 Aug. 1966, col. 437.
[15] 734 HC Deb. 19 Oct. 1966, col. 208.
[16] Harold Wilson, p. 297.
[17] 65th Annual Conference . . . *Report* (1966), p. 271.
[18] Ibid. p. 251.

concluded that the broad picture remained vague.[19] *The Economist* described the statement as a 'progress report on a policy . . . of wait and see.'[20] Still, there could be little doubt about the direction of the government's thinking. The aim was that Britain should not again have to undertake operations on the scale of confrontation outside Europe.[21] The method, in the view of senior officers, was to ensure that Britain did not have the capability to do so. In South-east Asia Britain had a transitional role but the reduction in the forces stationed there would continue. In the Middle East Britain would withdraw from South Arabia on independence and her remaining obligations in the area could be fulfilled by a small increase in forces in the Persian Gulf. Finally, the C in C, South Atlantic, and the frigate on station would be withdrawn in the course of the next few months.

In the debate in the House, Healey pursued a middle course, emphasizing both the value of a continuing presence and the savings which might still be made. There was no question, he explained, that east of Suez was an 'in between' role. To renounce all capability for peacekeeping operations would be to violate formal obligations and to abdicate a power to contribute to world peace. At the same time both the number and scale of Britain's commitments must be reduced.[22] Later he went on to explain that his disagreement with Mayhew and other speakers was not about eventual withdrawal but about fixing a date in advance: 'Before we fix a date in this way, we must have an idea of what will happen when we go. We must give our diplomacy a chance to construct a different basis for the security of the countries which we are leaving.'[23]

The Conservatives strongly opposed any early withdrawal but in the absence of an unequivocal statement of government policy their attack splintered in different directions. Their difficulty was increased because the government appeared to be following a trail blazed earlier by Powell and therefore the shadow defence minister's challenge carried little conviction. Powell attempted to sidestep the issue by concentrating his attack on other points. The government's savings were bogus savings

[19] 17 Feb. 1967.
[20] 18 Feb. 1967, p. 589.
[21] *MoD, Statement on Defence Estimates 1967*, Cmnd 3203 (1967), p. 7, para. 26.
[22] 742 HC Deb., 27 Feb. 1967, coll. 115–18.
[23] Ibid. 28 Feb. 1967, col. 395.

because they were cuts on an imaginary Conservative budget of £2,400 million.[24] What was important was that, with the exception of Aden, commitments remained as before. The real changes related to capabilities.[25] In other circumstances these arguments might have been damaging but they were not when the government could counter that the Conservatives were evasive on the major issue. What caused more concern was opposition in the ranks of government back-benchers. After the publication of the White Paper, a group of Labour MPs had submitted a resolution calling for earlier cuts in east of Suez commitments than were envisaged in the Defence Statement.[26] Over the next week other back-benchers announced their intention of not voting for the White Paper though it quickly became apparent that the critics disagreed amongst themselves almost as much as they did with the government. On 22 February a full meeting of the Parliamentary Labour party was held at which it was agreed to take note of the motion.[27] Against this background, the government adopted the unusual course of producing for the annual debate an explanatory motion welcoming the White Paper as a contribution to the continuing exercise of reducing the burden of British commitments, forces, and expenditure overseas.[28] This motion was approved by 270 votes to 231 but it was estimated that perhaps as many as 62 back-benchers had deliberately abstained. Significantly, this was the largest demonstration of dissent since the government had taken office in 1964.[29]

The End in Sight

The main part of the defence review was completed by the Defence and Overseas Policy Working Party of officials at the end of March 1967. The papers, together with a covering note by Sir Burke Trend, Secretary of the Cabinet, were then forwarded for consideration by the Defence and Overseas Policy Committee, under the chairmanship of the Prime Minister. In April the decision was taken in principle to reduce

[24] 742 HC Deb., 28 Feb. 1967, col. 395.
[25] Ibid. coll. 127–8.
[26] *Guardian*, 17 Feb. 1967.
[27] *Guardian*, 23 Feb. 1967.
[28] 742 HC Deb., 27 Feb. 1967, col. 97.
[29] *Times*, 1 Mar. 1967.

the forces in the Far East to about half during 1970–71 and to withdraw them altogether in the mid-seventies. This decision did not, however, represent a complete washing of British hands as it was closely related to proposals about aid, continued training and the maintenance of a specific military capability for use in the area. The course of the Committee's deliberations cannot be mapped in detail but there is little doubt that ministers were primarily influenced by general economic and political considerations and that specific pressures both at home and abroad were decidely of the second order. The economic factor was the major determinant but at the same time there was a decided shift in ministerial opinion about Britain's capacity to maintain a major military role east of Suez and about the extent to which that role accorded with Britain's real interests. On the former point, the changing assessment of what could be accomplished in Asia by an outside power of British dimensions was influenced by the United States experience in Vietnam, both in terms of its military demands and its political ineffectiveness. On the latter point, there was a growing conviction that Britain's interests were primarily European which was related to the cabinet's decision to apply for membership of the European Economic Community in May.[30] Denis Healey's position during these deliberations is not entirely clear but there is no question that he achieved less than many of his military advisers desired. One very senior officer summed up the situation by observing that whether Healey should or should not have resigned, 'the water was over the dam.'

By April then the basic lines of the revised defence programme had been determined but it remained to work out the details and to settle what would be made public. In addition, it appears that no clear decision had yet been taken about the extent of Britain's continuing strategic interest in the area after the withdrawal of forces from Malaysia and Singapore. Although these policy questions remained open, work began almost immediately on the mechanics of the reduction. The Ministry had now to consider the phasing of the withdrawal and to determine what effects it would have locally and how they might be alleviated.

On the political side, ministers were left with the awkward task of explaining the abrupt change in British policy to

[30] Patrick Gordon Walker, *The Cabinet*, pp. 128–9.

Commonwealth partners in the Far East and to the United States. Thus began three months of intense diplomatic activity during which visits were exchanged, pressure applied, and support canvassed. The first step was a visit by George Brown to Washington for the annual SEATO conference from 18 to 20 April. In meetings with Dean Rusk, Paul Hasluck, and Keith Holyoake, all on the same day, the Foreign Secretary conveyed the message 'half out by 1970–71 and all out by 1975'.[31] Apparently the first phase of the programme did not cause too much distress but there was strong argument about the second stage. The Americans in particular pressed hard that there should be no announcement of complete withdrawal so long as the war in Vietnam continued.[32] Two days after Brown left Washington, Healey was in the Far East for a five-day visit to Singapore and Malaysia. Again the general picture was explained but the Secretary of State declined to give details of the proposed reductions there and then. He added that the cuts envisaged up to April 1968 could be made without dissent from allies but difficulties would arise after that as the nature of the capability to be retained would then need to be defined. The main part of the discussions concerned the proposed reductions to 1970–71 but on the larger issue Lee Kuan Yew, Tunku Abdul Rahman, and Tun Abdul Razak all expressed their view that it would be most unfortunate to announce any withdrawal in advance.

On his return from the Far East, Healey told the House of Commons that by April 1968 it would be possible to reduce the total number of defence personnel by about 20,000 compared with the total at the end of confrontation.[33] What this meant, and in fact Healey had already spelt it out in Singapore, was that a reduction of a further 10,000 (including locally enlisted personnel) would be made over the coming year, leaving a service strength of some 30,000.[34] In addition, Healey said, preliminary discussions had been held about the scope of further reductions over the next two or three years.[35] Later that

[31] See *Sunday Times*, 23 Apr. 1967.
[32] Newspaper reports that Brown assured allies that the government was not contemplating any dramatic reduction in Britain's military presence in the area (*Guardian*, 21 Apr. 1967, *Economist*, 22 Apr. 1967), were without substance.
[33] 746 HC Deb., 1 May 1967, col. 91.
[34] *Times*, 28 Apr. 1967; *Financial Times*, 28 Apr. 1967.
[35] 746 HC Deb., 1 May 1967, col. 91.

month a small team of British experts visited Singapore on a fact-finding mission to establish the basis for aid and transitional arrangements.

The cabinet now turned to examine the question of withdrawal in more detail. Although the evidence is incomplete, it appears that there were heated arguments about whether a firm date should be announced and what the wording should be. The Foreign Office led the fight against a public commitment in advance and it had the backing of Britain's allies in the area and the support of the Secretary of State for Defence and the Chiefs of Staff. But there were other ministers—notably Roy Jenkins, Barbara Castle, and Richard Crossman—who were insistent that a terminal date should be published. On this occasion the overseas departments carried the day but opinion remained divided. In particular Denis Healey's stand brought him close to the political wilderness and increasingly isolated him from many of his colleagues.

During June and early July Commonwealth statesmen made determined efforts to strengthen Healey's hand and prevent an announced and early withdrawal from Singapore and Malaysia. The first move was made by the Australian Prime Minister, Harold Holt. In mid-June he visited Washington to lobby American support and then London to convey Australian views directly to the Prime Minister. He left with Wilson a 2,000-word statement setting out the Australian position, which he told reporters might be helpful in forthcoming cabinet considerations.[36] Lee flew to London on a similar mission a few days later. Reportedly towards the end of his visit he told a private meeting of Labour back-benchers that he had failed to shake the resolve of the British government to speed plans for withdrawal.[37] On 4 July the Tunku arrived for talks, declaring that British forces in Malaysia should be maintained at pre-confrontation levels.[38]

The government's decisions were announced in the Supplementary White Paper on Defence published on 18 July. The aim of British policy was to foster indigenous developments, thus allowing British forces to withdraw from the Middle East and the Far East. To this end deployment plans had been revised

[36] Melbourne *Age*, 13 and 17 June 1967.
[37] *Straits Times*, 28 June 1967.
[38] *Guardian*, 5 July 1967.

and commitments would be adjusted accordingly. In Singapore and Malaysia the forces would be reduced to about half during 1970–71 and it was planned to withdraw altogether from the bases there in the middle 1970s. The precise timing would depend on progress in achieving regional stability. However, it could not be assumed that thereafter the services would never again have to intervene in the Far East and the government therefore planned to maintain a military capability for use in the area, even when forces were no longer permanently based there. The proposals outlined in this paper, it was said, marked the end of the process of defence review.[39]

The broad picture was now clear but in certain respects the White Paper was either vague or silent about detail. In the first place, there was no mention of the commitment in the Persian Gulf and nothing to indicate that the government had firm plans for military contraction in that area also. Despite censure from *The Times*,[40] and some pointed questioning from Labour back-benchers, the parliamentary debate ended without the government showing its hand on this issue. Secondly, there was the uncertainty that surrounded withdrawal from the Far East in the 'middle 1970s'. In the Commons the Prime Minister later explained that this meant withdrawal between 1973 and 1977, the exact date depending on conditions in the area. Asked by Heath whether the government intended to withdraw even if there were not stability in the area in 1977, Wilson replied, 'Yes, Sir'.[41] Thirdly, there was the question of the nature and extent of the military capability which was to be maintained for use in the area after withdrawal. Some indication of the government's thinking was forthcoming in the Commons debate when the Prime Minister and the Secretary of State for Defence spoke of 'on the spot amphibious forces' together with air-mobile reserves in the United Kingdom.[42] Beyond that it is difficult to write with assurance, for publicly the matter was left there and in Whitehall the reports differed. On one account, however, special capability involved identifiable and additional units to those which would other-

---

[39] MoD, *Supplementary Statement on Defence Policy 1967*, Cmnd 3357 (1967), p. 12, para. 1.

[40] 'The Unanswered Problem', 19 July 1967.

[41] 751 HC Deb., 27 July 1967, col. 1103.

[42] See ibid. coll. 991, 997–8, and 1108. After the withdrawal from Aden, an additional brigade would be attached to the strategic reserve.

wise have been maintained; it involved additional combat aircraft and some additional intermediate transports, a larger army, and more general-purpose ships.

The White Paper held out the promise of a saving of some £300 million on the projected budget by the mid-seventies and a reduction in service manpower of about 75,000. Local defence expenditure overseas was expected to be reduced by about £32 million in 1970-71 and a further saving of at least £60 million was predicted by the mid-seventies.[43] There is no reason to doubt that the economic factor was the central consideration behind the government's decisions but it was scarcely all-determining. With some persuasiveness, critics could argue that the short-term savings were too marginal and the longer-run savings too distant for the economic motive to dictate the final shape of the strategic scheme east of Suez.[44] Accepting the economic origins of the review, a more perceptive interpretation would emphasize the increasing intrusion of general political considerations. In particular there was the increasing scepticism on the part of the cabinet about the likely effectiveness of Britain's military role, and this line of thinking was strengthened by Britain's inability to affect the course of the six-day Arab-Israeli war in June.[45] Equally relevant was the movement of opinion in favour of a redefinition of Britain's interests and responsibilities based on the proposition that the United Kingdom was a European and not a world power. To some extent these points were driven home by the pressure from within the party, which appears to have been more effective with the annual conference only three months away.

Judged solely on political grounds, the July formula was by and large a success. By steering a middle course the government avoided a confrontation both at home and overseas. Allied leaders expressed their disappointment but the language was moderate and the tone mild. Labour critics made plain their dissatisfaction and some 57 tabled an amendment proposing a more rapid withdrawal but when it came to the division on the government motion approving the White Paper only about 19 actually abstained.[46]

[43] Mod, *Supplementary Statement on Defence Policy 1967*, Cmnd 3357, p. 11.
[44] See esp. *The Economist*, 22 July 1967.
[45] Patrick Gordon Walker, *The Cabinet*, p. 128.
[46] The government motion was carried with a majority of 67. The opposition amendment regretting that the proposals in the White Paper gravely impaired the

The Final Settlement

Despite the confident assertion that the July statement marked the end of the process of defence review, the government's latest scheme rapidly lost conviction and in less than six months it had been replaced by a shorter time-table and a policy of complete disengagement. The turning-point came in November, and the abandonment of the July position was announced in January 1968. The key to understanding the government's reappraisal during these months lies in the worsening economic position and the increasing political force of those who argued for early withdrawal.

The first inroad was made concurrently with the devaluation of sterling on 18 November. Together with other measures designed to reduce government expenditure, the Chancellor announced that defence spending would be cut by over £100 million in 1968–69. In terms of the government's strategic scheme for the Indian Ocean the most serious cut was the decision not to proceed with the Aldabra project but there were other economies, especially the reduction in the number of Buccaneers on order and the earlier phasing out of HMS *Victorious*, which created difficulties also. Nonetheless, the Chancellor expressed confidence that the reductions could be made within the framework of existing policy,[47] and this assessment was confirmed by Healey a week later when he insisted that 'We can have no reversal of the July decision.'[48]

Welcome though these cuts were to Labour critics, there was considerable uncertainty about their substance and economic significance. Michael Foot openly queried whether they were genuine savings, observing that 'Healey's £100 million turns up like a free coupon in every package.'[49] The Secretary of State retorted later that so far as some of his colleagues were concerned, making defence cuts 'is rather like throwing herrings to a sea lion. It gulps them down and a second later is back asking for more.'[50] But if parliamentarians rightly suspected some sleight of hand, there was no question that the reductions

---

capacity of the services to meet all the demands that might be made on them was defeated in the Commons with a majority of 90 but carried in the Lords.

[47] 754 HC Deb., 20 Nov. 1967, col. 938.
[48] 755 HC Deb., 27 Nov. 1967, col. 59.
[49] 754 HC Deb., 20 Nov. 1967, col. 1169.
[50] 755 HC Deb., 27 Nov. 1967, col. 68.

were significant in military terms. In particular, the decision not to proceed with the Aldabra staging post, although it only marginally affected plans for the actual run-down of forces in the Far East, would substantially reduce strategic flexibility and therefore create difficulties for the maintenance of a special capability after withdrawal.[51] Despite the problems created by the November reductions, however, military leaders believed that the July scheme remained workable.

Scarcely had military planners begun considering the implications of these reductions when a new review—the fourth in three years—reopened the issues settled in July. Following speculation in the press, on 18 December Wilson announced a stringent review of all areas of policy where substantial expenditure was involved, including defence.[52] According to the Prime Minister, a major diversion of resources to exports, import replacement, and investment was required to improve the balance of payments, and thus to take full advantage of the opportunity created by devaluation. From the start it was apparent that the process of securing further cuts would be a delicate political exercise. Wilson records in his memoirs: 'There was no guarantee that we could get a package of the required scale, with the necessary political balance, even through Cabinet, let alone through the Parliamentary party.'[53]

The Prime Minister's announcement was followed by a month of urgent planning and abrasive argument which determined the pattern of Britain's withdrawal from the Indian Ocean. Throughout the deliberations the Secretary of State for Defence and the Chiefs of Staff were adamant that there could be no further force reductions without commensurate cuts in commitments. In support of their arguments the Chiefs of Staff pointed to contingency plans of various kinds and to the danger of a limited commitment developing into a wider one, and they concluded that a continued Far Eastern presence based on smaller forces was out of the question. Healey stood firmly alongside his military advisers and was understood to be prepared to resign over the issue if necessary. As a result, proposals from the Foreign Office and the Commonwealth Office that

[51] The fact remains, however, that the case for and against Aldabra was never really proved one way or the other. In the end the decision taken was much influenced by American lukewarmness and the pressure from the ecology lobby.

[52] 756 HC Deb., 18 Dec. 1967, col. 921-3.

[53] *The Labour Government 1964-1970*, p. 479; see also pp. 481-2.

a continued presence could be maintained if the military scaled down its force levels were never fully considered and no plans were produced which considered the feasibility of such a project, despite a minority military view that such a compromise might be workable.

Given the mood in Whitehall it quickly became evident that there was little prospect of maintaining a special military capability for intervention east of Suez after the withdrawal of British forces. Within the Ministry of Defence there was no substantive examination of the issue and apparently the economic limitations, the political climate, and the requirement for quick decisions all worked to foreclose consideration of a modified arrangement. A good deal of attention was devoted to what could be accomplished with the general military capability that would be maintained irrespective of decisions about the east of Suez role and this was explained to the Commonwealth countries concerned. However, the fact was that in terms of diplomatic reassurance this gesture was of very limited account.

From the outset of the review it was apparent that the timetable for withdrawal from the Far East would be advanced and that a date would be fixed for withdrawal from the Persian Gulf—the latter an issue which had lain fallow since the 1966 White Paper. The Far Eastern problem was the more awkward and several variations in the rate of withdrawal were studied and debated. For a time it seemed likely that withdrawal would be set in 1973 but after further consideration 31 March 1972 was selected as the terminal date. This was later brought forward to 31 March 1971 and it was this date which British ministers presented to overseas allies early in January. George Thomson was delegated the unhappy task of explaining the government's revised defence policy to Malaysia, Singapore, Australia, and New Zealand. The United States was informed by George Brown during talks in Washington. Goronwy Roberts, Minister of State at the Foreign Office, having two months earlier visited the Persian Gulf giving assurances that Britain would remain in the Persian Gulf as long as necessary to maintain peace and stability, now paid a return visit to inform the states concerned that after all withdrawal from the Gulf would follow in the wake of withdrawal from the Far East.[54]

[54] Apparently in November Goronwy Roberts had presented the Foreign Office view, not knowing that the drift of the cabinet's thinking was towards with-

The reaction overseas was sharp and indignant. United States officials took strong exception to the plans, especially those relating to the Persian Gulf, and reportedly the President sent a personal message to Wilson.[55] Malaysia, Australia, and New Zealand voiced their dismay in predictable fashion but did little to strengthen the hand of those ministers who had argued for a longer time-table and appropriate cushioning arrangements. Lee Kuan Yew, having earlier threatened economic reprisals, adopted a more practical course after Thomson's visit and flew to London for eleventh-hour discussions with British ministers. To the surprise of many, including his Commonwealth counterparts who appear to have accepted the government's plans as final, Lee won a postponement of withdrawal from March to December 1971 and some additional military aid.[56]

On Tuesday 16 January—known as 'Black Tuesday' within the Ministry of Defence—the Prime Minister announced the government's decisions. British forces would be withdrawn from the Far East and the Persian Gulf by the end of 1971 and thereafter Britain would retain no special capability for use in the area. The carrier force would be phased out once the withdrawal had been completed and the order for 50 F111s would be cancelled. However, a general capability based in Europe would be maintained which could be deployed overseas as circumstances required.[57]

In an attempt to minimize the magnitude of the January change of policy the Secretary of State later claimed that the real watershed in Britain's post-war defence policy was the July 1967 decision to withdraw from Asian bases in the middle seventies. By comparison, the January decisions were matters of timing rather than principle.[58] In one sense this was so. Yet

---

drawal. George Brown later disclaimed responsibility. 757 HC Deb., 24 Jan. 1968, col. 431.

[55] See *Sunday Times* and *Observer*, 14 Jan. 1968.

[56] The postponement of withdrawal meant that British forces would remain in the Far East for seven months after the last possible date for the next general election in the United Kingdom. This consideration was at the forefront of Lee's mind at the time. He made it absolutely clear in Whitehall that he considered that the withdrawal decision was brought about by internal political clashes within the Labour party, and he felt that, if the date for withdrawal could be postponed until after the election, there was a possibility that it might in some way be reversed.

[57] 756 HC Deb., 16 Jan. 1968, coll. 1580–5.

[58] 760 HC Deb., 4 Mar. 1968, col. 54.

timing, as Healey had frequently observed, was what the debate had come to be about. In any case Healey's rationalization took no account of the crucial decision that a special capability would not be maintained. And in July it had been the Prime Minister himself who had argued that the key to British policy lay in the maintenance of a special capability to intervene with strategically mobile forces.[59]

In the following years both the Wilson government and its Conservative successor in fact made provision for some continuing British involvement, but by then the die had been cast. The decisions taken between February 1966 and January 1968 had redrawn the perimeters of the British defence debate and set the direction of policy for the seventies. The shifts in course after January 1968 were primarily matters of adjustment and presentation, and as such must be regarded as part of the process of tailing off the east of Suez role rather than as representing any major change in thinking about Britain's place in the world.

[59] 751 HC Deb., 27 July 1967, coll. 1107–8.

Conclusion

A survey of the period 1947 to 1968 leads to the fundamental conclusion that defence arrangements were never adequately related to the time-table and consequences of decolonization. Defence contraction was seen as part of the process of political withdrawal only at the most general level and the connection between the two was never clearly spelt out. Despite some questioning on the periphery of policy-making, the end of the Indian empire was not seen as necessarily affecting British interest or commitment in security arrangements east of Suez; and for this reason military withdrawal remained something on the distant horizon, of little practical concern for matters of day-to-day policy-making. Over a period of almost two decades, successive governments showed a deep-seated reluctance to cut commitments or to limit the scope of the overseas military role. Similarly decisions about defence requirements were taken in apparent disregard of eventual withdrawal. Indeed, underlying much of the military thinking there seems to have been an implicit assumption that the apparatus of global defence was being remodelled for the longer term, if not in perpetuity. Thus the defence system originally designed to safeguard the Indian empire was maintained throughout the fifties to secure what were thought to be Britain's interests and responsibilities in the Middle East, the Far East, and in Africa. And in the early sixties, when Britain's colonial empire had gone the way of the Indian empire, it was refashioned, and in some ways strengthened, to meet the requirements of the post-imperial order.

The crucial year was 1947 and it was then that the defence implications of the retreat from empire required examination. On the one side the geographical presence, the military structure, and the moral force to sustain the broader role, and—on the other—the obligations and responsibilities which made it necessary, stemmed directly or indirectly from British rule in

India. With India, Pakistan, Burma, and Ceylon launched on their independent courses, the time had come for reappraisal. Yet this is not to argue that the security system in the Indian Ocean could and should have been dismantled almost immediately. What was required was some middle course for a transitional period—some intermediate policy between a defensive network cast in the imperial mould and the sweeping retraction implied by the latter-day Little Englanders who passed too lightly over the inherited burdens and swept aside the values and sentiments of the generation.

In the two decades after Indian independence the logic of the end of empire was reinforced by a number of practical considerations which steadily eroded the military basis of the world role and ensured its eventual demise. For the most part, it was possible to overcome the immediate difficulties in these years, but the long-term trend was fixed. On the one hand, the general capability of the services to intervene in Asia and Africa declined as the stock of weapons and equipment and the numbers in the forces became smaller. The falling percentage of the gross national product devoted to defence spending and the increasing cost of weapons systems and equipment programmes meant that each year the defence armoury grew progressively smaller. Similarly the pressures to reduce defence spending and to release men into industry resulted in a continuous reduction in military manpower. The decision taken in 1957 to abolish National Service greatly accelerated this process. By 1966 the army's strength was less than half the 1956 figure and no amount of rationalization could conceal the significance of this change for the maintenance of the world role. Indeed, it can reasonably be argued that the 1957 decision undermined Britain's position as a world military power inasmuch as the maintenance of a large standing army was the very basis of a broader defence posture. A third consequence of the restricted funds available for defence spending and the general cost inflation was that basic expenses—as for example pay, equipment, and research and development—absorbed an increasing proportion of the financial allocation with the result that less was available for operational expenses. Thus by the sixties considerations of cost as well as capability restricted the range of operations that could be undertaken.

The decline in Britain's attachment to playing a world role

is less easily documented. For most of the period this did not impinge directly at the political level but its influence can be seen in the growing reluctance to bear the burden of a large defence vote and to maintain large standing forces. The net result was that successive governments struggled to maintain the world posture without paying the strategic price. From 1965 to 1968 the profound change in outlook of the British nation became apparent and the government conceded that it had miscalculated the extent to which the public was prepared to make economic sacrifices for the vestiges of world leadership. Still, it remains true that the change in outlook which followed the loss of empire was not really important for most of the period because the world role was never put into the arena of political choice. That the east of Suez defence system survived for so long, therefore, was less a tribute to the willingness of the nation to bear the costs of empire without the dividends, than a consequence of the fact that the issue never saw the light of political day.

In the Indian Ocean also there were changes which greatly increased the problems of maintaining world strategy and the burdens it imposed. Most important were the eruptions and tensions which followed the dismantling of the European empires and the failure of the new states to establish either locally or regionally some indigenous system of stability to replace that which for a hundred and fifty years had been imposed from outside. What this meant was that far from fading away, Britain's commitments in the area became more onerous. As R. H. S. Crossman observed, the defence of the scattered remains of the empire became more burdensome than the defence of its earlier unity.[1] To compound the problem, a number of the new states, most notably Indonesia and Egypt, received large consignments of modern arms from abroad. Although at first the weapons supplied were usually obsolescent, by the early sixties many were of the latest types. Similarly, the strength of Britain's actual or potential enemies was enhanced by improved doctrine and training. The development of guerrilla strategy and tactics meant that the old methods and small forces could no longer control vast areas. The deterrent force of a British gunboat in the Persian Gulf in the nineteenth century or British aircraft in Iraq in the twenties

---

[1] 'Western Defence in the 1960s', *JRUSI*, 106/623, p. 328.

and thirties had little relevance in the fifties and sixties against well-armed and organized enemies, very often trained and supplied from outside.

It has frequently been suggested that a British military presence became increasingly less acceptable to the new states of Africa and Asia. As a general proposition this is a much over-simplified assessment. Many of the states within the ambit of British protection were content to remain there, although on occasions they felt constrained to speak to Whitehall with one voice and to the outside world with another. Moreover, the repeated predictions of certain commentators that the calls on British assistance would soon dwindle were not borne out in practice. Still, the fact remains that while a British presence was acceptable in some quarters, the rise of Afro-Asian nationalism placed formidable obstacles in the way of maintaining it. The difficulties about over-flying rights, training facilities, and base tenure all worked to increase substantially the costs and complications of deploying power 5,000 to 10,000 miles away from the home base.

In retrospect, the significance of these various factors for maintenance of the world role is immediately apparent. But perspective is very largely a product of time and for most of the period these difficulties were seen as problems to be overcome rather than as pointers to the inevitability of military withdrawal. As a result, there was little of the fundamental questioning of Britain's role which, with the advantage of hindsight, seems so clearly to have been required.

The survival of the east of Suez role in its broader form for some two decades after Indian independence was possible only because it was never seriously challenged. It is true that at times committees in Whitehall made attempts to reappraise the position, and in Parliament there were calls for withdrawal, but they aroused no great debate and generated little rethinking in the cabinet or the Defence Committee. The structure of British defence was too firmly weighted east of Suez and the role was too deeply rooted in Britain's outlook and history to be vulnerable to routine questioning and criticism. At this level it was not difficult to find persuasive reasons why the Indian Ocean role should be maintained. Economic interests, alliance obligations, and considerations of moral responsibility and world influence served at once to reinforce and to rationalize the continuance of a defence system in the East which, to paraphrase the words of one senior official, was there because it was there.

Against this background of inertia three more specific factors contributed to the maintenance of the world role. In the first place, British forces were almost continuously engaged in operations east of Suez during these years. With campaigns to be waged and won, there was little incentive to ask questions about the purposes or the viability of the system. In the short run the course was fixed. The long run went beyond the chart.

Secondly, the services themselves remained heavily committed to the world role and their views carried great weight with successive governments. The commitment of the military stemmed from their attachment to the imperial tradition and from their strong sense of responsibility to the successor states of the empire. But it was also a matter of service politics inasmuch as the east of Suez role provided a continuing justification for large forces and expensive equipment. Thus, when occasion offered, each of the three services used the world role as a means of securing the largest possible share of the defence vote. Another consideration was the importance attached to the world deployment of forces both in terms of recruiting and training areas.

Finally, and most important, there was the inability of successive governments to take long-term decisions and to relate defence policy to the other strands of overseas policy. For a period of almost twenty years defence policy was out of phase with colonial and foreign policy, and commitments remained broadly constant while capability progressively declined. In partial explanation it is possible to point to shortcomings in the administrative system, to personalities, and to the reluctance of Conservative governments to embark on the process of defence contraction. But the main factor must be sought in the inadequacy of successive cabinets, and perhaps in the inadequacy of the cabinet system itself, to decide issues involving long-term goals and crossing departmental boundaries.

The conclusion that Britain's military role as it was in fact perceived was inconsistent with the policy of decolonization in no way detracts from the value of the defence system which was maintained. The military achievement was in fact considerable. Notwithstanding the lack of clear political directives and the limited funds available for defence spending, the services developed a set of forces and a body of doctrine that was well suited to the task of lending military assistance to the new states of Africa and Asia. The structure of power which was originally built to safeguard the Indian empire was developed into a system of mobile forces designed to combat limited threats to the peace and insurgency movements around the rim of the Indian Ocean.

The process of adaptation did not begin until about 1954. In the immediate post-war period and during the years of the Korean war the dominance of general-war theory and the preoccupation with the defence requirements of Europe resulted in the neglect of strategic rethinking for the east of Suez area. After the Second World War, the apparatus of imperial defence was re-established in basically its pre-war form and very little thought appears to have been given to its relevance to the post-imperial order. Although all three services were concerned with the maintenance of stability in the area, the focus of attention was local rather than general and no body of doctrine was developed which defined the objectives and methods of the overseas role. However, each of the services, particularly the army, was building up a body of experience which was later to enable it to develop a small-war-counter-insurgency strategy.

The years 1954 to 1956 saw the emergence of new approaches to the problems of overseas security in the form of the airlifted strategic reserve and the tentative development of a limited-war role for the navy. However, the preoccupation with the nuclear deterrent meant that the limited-war role remained a secondary concern in Whitehall. Partly as a result, the new ideas were not fully worked out and their ramifications remained largely unexplored. Moreover, they had little importance in practice as few transport aircraft or suitable amphibious warfare ships were available and the chain of bases and garrisons and the manpower strength of the services remained adequate for maintenace of the traditional pattern of regional deployment.

Suez delivered the shock to the system which led to the development of a force structure and a body of doctrine appropriate to post-imperial conditions. Sandys' questioning challenged certain deeply ingrained aspects of service thinking.

The 1957 White Paper, although based on a mistaken reading of the utility of nuclear weapons, provided the structure within which the services could come to terms with the requirements of the sixties. The emergence of the air barrier forced the military to broaden their conceptual horizons and to consider the problems and tasks confronting them in the area within a regional framework. The result was that the late fifties and early sixties saw a process of continuous adjustment. The army built up a coherent doctrine of counter-insurgency campaigning; the naval force was adapted to the requirements of the east of Suez role; Transport Command was substantially strengthened and a number of the earlier difficulties relating to the air movement of troops were overcome.

This achievement was marred by two major shortcomings. The first was the failure of the base policy. In view of the immediate operational requirements and the financial limitations of these years it is a moot point whether the defence establishment had much room for choice. It is easy in retrospect to point to the increasing political costs and the declining military utility of large bases in sensitive areas without taking account of the difficulties in the way of developing an alternative strategy. Still, there were some who saw opportunities greatly to reduce Britain's dependence on fixed bases in Asia and Africa, and the fact remains that alternative proposals were neither satisfactorily costed nor seriously considered. The second failure was the inability of the services to reconcile their individual interest with the requirements of a national strategy. The preoccupation of the services with their respective roles led to overlapping functions and to the neglect of an adequate investment by one service in equipment which was mainly for the use or benefit of another. Similarly, the difficulties of coordination and command in the field must mainly be attributed to the reluctance of the services to brook any encroachment on their autonomy.

Despite these shortcomings the operational record of the services attests to their success in developing an effective system for the provision of military support to the successor states of empire. The extent to which the interests thus served were specifically British was always arguable, but few in the West questioned that Britain was making a substantial contribution both to international peace and to the stability of the new states of Africa and Asia. Viewed in this light, the returns from what was a comparatively modest investment were considerable.

Fired largely by the American experience in Vietnam, a new generation of analysts has suggested that Western military intervention in the Third World, based as it has been on the requirement for immediate stability, may in fact help to produce instability in the longer term. The debate has only begun, and it is instructive to reflect how little relevance it has to the terms of reference which framed consideration of post-war British policy in the Indian Ocean. In the evolution of that policy the relationship between ends and means was often blurred, but in the last resort the means determined the ends: just as the east of Suez role was largely a product of the existing defence system, ultimately lack of resources rather than intellectual rejection ensured its abandonment.

Select Bibliography

1. British Government Publications
    Defence Papers
    Relations with Other Governments
    Reports (except those from Select Committees on Estimates)
    Reports from Select Committees on Estimates
    History of the Second World War

2. Books and Pamphlets

3. Articles

All the items listed in Part 1 are published by Her Majesty's Stationery Office, London.

1. British Government Publications

Defence Papers

Admiralty. *Navy Estimates 1946* [for 1946–47] (1946); *Navy Estimates 1947–48* (1947); . . . *1948–49* (1948) and annually in the same kind of sequence until *Navy Estimates 1963–64* (1963). From 1964 a single set of Defence Estimates was presented; thus for 1964–65, 1965–66, and 1966–67 see *Defence Estimates*, listed under the entry Ministry of Defence, below.

—— *Explanatory statement on the Navy Estimates . . . by the First Lord of the Admiralty.* The series of Command Papers bearing this title begins in 1955; as it is a continuation of the series next listed (*Statement . . .*) the *Explanatory statement . . .* has been placed at the end of that series.

—— *Statement of the First Lord of the Admiralty explanatory of the Navy Estimates . . .* Command Papers, as follows: *1947–48*, Cmd 7054 (1947); *1948–49*, Cmd 7337 (1948); *1949–50*, Cmd 7632 (1949); *1950–51*, Cmd 7897 (1950); *1951–52*, Cmd 8160 (1951); *1952–53*, Cmd 8476 (1952); *1953–54*, Cmd 8769 (1953); *1954–55*, Cmd 9079 (1954); *Explanatory statement on the Navy Estimates . . . by the First Lord of the Admiralty*: *1955–56*, Cmd 9396 (1955); *1956–57*, Cmd 9697 (1956); *1957–58*, Cmnd 151 (1957); *1958–59*, Cmnd 371 (1958); *1959–60*, Cmnd 674 (1959); *1960–61*, Cmnd 949

(1960); *1961–62*, Cmnd 1282 (1961); *1962–63*, Cmnd 1629 (1962). From 1963 the kind of material previously given in these publications was included in the annual Statement on Defence; thus for 1963–64, 1964–65, 1965–66, and 1966–67 see the item Statements on Defence listed under the entry Ministry of Defence, below.

Air Ministry. *Air Estimates 1946* [for 1946–47] (1946); *Air Estimates 1947–48* (1947); . . . *1948–49* (1948) and annually in the same kind of sequence until *Air Estimates 1963–64* (1963). From 1964 a single set of Defence Estimates was presented; thus for 1964–65, 1965–66, and 1966–67 see *Defence Estimates,* listed under the entry Ministry of Defence, below.

—— *Memorandum by the Secretary of State for Air to accompany Air Estimates* . . . Command Papers, as follows: *1947–48*, Cmd 7053 (1947); *1948–49*, Cmd 7329 (1948); *1949–50*, Cmd 7634 (1949); *1950–51*, Cmd 7898 (1950); *1951–52*, Cmd 8162 (1951); *1952–53*, Cmd 8474 (1952); *1953–54*, Cmd 8771 (1953); *1954–55*, Cmd 9076 (1954); *1955–56*, Cmd 9397 (1955); *1956–57*, Cmd 9696 (1956); *1957–58*, Cmnd 149 (1957); *1958–59*, Cmnd 373 (1958); *1959–60*, Cmnd 673 (1959); *1960–61*, Cmnd 950 (1960); *1961–62*, Cmnd 1292 (1961); *1962–63*, Cmnd 1630 (1962). From 1963 the kind of material previously given in these publications was included in the annual Statement on Defence; thus for 1963–64, 1964–65, 1965–66, and 1966–67 see the item Statements on Defence, listed under the entry Ministry of Defence, immediately below.

Ministry of Defence. *Central organisation for defence.* Cmnd 2097 (1963).
—— *Defence Estimates: 1964–65* (1964); . . . *1965–66* (1965); . . . *1966–67* (1966).
—— Statements on Defence. Command Papers, as follows:
Statement relating to defence. Cmd 6743 (1946).
Statement relating to defence. Cmd 7042 (1947).
Statement relating to defence 1948. Cmd 7327 (1948).
Statement on defence 1949. Cmd 7631 (1949).
Statement on defence 1950. Cmd 7895 (1950).
[For 1951 see *Defence programme* . . . under the entry Prime Minister, below.]
Statement on defence 1952. Cmd 8475 (1952).
Statement on defence 1953. Cmd 8768 (1953).
Statement on defence 1954. Cmd 9075 (1954).
Statement on defence 1955. Cmd 9391 (1955).
Statement on defence 1956. Cmd 9691 (1956).
Defence: outline of future policy. Cmnd 124 (1957).
Report on defence: Britain's contribution to peace and security. Cmnd 363 (1958).
Progress of the five-year defence plan. Cmnd 662 (1959).

Report on defence 1960. Cmnd 952 (1960).

Report on defence 1961. Cmnd 1288 (1961).

Statement on defence 1962: the next five years. Cmnd 1639 (1962).

Statement on defence 1963 including memoranda to accompany the Navy, Army and Air estimates 1963–64. Cmnd 1936 (1963).

Statement on defence 1964. Cmnd 2270 (1964).

Statement on the defence estimates 1965. Cmnd 2592 (1965).

Statement on the defence estimates 1966, Part 1: *The defence review.* Cmnd 2901 (1966); Part 2: *Defence estimates 1966–67.* Cmnd 2902 (1966).

Statement on the defence estimates 1967. Cmnd 3203 (1967).

Supplementary statement on defence policy 1967. Cmnd 3357 (1967).

Prime Minister. *Central organisation for defence.* Cmd 6923 (1946.)

—— *Central organisation for defence.* Cmnd 476 (1958.)

—— *Defence programme: statement made by the Prime Minister in the House of Commons on Monday, 29 January 1951.* Cmd 8146 (1951).

War Office. *Army Estimates 1946* [for 1946–47] (1946); *Army Estimates 1947–48* (1947); . . . *1948–49* (1948) and annually in the same kind of sequence until *Army Estimates 1963–64* (1963). From 1964 a single set of Defence Estimates was presented; thus for 1964–65, 1965–66, and 1966–67 see *Defence Estimates,* listed under the entry Ministry of Defence, above.

—— *Memorandum of the Secretary of State for War relating to the Army Estimates . . .* Command Papers, as follows: *1947–48,* Cmd 7052 (1947); *1948–49,* Cmd 7332 (1948); *1949–50,* Cmd 7633 (1949); *1950–51,* Cmd 7896 (1950); *1951–52,* Cmd 8161 (1951); *1952–53,* Cmd 8477 (1952); *1953–54,* Cmd 8770 (1953); *1954–55,* Cmd 9072 (1954); *1955–56,* Cmd 9395 (1955); *1956–57* Cmd 9688 (1956); *1957–58,* Cmnd 150 (1957); *1958–59,* Cmnd 372 (1958); *1959–60,* Cmnd 669 (1959); *1960–61,* Cmnd 951 (1960). For 1961–62 and 1962–63 see the title immediately following.

—— *Memorandum on Army Estimates . . . by the Secretary of State for War: 1961–62,* Cmnd 1280 (1961); *1962–63,* Cmnd 1631 (1962). From 1963 the kind of material previously given in these publications was included in the annual Statement on Defence; thus for 1963–64, 1964–65, 1965–66, and 1966–67 see the item Statements on Defence, listed under the entry Ministry of Defence, above.

Relations with Other Governments

Colonial Office. *Accession of Aden to the Federation of South Arabia: exchange of letters between Federal and Aden Ministers and the Secretary of State for the Colonies.* Cmnd 1814, 1962.

—— *Ceylon: proposals for conferring on Ceylon fully responsible status within the British Commonwealth of Nations.* Cmd 7257, 1947.

Commonwealth Relations Office and Ministry of Defence. *Proposed defence agreement between the Government of the United Kingdom of Great Britain and Northern Ireland and the Government of the Federation of Nigeria.* Cmnd 1212, 1960.

Foreign Office. *Exchange of notes regarding relations between the United Kingdom of Great Britain and Northern Ireland and the State of Kuwait.* Cmnd 1518, 1961. (Treaty Series no. 93, 1961.)

—— *Pact of mutual co-operation between His Majesty the King of Iraq and the President of the Republic of Turkey.* Cmd 9859, 1956. (Treaty Series no. 39, 1956.)

—— *South-East Asia collective defence treaty.* [With protocol and Pacific charter.] Cmnd 265, 1957. (Treaty Series no. 63, 1957.)

—— *Special agreement between the Government of the United Kingdom of Great Britain and Northern Ireland and the Government of Iraq.* [With exchanges of notes.] Cmd 9544, 1955. (Treaty Series no. 50, 1955.)

—— *Treaty between the Government of the United Kingdom and the Provisional Government of Burma regarding the recognition of Burmese independence and related matters.* [With exchange of notes and annex.] Cmd 7360, 1948. (Treaty Series no. 16, 1948.)

Ministry of Defence. *Exchanges of letters on defence matters between the Governments of the United Kingdom and the Union of South Africa, June 1955.* Cmd 9520, 1955.

—— *Proposed agreement on external defence and mutual assistance between the Government of the United Kingdom of Great Britain and Northern Ireland and the Government of the Federation of Malaya.* Cmnd 263, 1957.

Reports (except those from Select Committees on Estimates)

Committee of Imperial Defence, Subcommittee on National and Imperial Defence. *Report.* Cmd 2029, 1924.

Committee on Representational Services Overseas. *Report.* (Chairman: Lord Plowden.) Cmnd 2276, 1964.

Keightley, Gen Sir Charles F. Despatch . . . Operations in Egypt—November to December 1956 [10 June 1957]. Suppl. no. 41172, 12 Sept. 1957, to *The London Gazette* of 10 Sept. 1957.

Ministry of Defence. Advisory Committee on Recruiting. *Report.* (Chairman: The Rt Hon. Sir James Grigg.) Cmnd 545, 1958.

—— *Government's comments on the report of the Advisory Committee on Recruiting (Cmnd 545).* Cmnd 570, 1958.

Mountbatten, Louis (V Adm Earl Mountbatten of Burma). *Report to the combined Chiefs of Staff by the Supreme Allied Commander South-East Asia 1943–1945.* 1951.

Tribunal on certain questions in regard to defence expenditure in dispute between the Government of India, the War Office and the Air Ministry. *Report.* Cmd 4473, 1933.

Reports from Select Committees on Estimates

House of Commons, Select Committee on Estimates:

Second report . . . session 1948–49: the defence estimates. 1950.

Seventeenth report . . . session 1948–49: the defence estimates. 1950.

Third report . . . session 1950–51: rearmament. 1951.

Sixth report . . . session 1950–51: Ministry of Transport; shipping and war terminal services. 1951.

Tenth report . . . session 1950–51: rearmament. 1951.

Second report . . . session 1951–52: rearmament. 1952.

Tenth report . . . session 1951–52: rearmament. 1952.

Third report . . . session 1952–53: call-up, posting and movement of national service men. 1953.

Seventh report . . . session 1955–56: naval research and development. 1956.

Second report . . . session 1956–57: supply of military aircraft. 1957.

Third report . . . session 1956–57: stores and ordnance depots of the service departments. 1957.

Third report . . . session 1957–58: the reserve fleet. 1958.

First report . . . session 1961–62: trooping. 1962.

Fifth report . . . session 1961–62: form of the estimates of the defence departments. 1962.

Eighth report . . . session 1961–62: the War Office. 1962.

Tenth special report . . . session 1961–62: trooping (observations of the Minister of Defence). 1962.

Fourth report . . . session 1962–63: spring supplementary estimates. 1963.

Tenth report . . . session 1962–63: military expenditure overseas. 1963.

Second report . . . session 1963–64: transport aircraft. 1964.

Fourth report . . . session 1963–64: form of the estimates of the defence departments. 1964.

Ninth report . . . session 1963–64: military expenditure overseas. 1964.

Fifth special report . . . session 1963–64: military expenditure overseas (departmental observations on the tenth report . . . in session 1962–63). 1964.

Seventh special report . . . session 1963–64: transport aircraft (departmental observations on the second report of the estimates committee). 1964.

Second special report . . . session 1964–65: military expenditure overseas (departmental observations on the ninth report . . . in session 1963–64). 1964.

Seventh report . . . session 1966–67: the movement of service personnel and stores. 1967.

Eleventh special report . . . session 1966–67: the movement of service personnel and stores (departmental observations on the seventh report from the estimates committee). 1967.

History of the Second World War
(UK Military Series except where otherwise stated)

Butler, J. R. M. *Grand strategy*, ii: *September 1939–June 1941*. 1957.

Collier, Basil, *The defence of the United Kingdom*. 1957.

Donnison, F. S. V. *British military administration in the Far East 1943–46*. 1956.

Ehrman, John. *Grand strategy*, v: *August 1943–September 1944*. 1956.

—— *Grand strategy*, vi: *October 1944–August 1945*, 1956.

Gwyer, J. M. A. *Grand strategy*, iii, pt. I: *June 1941–August 1942*. 1964.

Hancock, W. K. and M. M. Gowing. *British war economy*. 1949. (UK Civil Series.)

Kirby, Maj Gen S. Woodburn with others. *The war against Japan*, i: *The loss of Singapore*. 1957; ii: *India's most dangerous hour*. 1958; iii: *The decisive battles*. 1961; iv: *The reconquest of Burma*. 1965.

Postan, M. M. *British war production*. 1952. (UK Civil Series.)

2. Books and Pamphlets

Armstrong, Lt Col DeWitt C. (US Army). 'The changing strategy of British bases.' (Unpublished Ph.D. dissertation, Princeton Univ., 1959.)

Army League. *The British army in the nuclear age*. London, Army League, 1959.

—— *The army Britain needs*. Taunton, Somerset, Somerset County Gazette, 1964.

—— *British defence policy in South-East Asia*. Taunton, Somerset, Somerset County Gazette, 1966.

Attlee, C. R. *As it happened*. London, Heinemann, 1954.

Australian Inst. of Political Science. *Australia's defence and foreign policy*. Sydney, Angus & Robertson, 1964.

Barclay, Brig C. N. *The First Commonwealth Division: the story of British Commonwealth land forces in Korea 1950–53*. Aldershot, Gale & Polden, 1954.

Barker, A. J. *Suez: the seven day war*. London, Faber & Faber, 1964.

Bell, Coral. *The debatable alliance: an essay in Anglo-American relations*. London, OUP for RIIA, 1964.

Blundell, Sir Michael. *So rough a wind*. London, Weidenfeld & Nicolson, 1964.

Boycott, A. G. *The elements of imperial defence*. 3rd ed. Aldershot, Gale & Polden, 1938.

Boyle, Andrew. *Trenchard*. London, Collins, 1962.

Bromberger, Merry and Serge. *Secrets of Suez* (tr. by James Cameron). London, Pan Books/Sigwick & Jackson, 1957.

Brown, George (Baron George-Brown). *In my way: the political memoirs.* London, Gollancz, 1971.

Brown, Neville. *Strategic mobility.* London, Chatto & Windus for ISS, 1963.

—— *Britain and world security.* London, Fabian Society, 1966. (Fabian Research Series no. 258.)

—— *Arms without empire.* Harmondsworth, Penguin Books, 1967.

Bryant, Sir Arthur. *Triumph in the West 1943–1946.* London, Collins, 1959.

Buchan, Alastair (ed.). *China and the peace of Asia.* London, Chatto & Windus for ISS, 1965.

Bullard, Sir Reader. *Britain and the Middle East.* 3rd rev. ed. London, Hutchinson, 1964.

Callwell, Col C. E. *Small wars.* 3rd ed. London, HMSO, 1906, reprinted 1914.

Calvocoressi, Peter. *World order and new states.* London, Chatto & Windus for ISS, 1962.

Campbell, John C. *Defense of the Middle East.* New York, Harper for the Council on Foreign Relations, 1960.

Carrington, C. E. *The liquidation of the British empire.* London, Harrap, 1961.

Carter, Gwendolen M. *The British Commonwealth and international security: the role of the Dominions 1919–39.* Toronto, Ryerson Press, 1947.

Chatfield, A. E. M. (AF 1st Baron Chatfield of Ditchling). *The navy and defence: the autobiography . . . , ii: It might happen again.* London, Heinemann, 1947.

Childers, Erskine B. *The road to Suez.* London, MacGibbon & Kee, 1962.

Clutterbuck, Brig Richard L. *The long, long war.* New York, Praeger, 1966.

Cole, Capt D. H. *Changing conditions of imperial defence.* London, Sifton Praed, 1930.

—— Brig —— *Imperial military geography.* 10th ed. London, Sifton Praed, 1950.

Conan, A. R. *The sterling area.* London, Macmillan, 1952.

—— *Capital imports into sterling countries.* London, Macmillan, 1960.

Connell, John. *The 'office'.* London, Allan Wingate, 1958.

—— *Auchinleck.* London, Cassell, 1959.

Cooke, Colin. *The life of Richard Stafford Cripps.* London, Hodder & Stoughton, 1957.

Council on Foreign Relations, New York, and RIIA. *Britain and the United States: problems in co-operation.* London, RIIA, 1953.

Cross, James E. *Conflict in the shadows.* London, Constable, 1964.

Crowe, Cdr W. J. (US Navy). 'The policy roots of the modern Royal Navy 1946–63.' (Unpublished Ph.D. dissertation, Princeton Univ., 1965.

Crozier, Brian. *The rebels: a study of post-war insurrections.* London, Chatto & Windus, 1960.

Dalton, Hugh (Baron Dalton). *High tide and after: memoirs* [iii] *1945–1960.* London, Muller, 1962.

De Kadt, Emanuel J. *British defence policy and nuclear war.* London, Frank Cass, 1964.

Divine, David. *The blunted sword.* London, Hutchinson, 1964.

—— *The broken wing.* London, Hutchinson, 1966.

Driver, Christopher. *The disarmers.* London, Hodder & Stoughton, 1964.

Economic Cooperation Administration, Special Mission to the United Kingdom. *The sterling area: an American analysis.* London, ECA, 1951.

Eden, Sir Anthony. *The memoirs,* iii: *Full circle.* London, Cassell, 1960.

Elliott, Maj Gen J. L. *A roll of honour: the story of the Indian Army 1939–1945.* London, Cassell, 1965.

Epstein, L. D. *Britain—uneasy ally.* Chicago, Univ. of Chicago Press, 1954.

Estorick, Eric. *Stafford Cripps.* London, Heinemann, 1949.

Fergusson, Bernard. *The watery maze: the story of combined operations.* London, Collins, 1961.

Finer, S. E. and others. *Backbench opinion in the House of Commons 1955–59.* Oxford, Pergamon Press, 1961.

Fitzsimons, M. A. *The foreign policy of the British Labour government 1945–51.* Notre Dame, Indiana, Univ. of Notre Dame Press, 1953.

Fletcher, Raymond. *£60 a second on defence.* London, MacGibbon & Kee, 1963.

Foot, Sir Hugh. *A start in freedom.* London, Hodder & Stoughton, 1964.

Foot, M. R. D. *Men in uniform: military manpower in modern industrial societies.* London, Weidenfeld & Nicolson for ISS, 1961.

Franks, Sir Oliver. *Britain and the tide of world affairs.* London, OUP, 1955.

Gale, Gen Sir Richard. *Call to arms: an autobiography.* London, Hutchinson, 1968.

Garbutt, Paul E. *Naval challenge 1945–1961.* London, Macdonald, 1961.

Gibbs, N. H. 'British strategic doctrine 1918–1939', in M. Howard, ed., *The theory and practice of war.* London, Cassell, 1965.

Goldstein, Walter. *The dilemma of British defense: the imbalance between commitments and resources.* Columbus, Ohio State UP, 1966. (Mershon Center for Education in National Security, pamphlet series no. 3.)

Gordon, Hampden. *The War Office.* London, Putnam, 1935.

Graham, Gerald S. *Great Britain in the Indian Ocean 1810–1850.* London, OUP, 1967.

—— *The politics of naval supremacy.* Cambridge, CUP, 1965.

Gretton, V Adm Sir Peter. *Maritime strategy.* London, Cassell, 1965.

Grey, C. G. *A history of the Air Ministry.* London, Allen & Unwin, 1940.

Gwynn, Maj Gen Sir Charles W. *Imperial policing.* 2nd ed. London Macmillan, 1939.

Gwynne Jones, A. 'Training and doctrine in the British army since 1945', in M. Howard, ed., *The theory and practice of war.* London, Cassell, 1965.

Hamilton, W. B. and others (eds). *A decade of the Commonwealth 1955–1964.* Durham, NC, Duke UP, 1966.

Hardinge, Charles (1st Baron Hardinge of Penshurst). *My Indian years, 1910–1916.* London, John Murray, 1948.

Harris, Richard. *Independence and after.* London, OUP for Institute of Race Relations, 1962.

Hart, B. H. Liddell. *The revolution in warfare.* London, Faber & Faber, 1946.

—— *Defence of the West: some riddles of war and peace.* London, Cassell, 1950.

—— *Deterrent or defence: a fresh look at the West's military position.* London, Stevens, 1960.

Hayter, Sir William. *The diplomacy of the great powers.* London, Hamish Hamilton, 1960.

Heussler, Robert. *Yesterday's rulers.* London, OUP, 1963.

Hewins, Ralph. *A golden dream: the miracle of Kuwait.* London, W. H. Allen, 1963.

Hickinbotham, Sir Tom. *Aden.* London, Constable, 1958.

Hollis, Gen Sir Leslie. *One Marine's tale.* London, Deutsch, 1956.

Hoskins, H. L. *British routes to India.* New York, Longmans Green, 1928.

Howard, Michael (ed.). *The theory and practice of war: essays presented to Captain B. H. Liddell Hart.* London, Cassell, 1965.

—— *The central organisation of defence.* London, RUSI, 1970.

Indian Council of World Affairs. *Defence and security in the Indian Ocean area.* London, Asia Publishing House, 1958.

Ismay, H. L. (Gen 1st Baron Ismay of Wormington). *Memoirs.* London, Heinemann, 1960.

Issawi, Charles and Mohammed Yeganeh. *The economics of Middle Eastern oil.* London, Faber & Faber, 1962.

Jacob, Maj Gen Sir Ian. 'The United Kingdom's strategic interests', in RIIA, *United Kingdom policy: foreign, strategic, economic.* London, RIIA, 1950.

Jane's Fighting Ships. London, Sampson Low, Marston, annually.

Jeffries, Sir Charles. *The Colonial Office.* London, Allen & Unwin, 1956.

—— *Transfer of power.* London, Pall Mall Press, 1960.

Johnson, Franklyn Arthur. *Defence by committee: the British Committee of Imperial Defence 1885–1959.* London, OUP, 1960.

Johnson, Paul. *The Suez war.* London, MacGibbon & Kee, 1957.

Johnston, Sir Charles. *The view from Steamer Point.* London, Collins, 1964.

Jones, Arthur Creech (ed.). *New Fabian colonial essays.* London, Hogarth Press, 1959.

Joubert de la Ferté, Air Chf Mshl Sir Philip. *Rocket.* London, Hutchinson, 1957.

Karnik, V. B. (ed.). *China invades India.* Bombay, Allied Publishers, 1963.

Kaufmann, William W. *The McNamara strategy.* New York, Harper & Row, 1964.

Kennedy, D. E. *The security of southern Asia.* London, Chatto & Windus for ISS, 1965.

King, Gillian. *Imperial outpost—Aden.* London, OUP for RIIA, 1964.

Kingston-McCloughry, AVM E. J. *Global strategy.* London, Cape, 1957.

—— *Defence.* London, Stevens, 1960.

Kirkman, W. P. *Unscrambling an empire: a critique of British colonial policy 1956–1966.* London, Chatto & Windus, 1966.

Labour Party. Sixty-fourth Annual Conference . . . Sept. 27–Oct. 1 1965. *Report.* London, Labour Party, 1965.

Lee, J. M. *Colonial development and good government.* London, OUP, 1967.

Leeman, Wayne A. *The price of Middle East oil.* New York, Cornell UP, 1962.

Legum, Colin. *Pan-Africanism.* London, Pall Mall Press. 1962.

McKitterick, T. E. M. and Kenneth Younger (eds). *Fabian international essays.* London, Hogarth Press, 1957.

Maclean, Donald Duart. *British foreign policy since Suez 1956–1968.* London, Hodder & Stoughton, 1970.

Macmillan, Harold. *Memoirs,* iii: *Tides of fortune, 1945–1955* (1969); iv: *Riding the storm 1956–1959* (1971). London, Macmillan.

Macmillan, W. M. *The road to self-rule.* London, Faber & Faber, 1959.

Mander, John. *Great Britain or Little England?* London, Secker & Warburg, 1963.

Mansergh, Nicholas. *Survey of British Commonwealth affairs*, iv: *Problems of wartime co-operation and post-war change 1939–1952*. London, OUP for RIIA, 1958.

Marder, A. J. *The anatomy of British sea power: a history of British naval policy in the pre-dreadnought era, 1880–1905*. 1st ed. reprinted. London, Frank Cass, 1964.

Marlowe, John. *Arab nationalism and British imperialism*. London, Cresset Press, 1961.

Martel, Lt Gen Sir Gifford. *East versus West*. London, Museum Press, 1952.

Martin, L. W. *The sea in modern strategy*. London, Chatto & Windus for ISS, 1967.

—— *British defence policy: the long recessional*. London, ISS, 1969.

Mayhew, Christopher. *Britain's role tomorrow*. London, Hutchinson, 1967.

Miers, Richard. *Shoot to kill*. London, Faber & Faber, 1959.

Millar, T. B. *Australia's defence*. Melbourne, Melbourne UP, 1965.

Miller, J. D. B. *Britain and the old Dominions*. London, Chatto & Windus, 1966.

Modelski, George (ed.). *SEATO: six studies*. Melbourne, Cheshire for Australian National Univ., 1962.

Molesworth, Lt Gen G. N. *Curfew on Olympus*. London, Asia Publishing House, 1965.

Monroe, Elizabeth. *Britain's moment in the Middle East 1914–1956*. London, Methuen, 1965.

—— 'Mr Bevin's "Arab policy"', in A. Hourani (ed.), *Middle Eastern Affairs*, 2. London, Chatto & Windus, 1961. (St Antony's Papers no. 11.)

Montgomery, B. L. (FM 1st Viscount Montgomery of Alamein). *Memoirs*. London, Collins, 1958.

Morrison, H. S. (Baron Morrison of Lambeth). *An autobiography*. London, Odhams, 1960.

Moulton, Maj Gen J. L. *Defence in a changing world*. London, Eyre & Spottiswoode, 1964.

—— *British maritime strategy in the 1970s*. London, RUSI, 1969.

Northedge, F. S. *British foreign policy: the process of readjustment 1945–1961*. London, Allen & Unwin, 1962.

Nuclear dispersal in Asia and the Indo-Pacific region. Proceedings of seminar (5–6 Sept. 1964) sponsored by the Defence Studies Project of the Australian Inst. of International Affairs, at the Australian National Univ. Canberra, ANU, 1965.

Nutting, Anthony. *No end of a lesson: the story of Suez*. London, Constable, 1967.

O'Ballance, E. *The Sinai campaign 1956*. London, Faber & Faber, 1959.

Paget, Lt Col Julian. *Counter-insurgency campaigning*. London, Faber & Faber, 1967.

—— *Last post: Aden 1964–67*. London, Faber & Faber, 1969.

Panikkar, K. M. *Asia and Western dominance: a survey of the Vasco da Gama epoch of Asian history, 1498–1945*. London, Allen & Unwin, 1953.

—— *Problems of Indian defence*. London, Asia Publishing House, 1960.

—— *India and the Indian Ocean: an essay on the influence of sea power on Indian history*. 2nd impr. London, Allen & Unwin, 1962.

Porter, Brian. *Britain and the rise of communist China*. London, OUP, 1967.

Prasad, B. (ed.). *Defence of India: policy and plans*. Combined Inter-Services Historical Section, India and Pakistan, 1963; distributors, Orient Longmans, New Delhi. (In series Official History of the Indian Armed Forces in the Second World War 1939–1945.)

Pye, Lucian W. *Guerrilla communism in Malaya*. Princeton, Princeton Univ. Press, 1956.

Robertson, Terence. *Crisis: the inside story of the Suez conspiracy*. London, Hutchinson, 1965.

Rodgers, W. T. (ed.). *Hugh Gaitskell 1906–1963*. London, Thames & Hudson, 1964.

Rose, C. R. 'The relation of socialist principles to British Labour foreign policy 1945–51.' (Unpublished D. Phil. thesis, Univ. of Oxford, 1959.)

Rose, Saul. *Britain and South-East Asia*. London, Chatto & Windus, 1962.

Rosecrance, R. N. *Defense of the realm: British strategy in the nuclear epoch*. New York, Columbia UP, 1968.

RIIA. *Political and strategic interests of the United Kingdom*. London, OUP, 1939.

—— *British security*. London, RIIA, 1946.

—— *Defence in the cold war*. London, RIIA, 1950.

—— *United Kingdom policy: foreign, strategic, economic*. Appreciations by Professor Sir Charles Webster, Major General Sir Ian Jacob, and E. A. G. Robinson. London, RIIA, 1950.

—— *Collective defence in South East Asia: the Manila treaty and its implications*. London, RIIA, 1956; reprinted by OUP, 1958.

—— *British interests in the Mediterranean and Middle East*. London, OUP, 1958.

Schofield, V Adm B. B. *The Royal Navy today*. London, OUP, 1960.

Scott, Sir Robert. *Major theatre of conflict: British policy in East Asia*, London, Atlantic Trade Study, 1968.

Shinwell, Emanuel. *Conflict without malice*, London, Odhams, 1955.

Shwadran, Benjamin. *The Middle East: oil and the great powers*. New York, Praeger, 1955.

Singh, Brig Rajendra. *History of the Indian Army*. New Delhi, S. Attar Singh, 1963.

Slessor, MRAF Sir John. *Strategy for the West*. London, Cassell, 1954.

—— *The central blue*. London, Cassell, 1956.

—— *The great deterrent*. London, Cassell, 1957.

Snyder, William P. *The politics of British defense policy 1945–1962*. London, Ernest Benn, 1965.

Strachey, John. *The end of empire*. London, Victor Gollancz, 1959.

Strang, William (1st Baron Strang of Stonesfield). *The Foreign Office*. London, Allen & Unwin, 1955.

—— *Home and abroad*. London, Deutsch, 1956.

—— *The diplomatic career*. London, Deutsch, 1962.

Tedder, A. W. (MRAF 1st Baron Tedder of Glenguin). *With prejudice: the war memoirs*. London, Cassell, 1966.

Thetford, Owen. *Aircraft of the Royal Air Force since 1918*. 4th ed. London, Putnam, 1968.

Thompson, Sir Robert. *Defeating communist insurgency*. London, Chatto & Windus for ISS, 1966.

Thornton, A. P. *The imperial idea and its enemies*. London, Macmillan, 1959.

Truman, Harry S. *Memoirs*, ii: *Years of trial and hope*. Garden City, NY, Doubleday, 1956.

Tuker, Lt Gen Sir Francis. *While memory serves*. London, Cassell, 1950.

Tunstall, W. C. B., *The Commonwealth and regional defence*. London, Athlone Press for Inst. of Commonwealth Studies. (Univ. of London, Inst. of Commonwealth Studies, Commonwealth Papers no. 6.)

Verrier, Anthony. *An army for the sixties*. London, Secker & Warburg, 1966.

Vincent, Arthur. *The defence of India*. London, OUP, 1922.

Vital, David. *The making of British foreign policy*. London, Allen & Unwin, 1968.

Walker, Patrick C. Gordon. *The Commonwealth*. London, Secker & Warburg, 1962.

—— *The cabinet*. London, Jonathan Cape, 1970.

Watt, Sir Alan. *Australian defence policy 1951–1963: major international aspects*. Canberra, Dept of International Relations, Australian National Univ., 1964. (Working Paper no. 4.)

Weeks, Lt Gen Sir Ronald M. *Organisation and equipment for war*. Cambridge, CUP, 1950.

Williams, Francis. *Ernest Bevin: portrait of a great Englishman*. London, Hutchinson, 1952.

—— *A prime minister remembers: the war and post-war memoirs of the Rt Hon. Earl Attlee, based on his private papers and on a series of recorded conversations*. London, Heinemann, 1961.

Wilson, J. Harold. *The Labour government 1964–1970: a personal record.* London, Weidenfeld & Nicolson and Michael Joseph, 1971.

Windrich, Elaine. *British Labour's foreign policy.* Stanford, Stanford UP, 1952.

Woodhouse, C. M. *British foreign policy since the second world war.* London, Hutchinson, 1961.

Younger, Kenneth. *Changing perspectives in British foreign policy.* London, OUP for RIIA, 1964.

Zinkin, Maurice and Taya. *Britain and India: requiem for empire.* London, Chatto & Windus, 1964.

3. Articles

Adams, Capt J. H. (RN). Commando ship: her qualities and uses. *Navy*, 70/10 (Oct. 1965), pp. 327–9.

Alanbrooke (Alan Francis Brooke, FM 1st Viscount Alanbrooke of Brookeborough). Empire defence. *JRUSI*, 92/566 (May 1947), pp. 182–6.

Armstrong, DeWitt C. The British re-value their strategic bases. *JRUSI*, 104/616 (Nov. 1959), pp. 423–32.

Armstrong, H. F. The troubled birth of Malaysia. *Foreign Affairs*, 41/4 (July 1963), pp. 673–93.

Baldwin, Capt G. C. (RN). Interface in the air. *Navy*, 74/9 (Sept. 1969), pp. 302–3.

Barclay, Brig C. N. Historical background, general policy and tasks of the army. *Brassey's Annual 1950*, pp. 135–44.

—— The imperial army: composition, organisation and distribution. *Brassey's Annual 1950*, pp. 145–59.

—— Lessons of the Korean campaign, *Brassey's Annual 1954*, pp. 122–33.

—— Britain's strategic reserve and sea-borne task forces in action. *Brassey's Annual 1962*, pp. 33–40.

Barnes, Maj B. H. P. Future strategic importance of the Middle East to the British Commonwealth of Nations. *Army Quarterly*, 57/1 (Oct. 1948), pp. 161–77.

Barrett, Gp Capt G. G. The role of the RAF in the preservation of peace. *JRUSI*, 91/561 (Feb. 1946), pp. 77–82.

Beaton, Leonard. Strategy: east or west? *JRUSI*, 111/644 (Nov. 1966) pp. 281–90.

Bennett, Cdr G. M. Imperial defence. *JRUSI*, 91/562 (May 1946), pp. 165–75.

Beytagh, W Cdr W. Air power and air transport. *RAF Quarterly*, 17/1 (Dec. 1945), pp. 16–21.

Birdwood, C. B. (2nd Baron Birdwood). The defence of South

East Asia. *International Affairs* (London), 31/1 (Jan. 1955), pp. 17–25.

Blackaby, F. T. and D. C. Paige. Defence expenditure: burden or stimulus. *Survival*, 2/6 (Nov.–Dec. 1960), pp. 242–6.

'Blake.' The modern navy. *Blackwood's Magazine*, 290/1751 (Sept. 1961), pp. 193–204.

Bower, Maj Gen R. H. Air support for the army. *Brassey's Annual* 1954, pp. 180–8.

Boyd, Adm Sir Denis. The services in the Far East. *JRUSI*, 95/577 (Feb. 1950), pp. 41–7.

Boyle, MRAF Sir Dermot. The next 10 years. *Air Power*, 7/2 (winter 1959–60), pp. 91–8.

Brazier–Creagh, Brig K. R. Anti-terrorist operations in Malaya 1953–54. *Brassey's Annual 1954*, pp. 327–39.

—— The local defence of overseas territories. *Brassey's Annual 1956*, pp. 219–31.

—— Limited war. *Brassey's Annual* 1957, pp. 35–45.

Brecher, Michael. International relations and Asian studies. The subordinate state system of southern Asia. *World Politics*, vol. 15, 1962–3, pp. 213–35.

Brown, Neville. The military helicopter. *Brassey's Annual 1962*, pp. 75–83.

Buchan, Alastair. Britain and the nuclear deterrent. *Political Quarterly*, 31/1 (Jan.–Mar. 1960), pp. 36–45.

—— Britain in the Indian Ocean. *International Affairs* (London), 42/2 (Apr. 1966), pp. 184–93.

—— Britain east of Suez: the problem of power. *JRUSI* 112/647 (Aug. 1967), pp. 209–15.

Butwell, R. Malaysia and its impact on the international relations of South East Asia. *Asian Survey*, 4/7 (July 1964), pp. 940–6.

Cameron, Gp Capt N. The 38 Group concept. *RAF Quarterly*, 2/2 (summer 1962), pp. 101–4.

Carter, AVM W. Problems of modern command. *Brassey's Annual 1966*, pp. 120–8.

Cartmel, Gp Capt B. S. Maintenance of the RAF overseas. *JRUSI*, 92/565 (Feb. 1947), pp. 100–5.

Chamier, Wg Cdr J. A. The use of the Air Force for replacing military garrisons. *JRUSI*, 66/462 (May 1921), pp. 205–16.

Chappell, John. Trooping by air. *Navy*, 61/9 (Sept. 1956), pp. 270–4.

Clark, William. Britain east of Suez: the problem of influence. *JRUSI*, 112/647 (Aug. 1967), pp. 216–20.

Clarkson, Cdr R. A. Suez and Syracuse. *JRUSI*, 104/616 (Nov. 1959), pp. 443–9.

—— Naval heresy. *JRUSI*, 110/640 (Nov. 1965), pp. 316–20.

Collier, AVM A. C. Air transport. *JRUSI*, 90/557 (Feb. 1945), pp. 36–51.

Commonwealth manpower—a plea for a colonial army. *Army Quarterly*, 61/1 (Oct. 1950), pp. 53–61.

Conder, Lt Col H. R. R. Future developments in imperial defence. *JRUSI*, 92/567 (Aug. 1947), pp. 374–82.

Connell, John. The Middle East and Indian Ocean. *JRUSI*, 108/629 (Feb. 1963), pp. 23–30.

Cowley, Lt Gen Sir John. Future trends in warfare. *JRUSI*, 105/617 (Feb. 1960), pp. 4–16.

Craig, Lt Col T. S. Trooping today. *Army Quarterly*, 76/2 (July 1958), pp. 214–23.

Cross, Air Mshl Sir Kenneth. Transport Command 1943–1964. *RAF Quarterly*, 4/2 (summer 1964), pp. 85–92.

—— Transport Command today. *JRUSI*, 110/639 (Aug. 1965), pp. 210–16.

Crossman, R. H. S. Western defence in the 1960s. *JRUSI*, 106/623 (Aug. 1961), pp. 324–54.

Darby, Phillip. Beyond east of Suez. *International Affairs* (London), 46/4 (Oct. 1970), pp. 655–69.

—— The West, military intervention, and the Third World. *Brassey's Annual 1971*, pp. 65–79.

Davis, Gp Capt J. G. The employment of air forces in imperial defence. *RAF Quarterly*, 17/2 (Mar. 1946), pp. 77–82.

Day, A. C. L. The economics of defence. *Political Quarterly*, 31/1 (Jan.–Mar. 1960), pp. 57–62.

Deane-Drummond, Lt Col A. J. The army in the air transport age: a look into the future. *Army Quarterly*, 70/2 (July 1955), pp. 186–91.

De Weerd, H. A. Britain's changing military policy. *Foreign Affairs*, 34/1 (Oct. 1955), pp. 102–16.

Eden, Anthony. Britain in world strategy. *Foreign Affairs*, 29/3 (Apr. 1951), pp. 341–50.

Eley, Wg Cdr D. L. Helicopters in Malaysia. *RAF Quarterly*, 6/1 (spring 1966), pp. 5–10.

Foley, Maj C. J. Army equipment. *Brassey's Annual 1950*, pp. 171–8.

Foote, Maj Gen H. R. B. The re-equipment of the British army in the 1960s. *Brassey's Annual 1961*, pp. 348–53.

Foxley-Norris, Gp Capt C. N. The RAF today. *Blackwood's Magazine*, 290/1749 (July 1961), pp. 1–13.

—— AVM —— Future Command organisation. *RAF Quarterly*, 4/4 (winter 1964), pp. 253–61.

Franks, Sir Oliver. Britain and the tide of world affairs (Reith Lectures). *Listener*, 52/1341–6, 1954.

Frankland, Noble. Britain's changing strategic position. *International Affairs* (London), 33/4 (Oct. 1957), pp. 416–26.

Glubb, Capt J. B. Air and ground forces in punitive expeditions. *JRUSI*, 71/484 (Nov. 1926), pp. 777–84.

Goldberg, Alfred. The atomic origins of the British nuclear deterrent. *International Affairs* (London), 40/3 (July 1964), pp. 409–29

—— The military origins of the British nuclear deterrent. *International Affairs* (London), 40/4 (Oct. 1964), pp. 600–18.

Goold-Adams, R. Conventional forces and British defence policy. *Political Quarterly*, 31/1 (Jan.–Mar. 1960), pp. 7–16.

Gordon-Cumming, Gp Capt A. R. Fighters in Transport Command. *RAF Quarterly*, 4/4 (winter 1964), pp. 263–6.

Gordon-Finlayson, Air Cdre J. R. Defence problems of Aden. *Brassey's Annual 1957*, pp. 220–33.

Green, Lt Col A. (R. Aust. Army Corps). Military air transport—everybody's darling: nobody's baby. *Air Power*, 4/2 (Jan. 1957), pp. 109–15.

Gretton, V Adm Sir Peter. The future of the aircraft carrier. *Navy*, 69/9 (Sept. 1964), pp. 293–5.

—— A maritime strategy for British defence. *JRUSI*, 110/640 (Nov. 1965), pp. 301–10.

—— The future of the aircraft carrier. *Brassey's Annual 1965*, pp. 188–95.

Gwynne Jones, Lt Col A. British commitments overseas: modern strategic concepts. *JRUSI*, 108/629 (Feb. 1963), pp. 4–13.

Hall, Nowell. The problems of naval bases. Are fleet trains the answer? *Navy*, 61/8 (Aug. 1956), pp. 231–2.

Halliday, Cdr R. W. Commando ship at work. *Navy*, 70/2 (Feb. 1965), pp. 40–2.

Healey, Denis. When shrimps learn to whistle. *International Affairs* (London), 32/1 (Jan. 1956), pp. 1–10.

Hogg, Quintin. Britain looks forward. *Foreign Affairs*, 43/3 (Apr. 1965), pp. 409–25.

Howard, Michael. Strategy in the nuclear age. *JRUSI*, 102/608 (Nov. 1957), pp. 473–82.

—— Civil-military relations in Great Britain and the United States, 1945–1958. *Political Science Quarterly*, 75/1 (Mar. 1960), pp. 35–46.

—— Britain's defenses: commitments and capabilities. *Foreign Affairs*, 39/1 (Oct. 1960), pp. 81–91.

—— Bombing and the bomb. *Encounter*, 18/4 (Apr. 1962), pp. 20–6.

—— Military power and international order. *International Affairs* (London), 40/3 (July 1964), pp. 397–408.

—— Britain's strategic problem east of Suez. *International Affairs* (London), 42/2 (Apr. 1966), pp. 179–83.

Hudson, G. F. Will Britain and America split in Asia? *Foreign Affairs*, 31/4 (July 1953), pp. 536–47.

Hughes Hallett, R Adm C. C. Naval logistics in a future war. *JRUSI*, 95/578 (May 1950), pp. 232–45.

Jacob, Maj Gen Sir Ian. Principles of British military thought. *Foreign Affairs*, 29/2 (Jan. 1951), pp. 219–28.

'J.G.R.A.' Soldiering in the sixties. *Blackwood's Magazine*, 288/1740 (Oct. 1960), pp. 289–99.

Johnson, F. A. Politico-military organization in the United Kingdom: some recent developments. *Journal of Politics*, 27/2 (May 1965), pp. 339–50.

Johnson, AVM J. E. The role of Air Forces Middle East. *RAF Quarterly*, 5/3 (autumn 1965), pp. 169–75.

Kelly, J. B. The British position in the Persian Gulf. *World Today*, 20/6 (June 1964), pp. 238–49.

Kendall, Capt A. J. V. Air mobility for the soldier. *Air Power*, 7/3 (spring 1960), pp. 179–85.

King, Gillian. The problem of Aden. *World Today*, 18/12 (Dec. 1962), pp. 498–503.

Knorr, Klaus. Cost-effectiveness and research. *Survival*, 9/3 (Mar. 1967), pp. 83–6 and 101.

Krishnamachari, Sir V. T. Regional arrangements—the Indian Ocean area. *India Quarterly*, 2/3 (July–Sept. 1946), pp. 287–9.

Lee, AVM D. J. P. RAF fighters over Kuwait. *RAF Quarterly*, 2/2 (summer 1962), pp. 85–7.

Leifer, M. Anglo-American differences over Malaysia. *World Today*, 20/4 (Apr. 1964), pp. 156–67.

Levers, R Adm J. A. The maritime aircraft. *Navy*, 70/9 (Sept. 1965), pp. 292–6.

Lindsell, Lt Gen Sir Wilfrid. The development of India as a base for military operations. *JRUSI*, 92/566 (May 1947), pp. 221–31.

Luce, Sir William. Britain's withdrawal from the Middle East and Persian Gulf. *JRUSI*, 114/653 (Mar. 1969), pp. 4–10.

Lyne, Maj Gen L. O. The Middle East. *Brassey's Annual 1953*, pp. 107–13.

McHenry, D. E. and R. N. Rosecrance. The exclusion of the United Kingdom from the ANZUS Pact. *International Organization*, 12/3 (summer 1958), pp. 320–9.

Macintyre, Donald. Soldiers at sea. A study in strategic mobility. *Navy*, 70/4 (Apr. 1965), pp. 104–6.

McKitterick, T. E. M. What are British interests? *Political Quarterly*, 31/1 (Jan.–Mar. 1960), pp. 7–16.

Maclachlan, Donald. Which kind of war? *Survival*, 1/2 (May–June 1959), pp. 50–3 (first pubd in *Listener*, 12 Mar. 1959).

Manning the Defences. *Round Table*, 41/161 (Dec. 1950), pp. 44–51.

Manpower and Defence. *Round Table*, 39/156 (Sept. 1949), pp. 323–8.

Martel, Lt Gen Sir Gifford. The trend of future warfare. *JRUSI*, 92/567 (Aug. 1947), pp. 370–3.

—— The pattern of a future war: the land aspect. *JRUSI*, 95/578 (May 1950), pp. 221–31.

Martin, L. W. The market for strategic ideas in Britain: the 'Sandys era'. *American Political Science Review*, 56/1 (Mar. 1962), pp. 23–41.

Mayhew, Christopher. British foreign policy since 1945. *International Affairs* (London), 26/4 (Oct. 1950), pp. 477–86.

Mead, Brig. P. W. Army aviation. *RAF Quarterly*, 2/3 (autumn 1962), pp. 189–93.

Means, G. P. Malaysia—a new federation in South East Asia. *Pacific Affairs*, 36/2 (summer 1963), pp. 138–59.

Millman, Maj H. C. Sarawak and confrontation. *Army Quarterly*, 91/2 (Jan. 1966), pp. 186–91.

The Military Balance. London, Inst. for Strategic Studies, annually.

Modelski, George. International relations and area studies. The case of South East Asia. *International Relations* (London), 11/2 (Apr. 1961), pp. 143–55.

—— Indonesia and the Malaysia issue. *Yearbook of World Affairs 1964*, vol. 18, pp. 128–49.

Molesworth, Lt Gen G. N. Some problems of future security in the Indian Ocean area. *Asiatic Review*, 42/149 (Jan. 1946), pp. 26–34.

Montgomery, B. L. (FM 1st Viscount Montgomery of Alamein). A look through a window at world war three. *JRUSI*, 99/596 (Nov. 1954), pp. 507–23.

Moulton, Maj Gen J. L. Amphibious warfare in the late 1960s: seaborne/airborne operations. *JRUSI*, 107/625 (Feb. 1962), pp. 19–28.

—— Mobility in amphibious warfare. *Brassey's Annual 1962*, pp. 164–71.

—— A brush-fire operation—Brunei, December 1962. *Brassey's Annual 1963*, pp. 77–84.

—— The real cost. A study of the effectiveness of overseas forces. *Navy*, 69/11 (Nov. 1964), pp. 359–61.

—— Bases or fighting forces? *Brassey's Annual 1964*, pp. 143–51.

—— The role of British forces in a strategy of flexible response. *Brassey's Annual 1965*, pp. 23–32.

—— Aden and CVA 01. *Navy*, 71/4 (Apr. 1966), pp. 106, 108.

—— The 1966 defence White Paper and debate. *Brassey's Annual 1966*, pp. 1–10.

—— The Indonesian confrontation. *Naval Review* (Annapolis, Md., US Naval Inst.), 1969, pp. 140–71.

'Ned'. The fleet train. *Brassey's Annual 1953*, pp. 213–21.

Norris, Wg Cdr F. The roles of the Far East Air Force. *Brassey's Annual 1955*, pp. 308–15.

Panikkar, K. M. The defence of India and Indo-British obligations. *International Affairs* (London), 22/1 (Jan. 1946), pp. 85–90.

Pelly, Capt P. D. H. (RN). The pattern of a future war: the sea aspect. *JRUSI*, 95/578 (May 1950), pp. 221–31.

Portal, Air Cdre C. F. A. Air force co-operation in policing the empire. *JRUSI*, 82/526 (May 1937), pp. 343–58.

Robinson, D. MacIver. The logistic ship Sir Lancelot. *Brassey's Annual 1964*, pp. 165–71.

Robinson, Maj R. E. R. Reflections of a company commander in Malaya. *Army Quarterly*, 61/1 (Oct. 1950), pp. 80–7.

Sampson, Cdr T. S. The assault ship—HMS Fearless. *Brassey's Annual 1964*, pp. 162–4.

Saundby, Air Mshl Sir Robert. Sea power and the aircraft carrier. *Brassey's Annual 1953*, pp. 114–21.

—— Air power in limited wars. *JRUSI*, 103/611 (Aug. 1958), pp. 378–83.

Schofield, V Adm B. B. Britain's postwar naval policy. *Navy*, 63/8 (Aug. 1958), pp. 217–19; 63/9 (Sept. 1959), pp. 267–72.

—— and others. The state of Britain's armed forces. *Brassey's Annual 1966*, pp. 11–34.

Sendall, Maj W. R. We need a fighting fire brigade. Some deductions from Korea. *Navy*, 55/9 (Sept. 1950), pp. 272–3.

—— Royal Marines in the future: need for an amphibious striking force. *Navy*, 56/1 (Jan. 1951), pp. 4–5.

Shepherd, E. Colston. The carrier as a strategic weapon. *Navy*, 60/9 (Sept. 1955), pp. 272–6.

—— Air support for the army. *Brassey's Annual 1962*, pp. 138–43.

—— Safeguarding property and peace. *Brassey's Annual 1963*, pp. 212–18.

—— Implications of strategic mobility. *Brassey's Annual 1964*, pp. 181–5.

Slane, Maj P. M. Tactical problems in Kenya. *Army Quarterly*, 69/1 (Oct. 1954), pp. 45–52.

Slessor, Air Chf Mshl Sir John. Some reflections on airborne forces. *Army Quarterly*, 56/2 (July 1948), pp. 161–6.

—— MRAF —— Air power and the future of war. *JRUSI*, 99/595 (Aug. 1954), pp. 343–58.

—— British defense policy. *Foreign Affairs*, 35/4 (July 1957), pp. 551–63.

Smeeton, V Adm Sir Richard. Maritime air power. *Navy*, 71/9 (Sept. 1966), pp. 288–9 and 296.

Stevens, Capt T. M. P. The helicopter carrier. *Navy*, 62/10 (Oct. 1957), pp. 322–3.

—— Troop-carrying helicopters. *Army Quarterly*, 75/2 (Jan. 1958), pp. 203–9.

—— Lt Col —— A joint operation in Tanganyika. *JRUSI*, 110/637 (Feb. 1965), pp. 48–55.

Stewart, Michael. British foreign policy today. *Australian Outlook*, 20/2 (Aug. 1966), pp. 109–24.

'Tarbrook.' Britain's future strategic reserve. *Brassey's Annual 1958*, pp. 71–84.

Taylor, J. W. R. Give the army wings. *RAF Quarterly*, 4/1 (Jan. 1952), pp. 13–18.

—— How good are the RAF's new aircraft? *Air Power*, 3/4 (July 1956), pp. 245–58.

—— Military air transport in a nuclear age. *Air Power*, 4/3 (Apr. 1957), pp. 174–84.

—— Second-line deterrent. *Brassey's Annual 1959*, pp. 155–66.

—— No second deal thoughts on tactical transport for British army units. *RAF Quarterly*, 2/1 (spring 1962), pp. 3–12.

Thompson, Brig W. F. K. Progress towards an all-regular, long-service army. *Brassey's Annual 1960*, pp. 216–26.

Three questions on defence. *Round Table*, 47/188 (Sept. 1957), pp. 327–41.

Thursfield, R Adm H. G. The disposition of British sea forces. *Brassey's Annual 1954*, pp. 320–6.

Torlesse, R Adm A. D. The role of the aircraft carrier. *Brassey's Annual 1955*, pp. 72–82.

Verrier, Anthony. Strategically mobile forces—United States theory and British practice. *JRUSI*, 106/624 (Nov. 1961), pp. 479–85.

—— British defense policy under Labor. *Foreign Affairs*, 42/2 (Jan. 1964), pp. 282–92.

—— The end of independence. *JRUSI*, 109/634 (May 1964), pp. 136–40.

Waddy, Maj J. Ll. Helicopters for the army. *Army Quarterly*, 69/2 (Jan. 1955), pp. 194–200.

Walker, Patrick C. Gordon. The Labor party's defense and foreign policy. *Foreign Affairs*, 42/3 (Apr. 1964), pp. 391–8.

—— Has the West a place in Asia? *Survival*, 7/8 (Nov. 1965), pp. 301–4.

Wall, Patrick. The navy we need. *Brassey's Annual 1965*, pp. 222–31.

Whiteley, Gp Capt E. A. Allied defence co-operation in the Far East. *JRUSI*, 100/600 (Nov. 1955), pp. 532–49.

Whitestone, Cdr N. E. HMS Fearless. *Navy*, 71/1 (Jan. 1966), pp. 16–17.

Wilson, Lt Col A. D. The relevance of air mobility to the Middle East. *Army Quarterly*, 69/2 (Jan. 1955), pp. 161–84.

Woodhouse, Capt J. M. Some personal observations on the employment of special forces in Malaya. *Army Quarterly*, 66/1 (Apr. 1953), pp. 69–74.

Wright, Esmond. Defence and the Bagdad Pact. *Political Quarterly*, 28/2 (Apr.–June 1957), pp. 185–67.

Wykeham-Barnes, Wg Cdr P. G. The war in Korea with special reference to the difficulties of using our air power. *JRUSI*, 97/586 (May 1952), pp. 149–63.

Wyndham, Col E. H. The Near and Middle East in relation to Western defence. *Brassey's Annual 1952*, pp. 40–6.

Wynn, Humphrey. Helicopters and the fleet. *Navy*, 64/5 (May 1959), pp. 118–20.

Yool, AVM W. M. Air action in Korea. *RAF Quarterly*, 3/2 (Apr. 1951), pp. 111–14.

—— Air lessons from Korea. *Brassey's Annual 1951*, pp. 397–404.

—— The changing pattern of the RAF. *Brassey's Annual 1953*, pp. 327–53.

Younger, Kenneth. Public opinion and British foreign policy. *International Affairs* (London), 40/1 (Jan. 1964), pp. 22–33.

Index

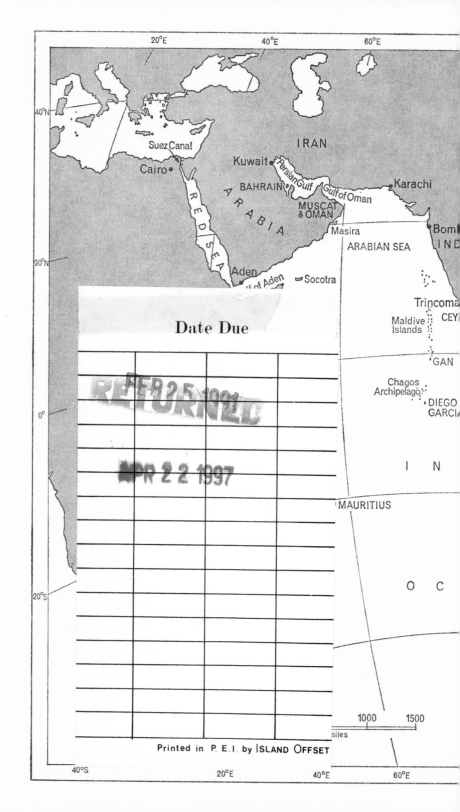

Printed in P. E. I. by ISLAND OFFSET